The Political Centrist

The Political Centrist

John Lawrence Hill

Vanderbilt University Press

Nashville

© 2009 by Vanderbilt University Press
Nashville, Tennessee 37235
All rights reserved
First edition 2009
Second printing and first paperback edition 2010

Cover design: Gary Gore
Text design: Dariel Mayer

This book is printed on acid-free paper.
Manufactured in the United States of America

Library of Congress Cataloging-in-Publication Data

Hill, John L. (John Lawrence), 1960–
The political centrist / John Lawrence Hill.
p. cm.
Includes bibliographical references and index.
ISBN 978-0-8265-1668-8 (cloth : alk. paper)
ISBN 978-0-8265-1669-5 (paper : alk. paper)

1. Centrist Party. 2. United States—
Politics and government—2001– I. Title.
JK2391.C46H55 2009
320.5—dc22
2008048045

We are . . . reformers in the morning, conservers at night.
Reform is affirmative, conservatism, negative. Conservatism
goes for comfort, reform for truth. . . . Conservatism makes no
poetry, breathes no prayer, has no invention; it is all memory.
Reform has no gratitude, no prudence, no husbandry. . . .
Conservatism tends to universal seeming and treachery, believes
in a negative fate, believes that men's temper governs them. . . .
Reform in its antagonism inclines to asinine resistance, to
kick with hoofs; it runs to egotism and bloated self-conceit;
it runs to a bodiless pretension, to unnatural refining and
elevation, which ends in hypocrisy and sensual reaction.

—Ralph Waldo Emerson

Contents

Acknowledgments

I THANK INDIANA UNIVERSITY School of Law–Indianapolis and the John S. Grimes Memorial Scholarship fund for their generous support for this work. I am also grateful to all the following, who have reviewed portions of this manuscript: Jeffrey Grove, Linda Kelly-Hill, Andrew Klein, Gerard Magliocca, R. George Wright, and Seth Zirkle. I extend a special thanks to the exhaustive research support of Steven R. Miller, librarian at the law school. I also want to thank my students Rasha Alzahabi, Justin Evans, David Gullion, Laura Kight, Joseph Lawson, and Allison Neil DeYoung for their research assistance, and Nicole Cox, Faith Long-Knotts, and Laurie Turner for their secretarial assistance.

The Political Centrist

Introduction:
The Center Holds

THE IDEA THAT POLITICAL ideologies can be placed along a continuum that runs from left to right is a legacy of the French Revolution. Delegates to the 1789 French national assembly were seated according to the interests they represented: the conservatives, representatives of the nobility and the church, were seated to the right while the representatives of the common people—those whom we would call "liberals" and "democrats" today—were at the left. The rise of socialist and anarchist theories and movements in the nineteenth century opened up the further reaches of the spectrum to the Left, while the counterdevelopment of authoritarian and fascist ideologies in the late nineteenth and twentieth centuries expanded the spectrum on the political Right to its current contours.[1] Yet there is something of a paradox underlying the idea that the Left-Right distinction tracks some particular set of political principles or criteria. While there are indeed deep and fundamental differences that distinguish the Left and Right and that place liberalism to the left of conservatism, socialism to the left of liberalism, and so on, it is also true, as Hannah Arendt and F. A. Hayek observed, that the totalitarian Left and the totalitarian Right resemble one another considerably more than either resembles the political Center.[2] As George Orwell put it, a left jackboot to the head is every bit as painful as a right jackboot.

In the United States today, the mainstream political spectrum runs from left liberalism to some form of paleoconservatism. Yet about half of us reject both the "liberal" and "conservative" labels. According to recent polls, fewer than a quarter of all Americans define themselves as "liberals," while only slightly more than a quarter call themselves "conservatives."[3] This leaves most of the rest of us, who define ourselves as politically moderate or centrist, in a kind of limbo. The political centrist's positions are often caricatured as a halfway house between liberalism and conservatism. "The only things in the middle of the road," claims populist author and activist Jim Hightower, "are yellow stripes and dead armadillos." The positions of the political centrist do not fall at the center on every issue, however, even if we could be certain where the center lies on particular issues. The centrist is not merely a pragmatic difference-splitter or political Solomon who believes that the best solution to any given problem is to sever the baby in two.

Misconceptions about political centrism trade on the idea that the centrist is perpetually in search of the political center of gravity—either in terms of his general political orientation or as a way of approaching particular issues. Yet ironically this charge has been made against virtually every political creed by some proponent of a still more radical position. The author of *The Conservative Mind*, traditional conservative Russell Kirk, denounced those "middle of the road" thinkers who follow "the way of the temporizer, pluming himself on having attained the Golden

Mean when in actuality he has only split the difference." The "middle course will lie," he argued, "wherever one extreme or the other decides to assign it." Kirk, however, was not writing about political centrists but about neoconservatives and other modernist conservatives whose politics he characterized as "the conservatism of mediocrity."[4]

Others have indicted conservatives such as Kirk on exactly the same charge. Libertarian F. A. Hayek repudiated conservatives as "advocates of the Middle Way" who have been willing to follow modern liberalism, though at a safe distance, embracing bigger government, the New Deal, and social welfarist policies of the twentieth century—all things conservatives once denounced. "With no goals of their own," Hayek insisted, "conservatives have been guided by the belief that the truth must lie somewhere between the extremes—with the result that they have shifted their position every time a more extreme movement appeared on either wing."[5] There is something to this charge, as we'll see in Chapter 3. Both liberalism and conservatism have moved significantly leftward over the course of the past two centuries. Today's conservatives are yesterday's liberals, and today's liberals are yesterday's socialist democrats.

Even those on the Far Left have been charged with being unprincipled compromisers. Among U.S. intellectuals, few consistently take positions further to the left than Noam Chomsky. Chomsky considers himself a "libertarian socialist" and has routinely maintained that contemporary America is a police state.[6] Yet Chomsky's views have been vilified as reactionary by anarchists to *his* left. As contemporary anarcho-primitivist John Zerzan put it, Chomsky's is "a severely, backward, non-radical perspective."[7]

The point here is not simply that every political position except for the truly extreme has been subject to the charge of temporizing. Rather, it is dangerous for a whole host of reasons to think about political orientation as running along a single continuum. While there is *something* to the Left-Right spectrum, at least in theory—and I'll suggest in Chapter 3 that this something has a great deal to do with each theory's orientation to equality—we should be alive to the problems that arise in thinking about the centrist's positions as falling at the center of the political spectrum. Thinking about centrism as a modus vivendi between liberalism and conservatism makes centrism appear to be nothing more than the politics of unprincipled compromise. It ignores the complexities of defining political orientation along a single axis. And it has the unsettling effect of making contemporary liberalism and conservatism appear to be more coherent and unified philosophies than they actually are.

Part I of this book dispels the myth that liberalism and conservatism are pure and monolithic ideologies in the United States today. Both are increasingly gerrymandered concepts, generic labels we give to one or another of two sets of opposed views united only by a loose family resemblance of positions and opinions—one straddling the socialist-liberal portion of the Left-Right political spectrum, the other the liberal-conservative portion. There are compelling reasons why so many Americans today see no reason to identify with either label.

SO WHAT IS POLITICAL centrism? It is three things all at once. At one level, it is a response to the breakdown of modern liberalism and conservatism. In the larger sense of the word, yes, centrists are liberals. But in this larger sense—the sense in which John Locke and Adam Smith and the classical liberals of the nineteenth century were liberals—virtually all U.S. conservatives today are liberals as well. We all believe in democracy, in individual freedoms, and in individual rights. In this sense we are all liberals. But "liberalism" obviously has a narrower, idiosyncratic meaning today. The liberal tradition has evolved from the highly individualistic, limited-state philosophy of Locke, Smith, and their followers to a more collectivist philosophy embracing big government and a much greater emphasis on equality as opposed to freedom. Centrists part ways with liberals in this narrower, modern sense on a plethora of issues. We believe that modern liberalism has strayed too far from many of the basic moral values which are essential to a good society: responsibility, merit, a commitment to the sacredness of the family, an emphasis on spiritual as opposed to material values, among others. When liberals treat even the most vicious criminal offenders as victims of society, when they refuse to grant any standing whatsoever to the interests of the fetus, when they embrace grossly disparate standards for people of different races to be admitted to a law school or to be hired for a job, when they advocate domestic policies which encourage further illegal immigration, and when they promulgate paternalistic dietary laws in the name of ensuring our health, liberalism begins to look like a very unliberal philosophy.

Yet centrists are not conservatives either. U.S. conservatism is an uneasy alloy of nineteenth-century classical liberalism and the true conservatism of antiquity, as with such thinkers as Aristotle, Cicero, and Thomas Aquinas. In some cases modern conservatism suffers from its liberal influences, while at other points it is precisely its conservatism that is to blame. The conservatives' version of materialism is seen in their permissive attitudes to corporate greed, their insouciance toward rising levels of economic inequality in the United States, their blindness to the destruction of the environment (including a persistent unwillingness still to acknowledge global warming), and their support for reckless foreign wars, to name a few examples. In some of these matters, conservatives run too far in the direction of the individualism of the classical liberal. In other ways, however, they suffer from a blinkered conservatism that stunts their capacity to appreciate the opportunities for change. Fifty years ago most conservatives resisted racial equality; today they resist the full social inclusion of gays and lesbians.

The tension between the socialistic and liberal elements of modern liberalism and the classical liberal and conservative elements of modern conservatism runs deep on both sides. Liberals and conservatives are frequently inconsistent in their internal philosophies, and they often adopt positions on the opposite sides of the same inconsistency. Take, for example, liberals' and conservatives' schizophrenic attitudes about the need to regulate certain spheres of human activity. Conservatives embrace a philosophy of nonregulation in the economic sphere while advocating the need for stricter government control in the personal domain—in matters involving sexual morality, marijuana use, or divorce laws, for example Why do conservatives believe that state regulation is so essential in the one sphere and so counterproductive in the other? Why did many conservatives once, relatively recently, believe that government had no legitimate right to try to change cultural attitudes when these attitudes reinforce bigotry and segregation, while simultaneously insisting that government must intervene to check what those opposed to abortion and assisted suicide now call the "culture of death"? Because modern conservatives have one foot in the classical liberal tradition that saw little role for government to engage in character shaping and the other foot in the older conservative tradition that taught that "statecraft is soulcraft," modern conservatives are ambivalent to the core on the question of the role of the state in shaping the values of its citizens.[8]

Liberals, of course, embrace the same inconsistencies from the other side. How can liberals believe that powerful cultural forces that shape our society—rap music, the sexualization of the Internet, rising out-of-wedlock births, and the continued high rate of divorce—should remain matters of personal choice beyond the reach of government, while insisting on the most rigorous intervention in the sphere of economic activity? Even within the narrower realm of personal morality, liberals are often torn between their libertarian and their paternalistic instincts, as when the debate turns to censoring pornography, legalizing drugs or prostitution, or imposing hate-speech codes. In fact, perhaps the deepest dilemma of modern liberalism is that it seeks to free people from every manner of constraint, a residue of its classical liberal inheritance, by using the potentially all-pervading influence of government.

One final incoherence in both philosophies is worth mentioning: liberals and conservatives today are all profoundly conflicted about the reasonableness of human choices and the significance of personal autonomy. Liberals lionize the value of personal autonomy and defend the sanctity of choice until the individual signs a subprime mortgage contract, or wants to ride without a motorcycle helmet, or opts to eat foods cooked in trans fat, at which point they frequently revert to an almost instinctive paternalism. This is because liberals are torn between two radically contradictory philosophies of human nature—the first rooted in the romantic idea that one's spontaneous choices are the deepest reflections of one's authentic self and the second grounded on modern sociological ideas that assume that human preferences are largely social constructions. So liberals tend to lean in favor of the authentic self when the individual's choices reflect the kinds of values they endorse, and to lean to the sociological view that holds that our choices are the products of false consciousness when they disapprove of the particular preference. Why, for example, do liberals insist that more information is an unmixed blessing when the issue is whether to discuss the proper use of condoms in a seventh-grade class, yet reject as coercive laws which require that a woman seeking an abortion be given information about fetal development or adoption alternatives? Conservatives, too, vacillate between the more conservative message that culture is all-important in shaping the mores and outlook of individuals and their classical liberal faith in the power of the individual to step outside the cultural framework to construct himself or herself ex nihilo.

These deep and glaring contradictions at the level of political philosophy—on

both sides—give the rest of us pause. They make us see that the world is complicated and that the truth frequently lies somewhere between the caricatured poses of
liberals and conservatives. So at the first level, centrists are responding to what we
take to be the intellectual bankruptcy of modern liberalism and conservatism. But
at a second level, centrists are reacting to the increased polarization of U.S. politics itself—a polarization generated by the liberal-conservative duopoly in political
thought.

THOUGH LIBERALISM AND CONSERVATISM are far from coherent and monolithic
theories of politics, we treat them as if they cogently define and divide the American political universe into two airtight and mutually opposed views of political reality. Yet their opposition is frequently a function of politics, not philosophy. What
explains the polarizing tendency in contemporary political thought? Why so often
do the media or ordinary Americans engaged in political debate fail to distinguish
finer gradations of political thought within each of the two traditions, even as we
also insist that these two traditions are distinct and inevitably opposed philosophies? Why *two* opposed political ideologies—no more and no less?

Political scientists refer to Duverger's law, which explains the tendency of majoritarian political systems—democracies that award 100 percent of political control to the group with as little as 51 percent of the vote—to evolve two parties
and no more.[9] Any group that seeks to capture a majority of the vote must, if it
does not already represent a majority, form majority coalitions with other, broadly
ideologically aligned groups. Two opposed groups form as each tries to capture the
middle—which is nothing more than capturing a majority of voters. It might seem
that Duverger's law bodes well for a centrist politics, but quite the opposite is true.
One side captures the middle not by triangulation, but by polarization. One always
has to choose sides, and there are generally only two sides from which to choose.
Consider the helter-skelter diversity of politics in the modern Democratic or Republican parties, the notorious schisms and fault lines between progressives and
populists on the Left, and libertarians and traditional conservatives on the Right.
The internal tensions on each side are covered over by a false, unified persona.

One consequence of this process is that positions on particular political issues in
the United States today tend to travel in clusters. The exigencies of political combat
often force those holding vaguely compatible positions on various political issues
to pull together under the banner of a common label, even though there are deep
tensions and inconsistencies between these allied positions. Why must people who
favor antidiscrimination laws protecting minorities (traditionally a liberal position),
for example, have to oppose any official public acknowledgment of religion—placing a crèche in a public park or the Ten Commandments on a courthouse wall
(a conservative position)? Why must those who hold progressive environmental
policies oppose any legal protection for the fetus, even in the latter phases of pregnancy? Why can't we prefer a more restrained judiciary, a position associated with
conservatism in the last fifty years, while holding more liberal positions politically?
Why is it inconsistent, for example, to believe that abortion should remain a legal

option up until a certain phase of pregnancy while insisting that the Constitution does not mandate this (or any) position relevant to abortion?

This tendency toward issue clustering has blunted the way we reason today, politically, socially, and morally. Rather than feeling free to embrace a set of positions which sometimes take the liberal side and sometimes appear conservative, moderates sometimes feel compelled to choose their poison, to conform their position to the cluster of positions associated with the Left or the Right. The problem with this is that it often forces them to embrace principles they do not hold. For example, most moderates in the United States have long concluded that laws criminalizing private consensual acts among homosexuals are outdated. Liberals have famously attacked these laws as a form of morals legislation, arguing that the state should have no authority whatsoever regulating behavior which is private. Conservatives respond by arguing that the state can regulate any behavior a majority of citizens believes to be immoral, even if conducted in private. The standard liberal position seems to commit us to the view that the state cannot regulate prostitution, incest, polygamy, drug use, and other arguably private activities, while the standard conservative position implies that we must support any view taken by the moral majority. Yet each of these positions is equally extreme and untenable, as I contend in Chapter 8.

H. L. Mencken once said that every difficult problem has a simple solution—and it's wrong. We centrists agree. In some cases, centrists are open to a pragmatic form of value balancing, not because we don't have a consistent set of principles but because the world is a complicated place in which values conflict. Consider the litmus test par excellence in contemporary politics—abortion. Liberals permit their pro-choice commitments to become a moral absolute—so much so that they are blinded to the barbarity of partial-birth abortion, a procedure routinely performed on a late-term fetus, who apparently consciously experiences the procedure for what it is—a horrific way to die. Liberals are afraid to draw sensible lines in the abortion debate for two reasons. Philosophically, they mistakenly believe that a commitment to reproductive freedom is an absolute, while politically, they fear the slippery slope effects of conceding any limitation on abortion rights. Of course, pro-life conservatives do the same thing from the other side, taking a position that requires that they equate a pregnancy ended in the first or second month with the first-degree murder of an adult human being. Again, both positions are extreme and untenable. Both, in their own way, fail to recognize the moral importance of the development of the fetus through pregnancy—the liberal by not recognizing the late-term fetus as indistinguishable from a baby and the conservative by not recognizing the difference between a baby and a blastocyst.

Centrists find room for a sensitive weighing of incommensurable values. We believe compromise positions are not simply politically expedient, they are—as a matter of substantive morality—often better justified than the extreme positions on either side. On abortion (Chapter 9), capital punishment (Chapter 11), illegal immigration (Chapter 12), and various other issues, a compromise position frequently advances the values of both sides significantly on the basis of sound principles which make powerful sense in each particular context. To this extent, this book is a call to reject the polarizing effects of the liberal-conservative duopoly of thought. It is an invitation to think through our political positions anew, from the perspective of a humane, sensitive, and above all commonsense political philosophy.

THERE IS, FINALLY, A THIRD LEVEL which draws moderates to the political center, and it is the most difficult to describe, though we will take this up all too briefly in Chapter 5. Underlying the surface politics of liberalism and conservatism lies a more trenchant divide between the secular and traditional views of the world. Each of these two conflicting paradigms for the human condition presents contrasting answers to the truly big questions in life: Does God exist? Is there a real morality, an objective foundation for right and wrong, or do humans construct their morality? Do human beings possess free will or are we ultimately causally determined to behave as we do? As I make clear in Chapter 5, we have to be careful not to overdraw these connections. Certainly some liberals are religiously more traditional, while some conservatives are downright postmodern in their view of the world, as I argue in Part I. But it would be a mistake to overlook the ways in which modern liberalism is shaped by a more secular view of the world, or the extent to which conservatism today reflects a natural-law, God-centered conception of the world. We see these differences most potently in public debates concerning the relationship of religion and politics, yet the influences operate in more subtle though equally powerful ways in other areas. Why do liberals and conservatives have such contrasting attitudes concerning the causes of crime or the purpose of punishment? To some extent, it is because liberals tend to view human beings as shaped by their environment, whereas conservatives place greater stock in free will and personal responsibility. Why are liberals more optimistic than conservatives about the prospect of engineering social conditions to eliminate war, poverty, violence, and other social evils? The answer lies in part, again, in the conservative's tendency to think that there is a certain incorrigible aspect to the human condition that we will never be able to eradicate. Whether this pessimism is cast in the paleoconservative's assumption that we are fallen or in the neoconservative's observation that collective action always has unintended consequences, the result will be the same. These same big-picture differences at the level of these two contrasting paradigms of the human condition also explain why liberals find progress where conservatives see only moral decay.

In some ways, then, the secular-traditionalist split is mirrored in the contemporary liberal-conservative divide. Yet, strangely, in other ways, liberalism and conservatism are themselves torn between these competing paradigms. Both groups hover peripatetically between the modern subjectivist ethic that holds that we humans construct our own morality and the more traditional belief that there are objective sources of morality such that morality is discovered, not constructed. Liberals are most likely to sound like the old natural lawyers, invoking absolute rights that exist independently of human laws, when opposing capital punishment or the torture of political dissidents. On other issues they appear happy to embrace the modern ethic of relativism. And conservatives sound most like natural lawyers when defending the fetus's right to life and opposing further government incursions into property rights. On other issues they, too, frequently defend a subjectivist ethic, as they often tend to do in matters involving economic choices. This takes us back to the incoherence of contemporary liberalism and conservatism.

For our part, many centrists embrace a more liberal version of the traditional paradigm. We believe in an objective morality but we don't believe, for example, that homosexuality is morally wrong. Many of us believe strongly in a personal God but we don't follow the line of the old natural-law thinkers who believed that they could discern God's will in every matter that touches the human condition. We believe in free will and are alive to the all-too-pervasive human tendency toward excuse making and self-deception, but we also understand that social and economic conditions do shape and limit people's options in ways that sometimes have to be taken into consideration, morally and legally.

So, on this third and deepest level, we often side with conservatives on principle, and liberals on the application of these principles.

Part I of this book (Chapters 1–4) traces the history and philosophy of modern liberalism and conservatism and attempts to show how these labels have each become freighted with such conflicting and overlapping meanings and positions that there is little of coherent unity in either position. In Chapters 1 and 2, I trace these two respective traditions, picking out particular exemplars—Locke, Mill, John Dewey, and John Rawls on the liberal side; Joseph de Maistre, Edmund Burke, David Hume, and Andrew Sullivan among the conservatives—to show the variety and development of each tradition. In Chapter 3, I examine the paradoxes of liberalism and conservatism today, while in Chapter 4, I discuss in somewhat greater detail why centrists reject libertarianism, left liberalism, and the varieties of modern conservatism.

Part I also sets up many of the theoretical debates underlying issues I discuss in Part II: Why does libertarianism commit its adherents to an open-border policy? How do liberals' and conservatives' conceptions of social order frame their views of the criminal justice system or the role of government in restructuring the economy? How do different sides think about freedom and equality? And what is the centrist's position in each case? Again and again we'll return to these foundational issues in Part II.

An initial cautionary remark is in order: I offer here an *approach*—what I think is a sound centrist approach—to thinking about the political and social issues of our day. But one need not agree with every position I take to consider oneself a centrist. What follows is hardly a litmus test or laundry list for political centrists. Nothing could be further from my deepest hope, which is to show that there are good sound principles for uniting around a core of centrist assumptions on the issues addressed. What I offer here is in part descriptive (i.e., this is what it means to be a centrist) and in part prescriptive (i.e., this is what I believe to be the better position on a particular issue). Certainly some who are drawn to the centrist persuasion will disagree with me on various issues, insisting that I am too "liberal" on gay marriage or too "conservative" on affirmative action. But centrists, like everyone else, are free to disagree with each other on the interpretation we give to our principles.

Part I
Beyond Liberalism
and Conservatism

Chapter 1
The Liberal's Paradox

ADAM SMITH MAY HAVE been the first to use the term "liberal" in the modern political sense in his *Wealth of Nations*, published in 1776. Yet it was not until the 1820s in Britain and the United States that the term "liberal" became part of our linguistic currency as a political expression.[1] There were no "liberals" during the American Revolution, for example, though many of the founding fathers—Jefferson is a good example—adhered to a form of republicanism brigaded with classical liberal principles.

Liberalism has taken three distinct forms historically, though it is the second of these that is usually associated with liberalism today. In its first phase, the classical liberal era ran from the late seventeenth century until some time around the end of the nineteenth century in the United States. The first true defense of classical liberalism was John Locke's *Second Treatise of Government*, published anonymously in 1690. Classical liberal ideas germinated throughout the eighteenth century and became the dominant approach to U.S. politics by the early to mid-nineteenth century. Classic liberalism's day in the sun was short-lived, however. By around 1900, the older, limited-government philosophy began to give way to the more egalitarian and interventionist ideals of the progressive liberal. Second-stage progressive liberalism became the dominant liberal ideology with FDR and the New Deal in the 1930s. Since then, "liberalism" has usually meant this form of left liberalism.

The third and most radical strain of liberalism, libertarianism, is of even more recent vintage. According to one account, Leonard Read coined the term "libertarian" in the 1950s when libertarians could no longer bear to use the word "liberal" to describe their own philosophy.[2] Libertarians often align themselves with the older classical liberalism, yet in some ways libertarianism is a much more radical philosophy. One example, as we'll see later, is that most eighteenth- and nineteenth-century classical liberals never doubted the government's role in preserving the morality of society—for example, passing laws prohibiting prostitution, adultery, homosexuality, drug and alcohol use, or other aspects of personal behavior. Libertarians do not believe government should have this power. Like progressive liberals, libertarians want government to stay out of the bedroom. And with classical liberals, they want government to stay out of the boardroom. Libertarianism is thus the most radically consistent form of antiregulatory liberalism. It is often (strangely) considered a form of conservative thought today, largely because libertarians share many conservatives' free-market principles. We examine libertarianism at greater length in Chapter 3, where I argue that it is anything but a conservative philosophy in most senses of the word.[3]

Defenders of each of the three branches of liberalism disagree about a great many things, but at the most general level they agree on two important points. First, all liberals seem to agree that the central political value of a liberal system ought to be *liberty*, though they disagree about how to define it. Second, all liberals agree in principle that the protection of freedom always requires some *restraint*, though they disagree about who needs restraining. All agree at a minimum that the limit of each person's freedom is the point at which it interferes with someone else's freedom. As the old expression goes, your freedom to swing your arm ends where my nose begins. It is primarily government's job to enforce this zone of restraint—by preventing you from taking my property or harming me physically or otherwise limiting my freedom, and by preventing me from doing the same to you. Most liberals will agree, then, that the government's function in restraining liberty—and this is crucial—*is done, at least in part, in the name of liberty.*

Herein lies the root of the paradox of liberalism: restraint is justified in terms of freedom. Adjust the definition of freedom accordingly, and you can justify any form or level of restraint. V. I. Lenin understood this perfectly. At the height of the Russian Revolution he declared, "It is true that liberty is precious—so precious that it must be rationed."

Recently New York City passed a ban on the use of trans fats in restaurants. Mayor Michael Bloomberg, who signed the bill into law, is something of a health fanatic. Bloomberg insisted that "nobody wants to take away your french fries and hamburgers—I love these things, too. But if you can make them with something less damaging to your health, we should do that." Another proponent of the bill was more candid. "Often people don't make wise food choices even when given the option. So we have to make choices for them. It's a positive move."[4]

This is just one example of the paradox of liberalism: the freedom of the individual to eat what he or she wants is restrained—in the name of the freedom of the individual. To those who may occasionally be willing to trade the health benefits of a non-trans-fat product for better taste, the liberal responds that trans fats are unhealthful. Eat too many of them and you may not live as long as you otherwise would. A shortened life span means that there is less time to make other choices and to enjoy your freedom in other ways. And while you live you may be less healthy than you could be, which will also limit your range of other choices. So, the logic goes, we restrain your freedom now in order to promote your long-term freedom to make those choices that you wouldn't have had a chance to make had you died prematurely. Of course, some of those other choices down the line may be limited for similar reasons, but that's another matter. Notice that we have made a crucial leap from the classical liberal approach to freedom: your freedom is limited not to preserve *my* freedom, but to preserve *yours*—the quintessential example of modern paternalism.

Whether you agree or disagree with these kinds of measures is not immediately my point. But when freedom becomes a commodity to be regulated and even maximized by the state, almost any form and level of restraint can be justified to that end. And that poses a paradox for thoughtful liberals.

We can think about the liberal's paradox in another way. The idea of a "right" means something different today than it did for the old classical liberals. When classical liberals used the term "right," they meant mainly freedom from government. To have a right to free speech or to the privacy of your home or to religious freedom meant that the government could not limit your freedom to speak or to live as you wish in your home or to practice your religion (or not) as you see fit. Rights were mainly rights *against government interference.* But, of course, even then, the idea of a right had to mean something more than this. When another person attempts to take your property or harm you, the classical liberal would agree that you have a right against this kind of personal invasion as well. So, even for the classical liberal, rights sometimes mean not just freedom from government, but freedom from *everybody* to do what it is you have a right to do. When the government recognizes your right to be free from government interference, it restrains itself. It does nothing. This is the idea of limited government. But when the government protects your right from a third party's interference, it must do something—it must intervene. So sometimes rights require that government do nothing, and sometimes they require that the government act.

This ambiguity gives rise to the modern confusion about rights. To put it a bit too bluntly, modern liberals tend to think about rights increasingly in the latter sense—to have a right is to have some freedom that the government will protect against every kind of infringement by third parties. We have a right to do our jobs free from the sexual harassment of our bosses and co-workers. We have a right not to be affected by secondhand smoke. Children have rights not to be physically disciplined by their teachers and, in some circumstances, even by their parents. The disabled have a right to access public buildings on the same terms as everybody else. We have rights to a minimum wage, to Social Security, and, perhaps before long, to some form of socialized health care.

Philosophers and lawyers sometimes draw a technical distinction between rights and privileges—those things we're left free to do and those things the government helps us do—but the truth is that, in many ways, this distinction has been blurred in our everyday way of thinking about things. Since every right must be protected by government, the distinction between rights and privileges has broken down. When the government prevents someone from taking your property (by sending the police) and when it intervenes to prevent you from being sexually harassed by your boss (by sending the Equal Employment Opportunity Commission to intervene), the only difference is the character of the activity that is being protected— keeping your property or working in an environment free of sexual harassment.

What this means is that the greater the number or scope of our rights, the *more* government we will need to protect them. This sounds counterintuitive, of course. We tend to think of rights and government as existing in tension with one another, as if more rights means less government. But this is the paradox. The greater *my* rights to be free from the things that you do, the more government that is necessary to protect me *from you.* If I have a right to be free from secondhand smoke wherever I go, the more laws that will be necessary to protect me—in bars and restaurants, in the workplace, et cetera. If I have a right to such social benefits as basic housing, health care, and a meaningful and remunerative job, more government will be necessary to achieve these things. At the extreme, there is no contradiction in the idea of totalitarian liberalism—a political state of affairs in which the state regulates most or all of our everyday activities in the name of maximizing our freedom. Tocqueville called this "soft despotism" in the nineteenth century, while H. G. Wells defended a similar idea in the 1930s, calling it (apparently without any sense of irony) "liberal fascism."[5]

The point here is not that government should never seek to do some of these things. We centrists believe that we live in a complex society and that some level of government regulation in some of these areas is sometimes beneficial, if not inevitable. But there is a self-defeating quality to the modern rhetoric of freedom and rights. Paradoxically, a society with fewer rights in the modern sense may sometimes be a freer one. This explains why modern libertarians, who are the staunchest enemies of expanding government, have a very limited repertoire of rights. It is the modern progressive liberal, who believes that there are rights to a great many things—from a smoke-free environment to national health insurance—who requires a much more expansive, interventionist government.

Liberalism, in other words, requires a kind of balancing act between the realm of positive rights, where government intervention is necessary, and the realm of negative rights, where we must be content to let the chips fall where they may without government intervention. Go too far in one direction, regulating human conduct at every turn, and freedom is reduced. Go too far in the other direction, of course—eliminating government altogether, as advocates of minimal government seek to do—and you wind up reducing freedom from the other side by disabling government from protecting essential positive rights. We may disagree about where exactly to draw the line between the two spheres, but all liberals agree that protecting freedom requires finding the right balance between them.

So why are modern liberals less willing than classical liberals to let the chips fall where they may? Why do they believe that freedom requires more, not less, government (except in areas of intimate relationships and in matters of self-expression)? The simple answer is that modern liberals have reinterpreted the essential mission of liberalism, and they have largely redefined what freedom means. In order to understand exactly how freedom has been redefined (for many of us now more or less accept some version of the newer definition), we must "commit political philosophy," as George Will once put it—and a little history, too. We begin with the year 1937.

Two Visions of Liberalism

If we had to choose the year classical liberalism died and was buried as the dominant form of liberalism in the United States, we couldn't do better than 1937. In a deeper sense, the writing had been on the wall for several decades, but in 1937 even the last bastion of classical liberal conservatism, the Supreme Court, gave up the ghost and embraced a new model of government. For three decades, from around 1900 to 1937, American constitutional politics were divided between a Supreme Court dominated by older classical liberals, on one hand, and state and

federal legislators who increasingly pushed for various progressive reforms, including maximum hour, minimum wage, and occupational safety laws, on the other.
The more conservative justices tried to hold back the tide of the new legislation by
interpreting various clauses of the Constitution in a way that was consistent with
the tenets of classical liberalism. Key to the worldview of these conservative justices
was the idea that many of the laws favored by progressives violated the freedom of
contract between the worker and the employer. By setting limits on the number
of hours a week a worker could work, or the minimum wage for which he could
work, the state was limiting the freedom of both parties to reach a bargain that was
acceptable to each.[6] Where the conservatives wanted to let more of the chips fall
where they may in these matters, the new liberals wanted more government and an
expanded array of individual entitlements.

After the stock market crash of 1929 and the Great Depression that followed,
voters elected Franklin Delano Roosevelt in 1932. Determined to beat the Depression, FDR and Congress passed a series of programs that fought unemployment
and that attempted to stabilize prices and wages. Many of these programs had the
whiff of socialism to conservatives, who opposed them because of the way they
interfered with contract and property rights, but to most of their supporters these
programs represented the new liberalism, a liberalism that sought to extend meaningful economic opportunities to all. For these programs to pass constitutional
scrutiny, two changes were necessary: the Court had to recognize a more expansive
role for the federal government, and it had to relax its rigorous classical liberal conception of property and contract rights.

The conflict between the progressive FDR and the conservative Supreme Court
came to a head in 1937. In two important cases in 1935 and 1936, the Supreme
Court had struck down two of Roosevelt's most important programs, claiming that
they were beyond the reach of federal power under the Constitution. In each of
these cases, the vote was close—five to four and six to three. Roosevelt resolved to
shake up the Court after these two defeats. Under cover of the rationale that six of
the justices were over seventy and needed extra assistance, he proposed to add six
new justices—all avid supporters of his programs—to the Supreme Court, creating
a total of fifteen (rather than the long-standing nine) justices. This would ensure
that he had a solid majority to uphold his programs.

Justice Owen Roberts had frequently been the fifth vote to strike down
Roosevelt's programs, and he had voted to do the same during the Court's conference on an important case, *West Coast Hotel Co. v. Parrish*.[7] But as the momentum
built for Roosevelt's "court-packing plan," as it came to be known, Roberts changed
his vote, siding with the administration in this and later cases. Roberts's last-minute
change of heart in this constitutional game of chicken between the president and
the Court effectively defused the court-packing plan and became known as "the
switch in time that saved nine"—the nine-justice system. Since then the dominant
vision of liberalism, on and off the Court, has been this newer version, which
views government, and particularly the federal government, as essential to achieving freedom.

The conflict between the Court's conservatives and Roosevelt's liberals concerned a host of more technical constitutional questions about such issues as the relationship of federal to state power under the Constitution's commerce power. Yet underlying the constitutional issues was a much deeper conflict between two visions of liberalism. This conflict had been simmering for well over a century. To understand the change we have to dig a little deeper—to the source of the philosophies of the classical and the modern liberal.

The Roots of Early Liberalism

The first systematic "classical liberal" (though, again, he would not have used the term) was John Locke (1632–1704). Locke's *Second Treatise of Government* can be considered liberalism's founding document, though there were certainly precursors. The essence of the *Second Treatise*'s liberalism, and that of the classical liberal tradition generally, derives from two basic ideas: the idea that there are inherent natural rights possessed by every human being and the notion of the social contract. To say that the individual has a right to something was, for Locke and for later classical liberals, very arguably to say considerably more than what most liberals mean by the idea of a right today. Natural rights are not created by the state, nor can a state deny or abolish them. Rights were seen as part of the moral fabric of the world. Governments can ignore natural rights, of course, but defenders of natural rights ideas will insist that the existence of these rights does not depend upon their enforcement by the state; in other words, they exist whether or not governments protect them.

Today we still sometimes talk in these terms, as if we believed in some system of natural rights, though few liberals today subscribe to the underlying philosophy of natural rights. Before the fall of the East German communist state, if we learned of someone being shot as they attempted to scale the Berlin Wall, we might have heard ourselves saying, "People have a *right* to leave their country." Today when a dissident in China is imprisoned for speaking out against the government, we get into our natural rights mode and insist that people have a right to speak out against their government. But of course neither defectors nor dissidents have any such right under their own legal system. Only if there is a transcendent body of natural rights can it make sense to speak of rights in this way. And most of the time, modern liberals don't believe that there are such rights. Not really. Where do these rights come from? How do we know what it is we have a right to (unless they're written down somewhere)? In what sense are they rights if they can't be enforced? And when we find ourselves in this latter, more skeptical frame of mind, we sound unmistakably modern in our outlook.

There is no getting around the fact that Locke's idea of natural rights was embedded within a God-centered conception of the world. As Locke, who was a devout Puritan, said in the *Second Treatise*, even in the state of nature, "though this be *a state of liberty*, yet it is not *a state of license*. . . . The state of nature has a law of nature to govern it, which obliges every one," so that "no one ought to harm another in his life, health, liberty or possessions for men [are] the workmanship of one omnipotent and infinitely wise maker."[8]

Today some libertarians and even a few nonlibertarian theorists argue that natural rights don't depend upon any particular theological view of the world. As libertarian theorist Murray Rothbard puts it: "One can easily arrive at libertarianism from a religious or Christian perspective. . . . Yet one can also arrive at all these self-same positions by a secular, natural law approach, through a belief that man can arrive at a rational apprehension of the natural law."[9] Rights simply exist and reason *will* reveal what these rights are, if only we follow the light of reason. But Rothbard and other theorists of secular natural law are rare today. Why? Because it has been almost impossible for most modern thinkers to reconcile a transcendent order of law with the prevailing view of the world that holds that there is no transcendent lawgiver. Without a transcendent lawmaker, there can be no transcendent law, and without a transcendent conception of the moral order, we must reconcile ourselves to the idea that law and morality are purely human creations. Nor do appeals to abstract reason seem to help for most. At a time like ours when reason seems to lead in so many different directions at the same time—to socialism for some, to libertarianism for others, and so on—how can libertarians demonstrate that their rationality is right and that everyone else's is wrong?[10] Not to be gratuitously nasty to libertarians, there is an unsettling dissonance between the libertarians' premodern conception of natural law, which binds everyone everywhere and for all time, and their very postmodern anything-goes approach to personal morality in other respects. At a minimum, we can say that natural rights grew up as part of a wider worldview that assumed the existence of a God-ordered world, even if some today think the cart can be unhooked from the horse that once pulled it.[11]

Locke didn't have this problem. He viewed the main function of government as protecting individual rights. In doing so, government preserved our God-given liberty. So what rights were there? Locke defended the triad of rights that had traditionally been protected by the English common law since the time of the Magna Carta: the rights to one's life, liberty, and property. "The great and chief end . . . of men's putting themselves under government," he wrote in the *Second Treatise*, "is *the preservation of their property.*"[12] Though these rights exist independently of any earthly convention, the social contract guarantees their protection by government.

Of the holy triad of classical liberal rights, it is surely the right to property that has caused the greatest contention in modern politics, though the meaning of "liberty" is also increasingly at issue, as we will see. Locke had claimed that one gains a right to property by mixing one's own labor with the natural bounty of the world: you cut down the (unowned) tree and build a house with it and it becomes yours. Since it is yours, you may do anything you wish with it, short of violating another's rights, including selling it to another. In this way contract rights came to be seen as an inseparable part of property rights. In this sense, the more conservative justices' ideas of freedom of contract in the 1930s were rooted in a philosophy that was more than two centuries old.

In a variety of ways, Locke began to connect political liberalism to economic capitalism. Given the strong emphasis on property rights, it was natural for classical liberals to support the free market. Locke anticipated some of the themes of the modern free marketer. A century before Adam Smith wrote his *Wealth of Nations*, Locke argued that people are inherently acquisitive and that property in private hands is ten times more productive than publicly owned property.[13] Later economic liberals from Smith to the twentieth century's F. A. Hayek would elaborate two other important themes connected to the free market. First, they argued that government intervention into economic affairs is often wasteful and counterproductive, that it undercuts the efficiency of private enterprise. Second, they insisted that the protection of property rights and economic wealth is important *politically* because economic power provides a counterbalance to the power of the state. The more government is able to interfere with the economy, the more this balance is upset. In short, political freedom requires economic freedom.[14] Adhering to this philosophy, the conservatives on the Supreme Court would have insisted that protecting property rights involved considerably more than playing defense for the well-to-do.

The Utilitarian Influence

While the idea of natural rights has always retained a strong symbolic hold on the liberal imagination, most modern liberals follow a different conception of rights, one rooted in the more modern, metaphysically skeptical utilitarian tradition.

Jeremy Bentham (1748–1832), the first systematic "utilitarian"—he coined the word—was a philosopher, a lawyer, a member of Parliament, and, through it all, an incredibly eccentric fellow. He was a child prodigy who was well into the study of philosophy, Latin, and violin by the age of five or six. He went to university at twelve and studied law beginning at sixteen, earning the degree but never practicing. Instead, he spent eight to twelve hours every day for much of the rest of his life writing (he never had much of a personal life), leaving literally tens of thousands of pages of manuscript at his death in 1832. Some of this material is still being reviewed and edited for the first time. Ever the wordsmith, along the way Bentham invented a variety of terms we use today—"international," "anarchism," "maximize," "minimize," and "codification," among others. But perhaps the quintessential testament to his strangeness as an individual came at his death. He willed a large sum of money to University College, London, a university for the socially excluded—nonconformists, Jews, Catholics—which he helped to found. His bequest was based on the condition that his "auto-icon"—his term for his mummified remains—be present at each annual board of directors meeting. Each year his remains are wheeled out to the board table, where it is announced that he is "present but not voting." (In 1975, students from another college stole his head and ransomed it for 110 pounds, to be paid to a charity.)

This man has had an inestimable influence on the liberal tradition.

Bentham's tens of thousands of pages written over the course of his long life were all based on one simple idea. The defining criterion for all morality, and the proper object of the legal system itself, he argued, was the idea of "the greatest good for the greatest number" of people, a phrase he discovered in Joseph Priestley's *Essay on Government*. Bentham used the term "utility" to refer to this principle, which he associated with maximizing happiness and minimizing pain. Through it he sought to give morality a kind of scientific foundation, one which theoretically permitted every moral claim to be weighed against every other claim according to a "hedonic calculus"—a calculus of happiness or pleasure—that could be used to govern any individual or collective decision: on any matter, whether you are contemplating some personal action or, as a member of Parliament (or Congress), considering voting for a law, if you want to know which is the best course of action, simply do that which will generate the greatest happiness for the greatest number (or which will reduce the greatest pain for the greatest number).

In many ways, utilitarianism and liberalism make copasetic bedfellows. For one thing, much of the modern liberal approach to the criminal law derives from utilitarian principles. The utilitarian sees no point in inflicting any pain on anyone—even those we might think deserve it—unless doing so generates a greater share of happiness for society generally. "All punishment is an evil," Bentham declared, because it gives pain to the person who is punished. Punishment is justified only in a cost-benefit manner: we punish the offender for his crime to deter him and other would-be offenders from committing future crimes. The harm inflicted on the offender in the course of punishment can be justified only if this punishment is more than offset by the harm we have saved others from—those who would have been victimized by crime were it not for the deterrent value of this punishment. Still, as important a role as deterrence plays in the modern criminal law system, it has the strange consequence of equating the harm experienced by a victim of crime with the harm an offender experiences in being punished. When people today criticize liberals for caring about offenders as much as victims, they are implicitly criticizing this utilitarian assumption that lies behind the liberal's (sometimes misplaced) humanitarianism. We will return to some of these issues in Chapter 11, when we discuss liberal and conservative attitudes to crime and punishment.

Utilitarians also tend to support the modern liberal's dismissal of morals legislation—for example, criminalizing homosexuality or private drug use. Laws should be passed only to prevent some discernible harm to others. What is the point of reducing the happiness of practicing homosexuals, for example, by threatening them with punishment for an act that harms no one else? What does society gain? the utilitarian asks. In this way the utilitarian is often on the same page as the libertarian and the modern liberal.

In many ways Bentham sounded like a classical liberal, and at other points like a very modern one. In the spirit of limited government he declared that every law is a restriction of liberty which can be justified only if the law generates more happiness than not having it. He defended the free market as a young man but grew more interventionist in old age. He advocated the separation of church and state, defended a robust conception of freedom of speech and press, and inveighed against censorship of every kind. In many ways these two systems of thought, liberalism and utilitarianism, serve each other's purposes well.

Yet in a deeper and more insidious way, utilitarianism worked against many of the most cherished assumptions of the classical liberal. Bentham was famously and sometimes furiously critical of the two central tenets of Locke's liberalism—natural rights and the social contract. As an agnostic who was generally dubious of things that couldn't be seen or tested, he blasted Locke's natural rights as "simple nonsense . . . rhetorical nonsense—nonsense upon stilts."[15] As for the social contract, it was a myth—and a dangerous myth that could be expected only to foment regular insurrections. "The origination of government from a contract is a pure fiction, or in other words, a falsehood." Striking a tone that sounded more like a conservative realist than a liberal, Bentham announced that the legitimacy of the state does not depend upon the consent of the individual; there is no mythical social contract. "All governments that we have any account of have been gradually established by habit, after having been formed by force."[16]

If there are no natural rights and no social contract, then where do rights come from? Bentham answered that they are created by the state. There are "no such things as rights anterior to the establishment of government." At the heart of the classical liberal conception of rights is the idea that what it means to have a right is that the state can't take it away from you, even if it is to society's collective advantage to do so. Even modern liberals want to hold on to this idea. In Ronald Dworkin's famous expression, rights are individual "trumps" against the collective interest or the will of the majority.[17] But for the utilitarian, rights are something like grants of privilege, from the state to the individual, to do certain things, when permitting the individual this freedom is conducive to collective utility. Bentham declared that individuals should be kept only "in the possession and exercise of such rights as it is consistent with the greatest good of the community that [they] should be allowed." There are no absolute checks on government, since "there is no right which, when the abolition of it is advantageous to society, should not be abolished."[18] In no uncertain terms, utilitarian thought presupposes that the state could act whenever doing so was in the collective interest as it determines the collective interest. Utilitarianism can potentially lead, in other words, in precisely the direction of totalitarian liberalism.

The utilitarian outlook has several unsettling implications for liberalism, though a kind of detente exists between the two theories. It's no coincidence that Bentham invented the word "maximize," for perhaps the greatest legacy of utilitarianism is that it's the state's role to maximize happiness, or welfare, or individual choice. In a stunning reversal of classical liberalism's central assumption that the state should be limited, under the influence of utilitarian thought modern liberals have embraced a largely managerial idea of the state that makes it a kind of central-ordering mechanism for society generally: the state is made responsible for a large share of what goes on in the sphere of civil society. Nor is freedom even the highest value for the utilitarian, as it is for the liberal. The utilitarian places happiness above freedom in his system of values. For the utilitarian, freedom can never be anything more than a *means* to happiness. And if limiting freedom rather than extending it generates more happiness or welfare, then the utilitarian must be committed to limiting freedom.

In fact, Bentham went so far as to suggest that, within civil society, the state cannot expand or contract the total amount of liberty—that, when it comes to freedom, it is all a zero-sum game. He declared that "no liberty can be given to one man but in proportion as it is taken from another. . . . How is property given? By restraining liberty"—that is, the liberty of the individual against whom the right is invoked.[19] Modern progressive thinkers have sometimes similarly suggested that the state can never really expand or contract liberty; all it can do is reapportion it, ration it, among individuals.[20] This suggests that government control can never be inimical to freedom. In a sense, Bentham brought liberalism uncomfortably close to Lenin's redistributive idea of liberty mentioned earlier.

But, of course, modern liberals are no followers of Lenin nor are they always utilitarians in their approach to social and political issues. For in their heart of hearts modern liberals still cherish the classical liberal's idea of a pristine realm beyond the reach of government. What liberalism needed was a great mind who could do the impossible—reconcile the limited-state theory of Locke and the classical liberal tradition with the utilitarianism of Bentham and his followers.

The Greatest Liberal of All

If there is a single transition point from the older classical liberalism to modern liberalism, it is John Stuart Mill's *On Liberty*, published in 1859. Every liberal should read *On Liberty*, and every conservative, too, if for no other reason than to understand the opponent's position. It is the greatest work of liberal theory and it is truly the transitional essay par excellence from classical to modern liberalism.

There are clear parallels between Mill's life and Bentham's. First, Mill's father, James, was a close friend of Bentham, and Mill himself was raised to carry on the utilitarian tradition. The elder Mill educated his son from infancy to be a prodigy. A stern taskmaster, Mill's father had Mill reading Plato by the age of six—in the original Greek. By ten Mill was writing a treatise on Roman law using the Latin he had mastered, and by the age of thirteen he assisted his father in writing a text on economic theory that was used in universities for the next several decades. When Mill was fifteen, he first read Bentham. It was then that he decided that the goal of his life was "to be a reformer of the world" along Bentham's utilitarian principles.[21] But the grueling childhood education, or possibly the utilitarian vision that had inspired it, was too much even for a prodigy. At the age of twenty Mill had what can only be described as a nervous breakdown. He relates in his *Autobiography* that this calamity was brought about by asking himself one simple question: " 'Suppose that all your objects in life were realized; that all the changes in institutions and opinions which you are looking forward to could be realized at this very instant: would this be a great joy and happiness to you?' And an irrepressible self-consciousness distinctly answered 'no.' At this my heart sank within me; the whole foundation on which my life was constructed fell down. . . . I seemed to have nothing left to live for."[22] The would-be world reformer first had to rehabilitate himself. For the better part of the next year he lived as if in a fog, and later wrote that it was the romantic poets—Wordsworth, Coleridge, and others of a more visionary or mystical nature—that brought him out of his funk. It was a very unutilitarian cure. Later in life, his wife, Harriet Taylor, continued to nurture this more poetic and individualistic side of his personality.[23]

Mill's spiritual odyssey is reflected in the two sides of *On Liberty*—the one side utilitarian and the other more individualistic. Utilitarianism remained a kind of frame or theoretical prism through which he filtered the more romantic and individualistic spirit of the book. Mill, like his father and Bentham, did not believe in natural rights. He always maintained that he was a utilitarian at heart and insisted that he would "forego any advantage" to be had in doctrines of "abstract rights." But his was an unorthodox brand of utilitarianism grounded on the idea of "utility in the largest sense, grounded in the permanent interests of man as a progressive being."[24] When talking about our external relations with the state or with others, he sounded most like a utilitarian. But he sounded like a romantic individualist when discussing freedom in its internal sense—in the sense of the flowering of each person's innate individuality. There was always a deeper side to freedom for Mill: freedom in its external sense—social and political freedom—was but a necessary condition to ensure that each individual could develop their true, authentic inner self. It is this inner aspect that makes Mill's thought so ennobling.

In terms of our external relations, Mill adopted Bentham's insight that there was no point in punishing acts that do not cause harm to others. The basic argument of *On Liberty* is that government should intervene only to prevent direct harm to others:

> The only purpose for which power can be rightfully exercised over any member of a civilized community, against his will, is to prevent harm to others. His own good, either physical or moral, is not a sufficient warrant. He cannot rightfully be compelled to do or forbear because it will be better for him to do so; because it will make him happier; because, in the opinion of others, to do so would be wise or even right. . . . The only part of the conduct of anyone for which he is amenable to society is that which concerns others. In the part which merely concerns himself, his independence is, of right, absolute. Over himself, over his own body and mind, the individual is sovereign.[25]

The "harm principle," as it has come to be called, entailed that two kinds of laws should never be passed in a liberal society—paternalistic laws (laws motivated by the desire to protect individuals from the consequences of their own decisions) and moralistic laws (laws which prohibit activities because they are commonly viewed to be morally wrong). Since paternalistic laws, at their best, prevent harm only to oneself, and since moralistic laws prevent no real harm to anyone (they are based on the offense but not the harm others experience), both violate the spirit of the harm principle.

It is very difficult not to feel a great deal of admiration for the harm principle. There is power and nobility in Mill's sentiments that run to the heart of the spirit of individualism in any sense. But, alas, Mill was an idealist who was drawn to bald pronouncements that he later qualified in a thousand ways in less conspicuous places. The harm principle implies a hermetic distinction between self-regarding and other-regarding behavior. But is there any such distinction?[26] When a spouse commits adultery, is the act really self-regarding, or should the state have the power to proscribe adultery? Doesn't prostitution or illegal drug use, activities which Mill thought fall beyond the reach of society, affect the tenor of the participant's life and, through it, the tone of society? The essential problem with the harm principle is that it rules out the possibility of collective harms to society: the harm principle recognizes harm only in the sense of direct, material harms to individuals.

Yet Mill sometimes cabined the individualistic consequences of his anti-moralistic principle. In some cases, he assumed the existence of a network of social obligations and duties which many today (perhaps under the general influence of his philosophy) do not accept. This is particularly clear with his view of the relationship between the family and society. For example, he explicitly endorsed laws which then existed in some European countries that required applicants for a marriage license to prove that they would be able to support their children.[27] Mill was motivated both by concern for impoverished children born into lives of "wretchedness and depravity" and for the public costs of caring for the children of indigent parents. Modern liberals are likely to view Mill's position on this issue as essentially conservative, but the disagreement underscores the extent to which Mill was willing to draw some hard lines in order to preserve the individualistic character of his view of social relations. A real commitment to individualism and to the harm principle requires that society must sometimes be able to prevent individuals from externalizing the costs of their behavior onto society. Interestingly, thirty years ago our own Supreme Court reached a conclusion diametrically opposed to Mill's, ruling that states cannot constitutionally deny the right to marry even to a person who has fallen years behind on child support payments for his previously existing children.[28]

We will explore some of the modern fallout from the harm principle in Chapter 8, but no one should doubt that it has had a powerful impact on the way liberals view the world. From liberals' distaste at judging the personal behavior of others to our constitutional right to privacy, which is a kind of harm principle lite, the reverberations of the harm principle are clearer than ever today.

Mill's ideas have also helped shape our ideas of freedom in a second way—in the way we think about inner freedom or the raison d'être for freedom. Why is freedom important, anyway? Mill provided a novel answer to the question. Classical liberals, as we have seen, thought of freedom as a negative value, as the absence of coercion, especially the coercion of the state. They followed Thomas Hobbes when he said that "the absence of external impediments is all that we mean by liberty."[29] But Mill insisted that nonconstraint or negative liberty was simply a *necessary condition* for freedom, not freedom itself. He connected freedom to what we might call the idea of "self-individuation," the idea, as he put it, that "individuality is the same thing with development and . . . it is only the cultivation of individuality which produces, or can produce, well-developed human beings." The cultivation of this individuality was, for Mill, our first duty, and social freedom the single most important condition for self-development. "Among the works of man which human life is rightly employed in perfecting and beautifying, the first in importance surely is man himself."[30] The essence of each person's individuality, moreover, develops from the inside out: "Human nature is not a machine to be built after a model, and set to do exactly the work prescribed for it, but a tree, which requires to grow and develop itself on all sides, according to the tendency of the inward forces which make it a living thing."[31] Self-individuation requires that one *become oneself.* And it may require that the rest of society validate this inner self in a variety of ways.

Mill's conception of freedom has deeply influenced the way we think about freedom and about ourselves. When we speak of the quest for authenticity, self-actualization, and self-individuation, we are invoking the Millian vision of freedom, the idea that there is a deeper purpose to our external political and social liberties. This deeper purpose is to provide a shield and a haven for the nascent self so that each person may, without the interference of society or the state, discover, unfold, and express their true self or inner nature.

As ennobling as Mill's vision of freedom as self-individuation is, the harm principle dramatically changed the way liberals conceive the relationship between the individual and society. The earlier classical liberals always held that freedom was threatened by the state, but not by society. Thomas Paine's comment in *Common Sense* was typical of this earlier attitude. Paine wrote that "society is produced by our wants and government by our wickedness; the former promotes our happiness positively by uniting our affections, the latter negatively by restraining our vices."[32] Society was no enemy of individual freedom for the classical liberal. Mill thought otherwise. He introduced the harm principle by declaring that it applied not only to the physical coercion of the state, but to "the moral coercion of public opinion."[33] Where classical liberals opposed the state to the individual and society, Mill conceived the individual as potentially at war with both. He was one of the first to inject into liberalism the romantic's distrust of society, tradition, settled practices, or anything else that might breed conformity or threaten the process of self-individuation. In Mill's thought, society takes on the character of the Other, rather than being an extension of the self as it was for classical liberals. Mill's vision provides a political gloss for the image of the isolated and alienated individual, a favorite theme of twentieth-century literature.

Mill also breathed new meaning into the liberal idea of freedom from government. Modern liberals sound most like classical liberals, demanding that government get off our backs in the name of a negative ideal of freedom, when they are defending the inner zone of privacy. And they do so in the name of freedom as self-individuation—the right of every individual to discover, develop, and express her true self. In *Planned Parenthood of Southeastern Pennsylvania v. Casey,* the 1992 Supreme Court case that reassessed *Roe v. Wade,* Justice Sandra Day O'Connor provided a spectacular example of Mill's influence on the contemporary liberal conception of freedom. In upholding a constitutional right of abortion, she wrote:

> These matters, involving the most personal and intimate choices a person may make in a lifetime, choices central to personal dignity and autonomy, are central to the liberty protected by the Fourteenth Amendment. At the heart of liberty is the right to define one's own concept of existence, of meaning, of the universe, and of the mystery of human life. Beliefs about these matters could not define the attributes of personhood were they formed under compulsion of the state.[34]

Here is the modern constitutional embodiment both of Mill's idea of a self-regarding realm of personal behavior and of its underlying raison d'être—the idea that freedom is the necessary condition for the perfection of each person's own unique and intrinsic individuality.

The New Liberalism Embraces Equality

Mill's influence reconfigured but preserved liberalism's commitment to the values of individualism and negative liberty. Yet in important ways Mill's thought represents a bridge from the classical values of individualism, limited government, and protection of property rights to the modern liberal embrace of collectivism, interventionism, and egalitarianism. His last two works before his death in 1873, *The Subjection of Women* and an unfinished defense of socialism (in a decentralized form), clearly presage modern liberalism's expanded commitment to social and economic equality. By the late 1880s, progressive liberals such as T. H. Green were busy developing the outlines of the new liberalism.[35] The central disagreement between classical and modern liberals was not just that modern liberals want more government, but that they want to use government to create conditions of greater freedom and equality. And this is the rub. Classical liberals believe that liberty requires equality—but only up to a point. Equality, for classical liberals, means equality before the law, or "formal equality." Beyond this point, classical liberals view liberty and equality as conflicting values. They insist that government efforts to promote equality in the social and economic spheres actually undermine freedom—by limiting property or associational rights, by redistributing property, or by limiting the rights of some in order to help others. Where classical liberals insist that government should remain neutral between different groups, progressives insist that government must sometimes take sides on social and political issues in order to affirmatively assist the poor or the disenfranchised.

Writing shortly after the turn of the twentieth century, at a point when the transformation from the old to the new liberalism was well under way, a sympathetic progressive, L. T. Hobhouse, declared that "liberty without equality is a name of noble sound and squalid result."[36] Within a few decades, John Dewey, the most important philosopher of progressive liberalism, insisted in a quasi-Marxian tone:

> The direct impact of liberty always has to do with some class or group that is suffering in a special way from some form of constraint exercised by the distribution of powers that exists in contemporary society. Should a classless society ever come into being, the formal *concept* of liberty would lose its significance, because the fact for which it stands would have become an integral part of the established relations of human beings to one another.[37]

Carl Becker, an intellectual defender of FDR's New Deal, proclaimed in a similar vein in 1941:

The essential problem of liberal democracy, therefore, is to preserve that measure of freedom of thought and of political action without which democratic government cannot exist, and at the same time to bring about, by the social regulation of economic enterprise, that measure of equality of possession and of opportunity without which it is no more than an empty form.[38]

Around the same time, President Roosevelt delivered a speech which capsulized the goals of the New Deal and highlighted the welfarist understanding of the new liberalism:

This Republic had its beginning and grew to its present strength under the protection of certain inalienable political rights—among them the right of free speech, free press, free worship, trial by jury, freedom from unreasonable searches and seizures. They were our rights to life and liberty. . . . As our nation has grown in size and stature, however . . . these rights proved inadequate to assure us equality in the pursuit of happiness. . . . We have come to a clear realization of the fact that true individual freedom cannot exist without economic security and independence. . . . We have accepted, so to speak, a second Bill of Rights under which a new basis of security and prosperity can be established for all.

Roosevelt went on to say that these new economic rights included "a right to a useful and remunerative job," the "right of every family to a decent home," the "right to adequate medical care and to enjoy and achieve good health," the "right to adequate protection from the economic fears of old age, sickness, accident and unemployment," and "the right to education."[39]

From the 1970s on, several liberal theorists have advanced still more aggressively egalitarian policies under the auspices of a quasi-Kantian idea of personal autonomy. In his *Theory of Justice*, regarded by many today as the most important defense of the new liberalism, philosopher John Rawls famously sought to temper liberty with his egalitarian "difference principle." The difference principle requires that social institutions that create disparities in life prospects between differently situated persons are "just if and only if they work as part of a scheme which improves the expectations of the least advantaged members of society."[40] In other words, policies and programs that permit disparities in wealth and privilege are allowable only if they can be shown to benefit those at the bottom relative to their position in the absence of these laws.

The difference principle turns out to have some far-reaching consequences. It requires a complete restructuring of the economy so that all proposed changes are certain to make the least advantaged better off than they were previously. It appears to require opening all borders since it applies to all human beings (though Rawls never directly draws this implication). And since the difference principle applies to all social institutions, Rawls struggled with whether it requires the abolition of the family, deciding finally that the liberal need not go quite that far. He did conclude, however, that his theory of justice requires the collective ownership of all individual talents and capacities. The difference principle, he concluded, "regards the distribution of natural abilities as a *collective asset* so that the more fortunate are to benefit only in ways that help those who have lost out."[41]

The former occupant of the Oxford Chair of Jurisprudence, Ronald Dworkin, seems to go further in one respect, virtually equating freedom and equality. In his essay "Liberalism," Dworkin asks: "What does it mean for government to treat its citizens as equals?" He answers: "That is, I think, the same question as the question of what it means for the government to treat all its citizens as free." Dworkin concludes that the essence of liberalism has always been that government must treat its citizens with "equal concern and respect." Treating citizens with "equal concern and respect" turns out to have a surprising variety of *substantively* egalitarian implications. It requires the aggressive redistribution of wealth, a presumption against inheritance, opposition to the death penalty, and strong commitment to affirmative action, among other positions. And, as with Rawls before him, Dworkin maintains that genuine commitment to equality means that one has no presumptive right to keep the fruits of one's personal talents and native capacities since these are ultimately the result of circumstances—the accident of biology, family connections, or a good environment. Dworkin argues: "In a society in which people differed only in preferences, then, a market would be favored for its egalitarian consequences. Inequality of monetary wealth would be a consequence only of the fact that some preferences are more expensive than others, including the preference for leisure time rather than the most lucrative productive activity." Because "talents are not distributed equally," government may intervene to equalize the differential effects of the genetic lottery. Because of inheritance, "the children of the successful will start with more wealth than the children of the unsuccessful." Government must intervene to equalize these differences. Dworkin concludes: "It is obviously obnoxious to the liberal conception . . . that someone should have more of what the community as a whole has to distribute because he or his father had superior skill or luck."[42]

These are jarring pronouncements for someone calling himself a liberal. It is striking how far this takes us from the classical liberal ideal. In fact, even middle-of-the-road liberals will find the idea of community ownership of individual talents and capacities inherently repugnant, if not shocking. Isn't *self-ownership* virtually the defining mark of a liberal political order? Consider what one of the most liberal of our founders, the man who declared that "all men are created equal" in the Declaration of Independence, said at another point: "To take from one because it is thought that his own industry and that of his fathers has acquired too much, in order to spare to others who, or whose fathers have not exercised equal industry and skill, is to violate arbitrarily the first principle of association, the guarantee to everyone of a free exercise of his industry, and the fruits acquired by it."[43] To suggest that the community collectively owns all individual attributes, as Rawls did, or that it is the community (in some collectivized sense) which distributes wealth, as Dworkin has, would have struck Jefferson as the double-speak of tyranny.

Even some who are sympathetic to the social goals of progressivism believe that some of the modern liberal tradition goes too far, that the new emphasis on positive freedom and equality is driving out the central values of the older liberal tradition. Liberalism has become too collectivistic, too socialistic. There is too much emphasis on government and too little on the values of self-reliance and community self-help, which are normally associated with negative liberty. This was the crux of Isaiah Berlin's great essay, "Two Concepts of Liberty," published in 1959. With the Cold War as backdrop, Berlin warned liberals not to stray too far from the negative ideal of freedom. He associated negative liberty with the free West and an extreme form of positive liberty with the totalitarianism of the Soviet Union. Positive ideas of freedom, he argued, tend to confuse freedom with other values. "Everything is what it is: liberty is liberty," Berlin reminded us, "not equality or fairness or justice or culture, or human happiness or a quiet conscience."[44] Positive freedom is ultimately a seductive value that leads, by degrees, from freedom to equality to security—and all under the protective aegis of an increasingly all-directing, and potentially even totalitarian, government.

Anything taken to an extreme—even freedom—becomes its opposite, as Hegel would have insisted. Once "freedom" is understood as equality, security, happiness, or the fostering of more and better choices, the most illiberal means may be necessary to promote it. As one of the clearest political thinkers of the last two centuries pointed out, the pursuit of "freedom," so understood, "restricts the activity of free will within a narrower compass, and little by little robs each citizen of the proper use of his own faculties." Over the "liberated," Alexis de Tocqueville further explained,

> stands an immense, protective power which is alone responsible for securing their enjoyment and watching over their fate. That power is absolute, thoughtful of detail, orderly, provident and gentle. It would resemble parental authority if, father-like, it tried to prepare its charges for a man's life, but on the contrary it only tries to keep them in perpetual childhood. . . . It gladly works for their happiness but wants to be the sole agent and judge of it. It provides for their security, foresees and supplies their necessities, facilitates their pleasures, manages their principal concerns, directs their industry, makes rules for their testaments and divides their inheritances. Why should it not entirely relieve them from the trouble of thinking and all the cares of living?[45]

This is the liberal's paradox.

Chapter 2
The Conservative's Dilemma

MODERN CONSERVATISM WAS BORN in reaction to liberalism, and conservatives ever since have self-consciously felt their central purpose to consist of raising an organized resistance to liberalism. Whereas the term "liberalism" was used as a political shibboleth beginning in the 1820s, the label "conservative" first appeared in its political sense in 1830, in an article in the British *Quarterly Review*.[1] A combination of Tories and some of the more conservative Whig politicians in Britain founded the Conservative Party a few years later. The word then crossed the Atlantic and, by the 1840s, U.S. statesmen such as Daniel Webster and John C. Calhoun began to describe themselves as "conservatives." Much of what American conservatism has stood for since then can be described in these same terms, as a kind of negation, a resistance to American liberalism: as liberalism has moved increasingly leftward, conservatism has resisted this drift. When William F. Buckley founded the *National Review* in the mid-1950s, declaring that its animating mission was to "stand athwart history, yelling Stop!" he captured what had always been the essence of American conservatism.

Yet the term originally meant very different things in distinct places. On the Continent in the nineteenth century, to be a conservative usually meant that one opposed the liberal and democratic revolutions of the eighteenth century. Conservatives there favored monarchy over republicanism and wanted to preserve an elevated role for the church in political and social matters. For such thinkers as Joseph de Maistre and Louis de Bonald, conservatism was adamantly set against all things modern. Maistre regarded the Enlightenment itself as the harbinger of social decay and political revolution, and speculated that it was the penultimate phase of history before the apocalypse. In Britain, conservatism expressed itself in a milder reaction to the momentum of the liberal and democratic changes of the late eighteenth and early nineteenth centuries. More than any other issue, the British Conservative Party was founded to respond to the Reform Bill of 1832, which dramatically expanded suffrage to the middle and lower classes in Britain. British conservatives favored a more limited democratic franchise, with Parliament to share a greater balance of power vis-à-vis the crown. Conservatives then were often split, as modern conservatives are, on economic policies. Many opposed the free-trade policies of classical liberals, sometimes for protectionist reasons (e.g., many were landowners who supported the Corn Laws, which prohibited the importation of cheap corn, a staple of the poor). But others were genuinely concerned about the degenerating social and economic conditions of the working class in Victorian England. In fact, conservatives sometimes sided with the socialist Left later in the century, leading Marxists to chide them as "Tory socialists."

In the United States, on the other hand, the liberal-conservative distinction has always been less concrete. And it has been less concrete not because liberalism here was more conservative than in Britain or on the Continent, but because U.S. conservatism has usually been more liberal.[2] Unlike its purer European variant, U.S. conservatism was not typically opposed to modernity or rooted in an anti-Enlightenment philosophy. Liberals and conservatives here shared the same modern democratic traditions, though U.S. conservatives interpreted these principles in ways that bear the indelible influence of an older tradition.

U.S. conservatives were small *d* democrats who believed in individual rights and who frequently defended the free market and generally supported a division of religious and political authority—just as U.S. liberals did. Looking back historically, it is sometimes almost impossible to say who the liberal or the conservative was in particular contexts. Were the Anti-Federalists, who favored a more democratic and egalitarian form of government but who were also states' righters who feared judicial activism, more liberal or more conservative than the Federalists?[3] Was Jefferson, the father of the modern Democratic Party, who favored limited government, who believed in the necessity of civic virtue over more materialistic values, who preferred the agrarian way of life over the corrupting influence of the city, and who argued that the redistribution of wealth was an arbitrary violation of "the first principle of association," really more the liberal than was Alexander Hamilton? Hamilton, father of the modern Republican Party, was in his time a nationalist who advocated more centralized power, believed in a more expansive government, and argued that government should intervene more freely in the economy—policies which are today considered liberal.

The great political divisions of the past simply do not line up well with our prevailing ideas about what it means to be a good liberal or conservative. And part of the reason for this is that U.S. conservatism is deeply indebted to the liberal tradition—but only in part.

U.S. conservatism is in fact rooted in two conflicting traditions, one premodern, the other modern. The first tradition springs from the political thought of antiquity and draws its political ideals from a specific metaphysical conception of the universe that holds that politics should bind man to the eternal order. This classical tradition has its source in such thinkers as Plato, Aristotle, Cicero, and various Christian theologians, including Thomas Aquinas. It holds that moral obligations arise from sources outside the human self, that the character of a community is determined by the moral character of its citizens, and that the state has a role in perfecting the character of its citizens, thereby preserving the constitution of the community. The second tradition, traceable to Hobbes and Locke in the seventeenth century and to the Enlightenment thinkers of the eighteenth, is by degrees increasingly liberal, secular, and individualistic. This second tradition usually holds that the most important political value is freedom, not order. While Locke retained the older idea of a transcendent moral order, others (e.g., Hobbes) insisted that morality is a human creation, which renders it relative to the needs of any given society. Where the older tradition required government to shape the character of its citizens in pursuit of the prescribed good life, the modern counsels government neutrality among the multitude of competing visions of the good life.

Modern conservatives are torn between these two traditions in a way that modern liberals, who are wholly committed to the second tradition, are not. Consider the labels we give to the various schools of modern conservatism—paleoconservatism, Burkean traditionalism, neoconservatism, a school of thought we will call skeptical conservatism, and, finally, classical liberalism. While there are no distinct lines between these schools—they represent shades of conservative thought—as we move through the series, we progress from the harder or more traditional forms of conservatism, rooted more heavily in the premodern tradition, to the more liberal forms of conservatism.

Owing to these differences of philosophy, conservatives themselves offer sometimes strikingly different definitions of conservatism.[4] Conservatives line up on opposite sides of almost every important question of philosophy. Does conservatism require belief in God, or is true conservatism to be distinguished from religious orthodoxy, as some recent self-described conservatives have argued?[5] Must conservatives believe in a natural law or some other such conception of a transcendent moral order, or can they be moral skeptics or relativists? Is conservatism a limited-state philosophy or does it require, to the contrary, an expansive, quasi-authoritarian conception of government?[6] Is conservatism a collectivist philosophy that provides that "the state is prior to the individual," as Aristotle taught, or is the individual philosophically prior to the state, as Locke thought? Was Burke closer to the essence of conservatism when he declared that society connected the living, the dead, and those not yet born in a quasi-spiritual, transgenerational contract, or was Margaret Thatcher right to insist that "there is no such thing as society?"[7] Is conservatism a paternalistic philosophy that holds the individual in rather low regard, or is it a philosophy grounded in the highest admiration for the values of personal autonomy and individual self-reliance?

We could multiply these questions almost indefinitely, but the point is clear: conservatism has stood for a bewildering array of political and philosophical commitments, which renders suspect the claim that there is a substantive core to conservatism. As J. G. A. Pocock put it: "Too many minds have been trying to conserve too many things for too many reasons."[8]

Of course, liberals disagree about some of these issues as well. But the liberal need not take a position on many of these questions. He is happy to leave the question of the existence of God or of a transcendent moral law to the individual. In fact, his philosophy not only permits this, it usually requires it. And on other issues—e.g., how to think about the relationship between the individual and society—modern liberals can afford to embrace an agnostic attitude. Conservatives, however, cannot—and they cannot for a reason that takes us to the heart of the conservative's dilemma. Conservatives presumably want to *conserve* the existing social order. But why? Two answers, basically, are open to conservatives. Either they want to conserve the existing social order because it is the *right* kind of order, or they oppose change for some other reason.

Over a half century ago, political scientist Samuel Huntington argued that conservatism is not a substantive political creed like socialism or liberalism or fascism. He maintained that there are no essential conservative principles or values. He claimed that conservatism is instead essentially a "positional" ideology. By this he meant that conservatives are chiefly concerned with preventing the destabilizing effects of social and political change: "When the foundations of society are threatened, the conservative ideology reminds men of the necessity of some institutions and the desirability of the existing ones."[9] Many other conservatives understand conservatism in exactly this way. They represent the skeptical school of conservatism I referred to earlier.[10] These conservatives are skeptical in the sense that they do not propose to offer a substantive philosophy and they often reject any conception of a transcendental moral order. They conserve less because what exists is right than because they fear the consequences of change itself.

Yet if conservatism is simply a positional philosophy, then there can be liberal conservatives and socialist conservatives and even anarchist conservatives—just so long as there is a liberal, socialist, or anarchist tradition waiting to be conserved. The positional idea of conservatism reduces it to a substantively empty philosophy. And if this is all that conservatism means, then positional conservatism will always suffer from two apparently fatal flaws—its relativism and its inability to inspire. Because positional conservatism has no deeper set of principles or commitments to which to appeal; it will always have to make its case against the unintended consequences of social change in terms of the same utilitarian philosophy that most liberals appeal to today. Thus, the case against change will always have a provisional nature about it. When there is good reason to believe that the benefits of social progress outweigh the costs, conservatives must yield their ground. If this is all that conservatism means in the end, then conservatism can hardly be called an inspiring philosophy.[11]

This, then, is the conservative's dilemma: Either conservatism is a substantive philosophy that conserves the existing social order because it is right, or it is a positional ideology that conserves for the sake of preventing change. Positional conservatism is empty and uninspiring while substantive notions of conservatism are diverse and conflicting.

This chapter traces the evolution of modern conservatism from classical political thought to the emergence of conservatism as a self-consciously held philosophy. I set the stage by describing the classical worldview from which conservatism emerged, and in succeeding sections sketch the political thought of perhaps the three most important conservative thinkers of the late eighteenth and nineteenth centuries, Joseph de Maistre, Edmund Burke, and David Hume, early exemplars of paleoconservatism, traditionalism, and skeptical conservatism.

Conservatives before Conservatism: The Classical Worldview

True conservatism is unthinkable in the absence of an idea of a *given moral order* of the world—an order providing a framework for human politics that must be *conserved.* Beginning with Plato, the classical political worldview took shape in a set of recognizable doctrines that linked history, politics, and the drama of human character in an overarching philosophical mosaic. Central to this worldview was a prevailing apprehension of what we might call the theory of social decay. The idea of social decay was probably already of ancient vintage when Plato presented one version of it in *The Republic*. Written in the fourth century B.C.E., when Athenian democracy was already in decline, *The Republic* was the first systematic attempt in Western thought to provide a template for the ideal society. Like all other things in the temporal world, Plato announced in *The Republic*, all social order is condemned to decay. Plato taught that societies move in a descending cycle of stages or characteristic forms. He began at the stage he found the most perfect—aristocracy or the virtue-loving society. Aristocratic societies, he argued, over time tend to unravel into degenerate forms of aristocracy—to timocracy, the honor-loving society, and from timocracy to oligarchy, the society in which the acquisitive instincts and the rule of the business elite reign supreme. From oligarchy, society degenerates still further into democracy, and from democracy into total anarchy.[12]

At each stage of decline, Plato taught, the social order reflects the changing constitution of society. The constitution of a society was not, for the ancients, a written document guaranteeing a particular form of government but was rather the dominant dispositions of individual character reflected in a society's institutions and its cultural ethos. Each form of society, Plato observed, embodies certain virtues or values that reign supreme and that are reflected in its institutions and mores. Intellectual and moral virtues are dominant in aristocratic societies, military prowess in timocratic societies, conspicuous acquisition and consumption in oligarchic social orders, and freedom and equality in the democratic society, he concluded. Since democracy was for Plato the second worst form of government, it should not surprise us that he associated democracy with what he considered the disordered democratic soul. He tells us that the "anarchic temper" characteristic of democracy honors "rulers who resemble subjects and subjects who are like rulers," where "the resident alien feels himself equal to the citizen, and the citizen to him," and where one finds the "spirit of freedom and equal rights in the relation of men to women and women to men." Plato taught that the degeneration of the political order was a reflection of a kind of moral decay of individual character. Anticipating such thinkers as Niccolò Machiavelli and Vilfredo Pareto, he thought that social decay begins with the social elites and spreads from above to the lower classes.[13]

The cyclical decline of social order reaches its nadir in anarchy. After a period of social desolation, only with the restoration of virtue does the cycle begin anew. In many versions, this reinstitution of virtue required the intervention of the man on the horse, a tyrant or a great leader. The ancients did not necessarily share our modern contempt for the tyrant or equate tyranny with illegitimate or immoral rule; some tyrants were thought to be good, if autocratic, rulers. It was the tyrant's role to put an end to the growing disorder and anarchy that the more aristocratically inclined attributed to the effects of democracy. It was perhaps impossible for the ancients not to recognize in the figures of Philip of Macedon and Julius and Augustus Caesar the great leaders, if not quite the social redeemers, augured by the myth of social decay.

This myth of the cyclical decline of society was discussed by Aristotle, defended by the Roman historian and political thinker Polybius, and accepted by Roman political thinkers such as Cicero. Polybius, who wrote in the second century B.C.E., a century before the end of the Roman republic, apparently had Athens and the other Greek city-states in mind when he wrote of the impermanence of states "which have again and again risen to greatness and fallen into insignificance." Of Rome he cautiously declared that it is difficult "to speak with confidence of their future" given the "natural origin, genesis and decadence" of each form of government in its respective impure forms.[14] A century later Cicero linked declining social morals to the decay of the Roman republic in the years immediately preceding its demise:

> Long before living memory our ancestral way of life produced outstanding men, and those excellent men preserved the old way of life and the institutions of their forefathers. Our generation, however, after inheriting our political organization like a picture now fading with age, not only neglected to restore its old colors but did not even retain its basic form. . . . What remains of these ancient customs on which [the poet] said the state of Rome stood firm? . . . And what shall I say of the men? It is the lack of such men that has led to the disappearance of such customs. Of this great tragedy we are not only bound to give a description, we must somehow defend ourselves as if arraigned on a capital charge. For it is not by accident—no, it is because of our moral failings—that we are left with the name of the Republic having long since lost its substance.[15]

How could the dissolution of society be prevented? By preserving the ancestral morality of a society embodied in the character of its people and preserved by their customs, mores, and practices. But how was this to be done, exactly? Plato's solution was hardly conservative in the modern sense. He recommended the abolition of the family and the institution of property and prescribed rule by an intellectual aristocracy of philosopher-kings. He compared conservatives to "bees, wasps and ants," who follow tradition by habit rather than because they have thought things through as a philosopher should.[16] In this respect, Plato's thought represents perhaps the first example of the kind of social engineering loathed by modern conservatives. Yet his theory of politics adumbrates two important conservative themes— a preference for elitist over democratic political solutions and an insistence that the state must inculcate virtue in individuals by teaching them to discipline their passions and appetites.

Plato contended that order and reason should rule in the soul and in the state and believed that when self-interest or material concerns become the dominant force in politics, the process of social decay is already under way. In *The Republic* he argued that subordination of reason to the "passionate" and "appetitive" impulses of human personality precipitates an injustice in the soul which leads to the degeneration of the social order through its various stages of decadence. He compared the state to the dutiful father, "watering and fostering the growth of the rational principle" in the soul of his son, the citizen, while others attempt to stir his passions and appetites and take him off course. The state itself should be guided by a cadre of philosopher-guardians who are supposed to attain a level of moral and intellectual virtue that permits them to see further and more clearly than members of the other classes. Plato discounted democracy precisely because it gave each individual the same say in government irrespective of level of experience, learning, or rational ability. While modern conservative thought is hardly as elitist in orientation, from Burke's time on we will see a parallel, if more measured, skepticism about democracy.

It was Aristotle, who had been Plato's student, however, who many today consider the first true conservative.[17] Not only did Aristotle provide the definitive imprint to classical political thought for the next two thousand years, his philosophy also set up some of the most striking contrasts between the future conservative and liberal movements. Consider the liberal's and the true conservative's views of the relationship between the individual and society. Locke began from the assumption that the individual is prior to society, morally and logically. For him, society must be thought of as arising (at least hypothetically) from the agreement of individuals, and all our political institutions must be justifiable on the basis of the consent of the individual. This represents a radical reversal of Aristotle, who wrote that "the state is by nature clearly prior to the family and the individual since the whole is of necessity prior to the part."[18] For Aristotle, the state is necessary to sustain the good life, and so in a sense it is more important than any group of individuals. In this respect, true conservatism is an anti-individualistic philosophy. Conservatives from Aristotle on have insisted that, while the state exists to secure the good life for the individual, the claims of the community must come first in order to further the good of the individual.[19] Conservatives thus emphasize duty to one's nation over rights, patriotism over humanistic internationalism, and the importance of adherence to time-honored rules and practices even though these may sometimes bring about apparent injustice in individual cases.

The contrast runs even deeper. Where liberals, particularly from Mill on, frequently look upon society as an alien and oppressive instrument of conformity—where they seem to believe that the quest for true individuality requires that we fight against social forces to find our true authentic self—conservatives believe society is the very source of our humanity and even of our personal identity. Aristotle insisted that people cannot exist in a fully human sense prior to, or outside, society. It is society—"the state," as Aristotle understood the concept—that humanizes us.[20] Outside society, "when separated from law and justice," the human animal is "the worst of all"—"the most unholy and the most savage of animals, and the most full of lust and gluttony," while "man, when perfected [by society], is the best of all animals."[21] Compare this concept, for a moment, to Jean Jacques Rousseau's idea of the noble savage, which influenced nineteenth-century romantic thought and which has indirectly influenced modern liberalism. The noble savage lives in sympathetic harmony with others in the state of nature. According to Rousseau, it is civilized society which corrupts us and which gives us an empty and inauthentic existence of "honor without virtue, reason without wisdom and pleasure without happiness."[22] Rousseau dismissed even the possibility of a cure for our condition in modern society—"once a man is dead, one does not send for the doctor." Where Aristotle declared that "he who first founded the state was the greatest of all benefactors," Rousseau anticipated Marx's critique of the state as a reflection of class interests: "The first man who, having enclosed a piece of ground, bethought himself of saying, 'This is mine,' and found people simple enough to believe him," Rousseau declared, "was the real founder of civil society."[23]

These differences between liberals and true conservatives run still deeper—to radically different views of human nature and the moral order. The conservative is certain that there is an order to things out there—that there is a moral template for the universe that binds human beings and that gives us a particular kind of purpose to fulfill in life. Aristotle taught that individuals can, in a sense, perfect themselves by living in accordance with their assigned function in the great chain of being. Where liberals, following the movement of modern thought, insist that each of us chooses our own end in life, that human purposes are malleable, Aristotle taught that we have a built-in purpose or *telos*, the natural function which nature has prescribed to all human beings. Nature has given us a purpose to fulfill in life, and our fulfillment as individuals depends upon living in conformity with this purpose.[24] The Aristotelian idea of virtue consists of nothing more than acting in conformity with our natural purpose. We foster virtue, he taught, by inculcating good habits in the individual.[25] And in each of these matters the state has an important role to play in the moral and civic education of the individual.

After Aristotle, it fell to the Stoic philosophers, who flourished from around 200 B.C.E. until the second or third century C.E., to develop the idea of the natural law, a central ingredient of later conservative thought. The Stoics taught that natural law provides both the physical and the moral order in the *kosmos*, and that this moral order supervenes on human institutions. It stands as a fixed standard that we, as rational beings, can know. Cicero described the natural law in these terms:

> Law in the proper sense is right reason in harmony with nature. It is spread through the whole human community, unchanging and eternal, calling people to their duty by its commands and deterring them from wrong-doing by its prohibitions. . . . The law cannot be countermanded, nor can it be amended, nor can it be totally rescinded. . . . There will not be one such law in Rome and another in Athens, one now and another in the future, but all peoples at all times will be embraced by a single and eternal and unchangeable law.[26]

Cicero followed another Aristotelian theme: he taught that virtue and right reason require that we follow a middle way between extremes. "All excess . . . over-luxuriance," Cicero wrote, "turns as a rule to its opposite. . . . Excessive freedom topples over into excessive slavery." Freedom consists of tracing a middle course between excessive deference to authority and the anarchic inclination to licentiousness, each of which represents a form of bondage—an idea that was still vital to the political thought of the framers of our own Constitution in the eighteenth century.[27]

These early conservative themes—the problem of social decay, the priority of the whole state over the individual, the role of politics in humanizing us and in inculcating good character, and the idea of the natural law—were all disseminated through various traditions, especially through the Roman law, which influenced medieval European law and through it, the English common law. Thomas Aquinas's reconciliation of Aristotelian and Roman Catholic theology became the cardinal postulate of the natural-law tradition of the seventeenth and eighteenth centuries. These ideals continue to reverberate, however more faintly, in the modern conservative tradition.

The Roots of Modern Paleoconservatism:
The Case of Joseph de Maistre

Modern conservative political thought emerged in the late eighteenth and early nineteenth centuries as a response to the Enlightenment and its political offshoots, liberalism and democracy. In its Christianized form the more orthodox form of conservatism held that God has ordered the universe, that he continues to oversee and to intervene in the world of human affairs, that he has a specific plan for our social order, and that we are responsible for discerning and doing his will in the world. The orthodox conservative holds a providential conception of history: God works through history and, while the world is constantly changing, only those changes sanctioned by God should be given effect in the world of human affairs. Tradition, in particular, provides clues to understanding God's will for the social and political orders.

Joseph de Maistre (1753–1821) is perhaps the most original, if extreme, of post-Enlightenment orthodox conservative thinkers. Maistre wrote to indict not only the French Revolution and its Napoleonic aftermath, but also modernity itself. In few modern thinkers is there a more potent sense of the ubiquity of social decay and of the belief that this decline is because humanity has turned its back on God. In our own time, Maistre has acquired an unfounded reputation for being a kind of protofascist, in large part due to Isaiah Berlin's treatment of his thought.[28] Although Maistre was unquestionably a religious authoritarian who harbored a dark view of fallen humanity, he would have recoiled at the fascist's vision of politics. He shuddered at the idea of the plebiscitarian dictatorship and the charismatic demagogue represented by his nemesis, Napoleon, who in some respects foreshadowed Hitler and Mussolini. When Maistre declared that "everywhere Lucretius was a harbinger of Caesar," he meant that skepticism and materialism tend to lead to revolution and dictatorship. Nothing could be further removed from Mussolini's "philosophy of action" than Maistre's insistence that "those men who appear to influence [history] are only circumstances." The fascist's apotheosis of the will could not have a better contrast than Maistre's orthodox Christian conviction that pride and willfulness are the source of human misery and conflict, that humans are weak, and that "nothing can be altered for the better among men without God."[29] Maistre is the father of paleoconservatism, but to confuse him with Mussolini is to mistake the reactionary right for the radical right.[30]

The central theme of Maistre's *Essay on the Generative Principle of Political Constitutions*, written in 1809, is that human history unfolds in accordance with a divinely conceived plan and that humanity either accepts God and becomes an instrument of this plan or separates itself from God and faces futility, or worse: "Man in communication with his Maker is sublime; his activities creative. The instant he separates himself from God to act alone, on the other hand, he does not lose his power, for it is a privilege of his nature, but his activity is negative and leads only to destruction." Maistre admonishes those who think that they are the original and wholly autonomous authors of their own actions: "Because he is aware of his freedom, [man] forgets his dependence. . . . In a sense, it is as if the trowel thought itself an architect. Doubtless, man is a free, noble and intelligent creature; nevertheless, he is an instrument of God. . . . For the body is the organ and tool of the soul and the soul is the instrument of God." Through God's direct intervention, all political institutions "have arranged themselves so neatly although no man among the vast multitude which acted in this vast world ever knew what he was doing in relation to the whole or foresaw the outcome." There is an implicit trust that must be confided in God, in the course of events, though justice may unfold slowly and indirectly. Ultimately all political affairs are "guided in their course by an infallible power." History is "experimental politics," but it is God's purpose and man can do nothing "unless he seeks the aid of God, Whose instrument he then becomes."[31]

Maistre's providential view of history and politics entails that laws, political constitutions, and human institutions generally cannot be created in an a priori fashion. He advised rulers, reformers, radicals, or any who would presume to create new political institutions to reconsider their plan. Humans cannot create law, and political institutions built upon a foundation other than the fundamental law of God are doomed to fail. "The essence of a fundamental law," he wrote, echoing Cicero, "is that no one has the right to abolish it." Law made by people (*loi*) are not truly "laws" (*droit*), but only "ordinances." Moreover, such law "obligates no one unless a higher power guarantees its enforcement." Thus, "law is only truly sanctioned, and properly law, when assumed to emanate from a higher will."[32]

Maistre's conservatism and the case he made against reform follow a number of classical lines of argument rooted in a theological conception of the world. His notion of evil was Augustinian in nature: it is difficult or futile to change things for the better because "evil is only a negative quality," a condition signaling the absence of good. "Probably human powers extend only to removing or resisting evil in order to separate it from the good, which may then develop freely according to its nature." Moreover, the existence of evil actually plays a role in the pursuit of the good: "Nothing good is unsullied or unaltered by evil. Every evil is repressed and assailed by good, which continually impels existence toward a more perfect state." Evil can even have beneficial consequences. Maistre provided the example of the development in France of the judiciary, the origin of which can be traced to the corruption of the king's court: judicial offices were sold to the nobility in order to line the king's coffers, yet they resulted, Maistre argued, in an independent judiciary that would not have otherwise developed. In this sense, God puts vice to the service of virtue and to the betterment of the community. While all political constitutions have faults, these may be irremovable, even necessary, like the imperfection of a tuned keyboard: "Tune the fifths rigorously and the octaves will be dissonant." Dissonance is inherent and cannot be eliminated; the best that we can do is to distribute this dissonance throughout the instrument. "Imperfection is an element of the perfection possible."[33]

The orthodox conservative's resistance to change is ultimately grounded in the view that political changes are the province of God alone and what unfolds naturally, in accordance with the divine order, is right. Maistre contended that all deliberative human intervention in the social and political realm is potentially futile at best, destructive at worst, which explains "the innate aversion of all intelligent persons to innovation." "The most important institutions," he wrote, "are always the result of circumstance, never of deliberation." Time "is God's prime minister in the province of the world." In fact, time is the ultimate test of the legitimacy of all political institutions. Responding to liberals who argued that all monarchies originate in usurpation, Maistre counseled that "nothing great has great beginnings" and concluded that the true test of the legitimacy of a monarchy is not its origin, but its endurance through the ages. The durability of an institution was, for Maistre, the truest sign of God's sanction. History, like the unwritten English constitution for which Maistre had such praise, "only moves while standing still."[34]

Maistre's conviction that the modern world was decayed, spiritually moribund, is manifest throughout the essay. He thought the eighteenth century the worst of all ages, and the nineteenth simply its continuation. Without "the spice of religion," all arts and sciences are decayed; the theater has blasphemed; the modern novel has blasphemed; history and particularly science have blasphemed. Everywhere, modern society has "prostituted genius to irreligion." Presaging contemporary conservatives, he singled out the universities for a particularly scathing rebuke, especially for their corrupting influence on morals and national character. In the closing pages of the essay, when he returned again to the subject of the eighteenth-century philosophes' onslaught upon religion, he asked: "How has God punished this execrable raving?" He answered: "He punished it as He created the light, in a single word; He said 'So be it!'—and the world of politics crumbled."[35]

The Father of Conservative Traditionalism:
Edmund Burke

Writing just a few years before Maistre, but in response to the same events that drove Maistre to his desk, Edmund Burke (1729–1797), an Anglo-Irish statesman and political essayist, is considered by many the father of modern conservatism. Ironically, perhaps, Burke would not have considered himself a conservative at all—had the label existed in his time. Even a century later Lord Acton considered him "one of the three greatest liberals."[36] He was, after all, an old Whig. The Whigs were, in a sense, the liberals of their day, at least during the late seventeenth and eighteenth centuries. The term "Whig" (a Scottish term that referred to a Presbyterian horse thief) became a political epithet shortly before the English revolution of 1688–1689.[37] The Whigs had supported that revolution and the largely Protestant ouster of the last Catholic king in England. They had sided with Parliament against the crown and, with the rising class of traders and industrialists, against the entrenched privileges of the older landed elite. In the 1770s and 1780s, Burke defended U.S. and Irish independence—highly unpopular stands in his day—and opposed the spread of British imperialism in India and around the globe. These were liberal causes, but Burke's liberalism was the protoclassical liberalism of the WASP, the aristocratic liberalism which some have traced to the American Federalists and to the modern Republican Party.[38]

The central theme in Burke's thought is that societies are held together in one of only two ways—internally, by the preservation of a people's organic customs, traditions, and what he called "prejudices," or externally, by the "despotism" of an expanding government. His thought is a defense of the internal conception of political order, whereas radicalism, as he saw it, depended upon the external imposition of order. Preserving the internal order of society requires, most importantly, the preservation of a tradition, which connects the present to the past and the future, preserving the fabric of a culture through time while also permitting the slow and evolutionary working out of God's order in the world. With a mixture of Irish mysticism and Aristotelianism, he declared that society is

> a partnership not only between those who are living, but a partnership between those who are living, those who are dead and those who are to be born. Each contract in each particular state is but a clause in the great primeval contract of eternal society, linking the lower with the higher nature, connecting the visible and the invisible world, according to a fixed compact sanctioned by the invisible oath which holds all physical and all moral natures, each in their appointed place.[39]

With Cicero and Aquinas, Burke believed devoutly in a given moral template for human affairs, insisting that through inheritance, tradition, and prescription, "our political system is placed in a just correspondence and symmetry with the order of the world." Burke taught that by ensuring the natural evolution of our social institutions, tradition preserves "the method of nature in the conduct of the state."[40]

Yet if God remains the architect of our social institutions, human beings are less the trowel (as they were for Maistre) than the engineers of change. Burke conceded, perhaps as Maistre would not, that while the natural law was binding on our institutions, our concrete political cues come from terrestrial rather than heavenly sources. He insisted that "the practical consequences of any political tenet go a great way in deciding upon its value." While he believed in a transcendent moral order of the universe, time and again he declared that it was useless to turn to metaphysical truths to tell us what to do in a given situation. Any skeptical conservative could agree when he declared: "In reality there are two, and only two, foundations of Law; and they are both of them conditions without which nothing can give it any force; I mean equity and utility." Law, too, is a matter of convention, not a deduction from the eternal order. "If civil society be the offspring of convention, then convention must be its law. That convention must limit and modify all the descriptions of constitutions which are formed under it. Every sort of legislature, judiciary or executory power, are its creatures."[41] The connection between politics and the eternal order is mediated by conscious human activity that unfolds only gradually through the slowly evolving traditions of a society.

Burke poeticized Aristotle's soft collectivism, his insistence that the state is prior to the individual. Society, he wrote, "is to be looked on with other reverence; because it is not a partnership in things subservient only to the gross animal existence of a temporary and perishable nature." Burke was critical of the creeping materialism of his own time and scorned as "sophisters, calculators and economists" the Benthamites and materialists who thought that politics could be reduced to maximizing the material interests of the governed.[42] Burke's antimaterialism presaged one of the more interesting rifts in modern conservatism—between the traditionalists whose emphasis is on the preservation of the moral and spiritual dimensions of culture and the conservative economists who are driven by the values of material growth and economic efficiency.[43] For Burke, as for Aquinas five centuries earlier, the object of society is the satisfaction not merely of human needs but of our moral perfection, of which only God can judge. God is "the initiator and author and protector of civil society; without which civil society man could not by any possibility arrive at the perfection of which his nature is capable, nor even make a remote and faint approach to it." Politics are an art, but an art which has as its highest aspiration the moral perfection of humanity in the image of God: "He who gave us our nature to be perfected by our virtue, willed also the necessary means of its perfection. He willed therefore the State. He willed its connection with the source and original archetype of all perfection."[44]

We should underscore that when Burke used the term "the State," he was hardly referring simply to the political institutions of a society. His concept of the state was closer to Aristotle's than to ours: the state is all our socializing institutions; it encompasses "civil society." As for the state in the modern political sense, Burke assumed that it should have little role in day-to-day human conduct. When British prime minister William Pitt asked him what role the government should play in the event of a terrible famine—in our own time, we might think of some catastrophic natural disaster such as a Hurricane Katrina or a terrible earthquake—Burke responded that government should "confine itself to what regards the State or the creatures of the State"—only "those things that are truly and properly public." It is not the function of government to answer to the need of individuals in their private capacity, even in exigent circumstances.[45] Burke agreed with Aristotle and Locke, each in part, simultaneously: the state was prior to the individual, as Aristotle said, but in its political form it must be strictly limited.

Burke's conservatism, like modern conservatism generally, was a response to the revolutionary lurch of history in his own time, and to what he regarded as the demoralization of politics brought about by the revolutionary movements in France and elsewhere. He reserved his most withering scorn for the political metaphysicians—the Condorcets and the Rousseaus—who inspired a revolution on the strength of what he regarded as misplaced abstractions and oracular conjectures. "Nothing," he wrote, "can be conceived more hard than the heart of a thoroughbred metaphysician. It comes nearer to the cold malignity of a wicked spirit than to the frailty and passion of a man. It is like that of the principle of evil himself, incorporeal, pure, unmixed, dephlegmated, defecated evil."[46]

Of the rationalistic and radical theories that began flowing, in his view, like a polluted river from across the Channel, he declared that "the pretended rights of these theorists are all extremes, and in proportion as they are metaphysically true they are morally and politically false." We cannot look simply to abstract rationality detached from a concrete context since "nothing is good, but in proportion and with reference." Politics is a matter of sound and prudent judgment—judgment born of practiced experience and informed by the wisdom of tradition, the residue of generations, since "the individual is foolish, but the species is wise."[47] The real wisdom of a people dwells in its common "prejudices"—for Burke this term carried none of the modern taint. Nothing could be worse, in Burke's view, than to strip a community of its prejudices, which he considered a kind of intuitive wisdom that is "anterior to intellect." To eviscerate the prejudices of a community is to devalue its unique cultural identity and loosen the bonds that draw a community together. He thus accused the radical philosophes of denuding the community of everything that makes it a true community: "you have industriously destroyed all the opinions and prejudices . . . all the instincts which support government. . . . You lay down metaphysical propositions which infer universal consequences, and then you attempt to limit logic by despotism."[48] Once the internal bonds of community have withered, communities can be held together only externally by government.

The emphasis on tradition may appear conservative to us today in that it limits social and political change, but it also assures independence and autonomy to each nation and culture. Where Cicero had argued that "all peoples at all times will be embraced by a single and eternal and unchangeable law," Burke's conception of tradition permitted a multiplicity of different social forms which "vary with times and circumstances, and admit of infinite modifications."[49] No nation's culture and tradition can be changed politically, in a top-down manner, without rending the social fabric that holds all practices and customs and institutions in place relative to one another. The moral culture of a society, its true "constitution," is its foundation for all true conservatives.

We begin to see in Burke's thought the shift from a substantive defense of practices and institutions because they are right to a defense based on what conservatives call their "latent functions," their propensity to bind the social order. Common prejudices bind societies together, irrespective of the nature of these prejudices or the diversity of such prejudices held by different cultures. Similarly, tradition works against the atomization of society by rooting the individual in time, by locating the individual in a greater continuity that runs from the past to the future. One of Burke's deepest psychological insights was that "people will not look forward to posterity who do not look backward to their ancestors."[50] As the bonds of community connect the individual to others at any given time, so tradition connects us to our ancestors and our descendants. As this temporal continuity is sundered, Burke thought, the individual becomes lost in time, lost even to oneself.

The First Skeptical Conservative

Where Maistre and Burke accepted many of the most essential assumptions of the classical worldview, especially the premise that there exists a transcendent moral order to which our institutions must conform, we should not be surprised that others during this period began to graft political conservatism onto a more modernist philosophical foundation. The single most important such theorist, and the thinker who deserves to be considered the first skeptical conservative, was the Scottish philosopher, essayist, and historian David Hume (1711–1776.) Hume presented the case for conservatism in a form free of its theological and metaphysical trappings.

Hume might appear an unlikely candidate to be remembered as conservative; Russell Kirk explicitly denied that he was a conservative at all.[51] In contrast to Maistre's fervent Catholicism and Burke's devout Anglicanism, Hume was an agnostic who famously refused absolution on his deathbed. Where Maistre and Burke believed in some version of the natural law, Hume laid the axe to the very root of natural law theory by introducing into Western thought the "is-ought" distinction and the radical separation of facts and values. Where Maistre insisted that only divine will could be the basis for social order and where Burke defended tradition as a reflection of the natural order, Hume openly questioned God's existence and thought that social convention was all that distanced us from imminent anarchy. Where Maistre pronounced the eighteenth century "a sacrilegious conspiracy of every human talent against its Creator," Hume's philosophy represents the zenith of the most skeptical strand of Enlightenment thought.[52] It is little wonder that Maistre, writing a few decades after Hume's death, considered him a "teacher of evil."[53]

Yet it was precisely Hume's skepticism that moved him in the direction of political conservatism. Where Maistre and Burke each wrote in response to the French Revolution, begun in 1789, Hume died on the brink of the age of revolution—as Leslie Stephen sardonically put it, "appropriately enough in 1776."[54] Hume was driven to his conservatism not by events on the ground, but because he was dubious both of the religious fundamentalist's faith in God and the Whiggish liberal's faith in the individual and in progress. For better or worse, Hume was conservative because he suspected that humanity stands alone in the universe and holds its fate in its own hands.

Hume believed in no transcendent moral order. He thought that our notions of justice and morality arise from human sources alone. "Public utility," he wrote in his *Enquiry Concerning the Principles of Morals*, "is the *sole* origin of justice and . . . the beneficial consequences of this virtue are the *sole* foundation of its merit." The "rules of equity or justice depend entirely," he argued, "on the particular state and condition in which men are placed and owe their existence to that utility to the public which results from their strict and regular observance."[55] In this respect, Hume was an early utilitarian and a fellow traveler of the modern moral relativist. Yet what made him a conservative was that he believed that social utility was best achieved by steady observance of the long-established rules and norms of a society.

Order, stability, continuity, and the protection of settled expectations—these were the essential ingredients of an enduring society.

Aristotle declared that the state was prior to the individual, and Burke had concluded that the individual is foolish but the species is wise. Hume cast this same insight in less poetic, more utilitarian terms. He thought that evolved social systems must be permitted to function toward a set of ends and according to a plan that is greater than the purposes of particular individuals. Justice, he wrote, "is not the consequence of every individual single act, but arises from the whole scheme or system."[56] For this reason, like many conservatives today, Hume distrusted the "do-gooder," the whistle blower, or the "man of principle." He declared that "the more principle a person possesses, the more apt is he, on such occasions, to neglect and abandon his domestic duties."[57] He similarly rejected abstract claims for social justice, whether promulgated by the religious fundamentalist or by the crusading progressive, in favor of a reasonably secure, if imperfect, social condition. "The maxim, *fiat Justitia ruat Coelum*, let justice be performed, though the universe be destroyed, is apparently false."[58] The world is imperfect and imperfectible. For the most part, it is more important to do no evil than to strive for affirmative good.

Hume rejected both the right-wing preoccupation with merit and the left-wing quest for substantive equality as bases for social distribution. Merit cannot be the basis for distribution of social benefits for "so great is the uncertainty of merit, both from its natural obscurity and from the self-conceit of each individual, that no determinate rule of conduct would result from it."[59] In this, Hume anticipated the views of those economic libertarians like Ludwig von Mises, F. A. Hayek, and Milton Friedman who maintained that only the social utility of a person's works, as judged by the market, can be the basis for reward. Here the conservative's veneration of systemic processes over individual judgment is merged with the modern and more relativistic idea that there are no absolute standards of value, no given order by which to judge merit.

As for attempts to legislate equality, these are either futile or will eventuate in the impoverishment of the nation: "Render possession ever so equal, men's different degrees of art, care and industry will immediately break that equality. Or if you check these virtues, you reduce society to the most extreme indigence; and instead of preventing want and beggary in a few, render it unavoidable to the whole community." Milton Friedman could not have put it better in criticizing the progressive's quest. And with Maistre and Burke, Hume declared that what sounds good in theory is often "pernicious and destructive" in practice. He held the radical philosophe in the same low opinion as would Burke and Maistre a few years later. While "*saints alone inherit the earth*," Hume wrote, "the civil magistrate puts these sublime theorists on the same footing with common robbers."[60]

Anticipating Bentham and the neoclassical economists of the nineteenth and twentieth centuries, Hume rejected the idea of natural rights. He defended the institution of property not in terms of a Lockean right to keep the fruits of one's labor, but in order to encourage human industry in the future. "Whatever is produced or improved by a man's art or industry ought, for ever, to be secured to him to give encouragement to such useful habits and accomplishments." He favored the rights to pass on one's wealth to one's children for the same reason. Similarly, Hume contended that the law of contract is based not on some backward-looking notion of promise keeping, but on the forward-looking, utilitarian reason that contracts promote commerce and "secure mutual trust and confidence" among those engaged in commerce. Property and contract are, in sum, human constructions, creatures of society or the state. But for this reason they should be protected only to the extent that they serve the greater good, since "all questions of property are subordinate to authority of civil laws, which extend, restrain, modify and alter the rules of natural justice."[61]

While Hume thought that human beings are naturally moved by sentiments of sympathy and beneficence for their fellows, he also taught that human nature is deeply flawed and that paternalism is sometimes justified. Not only is an individual drawn frequently off the path of virtue by patent self-interest, but worse, "much more frequently, he is seduced from his great and important, though distant interests, by the allurement of present, though often very frivolous, temptations. This great weakness is incurable in human nature." Where Maistre would have located the defect in human pride, the more charitable Hume chalked it up in part to myopia, simple short-sightedness. With Aristotle, and as against his one-time friend Rousseau, Hume concluded that human goodness is nurtured, not corrupted, by civilization, custom, and habit. "Habit soon consolidates what other principles of human nature had imperfectly founded."[62]

Because Hume believed that human judgment was all too fallible, he shared most conservatives' antipathy toward social contract ideas and, more generally, toward the classical liberal's insistence that we can build our institutions from the ground up from individual choices. In "Of the Original Contract," Hume delivered a scathing attack on the idea that the legitimacy of our political institutions depends upon the tacit consent of the individual. The social contract was inconceivable, he argued, without its being underwritten by the very social order it is supposed to create. Since the obligation to obey promises is itself a social artifact, the social contract could not predate society. Hume viewed the classical liberal's social contract as an example of philosophical bootstrapping of the worst kind, and concluded that it is borne out by neither history nor logic.

More generally, the world does not run on rational choice, consent, or persuasion; it runs on force: "The face of the earth is continually changing, by the encrease of small kingdoms into great empires, by the dissolution of great empires into smaller kingdoms, by the planting of colonies, by the migration of tribes. Is there anything discoverable in all these events but force and violence? Where is the mutual agreement or voluntary association so much talked of?"[63] Since the conservative's bête noire is instability, anarchy, the power vacuum, and since anarchy is always ready to reassert itself, social order requires that force be met with force. In times of insurrection, Hume maintained, "every wise man wishes to see, at the head of a powerful and obedient army, a general, who may speedily seize the prize, and give to the people a master, which they are so unfit to chuse for themselves."[64] Discussion, democracy, and mutual consent are all fine things, but these more sublimated institutions are possible only once traditions and customs have stabilized what power has consolidated. Hume would certainly have agreed with James Fitzjames Stephen a century later that, beneath the patina of the democratic ethos, there is always the specter of force. Even in a democracy, "the minority gives way," Stephen continued, "not because it is convinced that it is wrong, but because it is convinced that it is a minority."[65]

Has Hume's skeptical conservatism had a legacy? On two fronts, many contemporary conservatives will find this brand of conservatism off-putting. Paleoconservatives, traditionalists, fundamentalists, and others will reject Hume's theological skepticism, while those rooted in the classical liberal tradition will object to his rejection of individualism and the social contract. Yet Hume's thought prefigures the skeptical conservatism of such thinkers as the British political theorist Michael Oakeshott and, more recently, Andrew Sullivan. In his book *The Conservative Soul*, Sullivan distinguishes "fundamentalism" from what he regards as true "conservatism." In contrast to the fundamentalist, Sullivan imagines the conservative as a kind of Socrates who "knows what he doesn't know." Conservatives are doubters, not true believers, Sullivan argues, and epistemological modesty is the very essence and driving force of conservatism. Where the liberal's skepticism expresses itself in the optimistic conviction that nothing has to be the way it is, that anything can be changed and usually for the better, the conservative's skepticism is the pessimistic skepticism of Murphy's law: if something can go wrong, expect that it will. "If there is any doubt as to whether your random next encounter will be with the Dalai Lama or Charles Manson," Sullivan writes, "your safest option is to bet on Manson."[66]

Where the moralist or the fundamentalist seems to know all the answers, the skeptic has no foundations, no clear direction to proceed. Philosophy and religion can give us little solace because of "the fundamental incompatibility of certainty with humanity, of philosophy with politics, of ideas with practice," Sullivan maintains. "Somehow, we have to live in the interstices." Sullivan, who is gay, writes poignantly if ambivalently of his Roman Catholicism, sounding themes that are frequently discordant with that faith. He tells us that "the greatest human error is to believe . . . that there is a truth 'up there' that must or can be transposed down here."[67] This is about as far as we can get from the sense of order and certitude of the classical worldview. We are marooned in a world without clear signs, consigned to grope our way collectively through the dark passages of history. Not surprisingly, this form of skepticism tends to move the skeptical conservative in a libertarian direction. With no foundations, and no clear moral destination, Sullivan argues that we must be content to permit individuals to follow their own vision of the good life, whether this is the vision of "the Hawaiian surfer, the New York raver, the Ann Arbor stoner, the Alabama hunter, or any true fan of baseball or cricket."[68] Freedom for the raver? For the Ann Arbor stoner? If this is conservatism, then it is only a stone's throw from the liberalism of John Stuart Mill.

Sullivan's greatest intellectual hero, Oakeshott, treated conservatism as a disposition, a philosophy of life that does not depend upon—in fact, is at odds with having—any particular foundation in theology or metaphysics. He wrote winsomely in his essay "On Being Conservative":

To be conservative, then, is to prefer the familiar to the unknown, to prefer the tried to the untried, fact to mystery, the actual to the possible, the limited to the unbounded, the near to the distant, the sufficient to the superabundant, the convenient to the perfect, present laughter to utopian bliss. Familiar relationships will be preferred to the allure of more profitable attachments, to acquire and enlarge will be less important than to keep, to cultivate, and enjoy; the grief of loss will be more acute than the excitement of novelty or promise. It is to be equal to one's fortune, to live at the level of one's own means, to be content with the want of greater perfection.[69]

Oakeshott's definition highlights not simply the conservative's aversion to change but, on the positive side, a disposition of settled gratitude concerning one's lot in life.

Still, there is the other side of skeptical conservatism. One of Oakeshott's most oft-quoted passages, which Sullivan repeats, gives a melancholy sense of the skeptical conservative's outlook on the world: "Men sail a boundless and bottomless sea; there is neither harbour nor shelter nor floor for anchorage; neither a starting point nor an appointed destination. The enterprise is to keep afloat on an even keel."[70] Unlike the liberal, who believes in infallible progress, and the fundamentalist, who believes that the world is in the hands of Providence, the skeptical conservative believes that we are free but alone in the universe and that history is purely contingent. Anything can happen—and what happens is often for the worse. In Oakeshott's philosophy, existentialism becomes conservative and conservatism becomes thoroughly modern.

Chapter 3
What "Liberalism" and
"Conservatism" Mean Today

TO UNDERSTAND WHAT MODERN "liberalism" and "conservatism"—as these terms are now used—have become, we have to begin by recognizing a truth that most contemporary liberals and quite a few conservatives, too, will want to resist. By any measure, both liberalism and conservatism have moved considerably leftward on the political spectrum over the course of the past two centuries. What counts as liberalism today is in fact a hybrid of the older negative liberalism, now largely confined to the personal domain, and a moderated form of Western-style democratic socialism. And the various strains of contemporary conservatism are a mixture of classical liberalism brigaded with emanations of the older conservatism. Just as liberalism today is often torn between its classical liberal roots and its increasingly socialistic teleology, conservatism often seems to stand astride the same fault lines that, two centuries ago, separated the older conservatism from classical liberalism.

How Liberalism and Conservatism
Have Moved Leftward

The leftward drift of liberalism and conservatism is evident even at relatively close range. Speaking of a time in his life when he had been a Democrat, Ronald Reagan insisted, "I didn't leave the Democratic Party; the Democratic Party left me." Of course, some of Reagan's own positions had changed over time, but it's fair to say that, by the 1960s, liberalism had become associated with a number of positions that would have struck liberals even a generation earlier as untenable, perhaps even irresponsible. Neoconservative Irving Kristol looked back on the 1960s and said that it was easy for a liberal to become a neoconservative then—"all you had to do was stand still."[1] Like many of his ilk, Kristol is a defender of the welfare state and of a constellation of positions that were central to the new liberalism of FDR.[2] But now this is called "neoconservatism." Those liberals who became conservative while standing still were increasingly exercised by two things—the extension of the New Deal's "big government" philosophy to an ever-expanding number of areas of everyday life, and the influence of the values of the New Left on the liberalism of the 1960s and 1970s. With William F. Buckley's conservatives, an increasing number of erstwhile liberals found themselves wanting to "stand athwart history, yelling Stop!"

Liberals have successfully redefined liberalism's central concepts and values so that liberalism today in many ways stands for positions almost diametrically opposed to the positions of liberals a century and a half ago. Ask liberals today whether they favor a limited state or a state that takes an active role in ordering the myriad forms of social and economic relations among individuals, and they will reflexively defend a large measure of state intervention. Query whether they favor the protection of property and contract rights and a laissez-faire approach to economic relations, and they will reject each of these out of hand as anachronistic ideals. Inquire further whether they are opposed, as Tocqueville, Mill, and Acton were opposed, to paternalistic laws that make the state the final arbiter of the best interests of the individual in a broad range of matters, and they will answer that they are liberals and not libertarians. As H. W. Brands, a defender of modern liberalism, puts it in *The Strange Death of American Liberalism*, liberals today "define themselves as defenders of the downtrodden against the rich and powerful, as upholders of equality in the face of inequality, as apostles of compassion and tolerance in a world distressingly devoid of both." Reflecting the liberal's reliance on government to achieve greater equality, he adds: "whatever else it entails, liberalism is premised on a prevailing confidence in the ability of government—preeminently the federal government—to accomplish substantial good on behalf of the American people."[3]

Contemporary liberals and their fellow travelers use a variety of rhetorical devices to camouflage the larger leftward trajectory of our political history. One tactic is to describe policies and positions by labels that are one or two positions to the right of what they actually represent—calling socialist policies "liberal" and conservative positions "fascist." The late postmodernist Richard Rorty used the "f" word liberally, concluding that "our country is not so much in danger of slipping into fascism as it is a country which has *always been quasi-fascist*."[4] Another tactic is to link an unwillingness to continue in the direction of more government and more redistribution to some historic "conservative" political transgression or embarrassment. "The legacy of slavery, America's original sin," writes Paul Krugman in *The Conscience of a Liberal*, for example, "is the reason we're the only advanced economy that doesn't guarantee health care to our citizens."[5]

Liberals should know better than to make these kinds of simplistic and (in Rorty's case) outrageous claims. The truth is that Liberalism Past has achieved each of its major goals in turn: the end of slavery, an expanded franchise for women and minorities, the New Deal reforms including Social Security, the end of Jim Crow, the passage of the civil rights laws, the Great Society reforms, affirmative action, dramatically increased acceptance of gays and lesbians, et cetera. At each point in the trajectory, a new goal has come into view. Few liberal advocates of civil rights laws at the time of their passage in the 1960s would have advocated modern affirmative action policies. Few who argued for the decriminalization of sodomy laws in the 1950s and 1960s would have dreamed that forty years later we would be having a genuine national debate about gay marriage.[6] Even the exceptions—the few points where liberals lost some important battle—prove the rule: The Equal Rights Amendment fell a state short of passage a quarter century ago. Yet virtually everything that the ERA Amendment was intended to guarantee has come to pass through court decisions and legislation. Over the long haul, liberals have won almost every major political battle and most Americans today are, for the most part, glad they did. But when Americans hold their applause—as many do today concerning unlimited abortion rights or affirmative action or the call for open borders or a still larger government—they are accused of being reactionaries or, worse, fascists.

As liberalism has moved to the left, modern conservatism has moved left as well, filling the vacuum left by what used to be called "liberalism." Eighteenth-century conservatives harbored views that few conservatives today could agree with, at least if they hope to have any influence in public affairs. Men like William Blackstone and Edmund Burke in England, and John Adams and Alexander Hamilton here in the United States, were notoriously dubious about extending the right to vote to those without substantial property interests. Burke insisted that "a perfect democracy is the most shameless thing in the world" and quipped that "twenty four million [the number of adult British subjects at the time] ought to prevail over two hundred thousand" [the number who could then vote] only if "the constitution of a kingdom be a problem of arithmetic."[7] How many conservatives today would hold such "aristocratic" views? Not many and, again, not openly.

Modern conservatives almost universally reject the more absolutist conservatism of those like Joseph de Maistre and Louis Bonald—the authoritarian conservatism that was opposed to all forms of liberalism two centuries ago. Robert P. George, a staunch Roman Catholic professor of political theory at Princeton, is a good example. George has been one of the most influential and vocal defenders of a conception of natural law rooted in the theology of St. Thomas Aquinas. He passionately defends a strong pro-life position, believes that homosexual acts should be illegal, contends that contraception should be unavailable to unmarried persons, and goes so far as to insist that noncoital sexual acts between a married couple are morally illicit. George nevertheless argues that "faithful Catholics not only may but *must* be liberals." While George is certainly not endorsing many of the positions associated with modern liberalism, he argues that Roman Catholic teachings over the course of the last century clearly require a belief in the dignity of the individual, the defense of democracy, the protection of individual rights, and even a commitment to some level of economic redistribution to help the poor.[8] And George's positions represent what some count as the Far Right in the United States today.

How many conservatives a century ago would have supported laws forbidding discrimination in public accommodations, as most nonlibertarian conservatives do today? (In fact, how many liberals would have supported this a little more than a century ago?) How many conservatives then would have accepted the right of women to vote, to hold political office, or to head major corporations? Who would have conceived that a "conservative" justice of the Supreme Court, one appointed by Ronald Reagan, would have authored an opinion holding unconstitutional laws prohibiting consensual sexual relations among homosexuals, as Justice Anthony Kennedy did in the *Lawrence* decision a few years ago?[9] If this is "conservatism," one wonders what it is that is being *conserved*.

The Liberal Influence on Modern Conservatism

Four of the five strains of contemporary conservatism—paleoconservatism, traditionalism, neoconservatism, skeptical conservatism, and the cluster of classical liberal theories—are children of the Enlightenment and owe at least as much to the liberal as to the classical conservative tradition. Only the paleoconservatives—reactionary conservatives, often of a religious cast—can claim the mantle as heirs of the classical political tradition.[10] Yet even paleoconservatives accept core modernist values, including democracy and a defense of the U.S. Constitution, underscoring the extent to which even the most rigorous forms of conservatism today accept the essential political consequences of the Enlightenment. The policies of the John Birch Society represent a good example of core paleoconservative values—anti-Communism, antiglobalism, anti-interventionism, anti–civil rights policies, and so on. Their motto: "Less government, more responsibility and—with God's help—a better world." Yet they are unabashed defenders of the U.S. Constitution and democracy.[11]

While we can trace the various strains of modern conservatism to distinct traditions—paleoconservatism to thinkers such as Maistre, traditionalism to Burke, skeptical Enlightenment conservatism to Hume, as we saw in the last chapter—the distinctions between these traditions today are far from pristine. In fact, the labels "libertarian," "neoconservative," and "paleoconservative" emerged as political designations only in the 1950s and 1960s.[12] Notwithstanding the important differences on particular policy issues, in truth there are only two questions—one philosophical and one political—which divide conservatives today.

The philosophical question: Is there a God or, more specifically, a moral template for the universe that governs human affairs? That is, is there a basic moral order that our political and social institutions need to *conserve*? Generally, conservatives who answer in the affirmative come closest to the classical political worldview discussed in the last chapter and tend to fall further to the right on a host of political and social issues. They believe in a given moral order in the world and may accept some robust conception of social decay. Most paleoconservatives and traditionalists—among whose members can be counted evangelicals and fundamentalists, for example—adopt an explicitly God-centered conception of politics. In his essay "Why I Am Not a Neoconservative," historian Stephen Tonsor writes:

> Most old-fashioned conservatives are free of metaphysical anxiety and as happy as clams in a world that bears the unmistakable imprint of God's ordering hand. They are free of alienation, and they have absolutely no hope of a utopian political order. They live with sin and tragedy not as a consequence of the inadequacy of social engineering, but as a consequence of man's sin and disorder. They believe that human institutions and human culture are subject to the judgment of God, and they hold that the most effective political instrument is prayer and a commitment to try to understand and do the will of God.[13]

Other conservatives are frequently lukewarm on the theological question. Neoconservatives seem to assume that belief in God and an eternal order is a good thing *for most people to have,* but frequently seem to be skeptical themselves.[14] Skeptical conservatives from Hume on either don't believe or wish to bracket the issue (though they will usually agree that widespread religious belief helps societies cohere). And classical liberals are also divided, though those who believe in a natural law obviously believe that there is in some sense a set of eternal moral truths, whether or not they accept a divine explanation for this.

Largely because of these differences on the theological question or, more broadly, on the question about whether morality is God given or merely a human construction, traditionalists and paleocons frequently do not consider the others "true conservatives," though they have been willing to form strategic alliances with them against liberalism. As Tonsor in his typically provocative manner puts it: "When the wagon train is attacked we arm the women and children even though they may, in their ineptitude, occasionally mistake a friend for a foe." But when the others—particularly the neoconservatives—attempt to redefine the philosophy of conservatism, it is time to draw the line. "It's splendid when the town whore gets religion and joins the church. Now and then she makes a good choir director, but when she begins to tell the minister what he ought to say in his Sunday sermons, matters have been carried too far."[15] The public split between paleo- and neoconservatism that erupted more than two decades ago is, in the deepest sense, largely a religious split, but not because neoconservatism is supposed to be a Jewish phenomenon while paleoconservatism is a fundamentalist or Roman Catholic affair, as some have claimed.[16] The deeper divide has to do with the debate between secular and sectarian conservatives, between those who believe that our political institutions must conform to a certain order and those who believe that morality and politics are purely human constructions.

The second, more political question that divides today's conservatives concerns the ideological tension between the constellations of attitudes separating libertarians and classical liberals from traditionalists and paleocons. This tension has to do with basic attitudes concerning individualism versus collectivism, and freedom versus order and authority. Here, again, the more collectivist and authoritarian leanings of traditionalists and paleocons push them toward the political Right. Fusionist libertarian Frank Meyer famously clashed with Russell Kirk, the father of modern traditionalism, though both were contributing staffers for Buckley's *National Review.* Meyer scathingly attacked Kirk's *The Conservative Mind* as Burkean socialism, and Kirk waved away Meyer's more libertarian *What Is Conservatism?* in a dismissive three- or four-sentence review in another journal.[17] While traditionalists and libertarians both despair of the movement toward an increasingly egalitarian society in which the state is given a progressively greater share of power in directing the everyday affairs of ordinary human beings, they oppose the drift for very different reasons. Libertarians oppose expanding government because they believe it infringes on individual rights, whereas many conservatives emphasize the way expanding government undermines individual initiative and erodes the delicate network of social relations within the sphere of civil society. The libertarian rejects government because it is an expansion of coercive authority, while the conservative rejects it, in part, for exactly the opposite reason: because an expansive government undermines traditional authority, particularly the authority inherent in the family, the church, and the mediating structures of civil society.[18]

At the heart of libertarianism are two very unconservative instincts. First, libertarians do not share most conservatives' resistance to social change; libertarians are not lovers of tradition nor do they find in the past a model for present society. Second, libertarians are strongly antiauthoritarian in their attitudes, while conservatives frequently defend the need for greater authority in social institutions.

Where conservatives often support capital punishment, for example, libertarians usually oppose it. As Murray Rothbard put it, "Murder is murder" and "does not become sanctified . . . if committed by the government."[19] In general, the conservative, but not the libertarian, is particularly concerned about preserving the moral fabric of society. Compare the libertarian's to the traditional conservative's attitudes to such activities as drug use, nontraditional sexual behavior (homosexuality, prostitution), feminism, flag burning, or separation of church and state issues. In each case the libertarian defends what the conservative condemns. And the conservative condemns these things in the belief that they reflect a breakdown in the moral fabric of society.

There have been some famous attempts to fuse the two philosophies. Frank Meyer's *In Defense of Freedom* is the most significant of these. Meyer wrote that "virtue cannot be enforced by political means." To the libertarian he concedes that freedom "is the end of political theory and political action." But to the conservative he admits that freedom "is not the end of men's existence." Virtue is. Freedom is a "decisive and integral condition, but still only a condition" of virtue. It is for politics to preserve this condition, our essential freedom, and for individuals to pursue virtue on their own, "un-assisted" by the state.[20] But ultimately—on the essential political and legal issues of state action—Meyer's "fusionism" rings more libertarian than conservative.

Most conservatives have instinctively understood that while libertarians and conservatives share common foes on the left, the underlying thrust of their respective political philosophies are deeply antagonistic to each other.[21] Conservatives are far less radical than libertarians in both the moral sphere (where they stand to the right of libertarians) and in the economic sphere (where they stand to their left.) If this latter conclusion seems surprising, consider the neocon's defense of the welfare state, the traditionalist's acceptance of antidiscrimination laws in employment, and most conservatives' acceptance of the principle of equal pay for women and minorities who perform the same jobs as men. Modern U.S. conservatism is a faint whisper of the earlier conservative spirit. With each movement leftward taken by liberalism, conservatism has been drawn involuntarily along the same trajectory, though at some distance.[22]

The remainder of this chapter explores four dimensions along which liberalism and conservatism have traditionally been distinguished—their respective attitudes toward individualism, social change, individual responsibility, and equality. What I hope to show is that while these are still valid ways of understanding the many disagreements between liberals and conservatives, in some ways they are misleading. In fact, there have been some striking reversals of thought—points where conservatives appear to embrace what was once considered the more liberal position even as liberals sometimes appear more conservative.

Reinterpreting Individualism and Collectivism

What was it about the earlier form of liberalism that made it so unconservative? What lies beneath Locke's defense of limited government and the right of revolution, Smith's and Bentham's defense of economic laissez-faire, and Mill's rejection of paternalistic and moralistic limits on the individual? And what makes the modern liberal's defense of the right of privacy and the emphasis on personal choice so liberal? The answer is that each of these ideals depends upon a commitment to individualism. Liberalism prioritizes freedom and individualism over the collective, while conservatism places collective social values—order, patriotism, a shared moral code—first. Yet this seems less accurate today, at a time when most liberals support an expanded state and most conservatives oppose it.

From Plato and Aristotle on, the classical tradition taught that the state or society is morally or logically prior to the individual, whereas early liberals from Locke on believed that the individual comes first—that social and political arrangements must be justified somehow in individual terms. Of course, no conservative theory is purely collectivist, and no liberal theory is purely individualistic. Every conservative from Aristotle on has believed that the mark of the good state is that it guarantees the good life for its citizens, and every liberal understands that the interests of the state must sometimes take precedence over the interests of particular individuals, as in times of national defense. Nevertheless, liberals tend to start from the individual and build up from there, justifying social and political institutions in ways that are tied more directly to the will of the individual, whereas true conservative theories assume that our primary emphasis should rest upon preserving a good society and that the well-being of individuals will follow from this.

Modern political thought began with the social contract tradition of Hobbes, Locke, and Rousseau, which taught that political institutions are legitimate only to the extent that they reflect the *express or tacit consent* of the individual. Of the three thinkers, Locke and the classical liberal tradition arguably remained the most faithful to this underlying idea, holding that all social institutions and arrangements must be built from the bottom up, from decentralized agreements between individuals.[23] This bottom-up conception of social arrangements winds up having several important consequences. It requires, first, that government be limited. Classical liberals from Locke to Tocqueville recognized that when even democratic government grows too large, it tends to submerge the choices of individuals on the ground, replacing them with a system of institutional constraints, laws, rules, structures, and so on that limit individual choice. The bottom-up model also means that, in all matters that fall beyond the sphere of government, social arrangements should *flow from*, rather than precede, individual choices. On the classical liberal model, individuals should be free to make contracts, groups should be free to associate, and societies should be free to evolve and unfold and even disband in accordance with the felt needs of their members.

Even when modern liberals began to reject this older dogma of the social contract, they retained something of this idea that social change should occur from the ground up, without a great deal of external social structures. As the progressive British journalist L. T. Hobhouse, perhaps looking more behind than ahead, put it in 1911, liberalism is based on "the belief that society can safely be founded on the self-directing power of personality."[24] While Hobhouse was convinced that more government was necessary than the classical liberal thought appropriate, *government* was not the key to liberalism. Like other early progressives, he was confident that, if properly educated and informed, individuals are capable of taking care of themselves and that, in an open society of self-directing individuals, history and progress would take care of themselves without a great deal of overarching paternal authority of government.

At the heart of conservatism, in contrast, is the idea that human choices must constantly be guided by outside forces—by institutions, practices, laws, customs, habits, and, through it all, not a small measure of authority. Since Aristotle, conservatives have taught that the inculcation of good habits is essential to developing character and that customs and traditions embody and preserve these patterns for our individual perfection. Mill thought much the opposite, arguing that "he who does anything because it is the custom makes no choice."[25] James Fitzjames Stephen, the Victorian conservative who famously criticized Mill's *On Liberty*, found Mill's highly individualistic notion of human nature "a sort of unattractive romance."[26] Stephen declared that there "is hardly a habit which men in general regard as good which is not acquired by a series of more or less painful and laborious acts." Far from freeing us from constraint, Stephen thought that the "life of all men" in society "is like a water-course, guided this way or that by a system of dams, sluices, weirs and embankments."[27] Conservatives are not prepared to let individual desires run their natural course; indeed, most conservatives are convinced that leaving things to the natural impulses of the individual leads to the problem of social decay. Where liberals since Mill's time have feared that social forces breed conformity and individual stagnation, conservatives insist that society humanizes us and gives us our true individual identities. Where liberals believe social institutions should free us by opening up social opportunities that permit us to achieve self-individuation, conservatives emphasize the role of these institutions in *educating* us and in *restraining* the excesses of the individual.

These differences concerning freedom versus authority and individualism versus social structure go to the heart of what originally separated liberals from conservatives. But today liberals and conservatives have switched sides on this issue in important ways. The belief in the capacity of ordinary individuals to choose and to plan for their own lives without the superimposition of an extensive network of overarching structure is at the heart of any philosophy worthy of the name "liberalism." Yet today this is more often the position of the conservative. Today it is more often liberals who contend that individuals need a great deal more guidance and support and structure by the state in every matter from planning their retirement to planning their diet. It is conservatives who are more likely to insist that we must trust individuals to take care of themselves and who assume that individuals are generally prudent and able to carry on without a great deal of support and guidance at least from political authorities.

Modern liberals are skeptical about whether society can safely be run on the "self-directing power of personality." Beneath this skepticism is the abiding suspicion that the older conservatives were right after all: the good society requires a large quantum of authority, imposed externally and brought to bear on an ever-expanding array of individual decisions. The source of this necessary authority has changed, of course. The old conservative relied on religion and customs and deeply ingrained social norms, whereas the new liberal relies on the state, but the motivation is largely the same in each case: society must be protected from the excesses of individualism, just as individuals must be shielded from the consequences of their own native impulses.

Modern liberals attempt to hold on to their commitment to individualism by reinterpreting it. Individualism has always been connected to freedom, but freedom now means something very different from what it once meant. The older idea of freedom did not distinguish between "personal" and "economic" liberties; they were different facets of the same concept. The modern idea elevates personal freedom to an absolute value while discounting economic freedom as an illegitimate form of "power." Even personal freedom, however, is now confined to *half* of what Mill would have considered the self-regarding sphere. Whereas Mill rejected moralistic and paternalistic limits on the individual, modern liberals accept the need for a large measure of paternalism. Modern liberals are less convinced than their classical liberal forebears that the individual is capable of taking care of himself in a world grown evermore complex and bewildering. What does modern liberalism want to free us from? Apparently, from the consequences of freedom.

As if to compensate for what the individual has lost through the multiplication of paternalistic and regulatory measures, liberals have redoubled their efforts to preserve a sphere of personal freedom from morals legislation or more generally from any collective imposition of value upon the individual—freedom in the "private" realm involving mainly sexual and reproductive decisions. This is the freedom Justice O'Connor referred to in declaring that at the "heart of liberty" is the right "to define one's own concept of existence, of meaning, of the universe, and of the mystery of human life."[28] In this respect, contemporary liberalism is more liberal than that of the classical liberal of the nineteenth century, who never doubted the power of the state to regulate private morality. But this is the exception. What has been dramatically curtailed is the older, extroverted individualism—the individualism that requires economic freedom, genuine freedom of association, the freedom of the individual to make decisions that affect his or her own material interests and that touch on the material interests of others. It is this freedom that runs counter to the needs of the modern regulatory state, and that modern liberalism has domesticated. The individualism of modern liberalism is more concentrated and introverted. Individuals are more free today as long as what they want to do is considered private, and it is considered private as long as it never touches the material interests or economic expectations of others.

Openness to Change versus Conserving the Status Quo

"What is conservatism?" Abraham Lincoln once asked rhetorically in aligning himself with conservatives. "Is it not adherence to the old and tried, against the new and untried?" Winston Churchill once sardonically observed that he "preferred the past to the present, and the present to the future," and Russell Kirk wrote in *The Conservative Mind* that "the essence of social conservatism is the preservation of the ancient moral traditions of humanity."[29] Liberals and conservatives have always intuitively understood that one of their most obvious points of division is that conservatives want to *conserve* the existing order, whereas liberals have always been suspicious of unthinking obeisance to tradition, continuity, the status quo. In the spirit of romantic libertarianism, Ralph Waldo Emerson proclaimed that "the centuries are conspirators against the sanity and authority of the soul."[30] Karl Marx went further, exhorting the Young Hegelians to engage in "a ruthless criticism of *everything existing*."[31]

Liberalism's commitment to individualism, its receptiveness to change, and its optimism about progress are closely intertwined. If what it means to be a liberal is that one must generally be opposed to a great deal of overarching social structures and institutions that limit individual choices, then liberals must be prepared also to reject those structures that constrain individual choices *through time*. Individualism tends to draw our focus to the present, to the preferences and choices of those now living. Collectivism in its various forms tends to connect us not only with others in society at any given time, but also with those who came before and those who will come after, which explains Burke's observation that those who do "not look backward to their ancestors" tend not to "look forward to posterity."

Since earlier liberals believed that social arrangements should unfold from the bottom up, the consistent classical liberal had to be prepared, as Hayek put it, "to let change run its course even if we cannot predict where it will lead."[32] Letting change run its course means deemphasizing enduring social structures in favor of spontaneous decisions, subordinating the traditions of the past to the considerations of the present. Consider Thomas Jefferson's quintessentially liberal skepticism about an enduring constitutional order:

> Some men look at constitutions with sanctimonious reverence and deem them like the ark of the covenant, too sacred to be touched. They ascribe to the men of a preceding age a wisdom more than human. . . . I knew that age well, it was very like the present, but without the experience of the present. [Let us not] weakly believe that one generation is not as capable of another of taking care of itself, and of ordering its own affairs. . . . The dead have no rights.[33]

Even since, it has usually been the liberals who believe in a "living" or "evolving" Constitution, whereas conservatives are moved by fidelity to the original document (as we'll see in Chapter 7). When conservatives interpret the Constitution by looking to the text or to the original intent, they are seeking something outside themselves, an enduring meaning—a meaning grounded in the past which transcends the exigencies of the present. The liberal, on the other hand, believes that each generation must be free to evolve its own interpretation of reality and any constitutional constraints that flow from this interpretation.

Liberals not only find change desirable, they are considerably more likely to believe that very little if anything constrains our capacity to remake our society—and ourselves. Conservatives, by contrast, usually maintain that the world imposes a legion of constraints on this capacity for self-remaking—constraints set by the natural law, by human nature, or by the sustainability of certain kinds of social and economic conditions. Conservatives are much more likely to believe, for example, that economic systems not based on individual incentive are bound to falter because human self-interest cannot be designed out of the human condition. For this reason, conservatives are averse to what they regard as top-down experiments in social engineering. It is the liberal who is more likely to insist that we can refashion human nature, at least to some extent, by redesigning our political institutions.

The conservative's belief that there are fixed limits to social change explains the oft-noted "epistemological modesty" of conservatives who believe that politics cannot be reduced to pat rational principles, who think that individual human knowledge is necessarily fallible and limited, and who worry about the "unintended consequences" of centralized political action.[34] Conservative economist Thomas Sowell has drawn a distinction between the "constrained" and the "unconstrained" visions of politics, which he claims represents the most fundamental contrast between Right and Left.[35] The essence of the conservative's "constrained" vision is that few things can be changed without significant trade-offs. Politics becomes "the art of the possible" for conservatives, and social change may be a zero-sum game. In fact, it may be less than a zero-sum game. John Kekes insists that conservatives "are not so foolish as to deny that great advances have been made in science" and in other areas, but he objects that these advances usually bring costs of their own. "The stock of human possibilities is enlarged, but the possibilities are for both good and evil, and new possibilities are seldom without new evils."[36]

This aversion to change has deeper metaphysical roots for the paleocons and the traditionalists, who seem to fear that every change carries with it the seeds of social decay. Paleocon Richard Weaver wrote over half a century ago that "cultural decline is a historical fact—which can be established"—and maintained that "modern man has about squandered his estate." Weaver believed, as many conservatives believe, that a great deal of what the liberal regards as progress is in fact its opposite, and that "people traveling this downward path develop an insensibility which increases with their degradation." This insensitivity precipitates a kind of moral vertigo: "in the face of the enormous brutality of our age we seem unable to make appropriate responses to perversions of truth and acts of bestiality."[37] It similarly seemed to traditionalist Russell Kirk that, "to our sorrow," we "live in an 'antagonistic world' of madness and despair" and that "our culture seems in the sere and yellow leaf."[38]

Conservative and liberal themes sometimes dovetail as well, as with the classical liberal's defense of a decentralized free market. The conservative's aversion to overly rationalized social and economic institutions means a preference for decentralized social and economic arrangements. Because classical liberals believe, with most conservatives, that no central authority can have the necessary knowledge to set the conditions of supply and demand, they prefer free-market economic arrangements over socialized and centralized economic ordering.[39] Yet the same arrangement allows for the bottom-up expression of the economic decision of individuals reacting to market conditions, a liberal theme. In essence, the classical liberal's preference for decentralized economic ordering simultaneously reflects the liberal principle of individual choice and the conservative principle that inevitable limits on knowledge prevent these decisions from being made by a centralized agency.

What really distinguishes modern from classical liberals (and conservatives) is that contemporary liberals increasingly accept changes mediated from the top down, by the overarching institutions of government, rather than changes that emanate from the bottom up, from the choices of individuals through the institutions of civil society, as we see next.

Social versus Moral Causes of Human Discontent

The liberal's greater belief in the power of change—the prospect that we can make society any way we want from the top down through our political institutions, given the knowledge and the will—brings about one of the most fundamental inversions in modern liberal thought. It causes liberals to shift their focus from the individual to society. It means that human sin and misery and all their causes and consequences—war, poverty, inequality, and injustice—have to be reinterpreted in systemic, rather than individual, terms. Conservatives survey what they take to be the inherent evils of the human condition and conclude that they are a consequence of human selfishness, evil, stupidity, envy, original sin—the flaws inherent in the human soul. Liberals trace these same ills to our collective failure to change, our unwillingness to re-engineer our social and political institutions to make the world a better place. Whereas the conservative is inclined to believe that the individual is forever failing society, the liberal insists that society has failed the individual. Paradoxically, the modern liberal's individualism—the idea that social institutions must be continually refined to meet every need, desire, and whim of its individual members—leads to the negation of the individual. Liberals who believe that the individual can only be changed from the outside in by re-engineering his or her social condition wind up celebrating the *value* of personal choice as their highest ideal while simultaneously discounting the *power* of personal choice as a force for positive change. This sense of individual powerlessness reinforces the more introverted individualism of modern liberals: freedom seems to have more to do with the newer values of self-expression and self-individuation and what one does in private than with the older values of self-reliance, civic virtue, or personal responsibility.

For modern liberals, the power of the individual is realized largely through collective action—from community organizing to political mass mobilization. It is as if the individual can only change himself by first (in concert with others) changing his world. For conservatives, this not only places the cart before the horse, it is downright futile. Human imperfection cannot be engineered away. The cure, if anything, is moral, spiritual, or at least cultural. This is why Stephen Tonsor insisted that conservatives "live with sin and tragedy not as a consequence of the inadequacy of social engineering, but as a consequence of man's sin and disorder."[40] T. S. Eliot once caricatured liberals' tendency to spend their time "dreaming of systems so perfect that no one will need to be good."[41] For the conservative, there is always the need to be good—the need to adjust ourselves to the world, not the world to ourselves.

Yet many conservatives today do not take their own message adequately to heart. They are quick to indict the senseless violence of inner-city culture, the dissolute sloth of the welfare queen, or the hypersexualized misogyny of the rapper. But they don't seem to register the unparalleled self-indulgence of today's wealthy, the insulated vanity of corporate moguls, or the utter disregard of Washington plutocrats for the thousands of human beings in some other country who will suffer for their decisions. When CEOs escape prosecution and walk away fabulously wealthy after decimating the retirement funds of their employees, when one president of the United States commits a shabby perjury to avoid the truth of a sexual affair, and when another commutes the sentence of a crony two hours after a court has made it evident that he will have to go to jail, the lessons of character are clear.[42] If individual human character drives collective social forces rather than the other way around, as the best of conservative philosophy teaches, then it is the character of those at the top, those in power or with the capacity to lead by example, who will do the most damage socially.

Equality versus Elitism

If one had to choose a single political or social value that serves as the best proxy for political orientation generally, for what it means to fall to the left or to the right on the political spectrum, it would have to be equality. The further to the left a theory falls, the more egalitarian it is. This explains why liberalism falls to the left of conservatism, and socialism to the left of liberalism. Liberals love equality, and modern liberals love it more than classical liberals and modern conservatives, even as modern conservatives are more egalitarian than the older conservatives.

Liberals favor a greater degree of social and economic equality. They usually favor more redistribution, higher rates of progressive taxation, higher inheritance taxes, and so on, and they want to see egalitarian values influence spheres of life where conservatives believe they have no place (e.g., in the parent-child, teacher-student, employer-employee relationship). The conservative's attitude to equality, in contrast, is decidedly lukewarm. Relative to the liberal alternative at any point in time, conservatism in every form has traditionally embodied a mildly, and sometimes a potently, elitist or aristocratic attitude toward human differences. Neoconservative Irving Kristol wrote that, when it comes to equality: "I will simply plead my Jewishness and say, equality has never been a Jewish thing. Rich men are fine, poor men are fine, so long as they are decent human beings. I do not like equality. I do not like it in sports, in the arts, or in economics. I just don't like it in the world."[43]

Conservatives oppose social and economic leveling in part because they believe that there is an irreducible tension between freedom and equality. "There is no principle more basic in the conservative philosophy," Robert Nisbet declared, "than that of the inherent and absolute incompatibility between liberty and equality."[44] Conservatives are not opposed to equality *tout court*, of course. They believe in equality of legal rights and a measure of political equality (see Chapter 10). But conservatives have historically resisted the liberal's effort to create more equality by expanding the franchise and by other means of creating social equality (e.g., the civil rights laws). When Russell Kirk wrote that the essence of conservatism includes a belief in the need for social "orders and classes," and when Micklethwait and Wooldridge concluded that conservatism entails a preference for liberty over equality, belief in "established traditions and hierarchies," and an element of elitism, each recognized the conservative's preference for a greater level of inequality.[45] In the social and economic sphere, conservatives are the last true believers in merit, personal responsibility, and desert. They believe that inequalities frequently (though not always) reflect differences in effort, in ability, in intelligence, and in virtue. Redistribution is morally wrong and politically objectionable to the extent that it takes from the deserving, who have earned their wealth or success, and gives to the undeserving. Of course, no intelligent conservative believes that this is invariably true; the fair-minded conservative recognizes that unfair social inequalities do limit the individual potential of those not lucky enough to be born to circumstances that give them strategic advantages in life. Modern conservatives share the view of the anonymous American patriot who wrote in 1776 that equality is "adverse to every species of subordination beside that which arises from the difference of capacity, disposition and virtue."[46]

A preference for equality goes a long way to explaining even some of the more esoteric differences between liberals and conservatives. Why is it that liberals are considerably more likely than self-described conservatives today to support animal rights or vegetarianism? Perhaps it is because they are more likely to feel that the differences between humans and animals are not so great as to justify the exploitation of animals, whereas conservatives often believe that the notion of animal rights is an absurd trivialization of the very concept of rights. It is no coincidence that anarchists and utopians frequently advocate vegetarianism as an extension of their opposition to every form of domination and exploitation, while media conservatives such as Rush Limbaugh frequently lambast animal rights activists.

What holds for the differences between people and animals, however, counts doubly for differences among people. Why are liberals more likely to take the side of the undocumented alien, whereas conservatives more typically reject what they call "amnesty" for those in the United States illegally? Because they are deeply convinced that what distances each person from the next is largely the accidental differences of birth, class, and nationality, liberals have always been more cosmopolitan and international in orientation, whereas conservatives are often more patriotic and more parochial. It is fully consistent with the liberal spirit that George W. Bush's vision was that of "an ownership society," while Hillary Clinton's was the "we're all in it together society."

The liberal's greater egalitarianism also explains why liberals and conservatives understand the values of social pluralism and diversity in very different ways. Because liberals value equality, they insist on a greater right of inclusion for women, minorities, and others in private groups and associations, whereas conservatives insist on the right of each association to decide its own membership, which inevitably requires a greater right to exclude. Conservatives insist that groups and associations can be politically meaningful only if they express the unique perspective or message of their members. Should a Baptist law school have to admit an atheist? Should a Jewish group have to admit an avowed Nazi? A general right of inclusion of every individual to every group would not only undermine the expressive message of the group, it would dilute the group's identity and undermine each group's capacity to represent its unique constituency. As William Galston aptly put it, pluralism requires "diversity between" groups, rather than "diversity within" groups.[47] Liberals respond by insisting that protecting associational rights can sometimes have highly inegalitarian results, as when a male-only business organization excludes women, or when the Boy Scouts prohibits gay scoutmasters.[48] The differences between conservatives and liberals on this issue underscore the conservative's more general claim that equality and freedom (including freedom of association) are often in high tension with one another.

Of these four contrasts between contemporary liberals and conservatives, this last one is the most important. In fact, when liberals make exceptions to their other commitments, it is almost always done in the name of equality. When modern liberals trash individualism, it is the economic individualism of the capitalist. When they moderate their usually unfailing support for free speech rights, as some do in supporting hate-speech codes and restrictions of pornography, it is because of the way racist or pornographic speech affects minorities or women. Conservatives, for their part, do not so much oppose equality as they oppose the institutional changes necessary to create greater levels of equality. Creating more equality requires expanding government, particularly the federal government, and conservatives are opposed to this because they recognize that it is never the tendency of government to grow smaller. They understand as well what a steadily growing government entails for human freedom, for individual initiative, and for the tradition and authority lodged in the interstices of civil society.

"Liberalism" today, in sum, stands for an increasingly state-centered paternalistic egalitarianism with a generous measure of personal liberty in the self-regarding sphere. "Conservatives" are those who, for any of several reasons and to one degree or another, resist the big-government, increasingly egalitarian tilt of modern liberalism. And they sometimes resist this because it conflicts with their own definition of liberty. Which philosophy is really the more liberal or conservative? As I hope this chapter has made clear, it all depends on what we mean by "liberal" or "conservative." These terms are anything but self-defining today. Certainly neither means what it meant two centuries ago. This should give us pause about the continued viability of these terms as cogent political labels.

We political centrists believe that we have to rethink the central meaning of the liberal tradition. We locate that meaning in a moderate conception of individualism, a tradition that makes freedom, responsibility, individual merit, and self-reliance its central guiding principles. Yet, as centrists, we believe that these values must be understood in contemporary context. Individual freedom is often enhanced by government policies, though perhaps not as frequently as liberals believe. Responsibility and self-reliance must be reinterpreted in more relational ways in a world where ordinary people rely on the availability of jobs and a decent economy. Merit must be measured not simply by where one ends up in life, but relative to where one begins. In each of these ways, political centrists look to the core values that made liberalism and conservatism appealing and successful visions of politics, reinterpreting these in contemporary context.

In important ways, then, centrists want to conserve the liberal achievements of the past century, and in some cases even extend these. In some other ways, however, we believe that we have reached a kind of tipping point in U.S. politics today. On these issues, we stand with moderate conservatives who oppose the leftward drift of U.S. liberalism.

Chapter 4
Why the Big "Isms" Fail

POLITICAL CENTRISM AVOIDS THE gravitational pull of each of the other three dominant strains of political thought in the United States today—progressive or left liberalism, the various forms of conservatism, and libertarianism. In Part II, I spell out our differences with liberals, conservatives, and libertarians on particular issues, but in this chapter I explore our deeper political and philosophical agreements and disagreements with each.

What's Wrong with Libertarianism?

I begin with libertarianism because it is the most consistently radical and individualistic form of liberalism. Libertarians are right about so much, and wrong about so much as well. They frequently begin from sound premises, and then reason their way to untenable conclusions. Personally, if I had to choose between living in either a purely libertarian state or a purely socialist state, even a socialist state such as modern Sweden that operates along democratic lines, I'd happily take my chances in a libertarian society. Like libertarians, centrists do not believe that it is the function of government to take care of its citizens. But unlike libertarians, we do believe government has an important role to play in caring for the most vulnerable members of society and in establishing the ground rules for a decent and well-functioning society for the rest of us.

Libertarians are right to be concerned about the growth of government, particularly the federal government. Within just a few short decades Americans will face catastrophic shortfalls in funding for social service benefits—Social Security, Medicaid, Medicare, and any new programs such as universal health care (see Chapter 6). It is not that we centrists are opposed in principle to government's providing these services, but we recognize that the resources just won't be there within a quarter century or so. More generally, libertarians are right to distrust big, centralized government—its wastefulness, its callousness, and, yes, the way government power potentially limits liberty and undermines individual initiative. Where liberalism was originally a limited-government philosophy, not an antigovernment philosophy, modern liberals have strangely and sadly lost this distrust of state power. In fact, modern liberals sometimes seem to distrust everything—corporations, churches, schools, even individuals—*but* big government. Earlier liberals and their modern libertarian descendants understood that corporations, private groups, and other organizations within civil society can become limited bastions of private power, but they insisted that the individual was protected from private oppression, in part, by pluralism and competition—by the fact that a well-functioning society has many different groups which will compete for the allegiance of members, stockholders, employees, and so on. Contemporary libertarians believe, with some legitimacy, that the greatest threat to liberty is an expanding government with a monopoly on state power. Their answer: limit government, protect a basic skein of fundamental rights, and the rest will work itself out. In this respect, libertarians are the true heirs of the classical liberal tradition. They just take its lessons a little too far.

Libertarians instinctively distrust the state and the politicians who would direct it. "If you wish to know how libertarians regard the State and any of its acts," wrote Murray Rothbard, one of the most uncompromising of libertarians, "simply think of the State as a criminal band, and all of the libertarian attitudes will fall into place."[1] Taxation is theft, pure and simple. Capital punishment is murder. Restraints on trade are unjustifiable restrictions on individual freedom. Libertarians think of the state as a person and, for every official act of state, ask: Would it be morally permissible for an individual to do what the state is doing? If the answer is no, then how, they will inquire, can it be right for the state to do it? Libertarians are particularly dubious of the primary wielders of state power, the professional politicians. Whether or not one agrees with Lord Acton that power inevitably corrupts, there is certainly a greater propensity for corruption when power is wielded by those who have made it their life's mission to *gain power*. "The probability of the people in power being individuals who would dislike the possession and exercise of power," declared Frank H. Knight, "is on the level of probability that an extremely tenderhearted person would get the job of whipping master in a slave plantation."[2]

Libertarians are right to stress the problems associated with the overcentralization of power, but they also systematically overlook the benefits that flow from good, moderate, well-circumscribed government. They are right that collective planning of various facets of the economy is often bound to fail or to present some intractable problems down the line, as with Social Security, though they are wrong to conclude that it is inevitably unproductive in every sector of the economy. They are right to point out that government regulations frequently drive up prices, though they are wrong to conclude that this ends the argument for regulation. They are correct to insist that *excessive* dependence on government undermines civil society and individual initiative, though they overlook the ways in which government action can sometimes foster the conditions necessary to individual initiative. They are right, finally, to believe that it is generally better to act on the principle that individuals tend to know their interests better than the state knows them— that we are usually better off when we learn from our own choices rather than having them imposed on us—but wrong to conclude that paternalism can never be justified.

In the broadest sense, libertarians are right to approach the human condition from a bottom-up (or methodologically individualist) rather than a top-down (or methodologically collectivist) perspective. We humans inevitably act from our own psychological center of gravity. We are motivated by incentives, where these incentives usually concern matters close to us—our own, or our family's, or our nation's condition (often in that order). To update an example from Adam Smith, the kindest and most humanitarian person may be moved by the plight of a million tsunami victims half a world away but is more likely to be kept awake at night worrying about an overbearing boss or the rising price of gasoline. To the extent that political or economic centralization tends to detach individual knowledge and action from its consequences, it is bound to produce social and economic inefficiencies, both material and immaterial.

So far, so good. As centrists, we are often inclined to accept a great deal of the libertarian critique of modern politics, and we sometimes might be tempted to ally ourselves with libertarian causes, if for no other reason than to offset the continuing drift toward increasing "statism," as libertarians call it. Yet libertarianism is a seriously deficient view in several respects.

To see what libertarians oppose is to see how truly radical their philosophy is. They are opposed, for starters, to the use of state power to remedy certain kinds of social inequality. For example, most libertarians are opposed to modern civil rights laws that make it a crime to discriminate in public accommodations on the basis of race. Libertarians insist that business owners should be free to contract with whomever they want, and for whatever reason. They also oppose many other programs and policies which centrists support: a moderately progressive income tax; welfare subsidies for those who are sick, disabled, unemployable, or unemployed for short periods of time. They oppose such benefits as low-interest government-sponsored student loan programs or even programs such as the G.I. Bill, believing that such support should be left to the private sector. More radically still, most libertarians oppose state involvement in licensing doctors, lawyers, and other professionals; consumer protection laws; banking regulations; food and drug laws; housing regulations; immigration restrictions; and a host of other laws the centrist believes are necessary in our increasingly complex and frequently anonymous social environment.[3] The libertarian's answer, in each of these respects, is: let the market take care of the problem.

The problem is that libertarians draw the wrong conclusions from their methodological individualism. Because only individuals exist (i.e., because clubs and corporations and other organizations are only groupings of individuals that have no existence apart from these individuals), libertarians see no role for the state beyond protecting individuals. Thus, they insist that the state has no role whatsoever in fostering the conditions of the good life within civil society. Libertarians believe that government is there to protect one individual from another, but that it should have no role in preserving the intermediate realm of civil society, the realm that exists between the individual and the state. The institutions of civil society, as it were, must stand or fall on the collective action of individuals unaided by any overarching government structure.

Centrists believe that government has a role in promoting the general welfare and that it does so in part by protecting individuals and in part by securing the necessary social conditions—the social ecology—of human flourishing. Support for everything from free public education to the prohibition of dangerous drugs to antidiscrimination laws rests on the role of government in promoting the general welfare. This is accomplished in part by reinforcing those social conditions important to individual choice and welfare.

This brings us to an issue that has bedeviled the liberal tradition since Mill's time (and an issue we'll take up in Chapter 8). Mill thought that government should have no role in criminalizing purely private activity but could regulate activities that came under the heading of the "general welfare." He thought, for example, that government shouldn't prohibit private acts of prostitution but could prohibit public solicitation, that it shouldn't excessively regulate contracts but should have a role in ensuring the basic safety and purity of milk and other food products, that it shouldn't regulate the internal workings of the family but could bar the equivalent of today's deadbeat dad from remarrying.[4]

But most libertarians go farther. They believe that government should not be involved even with shaping or reinforcing the background conditions of a good society (e.g., educating its citizens, cleaning up the environment), structuring opportunities to assist people in making the right decisions (e.g., providing day care to encourage welfare mothers to go back to work), or supporting social organizations that instill values of good citizenship (permitting a boys club to use public schools for midnight basketball). Libertarians are quick to admonish others that they are opposed to "plac[ing] the guardianship of morality in the hands of the state apparatus."[5] But centrists do not want to make government the source of our morality either. Yet we do believe that government can and should be used to help express and reinforce the background conditions necessary to inculcating basic moral values, which have their source in our traditions and in the everyday experience of individuals.

Centrists part ways with libertarians on many of these issues because, at a more abstract level, we do not share the libertarian's austere and sometimes inconsistent conception of human freedom.[6] Libertarians hold that freedom is limited by only two kinds of conditions—any kind of government regulation, and individual acts that amount to "gun at the head" kinds of coercion. But there is a disconnect here: Why does the libertarian insist that the slightest tax on the owner of capital—say the owner of a factory—amounts to an impermissible "taking" that infringes the freedom of the owner, while holding that a starving, unemployed man is not really "unfree" as long as his rights (in the sense that libertarians define them) have not been violated by another individual? Libertarians reach these conclusions by starting from the assumption that freedom is limited only by the violation of a right, and then by insisting that the factory owner has a right to keep all of what he owns and that the unemployed man may be in tough straits, but is not "unfree" in the relevant juridical sense. As the Left has regularly charged, this is a conception of freedom that is soft on the haves and relentlessly tough on the have-nots.

Centrists prefer a different conception of freedom, one that incorporates a moralized component. We believe that the capacity of the individual to make autonomous choices is limited in many ways—by political, social, economic, and personal factors. Human freedom is a fragile flower, equally trammeled by the society that overregulates and the society that underregulates. Ultimately, the line between being inconvenienced and being unfree will be a matter of adjusting our moral sensibilities about what kinds of conditions we should expect people to overcome and what kinds of conditions we should not expect anyone to bear.[7] The libertarian conception, in contrast, does not take into account the physical, social, and even moral dimensions of unfreedom.

Because centrists believe that many social and economic conditions limit freedom, we do not share the libertarian's faith that a largely unregulated social and economic sphere will generate optimal social and economic consequences from the standpoint of freedom. There are strong reasons for protecting workers within the confines of the corporation. As Richard Cornuelle, a thinker who is broadly sympathetic to libertarian ideas put it, libertarians have not "confronted the disabling hypocrisy of the capitalist rationale," a rationale which concedes broad freedom to employers and considerably less to their employees. The libertarian cannot explain why an invisible hand that "arranges resources rationally without authoritarian direction" stops "abruptly at the factory gate."[8] In a larger sense, centrists find it difficult to understand how the libertarian can consistently oppose the concentration of political power in the state while remaining unconcerned about the accumulation of great economic power in corporations.

To sum up all these objections: libertarians have a very thin conception of the common good, one that extends only to the protection of basic individual liberties (as they define them), while centrists believe that government should have a broader role in shaping the conditions of the good life. While centrists do not wish to see the state become the source of our values, we do not oppose the use of the state to express and to reinforce the most essential of these shared moral ideals. In this way the centrist charts a middle course between the Scylla of extreme individualism and the Charybdis of the more collectivist approach of welfare liberals.

What's Wrong with Conservatism?

I should begin with a confession, or what liberals might insist can be regarded only as a confession. I am a genuine admirer of the conservative intellectual tradition—the tradition of incisive critique of liberalism that ostensibly began with Burke in the eighteenth century, continued with thinkers such as Tocqueville, Lord Acton, and James Fitzjames Stephen in the nineteenth, and culminated in the twentieth with men like Paul Elmer More and George Santayana and, more recently, Irving Kristol and George Will.[9] When conservatives miss the boat, they *really* miss the boat, as Mill thought when he called conservatives "the stupid party." But when they are intelligent, they seem so much more acute than even the sharpest liberals. Or perhaps more wise. Which brings us to a strange little quiddity of modern conservatism: the better conservative thought—the intellectual conservatism of the great conservative thinkers—is often as trenchant and wise as the contemporary on-the-ground conservatism of the Rush Limbaugh–Ann Coulter variety is shortsighted and frequently mean-spirited. Conservative thought of the better variety possesses a moral depth that liberal theory lacks. The better conservative thought is frequently more engaged with the interior aspects of the human condition and our connections with others across generations. This is to say that the better conservative thinkers have always held that political ideas cannot be wholly detached from the moral, cultural, and even spiritual concerns of the individual. In this sense, "statecraft is soulcraft," as George Will has written. This wiser conservatism believes in the relevance of character and holds more than a trace of the older idea that the constitution of a society flows less from its political institutions than from the moral character of its people. Concepts such as good and evil, guilt and redemption, integrity and moral decay still figure prominently in the conservative's vocabulary and view of the world.

When the better conservatism has been wrong politically, it is less because conservatives have begun from the wrong principles than because they routinely misapply them. One can and should believe in the central importance of moral character while insisting that a person's sexual orientation is entirely irrelevant to his or her goodness as a person. One can ardently believe in the values of patriotism and fidelity to our country while defending the right of the dissident or the flag burner. One can live by the values of merit, personal responsibility, and self-reliance while acknowledging the role of community and government in helping to establish the conditions that make these values attainable in the lives of ordinary Americans.

What is most alarming is that many modern conservatives seem to have abandoned the best of this conservative wisdom. Conservatism, for example, was once a proudly antimaterialistic philosophy that exalted Jerusalem over Babylon, the values of the spirit over the quotidian matters of supply and demand. But modern conservatism has been captured increasingly by the right-wing economists, leaving it to a few enlightened liberals and communitarians to reinvigorate discussion about human values. What was President Bush's advice to the American people immediately after 9/11? Keep consuming. It's hard to imagine Edmund Burke's reaction to this comment, but I hardly think it would have been approval.

Along similar lines, how is it that environmental conservatism has become a liberal cause? Why don't many conservatives have any interest in conserving the earth's resources? Why, for example, have conservatives continued to insist that global warming is an illusion when 2,500 of the world's most distinguished climatologists have reached the conclusion that it is indeed a very real threat?[10] Conservatives' disregard for the environment has at times verged on the farcical, as when President Reagan's secretary of the interior, James Watt, insisted that trees should be cut down because they contribute to the hole in the ozone layer. (At least he apparently believed in global warming.) In sum, the conservative record on environmental matters has been as dismal as it has been perplexing.

The conservative's excessive undervigilance in matters of the environment is strangely at odds with a foreign policy that is nothing short of precipitous. The neoconservatives' war in Iraq has been a doubly unconservative affair. It overreacted to a nonexisting threat of weapons of mass destruction, squandering U.S. lives and resources in the process. And as pointed out in the last chapter, it flew in the face of a fundament of conservative foreign policy from Edmund Burke to Joseph Schumpeter: you cannot hope to democratize a tribal society by democratizing its political institutions; culture comes before politics, not the other way around. Some neocons continue to advocate militantly aggressive interventionism in that troubled area of the world. Norman Podhoretz continues to insist that Saddam Hussein represented a strategic threat to the United States as "the secular face of the two-headed monster against which we have been fighting" and has recently advocated that we follow up the invasion of Iraq by bombing Iran.[11]

Certainly if this is what it means to be a conservative, then so much the worse for conservatism. Of course, not all conservatives have supported military interventionism. Paleoconservatives such as Patrick Buchanan have stridently opposed the war in Iraq, just as earlier communitarian conservatives such as Robert Nisbet opposed the use of military force except in cases where U.S. interests are directly threatened.[12] Even some neocons have acknowledged that interventionism is a symptom of neoconservatism's liberal heritage, a legacy of liberalism's internationalism, its moralism, and its love for democracy.[13] The older conservatism of the paleocon has traditionally been both more isolationist in matters at home and less interventionist in matters abroad. Still, it's clear that most who call themselves conservative today have supported intervention in Iraq and elsewhere. In the twentieth century, at least ostensibly, conservatism has become the party of war, and liberalism (at least more ostensibly) the party of peace.

On more general principles, centrists can make common cause with conservatives only on very general points, frequently again disagreeing in matters of application. While we have no difficulty in agreeing with conservatives, for example, that many of our most basic social institutions and practices are entitled to a presumption of respect, we hardly believe that every tradition has earned its way by expressing the best kind of evolutionary wisdom a culture can produce. U.S. conservatives in the nineteenth and early twentieth centuries fought the extension of democracy to the poor, then to minorities, then to women. Conservatives in the 1950s and 1960s fought civil rights. As recently as 1964, Republican Barry Goldwater made opposition to civil rights central to his presidential bid. These were not traditions worth preserving.

I recently taught a class in legal and political theory to upper-division law students in my moderately conservative midwestern town. Several female members of the class repeatedly described themselves as "conservative" and routinely distanced themselves from any policy smacking of liberalism. I asked them whether they thought women would now have the opportunity to pursue a law degree if conservatives of even fifty or seventy-five years ago had had their way? Perhaps not, they thought. Conservatives have too often been on the wrong side of history by clinging to the time-honored evolutionary traditions of a morally blinkered culture. A tradition's evolutionary pedigree is no guarantee of its moral acumen; evolution has produced plenty of biological dead-ends, after all.

In the spirit of Jefferson and Mill, we centrists believe it inevitable that each generation will reevaluate this inherited experience from the standpoint of its changed condition in the world. In fact, if we are to venerate tradition because it represents the accumulated experience of generations, then, as Jefferson asked, aren't previous generations "very like the present, but without the experience of the present"? Don't we have a bit more of it than they did? Moreover, shouldn't we candidly acknowledge that some of the modern conservative's most cherished institutions—political democracy and a regime of individual rights—were not an organic outgrowth of tradition at all, but a sudden political mutation that required a period of revolution in many parts of the world? Our nation's founders may not have been social progressives, but they were political revolutionaries. U.S. conservatives should never forget that our own political order is far more a product of deliberation, innovation, and sheer human will than it is the natural result of any slowly evolving organic tradition.

So centrists are of a different mind than traditionalists and paleoconservatives concerning the usefulness of tradition as a guide to day-to-day political affairs. At best, we believe that adherence to tradition may provide the antidote to some of the worst excesses of contemporary left liberalism. We are also alive to the dangers of the unintended consequences of collective action, as are classical liberals, neo-conservatives, and skeptical conservatives. Centrists are conservative, if this means that we are skeptical of big government and prefer a more decentralized system of governance. We are conservative, if conservatism involves a rejection of the sundry forms of socialist collectivism that have tempted others, particularly many intellectuals, over the course of the twentieth century. We are conservative, if conservatism means a commitment to the values of common sense, self-reliance, individual freedom, and personal responsibility. We are conservative, in other words, in all the ways that moderate liberals have always been conservative.

Between conservatives' nostalgic resistance to any form of social progress and modern liberals' determination to impose their own conception of progress at any cost, and by any means, centrists seek a middle course that is open to cautious experimentation guided by the democratic process. But our disagreements with conservatives extend to more concrete matters as well.

Centrists are generally skeptical of the moral positions of paleocons, traditionalists, fundamentalists, and others to the extent that these are driven by metaphysical claims based purely on biblical revelation, putative knowledge about the will of God, or notions of the natural law. Indeed, we candidly believe that revelatory sources of religious wisdom are frequently cravenly exploited by the televangelists and their ilk. Two days after the 9/11 attacks, Pat Robertson hosted Jerry Falwell on Robertson's TV show, *The 700 Club*. Falwell expressed the opinion that the attacks and the ensuing deaths of three thousand innocent people were God's retribution for the excesses of a liberal, secular culture. He declared that the attacks were a divine response to "the pagans, and the abortionists, and the feminists, and the gays and the lesbians." Robertson agreed. Yet every first-rate theologian from Thomas Aquinas to Reinhold Niebuhr has deplored claims to know the will of God as a violation of the third commandment. While centrists take the view that individuals have the right to look to their own religious beliefs and convictions to inform their own approach to politics and morality, others have the right to require something more in the way of proof. For similar reasons, centrists often find themselves on the other side from most orthodox conservatives on such issues as homosexuality and the extreme pro-life stance in the abortion controversy.

We part ways from conservatives in a host of other ways, some subtle, some far-reaching. Our social aesthetic is more liberal and individualistic. We value the role of the dissident as gadfly and the dissenter as guardian of truth. We distrust, as most true conservatives do not, entrenched authority and we believe with Jefferson "that a little rebellion now and then" is good for a healthy society. One constitutional implication of our skepticism toward authority is that centrists resist conservative efforts to concentrate even more power in the executive branch, as supporters of the "unitary executive" have under the latter President Bush—another area where our instincts are more Jeffersonian than Hamiltonian.

We reject as well conservatives' antihumanitarianism, their tendency to place systemic goods (such as reinforcing collective moral norms) over individual well-being, though we acknowledge that this is often a difficult balancing act. Conservative journalist Peggy Noonan, for example, has written about a high school graduation she attended in 1972 when a pregnant girl graduated with the rest of her class. As she walked across the stage to take her diploma, the crowd stood and applauded. Noonan writes that when this happened she heard a "thousand-year wall" falling: "We as a society do not approve of teenaged unwed motherhood because it is not good for the child, not good for the mother, not good for us. . . . Note to society: what you applaud you encourage."[14] Perhaps this is true. Certainly centrists believe, with conservatives, that our attitudes and cultural ethos frame the way each individual comes to see the world. Because social approbation and opprobrium inevitably shape each individual's moral outlook, it is true that we should be careful about what we encourage. Yet we also feel the tug of poignancy that attaches to particular cases, the need to support those who find themselves in trouble. Were those who applauded this young girl encouraging the pregnancy or were they simply acknowledging her grit and determination to finish her schoolwork, graduate with her class, and go through with her pregnancy?

Still, such delicate situations often require a nuanced judgment about the equities involved. Thus, centrists believe that humanitarian concerns can sometimes be exaggerated and exploited. For this reason we resist running too far in the opposite direction by embracing every personal hardship as a social injustice, as some liberals do. Most centrists appear to have sided with conservatives, for example, on the recent challenge to Indiana's voter ID law, which made exceptions for the elderly, the disabled, and the poor. The law, passed as an anti–voter fraud measure, required that voters have proper identification to vote. Even with the exceptions, liberals contended that the law discouraged the marginally committed voter who lacked proper identification. The Supreme Court reasonably responded that obtaining a proper ID may be inconvenient for some, but if voting is indeed a sacred right, it is not too great a burden to ask voters to obtain proper identification.[15]

Unlike many conservatives, centrists are also anti-elitist in temperament; we don't respect positions, but we do respect people who have earned what they have through their own intelligence, talent, and hard work. Politically, we oppose change imposed from above, whether by the right-wing moralist or the left-wing social engineer. We believe more generally that in a democratic society the *motive force* for change must come from the grassroots level. While it may still be the role of our political leaders to "refine and enlarge" these views, as James Madison put it, we believe that government should express, rather than generate, our social norms. In this respect, of course, we find common cause with some conservatives and some liberals.

Many of our most vocal differences, however, are with the media conservatism of the Rush Limbaugh–Ann Coulter brand currently popular among a certain segment of the U.S. public. This is frequently a self-consciously anti-intellectual and resentment-driven conservatism that provides knee-jerk support for some of the least attractive and most intellectually dubious causes. Why does the perennial distrust of concentrated power that so inflames the conservative imagination where big government is concerned undergo such a remarkable metamorphosis when the conversation turns to the economic power of big corporations? One can, after all, be a sturdy defender of property rights without insisting that government should subsidize Con-Agra, or provide Halliburton with grossly inflated profits largely obtained through influence peddling and downright fraud. It is precisely the conservative's double standard in these respects that leads the more paranoid on the Left to conclude that U.S. democracy is a complete sham and that corporations infallibly manipulate political outcomes to their own ends. For our part, centrists do not believe that corporations are inevitably evil, but we do believe they suffer from some of the same defects that bedevil any insular, self-interested organization. For this reason they must be monitored and their power (internally and externally) regulated.

The real problem with popular contemporary conservatism of this style is not that it is conservative, but that it is instinctively closed minded and often gratuitously mean-spirited. Oliver Wendell Holmes once remarked that "the mind of the bigot is like the pupil of the eye; the more light you pour upon it, the more it will contract." This is an apt description of the popular conservative's approach to reality today: when weapons of mass destruction don't turn up, maintain that they have been destroyed or secreted across the border in Syria. When evidence of global warming mounts, distract the audience by raising Al Gore's son's problems with substance abuse. As conditions in Iraq deteriorate to the point where every religious and political splinter group has its own militia, and the government itself has no real control over most of the country, deny that this qualifies as a "civil war" because there are more than two sides fighting.

In the end, these concerns point to a profound disconnect between the reflective conservatism of the thinker and conservatism on the ground in the United States today.

So much the worse for conservatism on the ground.

What's Wrong with Left Liberalism?

This book aims at rehabilitating a conception of liberalism that incorporates aspects of the ethos of the older liberalism with the humanitarianism of the newer. Centrists cherish the essential values of the liberal tradition—freedom, personal autonomy, personal responsibility, self-reliance, a healthy skepticism of power (especially concentrated power), and equality, properly understood. Centrists hew most closely to the values that have traditionally been considered "liberal" in this wider sense of the term. Even when we seem to embrace the conservative, it's usually on exactly those points where the leftward drift of U.S. politics has made conservatism liberal and liberalism something else. In sum, it is for the most part, the "left" and not the "liberalism" in "left liberalism" that centrists oppose. We are troubled considerably less with where liberalism has been than with where it seems to be going.

Every political philosophy must be judged by the company it keeps. Alliances often betray the tilt, the potential orientation, or the latent sympathies inherent in an ideology. When paleoconservatives allied themselves with authoritarians, fascists, or Nazis, as they have historically in Germany, Spain, Argentina, Chile, and many other places around the globe, it was in part because there is an ideological consanguinity between aspects of paleoconservatism and authoritarianism. The same is true of modern liberalism. Liberals have frequently made common cause with the radical Left because there are ideological connections, shared aspirations, and similar diagnoses of the human condition which link modern liberalism with some forms of more radical left-wing thought.

It is telling that among academic left liberals today, many are more likely to be conversant with Jacques Lacan than John Locke; they're far more likely to be able to quote Foucault than the *Federalist* and Marx rather than Madison. And there is a certain mean-spiritedness in some quarters that is every bit as jaundiced and resentment driven as the current unpleasantness on the conservative Right. For example, contemporary left liberalism is allied in various respects with modern feminism, one branch of which consists of the radical feminism of such thinkers as law professor Catharine MacKinnon and the late author and activist Andrea Dworkin. Here is how MacKinnon, in opening her 1993 book *Only Words*, apparently views the state of relations between the sexes in the United States today: "You grow up with your father holding you down and covering your mouth so another man can make a horrible searing pain between your legs. When you're older, your husband ties you to the bed and drips hot wax on your nipples and brings in other men to watch and makes you smile through it. Your doctor will not give you drugs he has addicted you to unless you suck his penis."[16] Now, perhaps some progressives will respond that this goes too far, but certainly there are others who will insist that it's not far off the mark as a description of social reality. And even some of those who believe that this goes too far will sympathize with the basic sentiments: the response may be overblown, but there's *something* here, after all, they will say. And those who take this view will tend to see analogies where others see only rhetoric—they will insist that every restriction on abortion institutionalizes reproductive slavery, that marriage is legalized rape, and that the traditional idealization of motherhood is bourgeois false consciousness.[17]

Centrists resist the radical portrayal of sex in the United States for two reasons. First, we don't believe that it is an accurate representation of reality. What percentage of fathers and husbands and doctors must engage in the kind of behavior MacKinnon depicts in order for this to be an accurate representation of gender relations in the United States today? Thirty percent? Ten percent? One percent? This is not an accurate representation of what generally is, even if it is an accurate representation of what occasionally has occurred. But more to the point, even to the extent that MacKinnon's caricature captures some fraction of relationships among men and women, centrists diagnose the condition differently than feminists. The causes for men's historic maltreatment of women are not to be found in patriarchal social conditions; they are to be found in the interstices of the human soul. Every reasonable religion and every moral code worthy of the name have fought against the same awful tendency in human nature (whether we call it self-aggrandizement, pride, amour propre, or the will to power) by which one person raises himself up (at least in his own eyes) by laying another low. It's not a condition exclusive to men, though some men have certainly engaged in this at the expense of women historically. The point is that feminists badly miss the mark by reducing many of our most pressing social problems to issues of gender. They polarize our politics by insisting on an "us and them" approach to politics. Perhaps worst of all, their diagnosis misses the deeper human source of many of our social and political problems.

The same lack of restraint affects many modern liberals' approach to race. A decade or more ago critical race scholar Richard Delgado wrote a series of dialogues involving his literary alter ego, Rodrigo, a law student of color. In one dialogue, Rodrigo traces all modern social evils to the premeditated scheme of today's "Saxons," his term for northern Europeans. Rodrigo opines in the essay: "Northern Europeans have produced next to nothing—little sculpture, art or music worth listening to, and only a modest amount of truly great literature. And the few accomplishments they can cite with pride can be traced to the Egyptians, an African culture." He goes on to explain that black athletes "are simply faster and quicker . . . and, yes, I do believe the same holds true in the mental realm." Rodrigo cites as evidence for this the ghetto game of the dozens, the object of which is to see who can insult an opponent's mother in the fastest, most vicious way.[18]

It is beside the point that no respectable white author today could or should get away with making similar denigrating claims regarding nonwhites. What is more troubling is that sentiments like this find respect, sympathy, and succor among a certain cadre of left liberals. Liberals have a double standard on issues of race—the kind of double standard that sanctions the claim that African Americans can never be described as "racist" even when they hold views that would be considered racist if held by whites. There is a level of ultrasensitivity that condemns as racist any comment based on a generalization linked in any way to race, at least if the speaker is white. When Bill Clinton pointed out on the eve of Barack Obama's South Carolina primary victory that Jesse Jackson had won the same primary in 1984, opponents leapt to the conclusion that this was "racist code." Of course, Clinton was pointing out that South Carolina has a large African American population that reliably turns out for black candidates—which was accurate and which can be called "racist" only if it's racist to point out that most blacks vote for black candidates.

In another vein, consider feminist progressive law professor Martha Fineman's proposal that government aggressively democratize not simply economic conditions, but experience itself. To create conditions of genuine equality, she argues, we should be prepared to "equalize contexts" for every individual child. To this end she proposes the following arrangement:

> We might at birth assign each child a social security number along with a list of professions they might legitimately pursue, appropriately grouped into categories such as "service worker" or "professional." We could also assign the schools they would be permitted to attend. If an individual was not inclined to be satisfied with his or her lot later in life, she or he would have to find a willing person with whom to bargain or trade in order to alter the luck of the draw. To further equalize contexts, perhaps each child should be compelled to spend time in a number of different neighborhoods during childhood—two or three years in Westchester county would be balanced by equivalent time in Harlem, Alabama, Ohio and California.[19]

It's not clear whether Fineman's proposal entails the abolition of the family, but certainly the prospect that government should oversee the forced relocation of children in order to "equalize contexts" rivals even the most utopian schemes of Plato or Marx.

Yet, as radical as this idea is, it may be only a difference of degree from the instinct that animates more jejune species of "modern progressivism." While working as a staff attorney for the Children's Defense Fund, Hillary Clinton published an article in the *Harvard Educational Review* that proposed a sweeping overhaul of the legal system's approach to children's rights. In the piece, Clinton compares the legal status of children to that of slaves, of wives under older family law rules, and of those living on Indian reservations. She attacks the traditional "belief that families are private, non-political units whose interests subsume those of children." Since children "lack even the basic power to vote," their interests must be superintended not simply by government, but by the federal government. To this end, she argues that all educational funding and policy making be centralized at the federal level, to be overseen only by the federal judiciary. But her more sweeping proposal was that "the state's responsibility as a substitute parent" requires active intervention into the family by "boards composed of citizens representing identifiable constituencies—racial, religious, ethnic, geographical"—and staffed by "members [who] will be elected and should rotate to avoid institutional calcification."[20] More than two decades later, in a speech delivered at the United Methodist General Conference in 1996, the message was more muted: Americans, Clinton declared, "have to start thinking and believing that there really isn't any such thing as someone else's child."[21]

Like many issues discussed in this book, such proposals raise questions of moderation. It is one thing to say, as centrists are willing to do, that the government has a role to play in providing a social safety net for families in trouble; it is quite another to suggest that the family is a political unit to be superintended by a modern-day Committee for Public Safety representing various social constituencies. It is, again, deeply ironic that modern liberalism should run so far in the opposite direction from the insights of Mill, who feared government power so greatly that he opposed even public funding of elementary and secondary schools.

Contemporary liberalism, then, has a trajectory all its own—a direction, a velocity, that is guided by the alliances it has formed since the late nineteenth century with more radical, socialist, and utopian ideologies. To be sure, these more radical movements have never made the inroads in the United States that they have in European politics.[22] There is always some distance between the academic left and liberalism on the ground, as it is found in the modern Democratic Party. But modern academic liberalism is more "radical" in the original sense of the term—it may reveal the true roots of modern liberal ideology, its deeper orientation when freed of the necessity for pragmatic political compromise.

Even the less radical forms of modern liberalism have this deeper cast. From around the turn of the twentieth century onward, modern liberalism's seminal theorists and thinkers—Bernard Bosanquet, L. T. Hobhouse, John Dewey, Carl Becker, John Kenneth Galbraith, John Rawls, and Ronald Dworkin, among others—have labored mightily to demonstrate how we might pour the newer wine of a more collectivist and egalitarian philosophy into the older bottle of liberalism. John Rawls and Ronald Dworkin, perhaps the two most influential academic left liberals of the past forty years, accept a view of government power that, I believe, cannot be squared with genuine liberalism. Rawls, you may remember, argued that no government policy can be justified unless it makes the worst off in society at least a little better off. He believed that implementing a just society requires that we "regard the distribution of natural abilities as a *collective asset* so that the more fortunate are to benefit only in ways that help those who have lost out."[23] Similarly, Dworkin argues that "it is obviously obnoxious to the liberal conception, for example, that someone should have more of what the community as a whole has to distribute because he or his father had superior skill or luck."[24]

These are striking pronouncements. In saying that all talents are "collective assets," Rawls is explicitly rejecting the core liberal value of self-ownership. He is asserting that even the personal assets of each individual—those talents, dispositions, and capacities that are most central to the moral personality of the individual— may effectively be controlled, dispensed, and distributed by the state. Dworkin's view that "skill and luck" (and presumably all the things that go into developing one's skill—i.e., the education, toil, and sacrifice) are illegitimate bases for social distribution is considerably closer in spirit to Marx's "from each according to his ability" than to Madison's view that "the protection of different and unequal faculties of acquiring property" is "*the first object*" of government."[25] Since the New Deal, Americans seem collectively to have decided that we want a little more Marx and a little less Madison—and that may be fine up to a point. Centrists accept the New Deal and the notion of a limited social safety net subject to the constraints imposed by our limited resources. But we fear that we've reached a kind of tipping point where every new need becomes a right and where our demands for social justice are outstripping our collective capacity to provide for these.

The paradox of modern liberalism is that the more we directly pursue its central goals, the more they seem to slip through our hands. Like happiness, liberty can be achieved only by not being too self-conscious in our pursuit of it.

Just as many conservatives persist in clinging to their myth of social decay, liberals have a myth of their own—what I like to call "the myth of uncompleted momentum." The myth of uncompleted momentum is the conviction that liberalism has its own, still unrealized, manifest destiny that requires that things continue proceeding in the same direction they have in the past. In his autobiographical essay "Trotsky and Wild Orchids," the late postmodernist philosopher Richard Rorty exhorted us to continue "along the trajectory defined by the Bill of Rights, the Reconstruction Amendments, the building of the land grant colleges, female suffrage, the New Deal, Brown v Board of Education, . . . Lyndon Johnson's civil rights legislation, the feminist movement and the gay rights movement." He suggested that the trajectory will be complete only when liberalism has achieved a thoroughly secularized, socialized, classless society. Those who may wish to stop short of the full trajectory, he suggested, are "the same honest, decent, blinkered, disastrous people who voted for Hitler in 1933."[26]

This is the myth of uncompleted momentum: If it is progress to have moved from Jim Crow to *Brown v. Board of Education*, then it must be better still to move from antidiscrimination to affirmative action. If it was beneficial to provide Medicaid and Medicare, then it must be better still to provide universal health insurance. If it was right to limit the death penalty in a variety of ways as the Supreme Court has done over the past thirty-five years, it must be better still to abolish it in all cases. If it was appropriate to grant amnesty to almost three million undocumented aliens living in the United States in 1986, then it must be better to do it again, or to open the borders permanently. Contemporary liberalism seems to operate much the way a shark swims—it stays afloat only if it keeps moving.

It is in this sense that many centrists fear we have reached a tipping point. Some of these ideas—open borders, for example—are simply disastrous. Others—such as universal health care—may be splendid ideas in theory but ignore the problem of cost. We do not have unlimited resources. We are at a point economically where, before we adopt any new programs, we should first decide which of the older programs must now be jettisoned.

Centrists part ways from modern liberals in several other respects as well. We are dubious of the increasing secularization of modern politics (see Chapter 5), we hold to a conception of government that stops short of an all-embracing welfare state (see Chapter 6), and we are particularly opposed to the increasing use of the judiciary to override democratic resistance to progressive reforms (see Chapter 7). We stop well short of the modern liberal's conception of an unbounded sphere of private morality, though we often side with liberals on particular moral issues (see Chapter 8). We are not unqualified supporters of *Roe v. Wade*, and many centrists adopt a middle course between the extreme pro-choice and pro-life positions concerning abortion (see Chapter 9). Concerning equality, we stand against racism and sexism and homophobism, but we reject government affirmative action programs that apply different standards for different groups (see Chapter 10). We tend to take a law-and-order approach to matters of criminal justice, though we side with liberals on the asymmetries of the criminal justice system, including the treatment of white-collar versus blue-collar criminals (see Chapter 11). We oppose opening the border to the free flow of illegal immigration, though we advocate expanded access for those already here to certain social rights and privileges on condition that the U.S. border be secured (see Chapter 12).

In sum, centrists fear that the leftward drift of modern liberalism will end up undermining what we take to be the most essential values of liberalism. Progressives who travel the liberal trajectory to its end are not liberals in any sense at all. They are the modern-day adherents of a more radical and socialistic conception of society that has moved the more visionary political thinkers from the time of the Enlightenment.

This is not *liberalism*. But there is sometimes magic in a word.

Part II
Toward a Centrist View
of U.S. Politics

Chapter 5
Politics and the Big Questions:
On God, Morality, and the Human Condition

"AT THE CORE OF every moral code," Walter Lippmann wrote, "there is a picture of human nature, a map of the universe and a version of history."[1] The same holds true for every political code. All political theories make basic assumptions about the nature of the good, about whether there are objective moral rights and wrongs in the world, about whether human beings have free will or are determined in their actions, about whether we are basically altruistic or egoistic, and, most importantly, about whether the world is in our hands alone or whether there is a God to whom we ultimately have to answer. These moral, metaphysical, and psychological assumptions ground each theory and give that theory its plausibility in the grand scheme of human affairs. Marx's metaphysical assumptions are about as far as they can be from Aquinas's, and Locke is considerably closer to Cicero on some of the deepest questions than he is to fellow liberals Bentham and Mill. Metaphysics matters to politics, even when the metaphysical assumptions remain in the background. By the same token, metaphysics is dangerous to politics—dangerous because of the all-too-human tendency to take its lessons too literally or to pretend to know more than we actually know about the world. In this sense, as I hope to show, many centrists are believing skeptics or skeptical believers.

There are in essence really only two ways of thinking about the world (though there are many different versions of each of these). Neither, taken rigorously and literally, is entirely satisfactory to liberal and democratic political institutions. For simplicity's sake, we'll call these two ideas the traditional and the secular viewpoints. As I am using these terms, "traditionalism" and "secularism" represent two poles of a dichotomy. Each exerts a gravitational pull on the thought of many conservatives and liberals, respectively. Traditionalism tends to slide toward fundamentalism and political authoritarianism, while secularism leads in the direction—literally—of a soulless conception of human existence which understands human beings in purely naturalistic terms, that is, as complex machines. Taken to an extreme, traditionalism can become Saudi- or Iranian-style religious authoritarianism, while secularism can metastasize into Aldous Huxley's brave new world or the kind of socially engineered community envisioned in B. F. Skinner's *Walden II*. Most of us today are more familiar with the dangers of fundamentalist authoritarianism because it now exists in various places around the globe and because we see signs of its influence here at home. Yet there is good reason to conclude that the secular paradigm represents the more grave danger in the long run, precisely because secularism has been the ascendant philosophy for the past three centuries.

A genuine commitment to liberal democracy requires that we steer clear of either extreme. Both fundamentalists and secular materialists think they know more than they actually do—the one because they believe they know God's will, the other because they overestimate the capacity of science to explain the depths of the human mystery.

The Traditional and Secular Understandings of the World

The traditional view of the world is a God-centered idea of the world; it is a world with a reality that runs deeper than the observable, material dimension of existence. Traditionalists believe not only that God has created the world, but also that he has endowed it with an overarching moral order no less real than the physical order of the universe. There are objective rights and wrongs in this world, either rationally discoverable by human beings or revealed through a particular religious tradition, which are interwoven into the objective order of the world. Even traditionalists who stop short of belief in an intervening God—who adhere to some form of deism, popular among many of our nation's founders—believe that the watchmaker God has created the universe and provided a purpose and a meaning to human existence. Things have not happened randomly; the universe is not a contingent place, a cosmic accident. Things add up, morally and politically. We are not alone in the world, left to our own devices, and life is not absurd. Most importantly, there is a given moral order that limits what it is right or permissible for us to do, both individually and collectively. Human morality and politics must accord with this transcendent or given order.

Central to the traditionalist's understanding of the world is the idea that human beings are free in the deepest metaphysical sense. We have free will that permits each of us to choose our course of action from among the courses of action open to us. Our inherent freedom means that we are responsible for our behavior, and that we are answerable for our actions, in both this world and the next. There are, of course, physical limits to what each of us can do and there are moral influences on our behavior, but ultimately each of us bears responsibility for who we become and for how we behave. By establishing laws that act as a floor and not a ceiling for human conduct, government sets the outer boundaries for permissible human behavior and reins in, through threat of punishment, the all-too-human tendency to transgress social norms and moral duties. Beyond this, government has little responsibility for fine-tuning social and economic relations within the sphere of civil society. With Thomas Paine, traditionalists are apt to share a minimalist view of government that holds that "society is produced by our wants and government by our wickedness." As classical liberals and most conservatives have insisted, government's primary purpose is to prevent harm, not to attempt to maximize the good.[2]

In broad strokes, this is the traditional paradigm. Certainly not every traditionalist has adhered to every aspect of this description—Calvinists doubt that there is free will (though they still insist on holding people responsible for their actions), and antinomians have doubted that God imposes hard rules, preferring a religion of the spirit to a religion of the law. Christian socialists have certainly advocated more progressive governmental policies in the name of their religion. But something like this constellation of ideas has fairly dominated traditional Western political thought for much of the past two thousand years.

Secularists reject this picture of reality in almost every important detail. I am using the term "secularism" in its widest sense; in a narrower sense, secularism is a position that requires that we divide religious from political power, that we separate church and state. Secularism in the narrower sense makes no claims about the validity of religious or spiritual truths and has been a staple of the liberal tradition since at least Locke's "Letter on Toleration" published in 1689. But as many use the term today—and as I use it here—"secularism" has a wider meaning. It entails not simply the separation of secular from ecclesiastical authority, but skepticism of the traditional, religious view of the world. The secularist believes, as journalist Christopher Hitchens recently put it in endorsing secularism, that "earthly things are all that we have, or are ever going to have."[3]

The British writer and philosopher Iris Murdoch once wrote, "It is easy to say there is no God. It is not so easy to believe it and to draw the consequences."[4] Secularism is the attempt to draw these consequences consistently in the sphere of politics and morality. It is the working out of the implications of thinking about the world in purely naturalistic, materialistic terms. As Richard Dawkins put it in his recent book *The God Delusion*, the secularist's view is that "there is nothing beyond the natural, physical world, no supernatural creative intelligence lurking behind the observable universe, no soul that outlasts the body" and "if there is something that appears to lie beyond the natural world, we hope eventually to understand it and embrace it within the natural."[5] Secularists' materialism is reinforced by their positivism, the view that the only things in the world which are meaningful are those things which can be objectively verified, quantified, or measured. As Dawkins would have it, "spiritual" entities must either be reduced to observable physical phenomena or they must be ruled out of court as, literally, "non-sense"—that is, as not knowable through the senses.

The secular view of the world has several profound consequences. It implies, first, that we are alone in the universe, that there is no cosmic arbiter of human action, no supernatural sanction for the wrongs we perpetrate on one another, and no otherworldly reward for those who have managed to stay in the black, morally and metaphysically. "Absolute truth is a mirage," Oliver Wendell Holmes, perhaps the only openly atheist justice to sit on the Supreme Court, once declared. "I see no reasons for attributing cosmic importance to man. . . . I regard him as I do the other species . . . having for his main business to live and propagate, and for his main interests food and sex. A few get a little further along and get pleasure in it, but are fools if they are proud."[6] For the secularist, there is no cosmic significance to the human drama. We are in this alone.

The true secularist also rejects the idea that there is any moral order in the world. As Hitchens put it, the world is "random and contingent." There is no overarching or given moral order out there waiting to be discovered, as the natural lawyers thought. Rather, human beings construct their own morality. Nothing outside us limits what we can do; we impose our own boundaries on ourselves, collectively, through informal social sanctions and through law. But there is nothing deeper— no divine sanction or natural law, no external moral code that binds us morally and politically.

The secular view requires that we understand all human behavior in the same way we think about the growth of plants and the movement of animals—as part of the natural world. All human behavior must be understood, at least in some ultimate sense, as flowing from outside causes—from a person's heredity or environment or some combination of these. Rigorous commitment to a secular, materialistic view of the world usually entails skepticism toward the traditional idea of freedom of the will. Since all human behavior must be understood causally and deterministically, we seem to have to rule out the idea that our actions follow from truly unconditioned choices. This, in turn, winds up raising doubts about the idea of individual responsibility. If we are all causally determined to act as we do, then it ultimately may not make any more sense to hold us responsible for our acts than it would to hold a tree responsible for the way it grows. In fact, those who embrace a rigorous version of the secular paradigm are likely to become skeptical concerning the various ideas associated with the traditional view of the person, among them the idea that we possess a mind that is somehow distinct from the physical brain. From the seventeenth century on, modern philosophy has traveled the path of all these conclusions. Our civilization seems to stand today with one foot in the older paradigm and the other in the newer. We assume the existence of free will and individual responsibility in many of our most basic moral assumptions and in the law, yet these assumptions are increasingly challenged today by psychologists, philosophers, and others who believe that human behavior is largely or entirely determined by our biological and environmental influences. All this stems from growing modern skepticism about the soul or the self as a distinct metaphysical entity with free will and the capacity to reason.[7]

There are also powerful political implications that follow from this secular picture of the human condition. As I suggest later in the chapter, secularism may lead to what I call a managerial conception of the government, the idea that all human problems must be managed by the government and that all social ills are to be anticipated or remedied by social engineers. Where traditionalists usually accept a more minimalist and preventive conception of government, secularists view politics, as conservative philosopher Michael Oakeshott put it, as "a succession of crises, each to be surmounted by the application of 'reason.'"[8] Where the traditionalist believes that the human condition places ineluctable limits on our collective capacity to solve human problems, the secularist tends to believe that, with enough knowledge (which we surely will sooner or later acquire), every human problem is potentially resolvable through collective political action.

Of course, some conservatives—those such as David Hume, Jerry Muller, Andrew Sullivan, and other skeptical conservatives—fall closer to the secular paradigm, as we saw in Chapter 2. And some liberals—those who are religiously motivated—are sometimes ambivalent secularists. Nevertheless, the connections between modern liberalism and secularism, on one hand, and conservatism and traditionalism, on the other, are clear enough that they often are the driving force in the political prescriptions of each.

The Temptation of Fundamentalism

If traditionalists believe in God and an objective moral order of the universe, then the more extreme among them, religious fundamentalists, claim to have highly specific knowledge of what God wants in particular circumstances and what the moral order requires in all important matters. It is natural, of course, for believers to want to know what God wills and what is expected of us. And to the extent that one's belief has been inspired by a particular religious tradition, the tendency to pick and choose from the entire package of orthodox beliefs, embracing some and rejecting others, comes at the risk of subverting one's belief in the entire package. If the Bible is incorrect concerning specific historical claims about various historical events, then it may very well be wrong about such central Christian tenets as the crucifixion and resurrection of Jesus—or so this logic goes. In fact, skeptics and fundamentalists share one essential inclination: notwithstanding their profound disagreements in other respects, both seem to believe that one must accept either all of it or none at all. Fundamentalists feel compelled to accept every word of the Bible literally as the word of God, while secular atheists seem to believe that a challenge to any particular claim indicts the entire tradition.

"Fundamentalism" and "evangelicalism," terms that have evolved in the twentieth century to describe religious movements based on literal interpretations of scriptural texts, are connected to political conservatism in several ways.[9] As we saw in Chapter 2, the true conservative believes in a given moral order and rejects moral relativism, skepticism, and the humanist doctrine that "man is the measure of all things." Belief in a given moral order means that there exist distinct rights and wrongs about which there can be no legitimate disagreement. The clearer and more authoritative these injunctions, the less room there is for disagreement and the more likely the fundamentalist will see our current social situation as decayed morally. Fundamentalism runs counter to liberalism's social tolerance and moral pluralism, its acceptance of diverse lifestyles, and its defense of the right to dissent in all matters religious, moral, and political. To the extent that fundamentalists believe that disobedience may result in divine retribution, moreover, they believe that the political consequences of misbehavior for the community can be grave. Each of these tenets tends to reinforce the more authoritarian attitudes of fundamentalist conservatives.

Consider the "Manifesto for the Christian Church," a document published by the Coalition on Revival, a network of Protestant evangelicals of various denominations, which hundreds of Protestant ministers and civic leaders have signed over the past two decades. In an introductory section, the authors state that "the world is in desperate trouble and western civilization stands on the brink of self-destruction" and maintain that the men of our society have become "emasculated, tamed, dependent, self-centered and soft." The document then goes on to lay out the following protocols of faith:

> We affirm that the Old and New Testaments of the Bible were so inspired by God that the human authors wrote the exact words and sentences God inspired them to write without error and without misrepresenting God, history or the created world in any way. . . .
>
> We affirm that this God-inspired, inerrant Bible is the only absolute, objective, final test for all truth claims and the clearest verbal picture of reality that has ever come into the hands of mankind. . . .
>
> We affirm that the Bible is not only God's statement to us regarding religion, salvation, eternity, righteousness, but also the final measurement and depository of certain fundamental facts of reality . . . in the spheres of law, government, economics, business, education, arts and communication, medicine, psychology and science.

The document goes on to assert that "there is a cause-and-effect relationship between obeying the laws and commandments deposited in His Word and being blessed by God"; that "those people or nations that live in opposition to biblical laws will, sooner or later, be cursed and destroyed"; that "it is, therefore, to the great benefit of all mankind . . . to bring every society's legal and judicial system into as close an approximation to the laws and commandments of the Bible as its citizens will allow"; and that it is their mission "to go forth into the world and make Bible-obeying disciples of all nations."[10]

For those who hold these views, moral and political disagreements are not questions for individuals to wrestle with on their own. A community that permits homosexuality, abortion, pornography, fornication, or any of the other various acts that the devout consider sinful risks "the ban," as the Old Testament authors put it. We risk collective obliteration. In this sense, the very idea of a private realm is, for the religious fundamentalist, a kind of cosmic category mistake. No behavior is truly private—particularly if society tolerates it.

Of course, fundamentalism and conservatism are related in other ways, as others who have studied fundamentalism have noted.[11] Fundamentalist organizations typically are rigidly hierarchical in structure; demand more-or-less absolute deference to their political leaders, who are often authoritarian personality types; and routinely subordinate women and those who are otherwise "different." Each of these tendencies seems to be exacerbated in proportion to the level of certitude and rigidity with which fundamentalist views are held.

By the 1970s, many sociologists had concluded that religious belief was passing from the scene in U.S. society. They followed Max Weber in believing that modernization and secularization were inevitably linked.[12] But Weber couldn't have been more wrong in this respect. Sixty percent of Americans today say that religion plays an important role in their lives—twice the proportion of Canadians or Italians and five times that of Japanese. Only 12 percent are unaffiliated with any religion.[13] Of the religiously affiliated, more than half describe themselves as evangelicals. The National Association of Evangelicals claims thirty million members today and claims to speak for over forty million people nationwide.[14] A recent poll indicates that 58 percent of all Republicans are conservative Christians. The amount of influence they wield is genuinely astounding. In the 1990s, Ralph Reed's Christian Coalition was considered the seventh most powerful lobbying organization in the United States, right behind the National Rifle Association and right ahead of the American Medical Association. Today they are only marginally less powerful. In the 2000 election, 68 percent of white Protestant evangelicals voted for Bush and Cheney. This number rose to an astonishing 78 percent in 2004.[15] Given the closeness of both elections, the impact of the evangelical voting bloc can hardly be doubted.

"The tendency to claim God as an ally for our partisan values and ends," Reinhold Niebuhr once wrote, "is the source of all religious fanaticism." Unfortunately, for the same reason, religious revelation can be tapped as an unchallenged source of power, as we have seen repeatedly in the recent past. George W. Bush reiterated publicly that God had told him, and told him clearly, that the United States had a providential mission to fulfill in invading Iraq and toppling Saddam Hussein's dictatorship. John Dean reminds us in his book *Conservatives without Conscience* of the Reverend Pat Robertson's comments after Israeli prime minister Ariel Sharon's stroke. He told his *700 Club* audience that the "prophet Joel makes very clear that God has enmity against those who 'divide my land,'" referring to Sharon's role in withdrawing troops from Gaza and the West Bank. When President Reagan nominated Sandra Day O'Connor to the Supreme Court in 1981, the late Reverend Jerry Falwell claimed that God opposed the nomination. "Every good Christian," Falwell claimed, "should be concerned about this nomination." Other conservatives were not so certain. Former Republican presidential candidate Barry Goldwater responded that "every good Christian should line up and kick Jerry Falwell's ass."[16]

C. S. Lewis, whose own commitment to Christianity was as pristine as it was cogently defended, saw clearly the perils of claiming any particular insight into the will of God in matters social and political. He admonished political leaders to avoid at all costs hubristic claims to having direct religious knowledge of God's will or of the providential order of the world: "On those who add 'Thus said the Lord' to their merely human utterances descends the doom of a conscience *that seems clearer and clearer* the more it is loaded with sin."[17]

Perhaps this doesn't bode well for Mr. Bush.

The Drift to Secularism

If fundamentalists go too far in one direction, hoping to impose upon the rest of us their own interpretation of the meaning of religion, then some contemporary secular liberals run too far in exactly the opposite direction: they frequently wish to banish altogether any mention of the religious or spiritual dimensions of human activity from the public sphere. The American Civil Liberties Union (ACLU), for example, not only opposes the display of a crèche in a park or a nonreligiously adorned Christmas tree in a law school, but also opposes even the most inclusive display of religious ecumenicalism—displays that include the symbolism of many different religious traditions.[18] The sources of many liberals' concerns, in this respect, lie considerably deeper than the constitutional principle of separation of church and state. (Why is it, after all, that many liberals are constitutional purists concerning the separation principle while virtually dismissing the Second Amendment's protection of the right to bear arms or the Tenth Amendment's protection for the autonomy of the states?) The liberals' attempt to oust religion from public life is driven not by their constitutional principles, but by their metaphysics. Because secularists deny the existence of a nonmaterial realm, they are prone to be skeptical of any political justifications that rely on religious, spiritual, or empirically nonverifiable sources of human values.

Recently, it has become fashionable for some of the most influential liberal thinkers to claim that the religious views of a person, a group, or a community should not have any impact in the process of political decision making precisely because they are not publicly demonstrable. Religiously motivated persons with a pro-life position, for example, might not be permitted to appeal to their belief that the fetus has a soul that enters upon conception, since others do not share this view. In debates over whether sex abstinence education is better than handing out condoms to a seventh-grade class, again, a person could appeal to material concerns such as the prevalence of sexually transmitted diseases but could be foreclosed from appealing to the belief that sex among twelve-year-olds is immoral on religious grounds.

The single most important recent philosopher of liberalism, John Rawls, took exactly this position toward the end of his career. In *Political Liberalism*, Rawls argued: "Our exercise of political power is proper and hence justifiable only when it is exercised in accordance with a constitution the essentials of which all citizens may reasonably be expected to endorse in light of the principles and ideals acceptable to them as reasonable and rational." Rawls called this "the liberal principle of legitimacy," yet this principle is anything but liberal.[19] Rawls's liberal principle of legitimacy places specific constraints on political decision making. It requires, most basically, that before we can collectively discuss a political issue, we must begin from a lowest common denominator, from premises and assumptions that "all citizens may be expected to endorse."[20] Since some citizens do not believe in a nonmaterial reality, it is unfair, Rawls argued, to permit others to begin from a spiritual worldview when we are discussing public matters that concern all of us. We must begin from premises that we all share—which means, of course, that we must begin from the secularist's assumption that only the material world and material interests exist. If ever an argument front-loaded its conclusion in its premises, this does.

Rawls argued more specifically that "comprehensive doctrines"—his term for a general religious or philosophical worldview—cannot serve as a partial basis for reaching political agreement. "Religious and philosophical doctrines . . . are too diverse, especially in a free society, to enable those doctrines to serve as the basis for lasting and reasonable political agreement." Because "reasonable persons see that the burdens of judgment set limits on what can be reasonably justified to others," comprehensive religious or philosophical views can never be the basis for political action. While Rawls was careful to say that he was not advocating skepticism in one's private life, "we are to recognize the practical impossibility of reaching reasonable and workable political agreement in judgment on the truth of comprehensive doctrines."[21]

The upshot of this view is to closet religious feelings and motivations—to restrict them to the private realm and to bracket them from any public significance. Rawls's concern is that if laws are passed for reasons secularists do not accept, then secularists are not being treated equally as citizens and are effectively being coerced by having to follow laws which do not comport with their own worldview. Yet he does not explain why the reverse is not true. Isn't the religiously motivated person coerced when forced to begin from the secularist's premise that there is *nothing more* than the material world? Isn't it better—indeed, more liberal—to permit individuals to start from their own premises, whatever they happen to be?

Rawls's strongly secularist position is untenable for three reasons. First, it stacks the deck against religion. Rawls's position would permit only empirically demonstrable considerations that would be relevant to a secularist, excluding any consideration that fails to meet the requirements of the secular positivist. To say that secular arguments and motivations will be acceptable as a basis for public debate, but that nonsecular arguments will not, is to violate the equal rights of those who are moved by religious sources of inspiration. Indeed, it is to treat the religiously motivated unequally. It is to say that traditionalists must meet the requirements of meaning set out by secularists. In essence, Rawls's principle of legitimacy requires that all political action be justified in terms only of those things we all can hear and see and lay our hands on; it rules out of court, virtually by definition, nonempirical sources of meaning and knowledge. In this sense, he has front-loaded his conclusion into his premises.

Second, as a practical matter, almost any traditional justification for laws can be restated in secular terms. In the abortion debate, for example, the religiously motivated can usually cast their spiritual concern in secular terms. Pro-life Christians can assert that they want to protect the dignity of human life rather than the soul of the fetus, or prevent a general devaluing of life to which abortion practices may contribute. These are the kinds of arguments secularists can accept. (The latter argument is frequently made by critics of legalized assisted suicide.) Similarly, in the case of a law proscribing nonmarital sex (e.g., "fornication"), Christians can assert not that sex outside marriage runs against the tenets of their religion, but that they are defending the sanctity of marriage as the only legitimate province of sex or that they seek to limit the spread of STDs, or any of a variety of other potential rationales. The point is that the injunction against religiously motivated arguments is usually easily circumvented.

Finally, who is to say, as Rawls does, that secularism is not itself a "comprehensive" worldview or doctrine, just as religious traditions are? While the secularist has different criteria for meaning and truth than the traditionalist, the secular materialist worldview comports with Rawls's own general idea of a "comprehensive doctrine."[22] So it is not at all clear that Rawls can privilege the secular paradigm, even on his own criteria.

In different ways, both fundamentalists and secular liberals want to impose their version of reality on everyone else. Both want to deny the political relevance of each individual's spiritual convictions (or anti-convictions). The fundamentalist claims that we can act only on the basis of what *he* knows, and the Rawlsian claims we can act only on the basis of what *everyone* knows. What about what each of us has learned—subjectively, uniquely, individually? Why shouldn't this be the criterion, with each of us our own interpreter of the tradition that guides us?

If Justice O'Connor was correct to insist, in another context, that "at the heart of liberty is the right to define one's own concept of existence, of meaning, of the universe, and of the mystery of human life," then certainly this liberty should not stop at the point where it may have some public consequence.[23] Centrists believe that this is a better understanding of what the liberal tradition requires than what is sometimes considered the "liberal" position today.

The Further Consequences of Secularism

The secular worldview holds some even more striking consequences for our way of thinking about the human condition, law, and politics. Taken literally and rigorously enough, secularism is on a collision course with the most central values of liberalism, properly understood.

True secularists understand human activity in naturalistic terms. By this I mean that they interpret human behavior as they would other natural phenomena—the movement of the planets, the growth of biological organisms, and so on. Essential to naturalism is the idea that human behavior is causally determined, that our choices and decisions and actions are explainable and predictable in terms of the same network of deterministic laws that governs the rest of nature.[24] Human behavior may be more complex than that of animals or nonliving physical objects like the planets, but it is not different in kind from other things in nature. Where traditionalists divide the world between the human realm, characterized by our capacity to exercise free will, and the natural world, where the laws of science apply unerringly, secularists hold that human behavior is of a piece with all other natural phenomena. Whereas traditionalists are "dualists" in that they draw a line between the physical world governed by the laws of science and the world of the human spirit, secularists are more likely to believe that all human behavior is potentially predictable as a product of genetic and environmental factors.

There are a number of truly profound political consequences of the secularist's view. Secularists view all human behavior from the "outside in" in a way that obliterates the possibility of human freedom and responsibility. Consider the views of the behaviorist psychologist B. F. Skinner, a thinker who took the secular ideal to its rigorous logical extreme. Skinner's behaviorism theory was a preeminent force among progressive social policy thinkers during the middle third of the twentieth century. His opinion of the idea of freedom is telling. In *Beyond Freedom and Dig-*

nity and other works, Skinner consistently argued that the concept of freedom is a childish conceptual hangover from the prescientific era—the era dominated by traditionalists. He believed that "the critical condition for the *apparent* existence of free will is positive reinforcement." In other words, "the person *feels free and calls himself free*" when that person has been positively reinforced.[25] Freedom of the will is an illusion, he tells his readers, as everything in the universe is causally determined. "We cannot prove, of course," Skinner writes, "that human behavior as a whole is fully determined, but the proposition becomes more plausible as the facts accumulate, and I believe that a point has been reached at which its implications must be seriously considered."[26]

Of course, if we do not make choices we cannot really be held responsible for our actions, morally or legally—not in the sense that we have traditionally meant by holding someone responsible. How can we blame someone for doing what they were causally determined to do, after all? Because secularists reject the old "free will and individual responsibility" justification for punishment, they have been forced to find more utilitarian justifications for punishment. On the utilitarian view, the offender is punished not because he is to blame but because punishment will deter others from doing what he has done.[27] Consider Justice Oliver Wendell Holmes's chilling utilitarian defense of capital punishment: "If I were having a philosophical talk with a man I was going to have hanged, (or electrocuted), I should say, I don't doubt that your act was inevitable for you, but to make it more avoidable by others we propose to sacrifice you to the common good. You may regard yourself as a soldier dying for your country. But the law must keep its promises."[28] A rigorous secularism requires us to take the dangerous step of abandoning long-standing ideas of credit and blame, responsibility and desert, and shifts the responsibility for crime control from the person to society generally.

More troubling still, by challenging assumptions about freedom of the will, secularism threatens the very foundations of liberalism and democracy. Liberalism depends upon a Janus-faced conception of freedom—an idea of freedom which points inwardly, to free will, even as it points outwardly, to our political liberties. Why do we protect the rights of individuals to live as we wish, to make decisions about our own lives and our own families? Because we assume that these decisions carry a certain normative weight, grounded in the autonomy of the person. Determinism fundamentally undermines notions of individual autonomy. Rights have validity only if we can assume that individuals are rational (capable of knowing their own best interests) and free (able to pursue these interests without fear that every individual act is skewed by influences over which one has little control). To be a liberal and a determinist is to believe in half of the equation without the other half—to insist on the protection of our external political liberties while denying the internal premise on which these liberties depend.

Democracy depends upon this same commitment. The individual vote is protected as an expression not simply of the individual's interest, but of the individual's autonomy. As one of the premier theorists of democracy puts it, belief in democracy depends upon a "presumption of personal autonomy," the belief that each adult individual "should be assumed to be the best judge of his or her own good or interests."[29] Taken to its logical extreme, determinism ultimately undermines institutions of freedom by suggesting the need for top-down control, characteristically vouchsafed as in the interests of those who are governed.

Taken far enough, the secular view can justify invasive government intervention to shape the preferences and choices of individuals. Law professor Cass Sunstein famously argued in an article in the *University of Chicago Law Review* twenty years ago that an important role for government consists in correcting the "distorted preferences" of individuals—which, he concluded, are frequently pervasive.[30] Sunstein acknowledged in a footnote that the central liberal concept of autonomy possibly "should be abandoned altogether." "The fact that preferences are socially constructed," he thought, "may mean that there is no such entity as a purely autonomous preference." Later he had second thoughts, conceding that "if the notion of autonomy is abandoned, the realm of permissible legal interference may become limitless—hardly a comforting prospect."[31] Like other progressives, Sunstein is torn between his liberalism and his secular commitments—between his attraction to the idea of autonomy and his adherence to the principles of social constructionism and all that this commitment entails.

Acceptance of the deterministic hypothesis is lethal to the underlying philosophy of liberalism and democracy because it strikes at the heart of what they depend upon—the idea of the freely choosing individual. This presents contemporary liberalism with a real dilemma: the more we conclude that our decisions are the product of social or biological variables over which we have no control, the more natural the tendency to believe that they are not really ours. As legal theorist Charles Fried put it recently, if our "bedrock sense of [our] own subjectivity" is "an illusion, a social construction," then all the fundamental distinctions of liberalism— for example, being influenced versus being coerced, being persuaded versus being brainwashed—must collapse. "If we do not take responsibility for our own judgments, we might as well give up on thought and argument, in trying to convince others and in being open to being convinced by others."[32] I cannot think of any assumption as potentially lethal to a liberal social order as the idea that individuals need government to correct their everyday judgments.

Where does the secular conception of the human condition lead at its furthest reaches? One frightening possibility is that, taken rigorously enough, secularism leads to the idea of the beneficent, paternalistic, state-directed society that corrects all distorted individual preferences and allocates all economic benefits—indeed, distributes all the outputs of individual talents and capacities that are collectively owned.[33] Ultimately, the naturalism of the secularist leads liberals in the direction of thinking of society as a system that must be managed, through the use of rationally designed programs and institutions. Since human beings act in predictable (and potentially controllable) ways, we can come to understand all human failings—aggression, selfishness, ignorance, superstition, war, poverty, prejudice, and so on—as the *effects* of conditions outside the individual, of various social or economic or biological causes. Through the applied use of human reason we can, it might even be held, potentially engineer society to put each of these conditions behind us permanently to create utopian, or near utopian, social conditions.

Secularism, in sum, leads in the direction of a managerial conception of the state. Wasn't this Skinner's prescription, after all? We are not free, Skinner argued, and never can be—because human behavior is externally precipitated by environmental factors. The literature of freedom, Skinner claimed, has "failed to rescue the happy slave." The object of government must be "to free man, not from control"—for this is impossible—"but from aversive control."[34] The function of the behaviorist-inspired state is to create a social environment where people are happy and secure, and where they are free from coercion and manipulation. Yet achieving this kind of environment requires the government to have a guiding hand in virtually every feature of human existence. If ever there was a humanitarian justification for a to-talitarian society, this is it. If it is not a society quite like that in Orwell's *1984*, then at least it has striking parallels to Huxley's *Brave New World*.

Why has the secular and materialist conception of human nature exerted so much influence on modern liberalism? The reasons are complex, but perhaps the most important is that liberalism has been swept along by the same modernist currents that have carried much of the rest of the academic sciences since the eighteenth century. Several of liberalism's greatest heroes—Bentham and Mill, for starters—were committed philosophical atheists, materialists, and positivists. Having shrugged off liberalism's more traditional commitment to metaphysical dualism, nineteenth-century liberals from Mill on began to speak in two parallel languages simultaneously—the "free will and individual responsibility" language of the traditionalist when discussing politics, and the more deterministic language of the materialist when writing on the more abstract questions of human nature.

Most modern liberals continue to be torn between their traditionalism and their secularism. They intuitively understand that liberalism without the ideas of freedom of the will and personal responsibility is an oxymoron. In their more lucid moments they also understand that there are limits to human perfectibility, that top-down forms of social change often carry unintended consequences, and, more generally, that the managerial state holds negative consequences for a broader regime of human freedom. At the end of the day, liberalism and secularism are on a collision course with each other. Defending liberalism and democracy requires that we hold on to some of the basic assumptions of the traditional paradigm.

Where Centrists Stand

As should be apparent by now, the political positions of centrists are in part a consequence of our own big-picture understanding of the human condition. Centrists resist the gravitational pull of either extreme. Ours is an updated, commonsense, and humanitarian version of traditionalism. Centrists think in terms of a self that has free will, that is generally responsible for its actions, and that deserves the merit or blame that comes with the consequences of its actions and omissions. We believe that liberalism and democracy depend on this conception of the self. If it should turn out that this view of the self runs counter to the assumptions of the materialist—as it seems to—then so much the worse for materialism. And if the breach in the fabric of the web of materialism represented by the idea of the free self should lead some to consider the possibility of a broader spiritual reality—if our understanding of ourselves as inherently free should lead us to question the materialist's idea of the world, and if this, in turn, should provide for some a clue to the meaning of the universe and to the possibility that God exists, after all—then shouldn't each of us have the right to act on these conclusions in the sphere of politics? "Liberalism"—in the best sense of the word—demands nothing less.

This picture of human beings as free and responsible means that each of us must shoulder a large measure of responsibility for who we become and for our circumstances. This is not to deny the role of chance, of accidents, or of the power of one's background and environment in shaping the character and circumstances of each life. Of course we are guided and influenced, shaped and expanded and sometimes limited, by our social and economic conditions. But these conditions cannot be conceived in anything remotely approaching the determinist's view of the human condition. Centrists are commonsense moralists. We are likely to find that a good deal more excuse making takes places in politics, in the criminal justice system, and in matters of everyday morality than most liberals will concede. When a looter is apprehended stealing a TV set from a department store in the wake of a major hurricane, we are not likely to be moved by the plea that the looter's poverty was the cause. When an adulterous husband claims that his genes have left him with a genetic propensity to cheat on his wife, we are likely to find the causes in his character, not in his genes. When the seriously overweight person sues MacDonald's claiming to be a victim of the hamburger chain's advertising, the centrist will be skeptical. There may be exceptions, of course, but the burden is on the pleader. While we are willing to give a fair hearing to systemic explanations for human behavior—for instance, to claims that unemployment causes crime or that patriarchal attitudes are responsible for the fact that women do not earn as much as men—we are also likely to conclude that these unifactorial causal claims are much too simplistic, that there are a whole skein of social, cultural, and personal influences that should not be dismissed as factors.[35]

These various considerations lead centrists to an intermediate conception of government which envisions considerably more intervention than that which is defended by advocates of limited government. At the same time, however, centrists believe that government should not function as a central ordering mechanism for curing every real or perceived social ill, as we shall see next.

Chapter 6

Between the Night Watchman
and the Leviathan: The Centrist's
Conception of Government

JUST AS WE CENTRISTS avoid the gravitational pull of the purely religious and the rigorously secular in matters of morals and metaphysics, we avoid another set of dichotomous extremes in the sphere of politics. If our accumulated political experience gained over the course of the nineteenth and twentieth centuries has taught us anything, it has taught us two basic truths. On one hand, the era of the laissez-faire state is over—and rightly so. Government inevitably has a role in leveling the disparities created by capitalism, and in redistributing to the least well off a measure of the vast amount of wealth we have generated as a society. On the other hand, in the course of pursuing the first goal, modern government has grown too large, with no indication that this trend will abate anytime soon. More to the point, big government is frequently grossly wasteful and inefficient. The centrist state treads a middle course between the profligacy of collectivism and the parsimonious austerity of the classical liberal's limited state. Our guiding insight is not that redistribution within reasonable bounds is wrong, but that waste, inefficiency, and a variety of other evils that frequently accompany redistribution are wrong.[1]

The Runaway State

"The state," declared the nineteenth-century French economist Frederic Bastiat, "is that great fiction by which everyone tries to live at the expense of everyone else."[2] If this view might once have been dismissed as the exaggerated bluster of a classical liberal, today it appears to be an uncontroversial truism. In 1900, just over 5 percent of the average American's income went to federal, state, and local taxes combined. In 2007, thirty-three cents of every dollar earned went to the government.[3] In fact, the figure is higher for those in the upper middle class, who shoulder the greatest proportionate tax burden relative to their income.[4] The average American works until April 30 every year to earn that share of his or her income that will go toward taxes, and in some states "tax freedom day" is well into May.[5]

Paralleling this rise in taxation, federal, state, and local governments spend one-third of everything that we produce as a nation. The federal government alone consumes slightly over 20 percent of our gross domestic product. Taxation has also become more concentrated at the federal level. In 1900, about 60 percent of government spending took place at the state and local levels; today, the federal government spends more than twice as much (about 69 percent) as all the states and localities combined.[6] Among other things, more localized spending ensured that state and local representatives would not saddle their constituents with the kind of silly and wasteful spending that was approved in the 2004 budget.[7] All the while, the rate of spending continues to increase at both the state and federal levels. State spending rose by 89 percent in the 1990s, and federal spending increased by 38 percent between 2000 and 2005. Federal spending alone now tops more than $22,000 per household on average, up from $19,000 in 2000.[8]

Nor can the explosion in taxing and spending be laid at the door of liberal Democrats alone. Total government spending increased by more than a third during George W. Bush's first term in office, while discretionary spending was up by more than 50 percent. Nor was most of this related to the post-9/11 effect. Under Bush's watch, Medicaid spending increased by 49 percent, federal spending for housing and commerce by 58 percent, and federal spending for regional and community development by a staggering 324 percent. Bush's total budget was 8 percent higher in 2005 than in 2004, and 9 percent higher still the next year, 2006. Notwithstanding his promise to roll back government, Bush did not veto a single spending measure during his time in office until October 2007. In 2000, the Government Accounting Office estimated that the U.S. government was committed to spending over $20 trillion more that it had any hope of collecting in taxes. By 2005, after President Bush's first term, this figure had more than doubled, to $43 trillion.[9] Over the past half century, the only president to successfully cut government spending was Bill Clinton, a Democrat. George W. Bush and Richard Nixon, both Republicans, each oversaw the largest expansions of the federal government since the New Deal.

Worse, spending measures are routinely passed today in the spirit of a kind of corruption so insidious and so ubiquitous that it is commonly accepted as business as usual. The number of registered lobbyists in Washington, for example, has more than doubled since 2000 alone. Pork-barrel projects have increased sevenfold in less than a decade, from two thousand in 1998 to more than fourteen thousand in 2007.[10] The waste, corruption, and simple inefficiency of government spending account for why, in 2001, the federal government made over $20 billion in overpayments in Medicaid and other government contracts; why, in 2003 alone, it could not even account for a missing $24.5 billion; and why, in 2004, the Department of Agriculture could not account for $5 billion in receipts and expenditures. On a smaller scale, it explains how air force personnel were able to run up credit card debt, paid by the federal government, to the tune of $49,000 for gambling, $69,000 for cruises, and nearly $75,000 for exotic dancers and prostitutes. It may explain as well why federal investigators testing the soundness of federal loan programs were given $55,000 in student loans for nonexistent colleges.[11]

The situation grows more distressing when we consider what motivates some of this spending. For example, federal outlays are sometimes spent on projects foisted on an unwilling public. Remember the bridge to nowhere? Federal money was allocated to build a bridge from the town of Ketchikan, Alaska, population 8,900, to the virtually uninhabited island of Gravina, population 50. Before plans to build the bridge, a ferry service ran between the island and the mainland, but some riders complained about the wait time for the ferry (fifteen to thirty minutes) and the fee (six dollars). In response, Alaska's elected representatives secured a $320 million earmark to build this bridge. As outrageous a waste of money as this is, the story doesn't end here. People in Alaska protested—they wanted to give the money to New Orleans to help the rebuilding effort in the wake of Hurricane Katrina. Alaskans conducted a substantial letter-writing campaign to give back the money. As one outraged citizen wrote in the *Anchorage Daily News*: "Of course Alaska should and, hopefully, will volunteer to reject the money for the bridge to nowhere, and Congress will apply the money for the hurricane relief efforts." Their elected representatives would have none of it. They resisted the return of the funds as "impractical"—because the funds were part of the state-by-state allocation formula that guaranteed every state its fair share. Moreover, congressional leadership from other states resisted the refund idea as well, apparently fearing that Alaska would set a bad precedent by giving back its pork.[12]

Given these trends, the future does not look bright. A recent study by the Congressional Budget Office forecasts the amount of money necessary to continue funding simply Social Security, Medicaid, and Medicare. In 1962, the government spent the equivalent of 2.5 percent of our gross national product to fund these programs. Thus, about two-and-a-half cents of every dollar of wealth produced in the United States went to help the disabled and the elderly through these programs. Today, this has risen to about 8 percent. With projected demographic trends, the government predicts that this will nearly double again to 15 percent by 2035 and, by 2075, will reach 21 percent—surpassing the share of the economy now absorbed by all federal spending combined.[13] Centrists are not opposed in principle to these kinds of social programs, but we simply do not believe they can be sustained at present levels. Our nation lacks the resources to continue spending at this level, let alone the increased spending that would be necessary to fund an expanded social safety net, including some form of national health care system.

Why have things gotten so out of hand? One answer, of course, is that politicians look only to the short term—to their own election or reelection—in promising the public services that they know or ought to know we cannot afford. But there is a deeper dynamic that virtually guarantees the unrestrained and seemingly inexorable growth of government. Several years ago a commentator offered the following scenario as the best model for understanding why government is bound to continue taxing and spending its way into continuous and unlimited growth.[14] The problem has to do with the highly centralized manner in which taxing and spending decisions are made, and the dynamic goes something like this: Imagine that four men go to lunch every day at the same restaurant. At the outset, each pays for his own lunch. One person would like to order a pasta dinner but orders a sandwich instead; another would like a piece of chocolate cake for dessert but forgoes it. In each case, the additional pleasure just isn't worth the added expense.

Now suppose that the group of four decides to split the bill four ways regardless of each individual's expenses. Now that extra piece of cake—say, at a cost of four dollars—will cost the cake eater himself only one dollar, since the cost will be distributed among his lunchmates. He is tempted to order the cake and perhaps occasionally he does order it. But most of the time, two factors check the tendency to superfluous orders—a sense of civility or fairness and self-interest. The cake eater, if he is even moderately socially astute, understands that the arrangement is fair only if everyone, at least over the long haul, comes out more or less even. So he will not want to impose his extra costs on his friends. He also understands that his behavior will have an effect on the other three—if he orders cake regularly, the second lunchmate will order the more extravagant pasta dinner. So fairness and self-interest check the impulse to overspend.

Suppose one day that the restaurant announces it will from now on split the bill among *everyone eating in the restaurant at the same time*. Now the man who wanted to order a pasta dinner will order a steak instead. Why not? Once it is divided among all those in the restaurant, the additional cost to him will be only a few pennies. But, of course, everyone else realizes the same thing and bids up their own bill. On some days, the steak eater may not even want steak; he might prefer the sandwich. But he knows that he will be subsidizing everyone else's bills and so figures he might as well get his fair share. The cake eater, by the same token, is now on to even more extravagant desserts, but again the financial effects on him are marginal. In this way, the limiting effects of the ties of friendship are blunted since people at one table don't know those at the others. And the curb on spending imposed by self-interest has now been inverted: those who do not bid up their own bill as extravagantly as everyone else will understandably feel that they are being taken for a ride. Of course, when the bill comes, each individual pays three, or four, or ten times what he would have paid if he were responsible for only his own bill. The restaurateur—and no one will miss the analogy—has implemented a brilliant plan to inflate his margin of profit.

Isn't this, in a nutshell, exactly the dynamic that drives government spending? Whereas one of the most important consequences of decentralization is fiscal self-responsibility, this restraint goes out the window with the advent of highly centralized forms of taxing and spending.

The Argument from Compassion

Most people recognize that our system of taxing and spending is fundamentally broken and that much of this has to do with the practical dynamic of the federal budgetary process just described. But there is also a deeper ideological dynamic that contributes to our ever-escalating demands for a larger state. What drives this dynamic is not selfishness or the desire to get one's fair share. It is often just the opposite; it is compassion. But it is compassion that wants to make the state responsible for every tragedy caused in part by the failure or the inherent limits of bureaucracy itself.

A kind of self-escalating process propels the expansion of government. It is a process driven by the best of intentions, by some pressing moral concern—for example, the need to provide a social service to those unable to provide for themselves. The state responds with a remedy; it assumes responsibility for an area of human need and then, predictably, fails in some way. Sometimes the failure is due to human error—the negligence or oversight of bureaucrats—while sometimes other systemic problems make it more difficult for some beneficiaries to take full advantage of the service. These systemic difficulties are sometimes referred to as the "problem of access." When one or the other of these things occurs, the automatic response of the compassionate is to call for another expansion of services to remedy the gap. And so the process takes on a life of its own.

What follows are two examples, the first an instance of bureaucratic negligence from a case that went to the Supreme Court several years ago, the second and more recent an example of the problem of access. In each case, the response of the compassionate to the failure of government is—more government.

In the first example, *DeShaney v. Winnebago County Dept. of Social Services*, a father severely beat his four-year-old son, Joshua, on several occasions. One beating was so severe that it left Joshua severely mentally handicapped. There was evidence that a neighbor had notified the local social service agency in Winnebago County of previous beatings, yet the agency never intervened to protect the child from the father. Attorneys representing the child subsequently argued that the agency's failure to intervene represented a violation of the boy's due process rights under the Constitution, effectively making the state responsible, in a constitutional sense, for failing to prevent the private actions of the father.[15]

Only the government can violate an individual's constitutional rights: for reasons that should be clear to everyone, the state cannot be blamed whenever one person, in his or her private capacity, harms another person in his or her private capacity. This would make the state responsible for every crime and invasion of civil rights. It would effectively obliterate the line between private and public conduct. Still, Joshua's lawyers argued that the state (and not simply his father) had violated his rights—by failing to act to protect him. And they had a plausible argument. In this case, the county social service agency was arguably *supposed* to protect him, and it failed to do so.

A majority on the Supreme Court ultimately decided that the agency's failure to act did not violate the boy's constitutional rights. The Court worried that victims of crime would be able to sue the state for a constitutional violation every time the police did not respond quickly enough, for example. But there were strongly dissenting voices, on and off the court. The dissent claimed that the state had "abandoned" the boy and "placed him in a dangerous predicament" by failing to intervene to protect him. Justice William Brennan argued that it was precisely the state's creation of the social service department that made the state responsible for the condition of the boy. He argued that "Wisconsin law invites—indeed, directs—citizens and other governmental entities to depend on other departments of social services . . . to protect children from abuse; . . . children like Joshua are made worse off by the existence of this program when the persons and entities charged with carrying it out fail to do their job."[16]

There is logic to this argument, but we should be clear about where it leads. As the state expands to fill the interstices of civil society, its power and its responsibility each grow proportionately, reinforcing one another. As the state expands to create programs such as those of social service agencies, it becomes more responsible for lapses on the part of its agents and officials. Neighbors do not intervene, for example, because the state is supposed to do it. And as the state's responsibility for a widening array of real and perceived social wrongs grows, so there is greater need to expand the state itself to meet these needs. It is in this sense that every escalation of government invites further escalation in what becomes a potentially never-ending cycle.

Consider, next, the story of Deamonte Driver, a twelve-year-old Maryland boy who died in February 2007 because he wasn't taken to the dentist in time. An article in the *Washington Post* reported that Deamonte died after bacteria from an abscessed tooth spread to his brain. Near death, after weeks of complaining about the tooth, he was finally brought to a hospital. The article reports that the boy's "mother had been focused on getting a dentist for his brother, who had six rotted teeth." Two operations and six weeks of hospital care (which sources valued at $250,000) were not enough to save Deamonte.[17]

Since his death, Deamonte has become a poster boy for universal dental care. Yet Deamonte's mother was eligible for Medicaid, which would have covered dental visits. Her problem, however, was one of access. She suspects that the paperwork confirming her eligibility for Medicaid was sent to a homeless shelter where the family had been staying a while earlier. The *Post* article notes that fewer than a third of all children eligible for dental care under the existing Medicaid program in Maryland, the District of Columbia, and Virginia actually saw a dentist in 2005. While Deamonte's mother had not taken either boy to a dentist in several years after a previous dentist discontinued treatment of the brother, the article notes that several obstacles make access more difficult. Only one in six Maryland dentists accepts Medicaid; moreover, many recipients have problems with transportation, homelessness, and erratic telephone and mail delivery. The *Post* article quotes Laurie Norris, a lawyer for the Public Justice Center, based in Maryland, which tried to help Deamonte's family: "I certainly hope the state agencies responsible for making sure these children have dental care take note so that Deamonte didn't die in vain."

The federal government requires all states to provide Medicaid for medical and dental care for poor children but, for a host of reasons, some eligible recipients such as Deamonte's mother do not or cannot take full advantage of the program. If state agencies are responsible for making sure these children have dental care, how far does the state's responsibility extend? Should the state open free dental clinics in rural areas to ensure that residents of underserved communities do not have to travel great distances for dental care? Should the state require all dentists, as a condition of state licensure, to reserve a certain percentage of their schedule for Medicaid recipients? Should the state have social services agencies call families to remind them that it is time for a child's six-month dental visit? How far does the responsibility of the state extend to make sure that children receive the benefits to which they are statutorily entitled?

One boy's tragic and unnecessary death is now used to suggest that the answer to these problems is a system of universal health care. There is, again, a logic to the argument, but only if you accept that the state is ultimately responsible for children such as Deamonte—not simply to provide them the opportunity to receive care under an imperfect Medicaid system, but to guarantee that they will take advantage of these still more comprehensive programs. The argument from compassion flows from an incontestable premise to an irresistible conclusion: someone needs help; therefore, government has a responsibility to provide it. Yet at a point in history when it appears that we will not be able to meet our obligations with Social Security, Medicaid, Medicare, and other outlays, how do we expect to afford to fill all the gaps? And if filling the gaps is a priority, should some other programs be jettisoned to free up the funds to pay for these priorities, or should government simply keep expanding?

For a long time the argument from compassion was the exclusive reserve of the liberal, while conservatives were asking the more practical, pressing question—how can we afford this?

Today, under the banner of compassionate conservatism, even many Republicans apparently find it difficult to resist the appeal of the argument from compassion. It was not Nancy Pelosi but George Bush who declared in 2003 that "we have a responsibility that, when someone hurts, government has got to be there."[18]

But where does it end?

A Top-Down View of the State

Underlying the argument from compassion is a certain conception of the state that has crept into the U.S. political consciousness since the 1930s, though it is also indirectly connected to secular ideas of social order that have been on the ascendant since the late eighteenth century. The state, according to this view, not only should provide the basic bulwark of social order, but also should function more generally as a kind of corrective mechanism for much of what is not right with society. Think of the state not merely as a provider of certain basic functions—fighting crime, providing for the common defense, providing basic social services such as education, et cetera—but as a kind of central ordering mechanism for civil relations, an executive control for an increasing share of everything that happens within the context of civil society. Those who hold some version of the top-down idea of government hold government directly or indirectly responsible, because of either what it has done or what it has failed to do, for a growing proportion of individual hardships, injustices, and dislocation. It is the government's job, according to this way of looking at things, to remedy the consequences of unregulated social and economic relations when they fall short of some ideal or expectation. Progressive government is seen as a kind of superintendent over society, perfecting social relations by anticipating, preventing, or remedying real or claimed injustices. The top-down idea of government requires that government act to order—restructure, compensate, redistribute, and assuage with an unfaltering (if not invisible) hand. It is less an outgrowth of our most pressing social needs than it is a guarantor of their perfect satisfaction.

Something like this conception of government has become almost the default position for contemporary politics. Everyone knows that government cannot remedy every hardship, but increasingly we talk as if it should. No conservative or moderate has successfully articulated an argument that satisfactorily answers the argument from compassion. No one wants to be the one to say that government cannot be there for everyone at all times, that some hurts and harms and even injustices must remain unremedied—indeed, that they may not be remediable at all—or that some social problems must be left to individuals or groups in their nonpolitical capacities. The response strikes many as callous, even misanthropic.

Advocates of the top-down view of government have developed a sophisticated array of arguments to bolster their position. One version, popular among progressives throughout the twentieth century, argues that no hard-and-fast distinction can be drawn between what is natural and what is socially constructed. We cannot draw a neat line, for example, between what one does or achieves for oneself and what one has achieved only because of the institutions of the state. Liam Murphy and Thomas Nagel argue in *The Myth of Ownership*, for example: "We are all born into an elaborately structured legal system governing the acquisition, exchange and transmission of property rights, and ownership comes to seem the most natural thing in the world. But the modern economy in which we earn our salaries, own our homes, bank accounts, retirement savings and personal possessions . . . would be impossible without the framework supported by government." They argue that it is illegitimate to criticize tax policy from the standpoint of a baseline representing one's pretax income, for example, since "all such figures are the product of a system of which taxes are an inextricable part."[19]

This is true in a certain sense, of course, but it is also misleading. Individuals certainly possess what they have in part because of the protection of the laws of the state, and because of the way in which the state helps to organize economic relations in a beneficial way. Yet the top-down view of social ordering tends to elide the significance of the individual. Most individuals have what they have, after all, in part because they have invested in themselves and worked for what they have. The state is able to tax only what the individual has earned, and it is no more fair to say that we have no basis on which to claim being overtaxed than it is for us to disregard the support we receive from government programs. That we cannot draw a hard-and-fast line between what we do for ourselves, in some natural sense, and what the state helps us do does not mean that the state does it all. Nor does it mean that there isn't a point where overregulation stifles the creative, wealth-producing impulses of the individual. A share of our taxes may go to creating conditions that augment our pretax wealth, but it does not follow that most taxes fall into this category.

Another version of the top-down conception of government views all individual wealth as public wealth. This is, in fact, an argument that was made by anarchists such as Kropotkin in the nineteenth century. It implies that we are born indebted to society, so we have nothing we can say is truly our own. In the 1920s and 1930s, liberal progressives such as Robert Hale reworked this line of argument, claiming that all social and economic power held by the individual is really just a delegation of authority from the state. This is how Hale put it in 1923:

> In protecting property, the government is doing something quite apart from merely keeping the peace. It is exerting coercion wherever necessary to protect each owner, not only from violence but also from peaceful infringement of his sole right to enjoy the thing owned. In doing so, it gives the owner of property economic dominion over the worker. Unless . . . the non-owner can produce his own food, the law compels him to starve if he has no wages, and compels him to go without wages unless he obeys the behest of some employer.[20]

Yet it is no more true that government is responsible for all that happens in the social arena—that it compels the worker to starve, for example—than it is true that capitalists own what they own solely because of their own sheer grit and determination. The top-down view of progressives is as reductionistic as is the bottom-up view of conservatives, who sometimes seem to suggest that each individual is completely self-made. As Richard Posner parodies the progressive's top-down view of social reality: "When I eat a potato chip, I am really eating the government's potato chip with its permission, since it is the government that created, recognizes and protects my right in the chip."[21]

Individual wealth and success are always the result of a complex skein of factors that include individual talent and discipline, social capital (including one's education), help from family and others, and political and legal factors. Some progressives are as one-sided in believing that individual wealth and success is largely or wholly traceable to state action as some conservatives are to suggest that all wealth is generated without the help of government.

Why Some Economic Redistribution Is Morally Justified

I have had a good deal to say about what's wrong with the progressive conception of government—that it is too big, too wasteful, and much too centralized. This may make it appear that centrists only grudgingly accept economic redistribution as a pragmatic compromise or, worse, as a way to stave off a genuine social revolution, as some rationalized the New Deal reforms. But centrists support a measure of economic redistribution on moral principle. We do not have an easy formula for determining how much redistribution is morally appropriate or economically productive. (As I suggest later, this requires a national discussion that takes into account our current financial capacity and obligations.) But we do believe that in a society as wealthy and as gifted as ours, those who are economically better off, and especially those who live amidst opulence and luxury, should help offset at least some of the financial hardships of others, particularly the poor and the disadvantaged.

Those who oppose economic redistribution do so on two general grounds, one based on natural rights, the other on various utilitarian considerations. On the rights side, limited-state conservatives claim that taxation is confiscatory, coercive, and, to put it bluntly, legalized theft. On the utilitarian side, they will claim that redistribution is counterproductive—that it undercuts incentives, lowers production and growth, and thwarts efficient transactions, among other objections.

The argument from rights is often rooted in a pastoral, Lockean picture of society. Locke's approach to property rights and economic relations made sense in a world where each person begins from roughly equal wealth, with roughly equal prospects, and where each person or family depends more or less on their own resources and initiative to survive and, with any luck, to prosper. Within this milieu, at least in a fair world, the intelligent and the hard working will flourish while the feckless and the indolent will flounder. To force those who have worked for their increase to forfeit some of what they have to others who have not, particularly when most people are living at the margins of survival, struck Locke and other early liberals as grossly unfair. And so it was.

But this is no longer an accurate picture of social reality. First, most of us do not live anywhere near the margins of survival today. The average American's adjusted income is fifty times higher today than it was three centuries ago.[22] The margin between subsistence and the average level of wealth is also much greater today than at any time in the past. Even as late as 1900, 80 percent of the income of the average household in the United States and other Western nations was spent on food, clothing, and shelter. Today these goods account for less than one-third of consumption spending.[23] This means that a great deal more of our wealth goes to conveniences and luxuries—a second home, expensive vacations, fine dining, and so on. We simply live in a very different world than that of Locke and his eighteenth- and nineteenth-century classical liberal descendants.

The libertarian will respond that a right is a right, that if people have earned their income fairly and legally, they have a right to spend it any way they wish, on any luxury they wish. The libertarian will claim that government should not be in the business of telling millionaires that they must give up some of what they have in order to help the poor. But, of course, natural rights claims can be used to require redistribution, just as they are deployed against it. This is part of the problem with natural rights theory; it is far from self-evident that the starving man has no natural right to a small portion of the bounty of the superfluous wealth of the rich man.

The Lockean ideal of property rights no longer resonates with most people's view for a second reason. When one mixes one's own labor with the bounty of nature, chopping down a tree to build a cabin, for example, it is easy to see why early classical liberals should insist that one has a property right in the house. Locke's self-sustaining bucolic built the house, lives in it, uses it. Without it, he would not survive. The bonus check corporate CEOs receive hardly has the same moral and physical significance for them. It is an asset, in many cases little more than a number that reflects a changing balance in a checking account. My point is that there is a *lived reality* to our relationship with our property. Centrists agree with libertarians that property rights ought to be protected as human rights in the same manner that other rights are protected, but we believe the right protects not the property, but the human connection with the property.[24] The reason we protect property rights, in part, is that they reflect the individual's sweat investment, the amount of life one has literally had to sacrifice to convert one's labor into property. As the nexus between an asset and one's physical, psychic, and moral investment in the asset grows more attenuated, the moral significance of the property interest diminishes.

A cab driver once told me that he was showing a member of the Kennedy family around Chicago and pointed to a large skyscraper owned by the passenger's immediate family. The passenger had no idea that he or his family owned the building. There was no personal nexus between the owner and the asset in this case. In sum, we protect property rights in part as an expression of the person. Societies that abolish property rights foreclose an important avenue of self-expression and of projecting oneself into the world of physical commodities. But for this same reason, there is a less compelling reason for protecting property rights that do not reflect some personal connection between the individual and the property. This explains why most people intuitively distinguish between taxing personal income and taxing wealth earned in other ways—for example, through inheritance. And it also explains why most people distinguish between taxing the surplus wealth of the corporate mogul and the income of the secretary who earns $25,000 a year.

I should be clear at this point that I am not advocating the radical redistribution of all property that falls beyond the personal nexus as I have described it. My argument is more limited. By insisting that there is no qualitative difference between the $25,000 income of a secretary and the $25 million Christmas bonus of the corporate CEO, right-wing economists go too far in the direction of detaching economic rights from the *moral worth* of a person's labor. Of course, libertarians believe that this notion of the moral worth of labor is a meaningless concept, that all value is market value and nothing else. Yet if conservatives really wanted to protect the values of personal effort and initiative, both for their intrinsic moral worth and for their utilitarian benefits, they would support levels of economic redistribution that would encourage and reward the efforts of those who work without adequate remuneration.

In sum, centrists do not reject moderate economic redistribution. What we oppose is the more radical tendency of some progressives who have concluded that all personal attributes and talents should be treated as collective assets, much as Rawls and Dworkin have argued. We oppose as well the idea that it is the role of government to seek economic equality as an end in itself. Centrists believe that differences in talent and initiative can legitimately be reflected in differences of wealth, though we also believe that current disparities in wealth grossly exaggerate these differences.

The Centrist's Approach to Government

Together the Left and Right conspire, only half-unconsciously, to produce the problem of the runaway state. The Left wants to use democracy to change the world. It wants more of the state, and more of what the managerial state can do to offset the displacements and injustices brought about by social conditions. But its secularism increasingly prevents it from thinking in any but material terms about what politics can do. Compassion means money; the chief function of the compassionate, managerial state is to facilitate the transfer of wealth from one group to another. The libertarian Right goes too far in limiting government while the plutocratic Right, with its "clash of interests" version of democracy, assumes that if the state can't be limited, then at least it can be bought. Everyone should be entitled, according to this view, to do their level best to grab their share of the pie. What is lost in taxes can be recouped in other ways—through corporate welfare and other various government subsidies, through tax breaks, and by Halliburtonizing government contracts to provide grossly inflated profits at the taxpayer's expense. In this way, the Left and the Right contribute to the feeding frenzy that fuels the ever-escalating expansion of the state.

Those of us who are of the centrist persuasion advocate a conception of government that falls between the libertarian's call for a scaled-back, night-watchman, limited-state approach to government, and the liberal's top-down managerial conception of the state. Our government has a role in securing the blessings of liberty and providing for the general welfare—ideas that go well beyond providing for the common defense and protecting personal and property rights. But the state should not be understood as subsuming society and providing an equalizing force for every real or imagined social injustice.

The following five points will serve to convey centrists' general orientation to the role, scope, and function of government in the United States today. They appear in very general form here; in the next several chapters I develop some of the particular implications of each.

(1) *A non-aspirational conception of politics.* Our first tenet will shock some, particularly on the Left, but here it is: politics is not and should not be the primary vehicle of social transformation, let alone perfection. This, of course, is what true conservatives once believed, though few today seem to continue to believe it. Centrists are devoted to the democratic ideal, but we believe that politics should occupy a relatively limited place in human affairs. In contrast to conservative moralists, we do not believe that a primary function of politics is the moral perfection of humanity. At best, laws should only be used to express and reinforce basic community values. And in contrast to the communitarian Left, we certainly would not entrust to the political process any desire for human self-transformation.[25] This asks far too much of politics. Centrists are happy to leave the quest for self-transformation to the individual, perhaps in consultation with a priest or therapist.

What the political process can achieve is two things—it can help establish and preserve decent and humane social and economic conditions necessary for the good life, and it can be used to express and reinforce a community's deepest cultural values. Everything else should be left to what was once not too euphemistically called "civil society." The first of these means that government has an important role to play in helping to set in place the material conditions which give people fair opportunities to succeed in life. The second idea refers to democracy's role in achieving a kind of moral balance between our political and our social institutions. In sum, law can help to express and reinforce our social ideals, as we will see below.

(2) *The role of government in structuring opportunities.* Centrists have a conception of freedom that is congenial to a moderate role for government in mediating

social and economic relationships. Because we reject the classical liberal's austere negative idea of freedom, we believe that government must do more than get out of the way. Government has a part to play in harnessing the social and economic forces that drive individual fortunes. But because we reject the progressive liberal's tendency to equate freedom with positive entitlements, we believe that government's basic role should never be, simply and essentially, redistributive. Rather, redistribution must be justified in terms of its capacity to help structure social and economic conditions to maximize individual opportunities, to promote human flourishing from the inside out.

A role for government in structuring opportunities means that individuals still must do the work for themselves. Government can help remove some of the grosser social obstacles that limit individual achievement. This is why we support antidiscrimination laws that protect minorities, women, and the disabled. Beyond this, government has an important role to play in providing a basic social safety net, the generosity of which should be conditioned on a level-headed assessment of the nation's ability to provide these services. Centrists accept such New Deal reforms as Social Security, though we believe that Social Security as it currently exists must be restructured to address the mounting problem of funding. We also support state and federal loan and grant programs to help finance education and home ownership and as a reward for service provided to our nation, as with the G.I. Bill.

Centrists further believe that every person who is able has a right to work. We believe that government should guarantee this right to everyone who can work by creating public work projects for the unemployed. We would also like to see more done to help those who want to work but are prevented from doing so by other obstacles—by disabilities or by other personal constraints. We support subsidized child care for working mothers and training programs for the disabled, among others. We believe that every individual can make a contribution to society, to our common wealth, and we believe that we can collectively help foster the conditions for each to do so in his or her own way.

In recognizing that government has a role to play in structuring opportunities, centrists heed the kinds of economic incentive-driven arguments made by conservatives, but for reasons different from those of many conservatives. Our ultimate ends are not economic; they are *human*. We believe that incentives play an important role in human motivation and, for this reason, reject social schemes that undercut incentives to work—for example, welfare payments to those who are able to work which approach or exceed what could be earned under a decent, living minimum wage. We are most concerned about the deleterious effects on individual character brought about by an under-incentivized economic system. Work makes people feel productive; it gives them the most essential social ingredient of self-esteem—the sense of dignity that results from knowing that one has contributed something to society. Where people feel no incentive to work, they are likely to feel valueless as persons. And when large numbers feel valueless and apathetic, they will turn to what we have learned are the normal range of antisocial and self-destructive behaviors—crime, drug and alcohol abuse, domestic violence, irresponsible parenting, and a host of similar social ills. Centrists will therefore insist on a need-driven conception for welfare benefits and would require that others who receive government benefits work for these in some capacity. This is the other side of the idea that everyone has a right to work. In this way centrists agree with liberals that government can help prevent these social ills, even as we agree with conservatives that automatic entitlement programs are not the way to go. There is no contradiction here: a good society makes for good, happy, productive, and self-fulfilled individuals.

(3) *A wealth-relative approach to government.* Government's ability to achieve these goals, and particularly to provide a social safety net, depends upon our collective wealth. It is an obvious principle, though one that seems to be increasingly disregarded by politicians, that we should self-consciously embrace a wealth-relative conception of government. On one hand, we can provide much more today than could be provided in the nineteenth century because ours is a much wealthier society. For this reason, it is anachronistic for conservatives to speak of taxes in the same terms as those that existed at the time of the American Revolution. As we have already seen, there is a much greater margin between subsistence and the average standard of living in the United States today. We can afford and should be prepared to pay for more public services than those which could be provided in the past. A wealthy society can and should be willing and able to care for the neediest and to care for them to a greater extent than can a poor society.

On the other hand, what is equally obvious is that no government program should be proposed or passed until we have the resources—now and into the future—to pay for it. If this requires curtailing some present programs to fund other, higher priority programs, then these present programs should first be curtailed. Like many others, centrists are most likely to insist that the first things to go should be the various irresponsible pork-barrel projects that currently glut every congressional measure. We particularly oppose large government outlays to oil companies that are already profiting spectacularly at the expense of the average consumer and to huge corporate conglomerates such as Archer Daniels Midland and Con-Agra that receive billions of dollars in corporate welfare, usually in return for generous campaign support for their champions in Congress. Many of us will agree with libertarians, some conservatives, and more than a few liberals who believe that the hundreds of billions we spend annually by stationing military forces around the globe in places like Korea, Europe, and, of course, the Middle East would be better spent updating our infrastructure, shoring up Social Security, and providing other proposed social welfare benefits such as health care.

If we pursue the same course we have for decades now, we can be sure that levels of taxation are going to continue to rise, as they have throughout the twentieth century, while our relative wealth has begun to decline. We are taxing more overall today, even though the average American's adjusted wages are lower than they were in the 1970s. These trends are bound to continue to the point where our children can expect to relinquish to the government well over half of everything they earn. And, of course, as conservatives are fond of pointing out, such trends will affect us in other ways as well—by undermining the system of incentives that drives the engine of wealth production.

These considerations militate in favor of holding a national conversation about what level of taxation we are collectively willing to tolerate. Because we understand that levels of taxation are only going to continue to escalate, we should consider capping at current levels the total amount paid by taxpayers. This could be adjusted to provide for progressively higher rates for the wealthiest in society. When the wealthiest in society have to shoulder a lower proportionate rate of taxation than those in the middle class, as is usually the case today, there is something deeply askew with our tax policy.[26] At the same time, there should be a general cap on taxation relative to every income level, which would progressively increase with gross income. This would force government to adhere to a "no new program without funding" requirement. More importantly, however, it would limit the predictable—in fact, what seems up to now to be the inexorable—drift toward greater collectivization and centralization.

(4) *Toward a more decentralized government.* Centrists favor a more decentralized model of government, and of society generally. In particular, we want to see a measured return to the values of constitutional federalism. With federalism, as Justice Anthony Kennedy put it more than a decade ago, "the Framers split the atom of sovereignty," dividing the expression of popular power along two dimensions—breaking up power vertically between the states and the federal government, and horizontally among the states themselves.[27] Yet it has become increasingly fashionable recently for some, particularly on the Left, to question the framers' wisdom in designing a federal plan of government.[28] The left liberals' highly nationalized and centralized approach to government represents the constitutional analogue of their top-down, managerial ideal of the state.

Centrists favor a moderate decentralization of political power for several reasons. First, centralized decision making is frequently wasteful and inefficient. Decentralization ensures a closer nexus between taxing and spending, so that the beneficiaries of pork-barrel spending programs shoulder the burden for these programs in a way that puts a brake on runaway spending. Second, more decentralized government ensures a flexibility conducive to efficiency, innovation, and experimentation. Decentralization facilitates what Louis Brandeis called "the laboratory of the states." When Wisconsin can try one welfare policy and California another, we all benefit by being able to compare the long-term consequences of each. Similarly, geographical and economic conditions in Montana are different from those in Florida or Rhode Island. Local authorities should be free to adapt their laws to suit these widely varying conditions.

A return to true federalism promotes more than efficiency and innovation, however; it would mean that government is closer to the people. The opportunities to participate and to have some influence upon state politics are still today considerably greater than at the national level. Federalism promotes diversity between the states and fosters the expression of local mores and ways of life. The citizens of California can decide to create one set of laws, one kind of social ecosystem, while Georgia voters can create another (presumably more conservative). Federalism protects against the one-size-fits-all approach of national legislation and, in doing so, gives individuals the opportunity to live in a place that reflects their own values—or to vote with their feet and move to a place that better reflects them. Finally, centrists are concerned about concentrating increasingly large amounts of power in the hands of a small number of politicians and bureaucrats in Washington, D.C. We believe that decentralization is still the single best safeguard against what used to be called the problem of tyranny.

These four values—curbing wasteful spending, promoting local innovation and efficiency, keeping government closer to the people, and preventing the concentration of political power—militate in favor of a greater commitment to the values of federalism. In a more general way, centrists embrace a conception of society that radiates up from the grassroots level to government, as much as it radiates down from government to the grass roots. We are not radical decentralizers. We believe in the necessity of a strong national government, but it should be a more *limited* government. We believe that government works far better when power, responsibility, and authority travel in both directions, from the people to their government, as much as from government to its people.[29]

(5) *The moral-expressive function of law.* The most important thing a community can transmit are its values. Law in a democratic society should serve to express and support the values of the community, within the bounds imposed by a robust recognition of individual rights. While laws without a supporting culture cannot make us virtuous, culture without the support of law has little hope of restraining the worst kinds of vices. Government should not function primarily, as it does today, to structure and redistribute material wealth but rather should play a supporting role in the expression and protection of the deepest values of the community. These commitments represent the heart of the centrist's approach to politics and government.

Chapter 7
Centrist Constitutionalism:
Democracy and the Role of the Judge

Practicing Politics at the Bar

When the Supreme Court decided *Gonzales v. Carhart* in April 2007, liberals were more than a little bitter. *Gonzales* upheld a federal law banning "partial-birth abortion" in cases where the mother's life was not endangered.[1] It represented the first case since *Roe v. Wade* in which the Court upheld a prohibition on a specific abortion procedure. In reaching its decision, the Court had to severely limit—some might say, outright overrule—another decision, barely seven years old, striking down a similar Nebraska law.[2] How could the Supreme Court change course so quickly? And what had become of the doctrine of stare decisis, which requires courts to adhere to established precedents?

Gonzales had been decided only months after two new conservative justices, Chief Justice John Roberts and Justice Samuel Alito, had joined the Court. After the decision, Justice Stephen Breyer, who had dissented, took the unusual step of declaring openly from the bench: "It is not often in the law that so few have quickly changed so much." Ralph G. Neas, president of the liberal advocacy group People for the American Way, was more vitriolic, complaining that "this Court has shown the same respect for precedent that a wrecking ball shows for a plate glass window."[3] For their part, conservatives were almost jubilant. Richard John Neuhaus wrote in *First Things*, the Catholic journal of politics and culture, that the decision should be "warmly welcomed" by pro-life conservatives and cautiously opined that, while "there are no guarantees, *Gonzales* gives reason to think that . . . the abortion regime may be on its way, a painfully slow way, to extinction."[4]

The positions of liberals and conservatives were exactly reversed only four years earlier. In the summer of 2003, the Court handed down *Lawrence v. Texas*, which struck down state sodomy laws on constitutional grounds. To reach this result, the Court had to overrule *Bowers v. Hardwick*, a precedent set just seventeen years earlier. The *Bowers* Court had indignantly denounced the claim that there was a constitutional right to homosexual sodomy. In his concurring opinion, Chief Justice Warren Burger invoked the Judeo-Christian proscription of homosexuality and declared that finding a constitutional right to sodomy would be to "cast aside millennia of moral teaching." The opinion was so stinging in rhetoric and tone that even Charles Fried, then President Reagan's solicitor general, called it "stunningly harsh." Yet in 2003, just seventeen years later, the Court overruled *Bowers* and consensual acts between gays were now constitutionally protected.

Conservatives responded to *Lawrence* with predictable fury. Columnist Dewy

Kidd called *Lawrence* "one of the most convoluted, toxic decisions of the past century," a decision "so putrid, it should have caused a massive uproar from every Christian, minister, pastor and priest in this country and demand for removal of half the U.S. Supreme Court."[5] Equally predictably, liberals could barely contain their glee. Joanna Grossman, a law professor at Hofstra, announced that *Lawrence* had "overruled a notoriously hateful precedent" and looked forward to the possibility that *Lawrence* opened the door to invalidating still other laws, including those prohibiting fornication, gay marriage, and possibly adultery and bigamy.[6]

The lesson of these two cases is not simply that most conservatives and liberals pay only lip service to the principles of precedent, demanding that any concerns about stare decisis be shelved when expediency requires. The deeper problem is that both have increasingly folded their constitutional principles into their respective political visions. Conservatives today frequently defend a conservative philosophy of judicial restraint when this gets them to the kinds of political outcome they prefer. Conservative opposition to the constitutional right of privacy is consistent with the conservative political agenda, which rejects abortion, gay rights, and other activities now protected under the privacy right. Happily—for them—their political and their constitutional positions line up with one another. But the same is true for liberals. Liberals today usually favor a more activist role for the judge, one that permits judges to recognize expanded rights under the privacy right and more egalitarian outcomes using the constitutional principle of equal protection. As with conservatives, liberals have a constitutional philosophy that often seems driven considerably more by their politics than by any principled commitment to a theory of constitutional interpretation.

The politicization of the Supreme Court is so endemic today that the justices now frequently vote in blocs along strictly ideological lines. During the 2006–2007 Supreme Court term, twenty-four of the Court's sixty-eight signed decisions were decided by 5–4 votes. In nineteen of these twenty-four decisions, the liberals (Justices Breyer, Ruth Bader Ginsburg, John Stevens, and David Souter) voted together against the conservatives (Antonin Scalia, Clarence Thomas, John Roberts, and Samuel Alito). The man in the middle, Justice Anthony Kennedy, was in the majority of all twenty-four of these close decisions, dissenting only twice during the entire term.[7] While this may be good news for centrists, as Justice Kennedy reliably expresses centrist constitutional commitments, it exemplifies the extent to which politics drives jurisprudence on the nation's highest court.

Liberals and conservatives have both been guilty of politicizing constitutional law when they have had the power to do so. Conservatives were the judicial activists a century ago, during the Lochner era, when the Court's older classical liberals clashed with progressives and moderates who dominated state and federal legislatures. During this period, which ran from *Lochner* in 1905 until 1937, the Court's conservatives deployed an idiosyncratic interpretation of the due process clause to strike down minimum wage, maximum hour, and other progressive laws passed by state and federal legislatures.[8] The Court read a rigorous right of "freedom of contract" into the clause, which meant that laws that restricted the right to contract in any way were subject to constitutional attack. The *Lochner* era ended with the switch in time that saved nine, when FDR tried to pack the Supreme Court with judges who would uphold his progressive programs. With Justice Owen Roberts's switch, the era of conservative judicial activism was over. Yet by the 1960s, it was the liberals who had moved toward a more activist stance.

Since the 1920s and 1930s, liberals in particular have come under the influence of legal realism, a theory that holds that there are no real legal rules that bind judges.[9] As Jerome Frank, a leading legal realist of the 1930s famously declared, "Law is what a judge had for breakfast"—meaning that law is whatever a judge says it is, and what he or she says may be as much the product of indigestion as anything else. Realists hold that judges do not interpret law, they *make* it. They make no apologies for this view. Judges cannot help but make law, realists insist, because belief in a system of objective legal rules and principles is an illusion. As Frank, who underwent Freudian psychoanalysis, put it, the myths of legal objectivity and certainty are a product of "the childish desire to have a fixed father-controlled universe."[10]

Legal realism is grist for the judicial activist's mill. If there is no law, then nothing prevents anyone from bending the Constitution to whatever particular use one may wish to make of it—as long as it is for some left-of-center cause. When I was a law student at Georgetown, I took constitutional law with the eminent Supreme Court scholar Mark Tushnet. Tushnet was a devotee of the then-popular critical legal studies movement, a modern-day blend of legal realism and the critical neo-Marxism influenced by the Frankfurt School. One day in class, he criticized a "conservative" ruling by the Supreme Court, *San Antonio Independent School District v. Rodriguez.*[11] The case upheld a statewide financing plan for public schools that ensured that more money per student was returned to high-tax (and presumably wealthier) areas, while fewer dollars went to students in areas with a lower tax base. The challengers had argued that this funding scheme violated the rights of poorer students under the equal protection clause of the Constitution. The Supreme Court rejected this argument, holding that the state could tie the allocation of resources for public schools to the tax base of each area. After discussing the opinion, a student asked Tushnet how he would have decided the case had he been a justice on the Supreme Court. Tushnet's immediate off-the-cuff answer: "I would decide this case as I would decide every case—I would pick the outcome that was most consistent with Marxism."

As law students, this was a shocking thing to hear, since we assumed that our grade on the final exam had something to do with our understanding of the *law*, not with our commitment to the values of the *Communist Manifesto*. Those who, like Tushnet, are skeptical of the objectivity of law believe that judges should use legal rules the way a drunk uses a lamppost—for support rather than illumination (i.e., to support the position they've already arrived at, rather than to illuminate the appropriate reasoning). When large numbers of members of the legal profession, particularly its elites, start to feel this way, it's bad news for a more measured approach to the Constitution.

The second reason many liberal judges today are more activist is still more depressing. There has been a steady erosion, since at least the 1950s, of our faith in democracy, particularly local democracy. As a constitutional law teacher, nothing is more distressing to me than to witness the extent to which law students seem to embrace the idea, in a knee-jerk way, that whenever courts intervene to limit local democracy, it is always a win for the forces of freedom—as if part of our freedom were not the right to self-government. Fifty years ago, at the end of his long and distinguished career, Judge Learned Hand saw what was happening and warned that the rise of the imperial judiciary was equivalent to being "governed by a bevy of Platonic guardians."[12] Today, many liberals (including those in the legal profession) seem to prefer exactly that—to be governed by judges, not majorities. They have lost faith in democracy entirely. When the average law student today hears about local democracy, he thinks not about Jefferson, who referred to Virginia as his "country," let alone about the ancient Athenian polis, where democracy first took root in Western civilization. Rather, with every conflict between liberal courts and local majorities since *Brown v. Board of Education*, it is assumed that local majorities are inevitably parochial, insular, racist, homophobic, and generally backward. The courts are the liberators. They exist to liberate us from . . . well, from democracy.

What all this means is that there is more than a little fairness in the conservative's charge that modern courts are increasingly elitist and that many federal judges hold political views well to the left of the U.S. mainstream. If liberalism, as the contemporary Left understands it, cannot achieve its ends through the democratic process, then so much the worse for democracy. As Hodding Carter, President Carter's one-time press secretary, commented after the defeat of conservative Supreme Court nominee Robert Bork in 1987, Bork's treatment "forces liberals like me to confront a reality we don't want to confront, which is that we are depending in large part on the least democratic institution, small 'd,' in government to defend what it is we no longer are able to win out there in the electorate."[13]

Centrists often favor the outcomes of the liberal era of activist courts, but we accept them with a troubled conscience. We believe that public school segregation was morally wrong and politically a bad idea. We believe that the state has no conceivable interest in telling people whether they can use contraception, or what gender their sexual partners ought to be. But we are troubled because we recognize that these court-imposed outcomes have been purchased at the expense of a gradual erosion of the democratic process and a corresponding politicization of the judiciary. Centrists resist the marked proclivity on the part of liberals and conservatives today to collapse their *political* preferences into *constitutional* principles. A commitment to the Constitution and to democracy requires that we happily embrace a distance between what we would like to see done by Congress or our state legislatures and what we believe is mandated by the Constitution. It means that sometimes we must wait for democracy to catch up with our own (sometimes more liberal) political views.

The Countermajoritarian Difficulty

Our Constitution embodies a fundamental tension between two opposed principles. The first principle holds that, in a democracy, a majority gets to make the laws that govern society. The second and opposed principle is that certain matters—most importantly, specific individual rights—lie beyond the reach of the democratic process. The first principle manifests our collective liberty to govern ourselves, to set the basic conditions for our shared social existence, while the second preserves the basic rights and liberties of individuals. Celebrated constitutional law scholar Alexander Bickel called this (one hopes productive) tension between these two principles the "countermajoritarian difficulty."[14] The protection of the individual requires that we limit the tyranny of the majority, but the protection of the democratic process requires that we limit the proclivities of judges to intervene in that sphere where the majority has a legitimate right to make rules and to set the tone for society.

While the line between these two realms may seem relatively clear, it is not. This is because protecting rights requires judges to interpret frequently vague terms such as "equal protection," "due process," and "cruel and unusual punishment." The more expansively judges define these terms, the greater the role of the judiciary in making social policy. Conversely, the narrower they are construed, the more that is left within the field of free play of democratic politics. Herein lies the deeper meaning of Bickel's notion, for the countermajoritarian difficulty is particularly the judge's dilemma: in policing the boundaries between majoritarian interests and individual rights, judges' rulings do not have the effect of saying simply that one activity falls within the sphere of democracy while another activity (abortion or the right to freedom of speech) must be protected as a right. To some extent, judges' rulings alter the boundaries between these two spheres. Like the uncertainty principle in quantum physics, the very act of examining the distinction between the two spheres has the effect of altering the line between them. This is what Chief Justice John Marshall meant in *Marbury v. Madison* in 1803 when he declared that it is the judge's function to "say what the law is." In saying what the law is, judges may expand or contract the sphere of their own judicial authority. There is thus a self-referential quality to judicial decision making.

Every time a judge finds a new right, the liberal in us may cheer, but the democrat—small *d*—in each of us should be wary. Why should we be concerned? Why not recognize a presumption in favor of individual liberties, even if this requires giving judges more power? Don't we as individuals win when judges limit the power of the majority to set the standards for everyone else? Libertarians and left liberals both sometimes make this argument: to the extent that judge-made law means limited government, all the more should we favor judge-made law. Yet this is an incredibly short-sighted view. For one thing, limiting democracy does not always mean expanding individual rights. Libertarians were not quite as enamored of the judiciary when judges decided, in the wake of *Brown*, that equality requires not simply desegregation, but the forced busing of public school students from one locality to another. Nor did they like it when the Court came dangerously close to creating a constitutional right to welfare benefits.[15] One person's right is often another person's limitation. So even when judges expand the individual rights of some, they are contracting the rights of others—for example, the children who are forced to travel to schools in distant locations, or the citizens who are forced to pick up the tab for court-expanded welfare benefits.

There is an even deeper problem with the view that the more judges take charge of public policy, the more freedom we all have. Looking at freedom exclusively from the individual's side winds up undermining the single most important political right the individual has—the right to take part in self-government. Our freedom is, in part, the negative freedom of the individual to live without interference by government; this is the portion of our freedom protected by individual rights. But the other half is our positive freedom—the freedom we have collectively to govern ourselves, to make laws that create the kind of society that most of us want to live in. Preserving freedom requires that we achieve an optimal balance between negative and positive freedom, the freedom from government and the freedom to take part in shaping the conditions of our social world through democracy.

Consider two recent examples that highlight the power of judges to displace our right to self-government in two of the most important areas where the principle of majority rule ought never to be violated. The first concerns the issue of gay marriage. In 2003, in *Goodridge v. Dept. of Public Health*, Massachusetts's highest court became the first of several state supreme courts to rule that gays and lesbians have a right to marry under the state's constitution.[16] The court agreed with the law's challengers that the majority could not draw a rational line between permitting marriage between a man and a woman, and permitting marriage between two persons of the same sex. In deciding that equality prevented the majority from drawing this line, the court expanded its sphere of authority and diminished that of the democratic majority to decide who can marry whom.

The *Goodridge* decision is distressing because, if there is any social issue that the majority ought to have the right to pass upon, it is the question about which kinds of relationships are going to have the full social and legal support of the state and society. I can think of no issue more deserving of being decided by all of us, rather than by the courts, than what it means to be a family in the full social and legal sense. Moreover, the legitimacy of gay marriage depends upon its being accepted by the majority. A court-imposed regime may not be accepted by a majority that feels increasingly disenfranchised from its rightful role as policy maker. There is likely to be serious political fallout from these decisions. Thus, I believe that this decision should be left to the democratic process, even though I also believe that it is time for the majority to seriously consider permitting gay marriage. There are good grounds for extending the marital right to gays, but they are social and political grounds, not constitutional grounds. It does not follow from the fact that a policy may be good politically that it is required constitutionally.

Bush v. Gore provides the second example of judicial intrusion into the sphere of self-government. Indeed, *Bush v. Gore* was a frontal assault on the very citadel of the principle of self-government, since the Supreme Court effectively stopped the Florida vote recount that might have altered the result in the 2000 presidential election. What many nonlawyers do not realize, however, is that *Bush v. Gore* was the culmination of a line of voting rights decisions by which courts had increasingly intervened in the political process for good, liberal reasons.

In a series of cases dating from the 1960s, the Supreme Court decided that courts should play a role in overseeing certain aspects of the democratic process itself.[17]

In several states, population shifts over many decades resulted in an inequality in the number of constituents in different districts. One voting district might include 200,000 residents while another might have double this number, yet each had only one representative. This meant that voters in the second, more populated district were underrepresented relative to those in the first (more constituents per representative equals less representation per voter). Thus the voting power of the average individual in the second district was diluted relative to that in the first. As the Court pointed out in these cases, the voting asymmetry was unlikely to be resolved through the democratic process itself, since the representatives of less populated areas had the same voting strength as those of the more populated districts.

In the face of this problem, the Supreme Court developed the "one person, one vote" rule in cases following *Baker v. Carr*, decided in 1962. The decision, however, was highly controversial. There had been a long line of similar cases going back to the mid-nineteenth century in which the Court had consistently refused to intervene on these redistricting issues. The justices had refused to do so, most importantly, because they believed in strict separation of the two spheres of authority represented by the courts and the political process. In fact, Justice Felix Frankfurter wrote a passionate dissent in *Baker v. Carr*, warning that the Court's ruling "foreshadows deeper and more pervasive difficulties." Liberals, of course, hailed the decision as fair and equitable, but Frankfurter (himself a liberal in most respects) insisted that "relief must come through an aroused popular conscience that sears the conscience of the people's representatives."

What were the more pervasive difficulties Frankfurter foresaw? *Baker* set in motion a line of cases in which the courts intervened increasingly in the political process, redrawing district lines and setting numerical standards to govern the redistricting process. In some cases, courts even permitted the creation of strangely configured districts designed to gobble up enough minority areas to create minority-dominated districts where none previously existed. Their purpose was to ramp up minority representation in Congress or at the state level. Liberals generally applauded these decisions—until 2000. Ironically, the logic underlying this line of cases led to liberals' most hated decision in recent memory, the ruling in *Bush v. Gore*.[18] Once the courts were empowered to equalize districts, what should stop them from intervening in a state recount during a federal election in which counties were using different standards (e.g., hanging chads versus "pregnant" chads, etc.) to judge the validity of votes cast?

Bush v. Gore reminds us that conservatives can be judicial activists, too. Recent revelations make clear just how political the decision was. Justice O'Connor was reported to have looked "stricken" on election night when it appeared that Al Gore had won. The memos she wrote to Justice William Rehnquist before the opinion was handed down referred to "we" and "us" in talking about the Republican response to the election.[19] The veneer of judicial impartiality was gone as the conservatives on the Court cobbled together the necessary five votes to stop the recount. Of course, the irony within the irony was that the plurality opinion left the underlying inequality unresolved. If the Court was going to intervene, the better response in *Bush v. Gore* is found in the dissenting opinion by Justices Souter and Breyer, who argued that the Court should remand the case to the state court and require that one standard be chosen and uniformly applied across all counties. This ruling would have met equality concerns while also ensuring the legitimacy of the election. Instead, as Justice Stevens wrote in his dissent: "Although we may never know with complete certainty the identity of the winner of this year's Presidential election, the identity of the loser is perfectly clear. It is the nation's confidence in the judge as an impartial guardian of the rule of law."

Where *Bush v. Gore* represents the ultimate extension of judicial authority into the political process, *Goodridge* demonstrates the extent to which courts can work pervasive and fundamental changes in social patterns. Yet both reveal why the judicial process has become increasingly politicized in recent years. As courts increasingly expand their authority in politics and society, it is only natural for political and social forces to want to capture the courts in return. If political issues tend to become legal issues, as Tocqueville observed even in the 1830s, the reverse occurs as well. When courts assume increasing authority over political issues, the legal issues become politicized. As Jeffrey Rosen has recently written: "When judges take it upon themselves to decide the most divisive questions of politics, technology and culture, who can blame both liberals and conservatives for selectively embracing judicial activism when it suits their purposes? Now that constitutional politics has become a blood sport, many believe, bipartisanship of any kind has become an unaffordable luxury."[20]

Conservative Constitutionalism: Its Virtues and Its Limits

Both liberals and conservatives today minimize the significance of the Constitution, though in vastly different ways. Activist liberals minimize constitutional values by using constitutional clauses as foils to insulate contemporary liberal values from democratic revision. In doing this, they run the risk of making a mockery of the idea that any objective constitutional law exists. For their part, many conservatives endorse a theory of constitutional interpretation that condemns many of our most important constitutional values to obsolescence after a short time. To understand why this is, we have to delve a bit deeper into the conservative's approach to the Constitution.

Conservative constitutional theories seek to bind the judge most clearly to the text and history of the Constitution. They are conservative in the sense that they attempt to conserve the original understanding of the Constitution. The three labels most closely connected to conservative constitutionalism today are "strict constructionism," "original intent," and "textualism." These do not all mean quite the same thing, however. "Strict constructionism" refers to the philosophy of giving constitutional terms like "due process" and "equal protection" their narrowest readings, thereby leaving the most room for the democratic process. While President Bush used this label to refer to the philosophy he preferred, even many conservatives disavow it. Supreme Court Justice Antonin Scalia, for example, calls himself a "textualist" and rejects strict constructionism as "a degraded form of textualism." "A text should not be construed strictly, and it should not be construed leniently," Scalia has declared; "it should be construed reasonably."[21]

Justice Scalia's textualism requires that a judge follow two principles in interpreting the Constitution: first, the judge should be restricted to the text of the constitution. A judge should not go beyond the text in any way, reading into the Constitution new rights or meanings that do not appear on the face of the Constitution. Second, in interpreting the meaning of any particular clause of the Constitution, the judge should interpret it in light of its meaning at the time the clause was ratified. In interpreting the meaning of the Eighth Amendment's cruel and unusual punishment clause, for example, we look to what they meant in 1791, the year the Bill of Rights was ratified, by the term "cruel and unusual punishment." This does not mean that the original meaning of the clause cannot be applied to new developments, as is sometimes objected. If a new form of torture is developed in the twenty-first century, we can address it through the Eighth Amendment as long as the new form of torture would have satisfied the definition of "cruel and unusual" back in 1791.

Scalia's textualism and Robert Bork's originalism are subtly different from a third conservative approach to interpreting the Constitution, sometimes referred to as original intent theories. Original intent theorists believe that the intent of the framers themselves should determine the meaning of each constitutional provision. For the original intent theorist, the meaning of each clause is the meaning that was in the heads of the framers or ratifiers when they voted for adopting the clause, that is, what counts for these theorists is what James Madison or the other framers intended a clause to mean. Textualists such as Bork and Scalia reject this. As Robert Bork put it, "Law is a public act," so that "what counts is what the public understood" about the meaning of a constitutional clause when it was ratified, not the subjective intent of the framers.[22] As Justice Scalia has written, in interpreting the constitution,

> I will consult the writings of some of the men who happened to be delegates to the Constitutional convention. . . . I do so, however, not because they were framers and therefore their intent was authoritative and must be the law; but rather because their writings, like those of other intelligent and informed people of the time, display how the text of the Constitution was originally understood. . . . What I look for in the Constitution is . . . the original meaning of the text, not what the original draftsmen intended.[23]

Textualism is probably the dominant conservative approach of the three today, and it is the theory that I will focus on here. Textualism has two virtues. First, textualists take seriously the idea that, when we speak of constitutional law, as Judge Bork put it, "we ordinarily refer to a rule that we have no right to change except through prescribed procedures. That statement assumes that the rule has a meaning independent of our own desires."[24] In linking the meaning of a clause to some potentially ascertainable public meaning of a particular constitutional clause, textualism gives us a principle that the nontextualist cannot provide. Even the two other conservative theories fall short in this respect: strict constructionism does not tell us how to ascertain the meaning of a clause (it says only that constitutional meanings should be read narrowly), while original intent theories are subject to the objections either that we do not know what the subjective intent of the framers was or that different framers may have had conflicting ideas about the scope and meaning of a clause. James Madison and Alexander Hamilton, among the many others framers, may have had different subjective understandings of the commerce clause or the Ninth Amendment, for example. Original intent cannot tell us how to resolve this conflict, but textualism at least gives us a principle, even if it is often a difficult principle to apply: what counts is the public meaning of terms like "cruel and unusual punishment" or "equal protection of the laws."

Second, by giving us a test for determining the meaning of constitutional clauses, textualism limits the discretion of judges to read their own values into the Constitution. It ensures that the democratic process, and not judges, will make the law that governs us. In doing this, it protects judges as well, for it prevents the politicization of the judiciary.

Yet rigorous textualism can get a judge only so far in interpreting the Constitution. A textualist approach has several apparently insurmountable limitations that even the most principled textualist must recognize. First, some constitutional terms like "equal protection" and "cruel and unusual punishment" are, and always have been, vague terms which become vaguer when set to the task of governing particular cases. There may be different, and conflicting, public understandings of these terms, or these terms may simply be indeterminately vague. What does "equal protection" or "cruel and unusual punishment" mean, anyway? And what did they mean in 1868 and in 1791, respectively, when these terms became part of the Constitution? It is often simply illusory to suppose that there is one and only one clear and canonical meaning of a legal phrase—now or then.

Second, while textualists are never supposed to look beyond the text itself, even they must concede that constitutional meanings must sometimes be gleaned by looking to the deeper *purposes* of those who voted to ratify a particular clause. In this way, textualism sometimes slides into a theory closer in spirit to some liberal theories. But it also gives judges a great deal more discretion to find deeper meanings in the Constitution that do not appear on the face of the text. Justice Scalia tells us, for example, that with reasonable textual construction, "context is everything." While the First Amendment protects only freedom of speech and the press, he concedes that it should extend, for example, to a handwritten letter locked in a desk drawer, which is neither spoken aloud nor published.[25] Yet looking to the context appears to be just another way of admitting that the text alone can get you only so far in interpreting the Constitution.

Finally, there is a third problem with textualism, though textualists would not find it a problem at all. There are strong reasons for rejecting the textualist's insistence that the meanings of legal terms must be those that existed at the point in time when the particular provision was passed or ratified. Consider two particularly relevant examples concerning the equal protection clause. Today, it is obvious to most that the term "equal protection of the laws" should mean that a state cannot segregate public schools on the basis of race. It is equally clear that a state cannot give automatic preference to men over women in a variety of contexts—for example, consistently delegating to a son, rather than a daughter, the right to administer the estate of a deceased parent.[26] Yet almost all scholars today acknowledge that the ratifiers of the equal protection clause never intended to outlaw segregation, and everyone agrees that it was never intended to reach gender issues at all. A consistent application of textualist principles would mean that the equal protection clause could not reach these issues, as it should.[27] And this stance has the effect of making the Constitution increasingly less relevant today.

Most of us want judges at least to be able to update the meanings of constitutional provisions so that they reflect the modern zeitgeist. The understanding of the term "equal protection of the laws" may not have been understood to mean that men and women had to be treated equally in 1868, but we do understand it that way today. This should be reflected in our understanding of the Constitution. The framers may not have believed that "cruel and unusual punishment" prohibited executing children, but we certainly believe that today. And that the framers obviously did not anticipate the modern phone system or thermal imaging does not prevent a court from applying the search and seizure clause of the Fourth Amendment to wiretapping or to infrared aerial surveillance of the inside of homes.

Where does this leave us? Freewheeling judicial activism is potentially hazardous to democratic values, yet a degree of discretion is absolutely necessary to preserve the values of the Constitution and to ensure that the Constitution retains its moral and political significance in a changing society. Those who espouse conservative principles of constitutional interpretation have a view of judicial decision making that is unworkably narrow. But what is the alternative?

Liberal Constitutionalism: How Far Is Too Far?

How do liberal judges decide cases? What is their theory of constitutional interpretation? Over the past forty years or so, perhaps the dominant tack of liberal constitutional theory has been to echo the legal realist's point that there is no clear demarcation between law and politics. Liberals have embraced the idea that every court opinion is, as liberal legal theorist Ronald Dworkin once put it, an exercise in applied political philosophy. A judge's theory of the Constitution should highlight what that judge thinks are the basic overarching purposes and values of the Constitution. This means that, where conservatives emphasize the language and tradition connected with constitutional clauses, liberals look to their purposes and consequences. As we might expect, conservatives are more backward looking in orientation, emphasizing the values of predictability and fidelity to accepted understandings of the Constitution, whereas liberals are forward looking in that they believe the ultimate real-world effects of decisions must be taken into consideration. Because conservatives have a more constrained, role-bound view of social order, they believe that judges should play their role in following the letter of the law, leaving it to Congress or state legislatures to change laws that have harmful consequences. Liberals are more likely to believe that judges should not be so constrained and that they should anticipate the consequences of their decisions.

Another difference is that liberals tend to approach the Constitution more holistically than conservatives do. John Hart Ely, one practitioner of this approach, criticized the "clause-bound" approach of conservatives and argued that the Constitution should be interpreted as a unified document embodying a coherent theme, a set of deeper philosophical commitments that order and prioritize the various constitutional clauses. Ely's theory of the Constitution was that courts should function to dissolve the countermajoritarian difficulty. Rather than being in conflict with democracy, courts should interpret the Constitution in a way that makes us a more democratic nation. For this reason, Ely favored giving broad protection to free speech and press on the theory that these are necessary preconditions to the discussion and debate that should precede voting. He similarly favored the "one man, one vote" cases along with cases that ensured greater minority participation in politics. Yet he was skeptical of the privacy right jurisprudence of the Warren Court—cases such as *Roe v. Wade*—which he believed did not further the democratic ideal but were simply impositions of the judges' values.[28] In important ways, Ely's is a good example of a centrist approach to the Constitution.

More liberal legal philosophers have other theories. Ronald Dworkin argued that judges must each do their best to construct a comprehensive theory of the legal system that can consistently justify all the various rights, principles, rules, and policies that exist while giving them the morally best interpretation in their eyes.[29] Dworkin appropriately calls his judge Hercules, since one would have to be an intellectual Hercules to accomplish this task fully. Dworkin's own vision is that of a judge who interprets provisions of the Constitution in a way conducive to creating conditions of "equal concern and respect" among Americans. For Dworkin, this means protection of the privacy right, advocacy of affirmative action, First Amendment protection for pornography, and outlawing of the death penalty—all positions predictably in line with contemporary liberal values.[30]

More recently, Justice Stephen Breyer of the Supreme Court has developed another version of this liberal approach. Rather than deciding cases in a clause-by-clause manner, a justice should "develop a view of the Constitution as a whole." His approach favors "purpose and consequence" over "language, history and tradition." He suggests that judges must have a deeper theory of the purposes of the Constitution. "I see the document as creating a coherent framework for a certain kind of government."[31] In interpreting particular clauses, we should understand that provisions like the due process or equal protection clause are not precise, and that they "reflect fundamental aspirations and . . . moods" to which a judge must give effect.[32]

What would Justice Breyer's theory require exactly? In his 2005 book *Active Liberty*, he defends a judicial philosophy based on his idea that the Constitution seeks to foster a balance between negative and positive liberty, between the freedom from government and the freedom to take part in government. The right balance is what he calls "active liberty." In itself, this is an innocuous, if very general, claim about the meaning of the Constitution. But how are we to apply the idea of active liberty in particular cases? Here a certain looseness creeps in. Not surprisingly, Justice Breyer's interpretations of the principles of negative and positive liberty wind up reinforcing the values that every good contemporary liberal wants to see underwritten by the Constitution. Negative liberty means that there is a right to an abortion but not to the kinds of economic liberties the *Lochner* libertarians would have wanted to protect, for example. More of a reach still, Justice Breyer makes positive liberty, the right to participate in government, the philosophical basis for defending affirmative action. In defending the *Grutter* decision, in which the Court permitted the University of Michigan Law School to use lower admissions criteria for minority than for white applicants, Justice Breyer invokes positive liberty. What has positive liberty to do with affirmative action? Justice Breyer explains:

> What are these arguments but an appeal to principles of solidarity, to principles of *fraternity*, to principles of *active liberty*? They find some form of affirmative action necessary to maintain a well-functioning participatory democracy. . . . Too many individuals of all races would lack experience with a racially diverse educational environment helpful for their later effective participation in today's diverse civil society. Too many individuals of minority race would find the doors of higher education closed; those closed doors would shut them out of positions of leadership. . . . If these are the likely consequences . . . could our democratic form of government then function as the Framers intended?[33]

The problem with Justice Breyer's theory is not simply that his overarching philosophy does not come from the Constitution itself. (It doesn't, but to be fair, neither does the textualist's philosophy—the Constitution itself does not tell us how to interpret it.) Nor is it simply that there are as many of these jurisprudential metaphilosophies as there are intelligent and creative minds to dream them up. The deeper problem is that a judge can get anywhere he or she wants armed with so general a theory. This is because constitutional values such as self-government, equality, or freedom of speech are inherently malleable commodities when unmoored from the context provided by tradition and precedent. Positive liberty can get a judge to affirmative action, but it can also get us to many other things that are not guaranteed by the Constitution. Wouldn't guaranteeing a right to a college education, for example, promote a well-informed democracy?

The Right to Privacy

The single most important constitutional focal point of debates between liberals and conservatives in this area is the right of privacy. I would be remiss in suggesting that those of us drawn to centrist politics are any less divided on the legitimacy of the privacy right than are liberals and conservatives. The debate about the right to privacy seems to drive right down the middle of the U.S. political spectrum but, again for many liberals and conservatives, this is because of the political consequences of right-to-privacy decisions—because the kinds of activities protected by the privacy right (abortion, gay rights) are important to liberals and are often reviled by conservatives. For many centrists, the problem is more complicated. We often agree with liberals that the state has no business restricting various forms of personal behavior, but we are uncomfortable with judges creating new rights that have no basis in the text, history, or purpose of the Constitution. We are political liberals and moderate constitutional conservatives.

The right to privacy was first recognized in 1965 in the *Griswold* case.[34] In *Griswold*, the Court struck down a law that prohibited the use of contraceptives for birth control purposes. A plurality of judges struck down the law, though on a variety of different grounds. Even Justice Hugo Black, who dissented, found the law "uncommonly silly." Yet as Justice Black argued, it is one thing to regard a law as silly or unwise and quite another to think that judges have the power to strike it down.

Griswold's "right to privacy" and the cases that follow in its train are some of the most hollow constitutional decisions in the Court's history. If the privacy right was protected by the Constitution, why had it not been recognized previously? Moreover, if the justices were interpreting particular provisions of the Constitution, why was there so much disagreement about where this right came from? Justice William O. Douglas used *Griswold* to introduce his novel theory that the right to privacy was based on the "penumbras and emanations" of the First, Third, Fourth, Fifth, Ninth, and Fourteenth Amendments. Eschewing Douglas's astronomical metaphor, Justices Arthur Goldberg, Earl Warren, and William Brennan thought that the Ninth Amendment "lends strong support" to a claim ultimately based on the due process clause of the Fourteenth Amendment. Justice John Harlan thought that it was the Fourteenth Amendment's due process clause "standing on its own bottom," without support of other provisions of the Bill of Rights, that created the right. Justice Byron White appears to have thought that the law did not violate a "right" in the constitutional sense, but that the means used by the law did not achieve its intended end, so the Court could strike the law down as an ill-conceived measure on what constitutional lawyers refer to as "rational basis review." (White's approach was the most provident, since it permitted the Court to strike the law down without creating a general right that would be followed in future, more controversial, cases.) And Justices Potter Stewart and Black dissented, finding no constitutional violation at all.

The problem with *Griswold* is that there appear to be many different roads to the same preordained conclusion. The justices recognized an altogether new right, never before seen in constitutional discourse, and each arrived at his conclusion from distinct if novel legal premises. Rarely has an opinion appeared so result oriented. Each opinion was a conclusion in search of a justification—with several conflicting justifications as a result. The skeptic will be pardoned for wondering aloud how anyone can reasonably accept that what the judges were doing here was interpreting the law. This is a long way from holding that the equal protection clause prohibits public school segregation.

Several years later the Court finally achieved some consensus about which clause was the basis for the privacy right. They came around to Justice Harlan's view that the due process clause is the proper constitutional basis for this right, though the privacy right was long established by this point. Ironically, however, this is the same due process clause used by activist conservatives during the *Lochner* era to read a libertarian "freedom of contract" interpretation into the due process clause. In an earlier incarnation still, the due process clause was used in the infamous *Dred Scott* decision, which purported to recognize a constitutional property right in one's slaves. Good liberals may favor the kinds of values protected by *Griswold* and its progeny as opposed to the very different values protected at each of these earlier two points in history, but the real question remains: what makes the *Griswold* interpretation of the due process clause any more valid as a constitutional matter than *Lochner*'s? If *Lochner* was bad constitutional law from the Right, isn't *Griswold* equally bad from the Left?

The Court's privacy decisions have generated a much larger problem in the long run, since the *scope* of the privacy right remains contested. With no basis in the Constitution, no one could be sure what other activities it might reach. Justice Douglas limited the right in *Griswold* to the intimate decisions of married couples and asked whether we are willing to have the police "search the sacred precincts of marital bedrooms for telltale signs" of contraception use. But some worried that the right sounded much broader—that it might, in essence, constitutionalize Mill's harm principle. Some of the judges in *Griswold* wondered whether the right might reach laws prohibiting fornication, adultery, incest, prostitution, or polygamy, among others. A few years later, exactly this began to happen. In 1972, the Court recognized the right of unmarried persons to use contraception, leading some to wonder whether the Court was implicitly recognizing a general constitutional right to consensual sexual relations regardless of marital status.[35] A year after that the Court recognized a general right to abortion in *Roe v. Wade*, a decision Justice White called "improvident," "extravagant," and "an exercise of raw judicial power."[36] Yet the Court has never been able to offer a satisfactory explanation of why a privacy right which permits a woman to terminate a pregnancy does not give her a constitutional right to trade sex for money or to smoke marijuana or to engage in other consensual self-regarding behaviors. It can't explain why one now has a right to refuse unwanted medical treatment, even to starve oneself, but why terminally ill patients cannot ask for a lethal dose of morphine to end their suffering.[37] Because the right came out of nowhere, there was no context for delimiting its scope in a meaningful way.

Defenders of the right of privacy may well argue that these rights are marginal incursions into the democratic process, warranted by the need to protect fundamental liberties. But are they limited incursions into democracy? Giving judges broader power to make social policy tends to erode the democratic process in two significant ways often overlooked by liberal proponents of broad judicial power. When the Supreme Court extends constitutional protection to an activity that was previously not protected, it effectively brackets this activity from any democratic evolution, that is, to find a constitutional right to an activity is to place this activity permanently above the flux of majoritarian politics. This impedes democratic experimentation and change among states at any given time and nationally over the longer term. Before abortion was constitutionalized, for example, different states could try out differing regimes of regulation. The more liberal states could experiment with liberal approaches to abortion, while conservative states could do the opposite. Moderate states could implement intermediate regimes that would give significant protection to women while limiting what the states might regard as the more abusive abortion practices. Moreover, as the states experimented with various policies (and every indication is that the pre–*Roe v. Wade* trend was distinctly in the direction of liberalization), they could adapt and evolve these policies to suit the changing needs and mores of the electorate. There is arguably more choice in a decentralized approach than there is in a one-size-fits-all abortion policy.

With the constitutionalization of abortion law, however, both the horizontal experimentation with policy at the state level and the temporal evolution of policy through time come to an end. One rule, frozen in time, applies to the entire nation—short of a court reversal or a constitutional amendment. Ironically, then, an untethered notion of evolving standards of jurisprudence frequently leads to ossification of the law. It prevents democracy from taking its course and from changing with the times, as democracy should. It prevents the very evolution of the law that liberals often wisely want to preserve.

Centrist Constitutionalism: Four Minimum Commitments

A centrist approach to the Constitution means two things, at a minimum. First, and more generally, we must embrace an attitude that distances our constitutional principles from our political sympathies and antipathies. While law and politics may never be completely separable in the real world, neither should law become the handmaiden of politics. Creating this distance requires, second, that on issues of interpretation judges must steer a middle course between the rigors of originalism and the excesses of liberal judicial philosophy. But what might this middle course require?

One way to think about the judge's role is that a judge not only should be limited by the text but also should be free to update constitutional understandings to bring them into conformity with contemporary understandings. This means that we can accept the first but not the second tenet of Scalia's textualism and Bork's originalism. The text should be followed, but the meanings of clauses need not necessarily be restricted to the meanings they had when those clauses were ratified. An evolving textualism, as we might call it, ensures the stability and the objectivity of constitutional law while recognizing the reality of change.

A commitment to an evolving textualism holds judges, minimally, to four principles or rules of thumb in interpreting cases. There may well be other considerations that ought to guide a judge in interpreting the Constitution, but the following represent the most basic minimum requirements of a centrist constitutionalism.

(1) *Constitutional consistency.* No interpretation can be valid which is itself fore-

closed by the plain meaning of the Constitution. There can always be reasonable differences of opinion on many issues—about what a clause means, exactly, or about whether a particular clause should be interpreted to reach new issues. But it is quite another thing to interpret a clause in a way expressly foreclosed by the Constitution itself. Any interpretation that contradicts a result the Constitution plainly permits or forbids should be out of order.

While this may seem an obvious condition of faithful constitutional interpretation, it is frequently ignored. For example, the Fifth Amendment provides that "no person shall be held to answer for a capital or otherwise infamous crime" without indictment. And the due process clauses of the Fifth and Fourteenth Amendments themselves prohibit the taking of "life, liberty or property" without due process. Each of these provisions, in other words, specifically contemplates the death penalty as a constitutionally available alternative. Each was incorporated into the same Bill of Rights that embodies the "cruel and unusual punishment" clause of the Eighth Amendment. Thus, whatever the framers meant by "cruel and unusual punishment," it certainly did not prohibit the death penalty.

Yet some argue today that the Eighth Amendment does indeed now outlaw the death penalty. At a talk he gave at Georgetown University Law Center in 1985, for example, Justice William Brennan declared: "As I interpret the Constitution, capital punishment is under all circumstances cruel and unusual punishment."[38] Yet there is simply no way that Brennan's position can be squared with the text of the Constitution itself. The point here is not that the states should not be free to eliminate the death penalty if a majority in the state wishes to see this done. Many states have done so. Rather, states should be free to decide, one way or the other, whether to employ the death penalty in certain cases.

In sum, in interpreting vague constitutional principles and rights, no interpretation can be acceptable which directly conflicts with the plain meaning of the Constitution itself.

(2) *A presumption against entirely novel constitutional principles.* There should be a strong presumption against interpretations that create altogether new constitutional principles or rights not clearly grounded in the text of the Constitution. I do not mean that previously recognized rights cannot be applied to new situations. It is certainly within the zone of legitimacy, for example, to consider whether the free speech clause of the First Amendment should reach the burning of a draft card or the protection of sexually explicit publications. It is similarly permissible to entertain the possibility that the "cruel and unusual punishment" clause should prevent the execution of the mentally disabled or of persons under the age of eighteen. It is also permissible to consider the propriety of new remedies to protect previously recognized rights. The creation of the exclusionary rule, for example, permits a court to throw out evidence gathered in violation of the "search and seizure" clause of the Fourth Amendment. Each of these cases represents arguably legitimate extensions of our current understanding of the Constitution: old principles are being applied in new ways.

It is another matter, however, to create an altogether new substantive right, just as it would be to abolish a long-recognized right, particularly when this action is predicated upon previously unheard-of principles. This is why the creation of the right to privacy was objectionable. When it was first recognized, the privacy right was not an extension of an older right that was firmly grounded in the Constitution; it was an entirely new principle created by a Court that could not even reach consensus about which clause of the Constitution grounded the right.

This means that the initial recognition of the privacy right was an impermissible reach by the judiciary. But what does this portend for the privacy right today? Is it better to overrule a right that has long been recognized or to acquiesce in the gradual acceptance of a right that was highly questionable when initially recognized?

The right has for forty years been part of our constitutional tradition. Overturning it would not only reverse several established precedents and upset the settled expectations of the U.S. public, but also precipitate even more bitter and partisan political battles between the forces of the Left and Right. Under these circumstances, perhaps the least unsatisfactory alternative is to limit further expansion of the right without overturning it.

(3) *A social criterion for constitutional meanings.* Where judges must interpret constitutional clauses that reflect widely shared and understood public values— values like equal protection, free speech, or the avoidance of cruel and unusual punishment—they should avoid departing significantly from what a large share of the U.S. public would consider a reasonable understanding of the term. Judges should be able to update the Constitution by reading more contemporary understandings into these clauses, but these updated meanings should be meanings held in common, that is, meanings that would not be rejected by a large share of the U.S. public. Before a judge considers extending an existing right to a categorically new class of cases, he or she should be required to ascertain whether the rest of us, if consulted, would find the new interpretation objectionable. Would it fly in the face of contemporary U.S. customs, practices, or understandings? This would justify, for example, the extension of equal protection to women but it would not permit a court to reach the conclusion that the equal protection clause requires constitutionalizing welfare rights or, more remotely, that it requires the abolition of private property.

Some will immediately object that this as a populist limitation on judicial review. They will say that it injects a majoritarian element into our rights analysis. Since rights are countermajoritarian in nature, some will object that the majority's definition can't be the last word on the meaning of a right. But what is the alternative? To permit the judge to read his or her own idiosyncratic meaning into the clause? Requiring that judges consult a social criterion permits them to move beyond the limits of originalism, since commonly accepted social understandings of clauses will be contemporary understandings. Yet by tethering interpretations to currently accepted understandings, it prevents judges from reaching genuinely idiosyncratic interpretations of rights. Moreover, this principle is negative in character. It requires not that a majority agree with a specific interpretation, but that interpretations that fall well outside the mainstream of meaning be rejected. The purpose of this restriction, then, is not to give the majority a check on what judges do (when judges check the majority) but simply to provide a contemporary cultural touchstone when interpreting the Constitution.

(4) *A presumption against social legislation.* The fourth consideration looks to the political consequences or the aggregate social effects of proposed changes that a new constitutional rule would bring about. It requires a strong presumption against decisions that will have dramatic, wide-scale, and lasting consequences on basic social patterns, as well as against decisions that undermine the integrity of the political process. In a democratic society, a small number of unelected judges should not make decisions that radically change the structure of society or basic social patterns. This is the primary postulate of every democratic society. Similarly, courts should have a minimal, guarded role in the political process. Courts should not be deciding elections and should probably intervene in the political process only when it is clear that some political distortion is systematically frustrating majority rule.[39] Centrists may feel some tension here between their more liberal political sensibilities and their commitment to democratic values, but where the changes wrought are likely to be broad and fundamental, the issue is one that should be left to democracy.

The four principles elaborated here may give the centrist approach to the Constitution a vaguely conservative cast. But the last fifty years have witnessed an explosion of judicial intervention into areas previously left to politics alone. We live during a time when the arc of judicial authority is on the rise. The constitutional decisions of the past fifty years have already given the judiciary a permanent foothold in a number of areas. These decisions will not simply evaporate with time. Judges will continue to exercise authority in these areas. From the standpoint of these developments, putting the brakes on continued expansion of judicial power is not a conservative venture at all.

Chapter 8

From Gay Rights to Drug Legalization: The Tension between Individual Freedom and Social Morality

WHICH ARGUABLY PRIVATE ACTIVITIES should remain beyond the reach of the law? How strong a presence should the state have in the personal decisions of the ordinary individual? While centrists may agree with conservatives that issues such as gay marriage, abortion, or other private activities should be decided by the democratically elected legislature and not by the courts, this does not mean that we believe these activities should all be legally prohibited.

Consider the kinds of activities that libertarians and some liberals believe should remain beyond the reach of the law: using contraception, having an abortion, consensual sexual acts between adults, including adulterous and homosexual acts. The more libertarian among them often go further, arguing that prostitution, drug use, polygamy, incest, and assisted suicide, among others, should also be permitted activities among adults. The morals legislation debate has historically opened up a great intellectual Maginot Line between liberals, who believe that government should have no say in any of these matters, and social conservatives, who insist that the state should be able to reach and potentially prohibit all of these. On these issues centrists often find themselves in the middle between two unacceptably extreme, if opposed, positions.

Morals Legislation and the Liberal-Conservative Fault Line

The various traditions of liberalism part ways on the issue of the legitimacy of morals legislation. Where classical liberals usually accepted the state's role in regulating the health, safety, and morals of its citizens, a few early liberals dissented, arguing that society had no interest in regulating personal morality. Bentham had concluded that there was little point in punishing consensual, private acts such as homosexual sex because doing so was counterproductive from a utilitarian perspective. Morals prohibitions, he reasoned, subtracted from the overall happiness of society by preventing those who want to engage in these activities from doing so while giving nothing back to society in terms of collective utility.[1] The German political thinker Wilhelm von Humboldt may have been the first (around 1790) to defend an early libertarian argument for an absolute right to live as one wishes, consistent with a similar right for all others.[2] Yet it was John Stuart Mill (who cited Humboldt in the inscription of *On Liberty*) who opened up the gulf between modern liberals and conservatives by drawing a clear distinction between self-regarding and other-regarding behaviors and arguing that all self-regarding behaviors should be off limits to state regulation.[3]

Mill's "harm principle," as it came to be called, was pristine in its simplicity: He began his essay by asserting that "the sole end for which mankind are warranted individually or collectively to interfere with the liberty of any of their number is self-protection." The person's "own good, either physical or moral, is not a sufficient warrant." He insisted that "the only part of the conduct of any one for which he is amenable to society is that which concerns others." The harm principle drew a basic distinction between "harm-based" laws, which prohibit one person from harming another in a direct and material way (e.g., laws prohibiting murder, theft, fraud, and so on), and laws which regulate behavior that causes no direct, material harm to third parties. This placed off limits two kinds of laws—laws that seek to prevent individuals from making decisions that might potentially harm themselves (paternalistic laws) and laws that prohibit an activity because the majority believes it to be morally wrong (moralistic laws).

Mill concluded that moralistic laws prohibiting prostitution, drug use, homosexuality, gambling, and a variety of other issues fall into the self-regarding domain, although he also argued that the commercial and other effects of some of these activities could be regulated.[4] Underlying the harm principle was an expansive theory of human liberty that asserted that freedom was necessary for the flowering of self-individuation. The quest for self-individuation means that each of us must have the right to perform our own experiments in living as we see fit, in order to become a truly individualized self.

For liberals who follow Mill, the legal and political world is divided between two realms—one purely personal and completely beyond the reach of government and the other public and reachable by laws.[5] Yet true Millians are difficult to find outside the ranks of libertarians today. Most nonlibertarian liberals are considerably more paternalistic than Mill was. Liberals today often oppose legalizing prostitution or drugs, for example, partially on grounds that prostitution is inherently exploitative or that potential drug users underestimate the danger involved in using particularly serious drugs such as heroin or crack cocaine. Liberals today are simply more skeptical about the accuracy or reasonableness of human choices. Consequently, where Mill (and modern libertarians) opposes both morals legislation and paternalism, most progressive liberals endorse Mill's categorical ban on morals legislation while accepting a greater measure of paternalism.

For their part, traditional conservatives lean toward the opposite view, accepting morals legislation as necessary to preserve social order. Ironically, it is usually conservatives today and not liberals who are as dubious of paternalism as Mill was. Conservatives typically reject the neat, hermetic distinction between private acts and public consequences, for they suspect that there is a great deal more seepage from private acts to public consequences than liberals seem to concede. They are concerned, for example, about the spread of immoral behavior brought about by the bad example of those practicing it. They may also fear the way immoral behavior tends to generate other immoral or suboptimal behaviors—for example, the tendency for prostitutes to become drug addicts or alcoholics or the likeli-hood that substance abusers will lose their jobs and become public charges. And, of course, conservatives point out that private immorality often generates real harms indirectly—for instance, the way gambling or drug addiction can lead to ancillary crimes to raise money. At a deeper level, conservatives are skeptical of liberals' entire moral psychology, their view of human nature and the relationship between social authority and morality. They are skeptical of the liberal idea of an authentic self that can be freed only by removing the constraints of social oppression. Conserva-tives from Aristotle on have thought just the opposite about human nature—that our characters are formed by social influences and that this process requires a much larger quantum of social authority than the liberal believes is necessary.

These fault lines between liberals and conservatives first appeared in the re-sponse to *On Liberty* by one of Mill's earliest and most famous critics—the con-servative James Fitzjames Stephen. Stephen's reply, published as *Liberty, Equality, Fraternity* in 1873, the year Mill died, provides a battery of conservative counteras-sumptions and opens a window into the conservative mind. Stephen shared Mill's utilitarian assumptions and had enthusiastically greeted the publication of *On Lib-erty*, but later changed his mind. "Up to a certain point, I should be proud to describe myself as his [Mill's] disciple," he said, "but there is a side of his teaching which is as repugnant as the rest of it is attractive to me." Like later conservatives, Stephen was convinced that Mill's concept of human nature was "unsound." He doubted that people are naturally self-perfecting, even in the liberal's sense of self-perfection. In fact, Stephen thought that most people are feckless and irresponsible when unguided by social conventions and forces. "Estimate the proportion of men and women who are selfish, sensual, frivolous, idle, absolutely common-place, and wrapped up in the smallest of petty routines, and consider how far the freest of free discussion is likely to improve them." The liberal wants discussion and persuasion, and is offended at the notion of moral coercion. Yet everything good and noble, Stephen insisted, comes from habits originally formed more or less under coercive conditions. "The condition of human life is such that we must be restrained and compelled by circumstances in nearly every action of our lives." We should recog-nize that "both religion and morality are and always must be essentially coercive systems."[6] Stephen rejected out of hand Mill's harm principle, with its hard line be-tween self-regarding and other-regarding acts. "The strong metaphor that we are all members one of another is little more than the expression of a fact. A man would no more be a man if he was alone in the world," he echoed Aristotle, "than a hand would be a hand without the rest of the body." As for the idea of a privacy right, he had this to say: "It is one thing to . . . tolerate vice so long as it is inoffensive, and quite another to give it a legal right not only to exist, but to assert itself in the face of the world as an 'experiment in living.'"[7]

There are several well-known problems with the harm principle which more thoughtful modern liberals recognize, acknowledging the need for numerous amendments and qualifications.[8] One important problem is that the harm prin-ciple seems to prevent society from reaching private acts which lead to public harms. Mill thought that if private behavior (e.g., hard drug use) leads to public harms (e.g., crime), we can punish the crime when it occurs, but we cannot prevent the private cause of that crime (e.g., by prohibiting the drug use itself).[9] Fortunately, even most modern liberals see that when certain private acts regularly lead to public harms, the law should reach the precipitating private activity.

Similarly, the harm principle seems to prevent us from regulating individual activities which create only de minimis injuries when taken independently but which can produce serious collective injuries when aggregated. Suppose I pump small quantities of pollutants into the ground that filter out into aquifers and streams in small quantities. The effects are so diffused that my acts do not directly and materially harm any particular individual in the sense usually required by the harm principle. Yet if everyone did this, the aggregate effect on our environment would be disastrous. Most liberals admit that the harm principle must be amended to permit the law to reach private acts which become harmful when aggregated.

A more general problem is that most liberals agree that the law should be able to reach certain other social conditions which cannot be considered "harmful" at all in Mill's sense. Most agree, for instance, that we should be able to prohibit offensive activities, public acts that violate the sensibilities of the ordinary person— for example, indecent exposure.[10] Similarly, some believe that we should be able to prevent some kinds of conduct which do not qualify as a harm, either because the affected individual has consented to the act or because the social effect is not concrete enough to be considered a harm. Does prostitution "commodify" sexual relations between men and women? Do surrogate mother arrangements exploit the surrogate mother? Liberals are notoriously divided on many of these questions, indicating that they are not unqualified supporters of the harm principle after all.

More generally, even some liberals reject the very heart of the harm principle when they accept that the state has a legitimate role in promoting certain basic moral values. Liberals often want to protect different values than conservatives, but they want to protect certain values just the same: they support, for example, the moral effects of antidiscrimination laws, which not only prohibit discrimination in individual cases but also foster an ethic of racial and gender equality. Few liberals will deny that it is legitimate for government to eradicate racist values. Similarly, they will support laws which seek to engender a heightened sensitivity to sexual harassment, or an expanded awareness of threats to the environment. Why is this any different in principle than when the conservative wants to protect the value of life or promote the traditional family unit?

Liberals' support for the harm principle is more symbolic than real. With the exception of homosexuality and abortion, when most liberals will temporarily resume their Millian guise, they are frequently even less averse to "regulating morality" than conservatives are. It is just that they want to protect different values than conservatives. But let's go to the heart of the problem with the harm principle and address why it is sometimes socially imperative for society to reach behavior which is private and arguably nonharmful (in Mill's sense). Suppose that a new drug is invented. Call it Nirvana. Suppose Nirvana can be manufactured very cheaply so that a person can get high on it for roughly the cost of a pack of cigarettes. Because of its low cost, there are few fears that crime will result from those who need to get money to buy the drug. Suppose, further, that the drug's effects do not include impairment of motor or cognitive skills, nor will it adversely affect the perceptual or reactive centers of the brain. The drug will not cause dangerous or erratic behavior in its users. There will not be a rise in traffic accidents or the other consequences that usually result from the effects of a drug on our motor skills or emotional centers of the brain. Instead, Nirvana affects only the mood center of the brain, inducing a state of intense euphoria that lasts for hours. During the high the user is able to work or to perform various day-to-day functions, but doing so subtracts from the intensity of the pleasure. The drug is not physiologically addictive but it is so intensely pleasurable that many who try it even once will decide to devote their lives entirely to its use. Since users are not impaired when using it, they are able to work, but because the effects of the drug are maximized by abandoning other activities and concentrating on the experience itself, it is expected that many who try the drug will largely give up all other outside pursuits to devote themselves to its use.

Suppose the predicted effects on social order from widespread use of Nirvana are dramatic. Users will not be interested in normal family relations; sex will be unimportant; the life of the mind, education, social issues, and politics—each of these will be neglected by large numbers if the drug is permitted. Indeed, society as we know it would be irreparably transformed in the most dramatic way. In fact, we might even predict that this entire society would die out after a generation or two, leaving no trace of the previous social order. Though the use of this drug harms no individual in Mill's sense, its collective use would dramatically alter, and perhaps destroy, society. This is an example of exactly what the harm principle protects—private activity that does no direct harm to any individual third party—with disastrous social consequences. Certainly some may stand fast on their Millian principles, insisting that if everyone really prefers to live under the influence of this drug, even at the cost of our very way of life, then so be it. But for those who feel differently, we cannot rule out, as a matter of principle, the notion that society sometimes has an interest in what people do with their private lives. If this is correct, then the liberal's harm principle cannot be our guide. We are forced to agree with those conservatives who believe that there can be no theoretical boundary that protects a zone of privacy from the sphere of public power.

But does it follow from this, as some of these same conservatives will insist, that society should be able to regulate any activity whenever a majority believes it to be immoral? In 1957, the British Wolfenden Commission, which the British Parliament had asked to study the question of decriminalizing prostitution and consensual homosexual sodomy, published conclusions virtually identical to those Mill had defended in *On Liberty* almost a century earlier. The Wolfenden Report proposed that private acts between consenting homosexuals should be decriminalized, as should prostitution, though public solicitation by prostitutes should be prohibited. The report inflamed widespread popular debate on the issue of morals legislation and inspired a now-classic exchange between the conservative British jurist Lord Patrick Devlin, who attacked the report, and the don of jurisprudence at Oxford, H. L. A. Hart, who largely defended its liberal conclusions. The debate put Hart on the side of Mill, and Devlin on the side of Stephen.

Devlin criticized the findings of the Wolfenden Committee, maintaining that a shared social morality was necessary to the coherence and continuation of society, and that a "loosening of morals" leads to moral individualism, cultural decay, and social disintegration. "A society is not something that is kept together physically; it is held by the invisible bonds of common thought," Devlin wrote. "If the bonds were too far relaxed the members would drift apart. A common morality is part of the bondage." "Every society," he wrote, "has a moral structure as well as a political one." Consequently, "society may use the law to preserve morality in the same way as it uses it to safeguard anything else that is essential to its existence." A "society may do as much to preserve its moral code as it does to preserve its government. . . . The suppression of vice is as much the law's business as the suppression of subversive activities." Devlin argued that preserving social order requires that the law give vent to the majority's "intolerance, indignation and disgust" toward the acts of homosexuals and prostitutes. He argued, finally, that in a democracy laws should reflect not the "rational" or the "correct" beliefs about right and wrong—since this will always be disputed—but simply what the majority happens to believe is right or wrong: "It is not necessary that [the community's] appreciation of right and wrong, tested in the light of one set or another of those abstract propositions about which men forever dispute, should be correct. If it were, only one society at most could survive. What the lawmaker has to ascertain is not the true belief but the common belief."[11] It is striking that in this respect, Devlin's conservatism sounds dangerously close to the cultural relativism of which conservatives often accuse liberals.

In a rejoinder to Devlin, Hart delivered a series of speeches later published as a book entitled *Law, Liberty and Morality*, which defended the Commission's report on quasi-Millian grounds.[12] Hart largely demolished Devlin's argument from social decay. To Devlin's claim that a loosening of morals leads to the disintegration of society, Hart responded that "no reputable historian has maintained this thesis and there is indeed much evidence against it." Hart argued that Devlin "appears to move from the acceptable proposition that *some* shared morality is essential to the existence of a society to the unacceptable proposition that a society is identical with its morality" at any given point in time, "so that a change in its morality is tantamount to the destruction of society." Even if a society's conventional morality were to change, this would not subvert or destroy the society: "We should compare such a development," Hart wrote, "not to the violent overthrow of government but to a peaceful constitutional change in its form, consistent not only with the preservation of a society but with its advance."[13] As to Devlin's appeal to democracy, Hart argued that Devlin's "central mistake" is the "failure to distinguish the acceptable principle that political power is best entrusted to the majority from the unacceptable principle that what the majority do with that power is beyond criticism and must never be resisted."[14] Confusing these distinct principles amounts to what Hart called "moral populism."

The Centrist's Stance

Centrists reject both the conservative's claim that society should regulate personal behavior whenever a majority disapproves of the lifestyle choices of a minority, and the liberal's belief that society may never regulate behavior that is private or self-regarding. In contrast to both, centrists tend to hold that the private and public realms are separate yet interdependent. The line between the private and the public, the self-regarding and the other regarding, is neither hermetic nor reducible to a simple principle. Our commitment to balancing individual freedom and social order will always reflect an array of messy and often incommensurable moral and empirical considerations. Practical judgment in weighing these considerations is indispensable. We must decide collectively, pragmatically, and often painstakingly. And we should be wary of any attempts by purveyors of easy solutions to cut broad swaths in public policy by offering monistic principles for deciding these issues.

We should think of the public and private realms not as distinct and impermeable, but as overlapping domains that shade into one another. Rather than appealing to stark principles that purport to set certain kinds of activities either within or beyond the scope of government power, centrists believe that these are often questions of degree. Moreover, balancing the values of freedom and basic social order will, to some extent, be like comparing apples and oranges. There is no neat metric that permits us to reduce the claims of the individual and of society to one lowest common denominator. Different values such as freedom, equality, and social order are, as Isaiah Berlin insisted, simply incommensurable. In this respect, we differ from classical utilitarians, who believed that the utility of every claim could be more or less quantified and weighed according to a hedonic calculus. There will always be something impressionistic in the process of weighing the individual's claim to engage in some activity against society's claim to prohibit or regulate it. But there are several things that need to be said on each side of the balance.

First, centrists have a capacious understanding of freedom. No other value is more important to us than individual freedom. We value freedom both because we think that it is intrinsically important for individuals to be able to shape their own lives and destinies and because freedom is essential in a pluralistic society. Stephen thus was wrong to believe that we should see the social world primarily as an expression of force and that individual development must consistently be coerced under the aegis of overweening authority. And Devlin was wrong to believe that the "social bond" should become the predicate to engineer conformity. Mature individuals usually know better than do others who they are and what is best for them. A society where people can pursue their own innate leanings, inclinations, and talents is a happier and more productive society than one in which people are told which professions they may go into or how they should live. Being individuals, we all have a unique window into the world in that we each experience the world a little differently than everyone else. When Mill declared that we are built more like a tree than a steam engine—that we do best when we grow from the inside out and that a large measure of freedom is necessary to permit this growth—he made a lasting contribution to our understanding of the moral psychology of human freedom. But like many principles, Mill's has been susceptible to abuse. People tend to know what they are good at, what they intrinsically love, but not all our choices reflect our identities in the same way. Some liberals run astray in believing that every individual choice is an infallible expression of the deepest impulses of individual authenticity. They are wrong to run to the opposite Rousseauian extreme from

Stephen—to believe that coercion or authority is never warranted in limiting the range of available options for adults. We centrists are drawn to the metaphor that there is a kind of nexus, an elastic link, between one's core personality and one's choices and behaviors. In some cases, where our choices express our deepest individual impulses, the nexus will be quite short and the case for protecting the choice at its strongest. In other cases, the nexus between who we are and what we decide may be considerably more attenuated, as when someone decides to take some action on the basis of a fleeting whim or under social conditions which distort the individual's decisions. Sometimes, in other words, our choices are only *what we do* while at other times they reflect *who we are*. Thus, the Millian thesis not only tends to bifurcate our actions rigidly into the mutually exclusive realms of private or public, but also suffers from a one-dimensional moral psychology which accords the same degree of validity to choices which flow from the most central aspects of our self-identity with those which are the result of purely transitory preferences.

To sum up, we might say that not all freedom claims are created equally. In weighing the significance of the individual's interest in liberty to engage in various behaviors, we should consider such questions as the following: How important is the regulated activity to human beings generally as a physical or psychological matter? To what extent is the activity connected with a person's deepest sources of self-identity and self-respect? Finally, what are the political, social, and economic dimensions of the activity? For example, does prohibiting the activity affect individuals' capacity to take part in shaping their social and political world or in earning a living? Where conservatives tend to ignore these considerations, liberals tend to treat them all as equally compelling. Centrists believe that distinctions must always be drawn, and that this can be done only on the ground, contextually, on the basis of a host of often conflicting considerations.

What about society's interest in regulating behavior? The Nirvana drug example demonstrates that society must sometimes regulate conditions on the basis of their generalized social effects. There is no other way to think about this than as a form of morals legislation; society regulates to preserve our current way of life from a threat which affects us not by directly harming third parties, but by harming all of us in a more generalized way (through our own behavior). But our conception of moral harm is a humanitarian conception. To constitute a moral harm, the regulated activity would have to pose a real threat to human flourishing. If the activity undermines the values essential for individual well-being and social order, society can regulate it. But if it represents merely an eccentric or unusual lifestyle choice, there is no reason to seek to regulate it. To put it slightly differently, the state should regulate or prohibit an activity only when there is a strong *reason* to do so. In contrast to the conservative attitude, centrists do not believe that mere appeal to tradition or prejudice should be enough to prohibit some activity. "This is the way it's always been done" is not a sufficient reason to prohibit or to regulate. The argument for prohibition will have to be made in terms of real social harms, not outworn prejudices.

Centrists part ways from liberals in a second way: we have a broader idea of what constitutes a social harm. Contemporary liberals who follow Mill insist that we should never prohibit a behavior simply because of its influence on other people's attitudes or dispositions, because it sets a bad example, or because of its effects on the tone of society.[15] Suppose, for example, that we could be sure that legalizing prostitution would change for the worse our collective attitudes toward sex and love—that it would monetize or objectify the character of sexual relations between men and women generally. (I happen to doubt that this would occur, but suppose we can agree that it would.) Millian liberals will argue that this is not a sufficient reason to continue prohibiting prostitution—the effect on the general tone of sexual relations is not a real harm in the Millian sense. Yet centrists will agree in principle with other liberals, with some feminists, and with communitarians who believe that this would present a sufficient reason not to decriminalize prostitution if the consequences were reasonably likely. If significant enough, the collective or aggregate effects of changes in society that fall short of individualized harm are still within the province of regulation. Most centrists will also agree that in some cases the only way to prevent certain identifiable public harms is by rooting out their private causes.

The remainder of this chapter applies the foregoing discussion to three contemporary moral issues—the treatment of gays, prostitution, and the debate over drug legalization. Two caveats are in order. First, the conclusions I draw here are my own. Not all centrists agree with each of these, though I believe many will find them generally on track. Second, my purpose here is simply to capture the flavor of centrists' reasoning. I do not claim to exhaust all the considerations pertinent to these issues.

The Question of Gay Marriage

We should begin by frankly acknowledging that religious sentiments have traditionally played a strong role in the legal proscription against homosexuality. The English common law treated homosexual sodomy as a felony, which meant that for centuries it was punishable by death. In the 1760s, the greatest commentator on the common law, William Blackstone, called sodomy "the infamous crime against nature," a "crime not fit to be named." He took the position that sodomy was an offense of "deeper malignity" than even rape.[16] Ever the pragmatists, however, the English relaxed their indignation under certain circumstances. The common law permitted a reduction of the crime of sodomy from felony to misdemeanor when the participants in the act had been at sea for greater than ninety days.

Modern attitudes have been quite different, of course. In the 1950s, the American Law Institute recommended decriminalizing homosexual acts, and over the next forty years, about thirty-three states rescinded their antisodomy laws. Then in 2003 the Supreme Court decided *Lawrence v. Texas*.[17] *Lawrence* held that states could not constitutionally prohibit private consensual sexual relations among gays, concluding that state sodomy statutes were invalid because they advanced no legitimate state interest. As with its onetime opposition to the use of contraception, a majority of Americans today appears no longer to hold the moral or narrowly religious views which once supported the proscription of consensual homosexual acts.

While the *Lawrence* case effectively takes the question of criminalizing homosexual acts off the table, it has quickly led to the question of legalizing same-sex marriage. Many, and perhaps a good number, of centrists may want to draw the line here, permitting gays to express their sexual preferences but not fully welcoming them into the community. But it's not clear why we should draw this line. Only if we can point to some concrete, generalized harm to society in permitting gay marriage is there even an argument. In fact, in considering the balance between the liberty interests of gays and the social costs of permitting gay marriage, the argument in favor of permitting gays to marry is considerably stronger than opponents seem to recognize.

Starting on the freedom side, the right to marry is a fundamental right linked, in law and in custom, with some of our most essential human needs and longings. It is the single most emblematic mark of attaining adulthood in our society; it is the gateway to parenthood, and it is through marriage and family that individuals are fully integrated into the community. "No other institution has the power to turn narcissism into partnership, lust into devotion, strangers into kin," as Jonathan Rauch puts it in *Gay Marriage*, a book one reviewer described as the "conservative case for gay marriage." Marriage, Rauch writes, gives us "stakes"; it gives us a home. "We are different people when we have a home, more stable, more productive, more mature, less self-obsessed, less impatient and less anxious. Marriage is the great domesticator." Because marriage and family tie us most directly to the wider community, to deny this right to gays and lesbians is to ensure that they will always remain not simply outside our community but, in a real sense, rootless. Married people generally live longer; they are healthier and more successful than single people. Because marriage ensures that "there is always someone out there for whom you're always first in line," it gives those who are married the emotional foundation to flourish in all of life's ventures.[18] The benefits of marriage, in sum, are linked to our deepest sources of identity and happiness and, at the same time, emanate outward to our social, economic, and political well-being.

What are the potential social harms of gay marriage? Conservatives sometimes become frenetic at the prospect of legalizing gay marriage, connecting it with the end of the American way as we know it. Maggie Gallagher, whose *Enemies of Eros* twenty years ago was an impassioned, persuasive plea in defense of the beauty and sanctity of marriage, wants nevertheless to deny the benefits of marriage to gays and lesbians. She recently wrote that permitting gays to marry "means losing the marriage debate. It means losing limited government. It means losing American civilization."[19] This goes too far—way too far. Conservatives are right to insist that the maintenance of our civilization depends upon our values and our character as a people. They are right to insist that civilization depends upon our intelligence, our productivity, and our goodness. But people's sexual orientation has nothing to do with their character, their honesty, their integrity, or their moral goodness as individuals. Permitting gays and lesbians to marry in no way imperils our essential values. If anything, it enhances them.

Conservatives sometimes claim that permitting same-sex marriage would fundamentally alter our idea of marriage, and certainly this is true—marriage would no longer be restricted to one man and one woman. But it is difficult to see what harm would follow from permitting this change. It is ironic to consider homosexuality a threat to the family when many gays and lesbians want to marry and start families and are prevented from doing so only by their current legal status. The notion that the U.S. family is threatened by permitting homosexuals to live as they wish is another version of the fallacy Hart found at the core of Devlin's views about social morality: the family is destroyed by permitting homosexual families only if we define "family" in exclusively heterosexual terms. In this case, the conservative wins the argument only by begging the question about what it means to be a family. More to the point, as Rauch points out, the surest way to lose the marriage debate or to devalue the currency of marriage is to "surround it with competitors which offer most of the benefits but few of the burdens, as is happening with domestic partnership programs."[20] If individuals, straight or gay, want the benefits of marriage, we should require that they be married.

Prostitution

Liberals have defended legalized prostitution for the past 150 years—long before anyone would have dreamed of legalized gay marriage—and yet today they probably remain more divided about prostitution than they are about gay marriage. Liberals are likely to feel that gays who want to marry arguably have a more legitimate claim than those who want to patronize prostitutes, especially since sex has become more available with the advent of the sexual revolution. As one commentator has observed, whereas medieval prostitutes offered their customers normal sex, contemporary prostitutes specialize in kinky sex precisely because there is a smaller market for the normal variety.[21] More than half a million women work as prostitutes in the United States today, while (according to one estimate) as many as 75 percent of men have patronized a prostitute at least once in their lifetime.[22] Still, it is probably true that most customers, especially those who are married or involved in long-term relationships, do not act out of a sense of real sexual need but are looking for the unusual, the kinky, or the unbounded.[23]

It is probably fair to conclude that considerations of human need and the vindication of one's essential self-identity do not provide the same level of support for liberalization here as they do with homosexual marriage. One is not born a prostitute or a customer as some are born gay. Neither prostitutes nor their customers identify with their roles in the same way that gay persons inevitably see themselves as gay. Prohibiting prostitution does not involve a basic denial of anyone's self-identity nor does it undermine anyone's sense of self-respect. Nor does prohibition involve a denial of other political rights connected to the activity. At points in our history, atheists could not sit on juries and Communists could not join associations for advancing their cause. Prohibiting prostitution is not connected to a denial of these other civil rights. Yet the fact that prostitution is an economic activity means that prohibiting it will affect the economic interests of prostitutes. Obviously, prostitution is not the only way to make a living, but for many prostitutes it is the most lucrative way. As Priscilla Alexander, a co-organizer of a prostitutes' rights organization, puts it, the "specific reasons that prostitutes have given for choosing their work . . . have included money, excitement, independence and flexibility, in roughly that order."[24] The economic dimension of the activity means that, from the freedom side of the equation, prostitutes probably have a much stronger claim to engage in the activity than do their customers.[25]

What about the harms side of the equation? We should begin by noting that, Devlin notwithstanding, prostitution does not generate the feelings of "intolerance, indignation and disgust" that he believed must be vindicated in order to preserve the social bond. One Justice Department survey ranked people's perception of the level of seriousness of 204 crimes, ranging from first-degree murder to school truancy. Those surveyed ranked prostitution 174th on the list.[26] Most Americans today are troubled less by a feeling that prostitution is intrinsically immoral than by its secondary effects—its link to the spread of STDs or to street crime.

Yet feminists and conservatives have teamed up to argue that many women are coerced into prostitution, that they are subject to a much higher level of violence once in the profession, and that possibly as many as half of all women who become prostitutes were victims of childhood sexual abuse. One feminist describes the "culturally supported tactics of power and control which support the recruitment or coercion of women and children into prostitution." This imposing array of social "tactics" includes "child sexual abuse, rape, battery, educational deprivation, job discrimination, poverty, racism, classism, sexism, heterosexism and unequal enforcement of the law."[27]

Add to this argument the feminist's claim that prostitution tends to commodify women as sexual objects. Margaret Radin warns that if sex were "openly commodified,"

> new terms would emerge for particular gradations of sexual market value. New discussion would be heard of particular abilities or qualities in terms of their market value. With this change in discourse, when it becomes pervasive enough, would come a change in everyone's experience, because experience is discourse-dependent. . . . It might make the idea of nonmonetized sharing impossible; . . . we do not wish to unleash market forces onto the shaping of our discourse regarding sexuality.[28]

Conservatives and, again, feminists claim still another generalized social harm: acceptance of prostitution represents a threat to orthodox sexuality and to the family. In this last regard, George Gilder tied these threatened social harms, applicable to prostitution and more generally to the sexual revolution, to the familiar conservative theme of social decay: "In a world where women do not say no, the man is not forced to settle down and make serious choices. His sex drive—the most powerful impulse in his life—is never used to make him part of civilization as the supporter of a family. . . . His sex drive only demands conquest, driving him from body to body in an unsettling hunt for variety and excitement in which much of the thrill is in the chase itself." Ultimately, Gilder concludes, "when too many men are subverted, the society itself is jeopardized."[29] Feminists Linda Hirshman and Jane Larson predict largely the same thing, though they are concerned less about society at large than about the interests of women. Prostitution "strengthens the bargaining position" of the prostitute, but this "comes at the expense of the collective bargaining power of women in dealing with men." In contrast to Posner's claim that prostitutes today fill a market niche for kinky sex, they suggest that prostitutes "damage the interests of nonprostitutes, bidding down the price of heterosexual access." Prostitution represents "a standing offer to violate the marriage contract of sexual fidelity and thus particularly injures the interests of wives. Where prostitution is curtailed, wives are better situated to force their husbands to bargain with them for sexual access."[30] Notwithstanding these concerns, Hirshman and Larson recommend that prostitution be decriminalized.

What are we to conclude about these kinds of arguments? First, some of these claims, such as that most prostitutes were coerced into the profession, appear overblown and understate the obvious economic and existential motives for engaging in prostitution.[31] Prostitutes themselves cite the allure of dramatically increased earning capacity as the most important reason for becoming prostitutes.[32] Other claims, including occupationally related violence, can be addressed more readily by regulating prostitution than by consigning it to the black market. The claims from commodification of sex and the breakdown of the family envision harms that are more diffused and speculative. Centrists are receptive to looking at these kinds of arguments about generalized social harms but may be skeptical that such predictions are realistic in this instance. Whatever effects prostitution may have on our sexual attitudes or on family structure, they are likely overshadowed by a host of more pervasive social influences, from the media to the Internet, that already exist. The argument from commodification in particular may well reverse the cause-and-effect relationship between prostitution and commodification: men's tendency to objectify women sexually may be better understood as a cause, rather than an effect, of prostitution. Nevertheless, these issues are complex and they are, of course, issues where differences of opinion are often reasonable.

Perhaps the best overall conclusion that we can draw about legalizing prostitution is that, on the liberty side of the equation, the customers' interests do not rise to the level of those of gays in the gay marriage debate. Yet the prostitutes' interest deserves greater weight, as it involves a matter of livelihood or, at least, a matter of what he or she may regard as the most lucrative livelihood. This alone is not decisive, of course—drug dealers can make the same argument. Yet it indicates that while prostitutes do not identify with their roles in the same way that gay persons identify with being gay, there is an economic dimension to their claims that cannot be overlooked. On the harms side, the case is equivocal at best. In the end, however, the argument for legalizing prostitution is strongest when cast not in libertarian terms, as the liberty of individuals to do with their body what they wish, but in terms of society's ability to ameliorate the harms associated with it. This has been the approach of many other Western countries. In Great Britain, public solicitation is illegal, but prostitution has been decriminalized; most prostitutes today advertise through the Internet or through agents. Since 1972, Canada has followed a similar model, permitting prostitution but banning public pandering. Most Australian states have decriminalized prostitution since the 1970s. Sweden, Japan, and various other developed countries have also followed the regulatory model and decriminalized prostitution.[33] In sum, the regulatory model seems the most appropriate approach to prostitution.

The Drug Legalization Debate

More than perhaps any other issue, the drug legalization debate has fomented a spectacular division *within*, rather than *between*, the political Right and the political Left. On the Right, social conservatives are adamantly opposed to drug use and to any discussion of legalization. When former drug czar William Bennett was asked whether we should consider beheading drug offenders he responded, "Morally, I don't have any problem with it."[34] Yet right-wing libertarians and neoclassical economists favor legalizing all drugs, arguing that legalization will dramatically lower the price of drugs, reduce drug-related crimes, and save us the resources now spent on the war on drugs, including the costs of incarcerating hundreds of thousands of people a year in the U.S. prison system.[35] On the Left, liberals are divided between those left libertarians who believe that drugs should be legalized and most other liberals, who favor, for a number of humanitarian and paternalistic reasons, a system which we might call therapeutic criminalization—a hybrid approach that is part criminalization, part mental health model.[36]

On the freedom side of the balance, advocates of drug decriminalization argue that people may do with their lives and their bodies as they wish, and that the choice to use drugs can be as autonomous as other life choices. Citing a generalized right to "self-ownership," libertarian David Boaz argues that "if there are any limits to the state's power over individuals, surely the state should not be permitted to regulate what we put into our own bodies." He claims that the "right of self-ownership certainly implies the right to decide for ourselves what food, drink or drugs" we will ingest.[37] Progressive liberal David A. J. Richards prefers an "autonomy-based concept of treating persons as equals." Richards has argued that the life scheme of drug users is, from their own subjective viewpoint, fully rational and autonomous. He maintains that "the psychological centrality of drug use for many young addicts in the United States may, from the perspective of their own circumstances, not unreasonably organize their lives and ends." Criticizing drug users for making drugs the central part of their lives "can bear no more just normative weight than the criticism of love or wealth as addictions."[38] A life of drug use is, presumably, as valid a lifestyle choice as a life devoted to the pursuit of financial independence, wisdom, or love.

The problem with Richards's view of the human condition, however, is that it makes every choice as valid as every other choice. In fact, if the life of the hardened drug addict is fully autonomous, it is difficult to know what *wouldn't* be. Richards criticizes Immanuel Kant, who made the concept of autonomy central to his theory of ethics, for comparing drug use to slavery and for insisting that addiction represents an alienation of our capacity for autonomy. Richards insists that Kant's view of moral personality was "unimaginative" while his condemnation of drug use was "morally perverse," because "even psychological devotion to drugs may express not a physiological bondage, but critical interests of the person."[39]

Yet the right to use drugs is hardly as important a freedom as the right to freedom of expression or religious liberty, the right to choose a profession or the right to marry. If we were to ask a libertarian to prioritize these liberties, I do not believe that we would find many who would relinquish freedom of speech or the right to a fair trial in order to preserve a right to use drugs. Nor is the *ex ante* desire to use drugs the product of a pressing physiological need or the authentic expression of one's deepest identity. The point is, again, that not all freedom claims are created equal. Of course, this doesn't mean that all drug use must be prohibited either. Before we can say anything about this, we have to take a look at the social costs of drug use and addiction, as well as the costs of interdiction.

One of the most popular arguments marshaled by those who favor drug legalization is that alcohol exacts a far greater social toll than drug use. The National Highway Traffic Safety Administration estimates that in the last quarter of the twentieth century, more than 110,000 Americans died as a result of alcohol use.[40] Advocates of drug legalization point out that drug-related deaths are far fewer and that alcohol-related crimes, including homicide, rape, and assault, are many times the rate of crimes resulting from illegal drug use. From this they draw the flawed conclusion that alcohol is the problem, not drugs. What they overlook is the obvious fact that drug-related violence and accidents are considerably lower than alcohol-related violence and accidents precisely because alcohol is readily available while drugs are not. More people use alcohol, and use it much more frequently, than use illegal drugs because drugs are considerably more difficult to obtain. Advocates who draw the comparison between illegal drugs and alcohol ought to draw the conclusion not that drugs should be legalized, but that alcohol should be further restricted. As longtime opponent of drug legalization James Inciardi has argued, "To assume that the legalization of drugs would maintain the current, relatively low levels of drug use when there are high rates of both alcohol and tobacco use seems rather naive." In fact, if drugs were legalized and were commercially marketed, we should expect levels of use to increase as the result of "the ability of the entrepreneurial market system to create, expand and maintain high levels of demand."[41]

If drugs were legalized, the best guess is that some drug-related crimes (those motivated by the need for money to buy drugs) would fall dramatically, a reflection of the lower cost of drugs. What we should expect to increase are the kinds of social costs that we now find with alcohol: crimes caused by offenders who are under the influence, fatalities and injuries from traffic accidents, and general public health costs as we attempted to deal with the effects of addiction. Legalizing all drugs would be a sure way to reduce many of the social costs on the crime side while dramatically increasing the public health costs. Generalized drug legalization, in sum, is a dangerous prescription for the health and well-being of our society.

Yet it obviously doesn't follow that all drugs are equally dangerous. Just as libertarians go too far in defense of a generalized right to use drugs, so conservatives lump all drugs together equally in their condemnation of their effects. While heroin, cocaine, crack, and methamphetamine, among others, are highly dangerous drugs and should remain illegal, nothing stands in the way of adopting a more benign approach to marijuana, for example. Many who oppose a more lenient approach to marijuana today do so in part because marijuana use was historically linked to countercultural attitudes of the 1960s and 1970s, to the antiwar movement, and to a variety of other behaviors conservatives oppose. It didn't help that marijuana use became popular at the same time that other, more dangerous drugs became widely available, so that marijuana came to be seen as a gateway drug to the others.

Conservative antipathy to marijuana is thus in part the product of a historical anomaly. Most of us who grew up in the 1970s and 1980s, including an increasing number of judges and state and federal legislators, have smoked marijuana and understand that the most dangerous effects of occasional use are akin to those of heavy cigarette smoking.[42] The current hysteria surrounding marijuana is plainly overblown, a feature of the wider consequences of the war on drugs. Along these lines, most centrists are likely to find wanting recent federal efforts to prohibit the medical use of marijuana when prescribed by a physician. The position previously taken by the Bush administration in this regard appears an unwarranted and puritanical intrusion into the patient-physician relationship and also appears to ignore a good deal of evidence that marijuana can be genuinely helpful in relieving the symptoms of cancer, AIDS, and other serious medical conditions.

ON MANY OF THESE questions of legislating morality, centrists may disagree, as others do, concerning where some of the lines should be drawn. We may draw differing conclusions on some of the particulars. But we reject both the generalized view of liberals who believe that the state has no business in setting broad parameters to human behavior and the claims of conservatives who want to use the state to eliminate what they take to be every form of human vice.

Chapter 9
A Centrist Approach to Abortion

Abortion in Social and Historical Context

No other subject has quite so divided liberals and conservatives as abortion. This is due, in no small measure, to the political atmosphere that has followed the Supreme Court's decision in *Roe v. Wade* and to its obvious connection to women's rights, on one hand, and to views of others concerning the sanctity of human life, on the other. The U.S. public is deeply divided about abortion. A recent Gallup poll reported that 20 percent of Americans thought abortion should be illegal under all circumstances while 24 percent thought it should be available under all circumstances. The great majority, 55 percent, felt that abortion should be available under certain conditions, but should not be generally available.[1] Thus, 75 percent of all those polled rejected the extreme pro-choice position even as 79 percent rejected the staunch pro-life position in favor of one in which abortion is sometimes available.[2]

It is estimated that roughly 1.3 million abortions are performed in the United States each year.[3] Recent census data indicate that there are 319 abortions for every 1,000 live births in the United States. Put differently, nearly one in four pregnancies (excluding those that end in miscarriage) are intentionally terminated. Of all abortions, roughly 90 percent are performed before the thirteenth week of gestation, about the time when quickening (the point when the mother first detects fetal movement) takes place. The remaining 10 percent take place after quickening, with a tiny number—probably no more than 1 percent of all abortions—taking place at or after viability.[4]

Liberals and conservatives today each harbor their own peculiar misconceptions about the regulation of abortion historically. Conservatives sometimes suggest that permissive attitudes to abortion are the aberrant result of sexual liberation since the 1960s. They seem to assume that a more restrictive abortion policy was the original U.S. policy. Yet quite the contrary is true. The colonists followed the permissive English common law rule that permitted abortion up until the time of quickening. (If this rule were followed today, roughly 90 percent of all abortions would be legal.) The legal regime began to trend toward the more conservative rule only in the 1840s, when Massachusetts and Virginia passed statutes making any abortion a misdemeanor unless it resulted in the death of the mother, in which case it became a felony. By the 1880s, most other states had followed suit. While a variety of social factors contributed to the legal change, including a resurgent evangelical movement after the Civil War, the first statutes were passed in response to the deaths of women who had sought (then legal) abortions.[5]

Liberals have a similar misconception, though they draw the opposite conclusion. Since they assume that abortion was illegal throughout American history, they believe that women's rights can be protected only by constitutionalizing the right to an abortion. The logic seems to be: either protect the right absolutely under the Constitution or be prepared to give it up altogether. Yet, in 1967, a trend toward liberalization of abortion laws began, when Colorado adopted a proposal to permit abortion in cases when the physical or mental health of the mother was threatened by the continued pregnancy, when the fetus would be born with a severe physical or mental defect, or if the pregnancy had resulted from rape or incest. While these may sound like limited exceptions, the mental health exception, in particular, could be quite broadly defined (as we will see shortly). By 1972, thirteen states had similar statutes and four other states (New York, Hawaii, Washington, and Alaska) had completely decriminalized abortion. A year later, when *Roe* was decided, all but five states had bills to liberalize abortion pending in their state legislatures.[6] In all likelihood, the trend toward liberalization would have continued had *Roe* not been decided, just as laws concerning divorce, homosexuality, and the death penalty have been liberalized since the 1970s.

In fact, it is a fair bet that much of the politicization that has occurred in the wake of *Roe v. Wade* is precisely the result of the frustration felt by conservatives, and the equally strong counterreaction of feminists and liberals, generated by the winner-take-all effect of constitutionalizing abortion. As long as abortion remained a matter to be decided on a state-by-state basis, conservatives could be content with the limited victories afforded by having some influence in some states, just as liberals could be satisfied to the extent that they could influence others—particularly since the trend would likely have continued in their direction. Nor could conservatives complain that the will of the majority was being thwarted. Since *Roe*, however, the positions of liberals and conservatives have taken on an increasingly categorical nature: either the pre-embryo must be absolutely protected from the moment of conception, as many conservatives maintain, or we must recognize an absolute right of women to have an abortion virtually until natural childbirth, as many liberals and feminists hold.

I propose an intermediate approach to the standard liberal and conservative positions that preserves intact much of what liberals want to preserve in a woman's right to choose while at the same recognizing that the fetus does have an interest worthy of protection during the latter phases of pregnancy. Moreover, the line I will draw is, I believe, more principled than those adopted by most liberals and conservatives today: the proper starting point in discussions of abortion should be the consideration of the fetus's capacity for sentience—its ability to feel pain and to respond in a conscious manner to external stimuli. This is not the only consideration, of course, but the capacity of the fetus to feel pain at a certain point during pregnancy should give pro-choice proponents some pause about advocating abortions after this point. And, before this point, conservatives should find it more difficult to justify their own position.

Two Central Issues

Many of the arguments made on both sides are of a more utilitarian nature: they concern the consequences of abortion policy generally. One of the more important arguments frequently made by those favoring the pro-choice position is that criminalizing abortion means that a certain percentage of women who are forced to obtain illegal abortions will die or be seriously injured in back-room procedures.[7] More controversially, two economists have recently suggested that the availability of abortion since the 1970s has resulted in a reduction in the crime rate since the 1990s. The authors speculate that a decline in the number of unwanted babies translates into a decrease of those most likely to commit crime—those raised by mothers who did not want them.[8] Conservatives have sometimes made exactly the opposite argument, insisting that a regime of legalized abortion has fostered a cultural ethos of desensitization to the value of human life.

I focus here not on such utilitarian arguments but on the moral or philosophical center of the abortion controversy. When lawyers, theologians, and moral philosophers discuss the abortion issue, it is customary for them to approach the problem from the standpoint of two issues: First, should (or at what point should) the fetus be considered a person, a being worthy of moral consideration and, perhaps, legal protection? Second, whether or not the fetus is a person, should (or up to what point should) women have a right to an abortion?

The answer one gives to the first question does not necessarily determine one's answer to the second. Some conservatives believe that the fetus is a person from conception and from this conclude that there is no right to abortion, while liberals frequently claim that the fetus is not a person and automatically conclude that the right to abortion is thereby established. Neither conclusion necessarily follows. There have been ingenious arguments that plausibly establish that a woman has a right to an abortion even if we assume that the fetus is a person from conception onward.[9] And it is equally arguable that the fetus should receive some level of legal protection even if it does not yet qualify as a person, because it is a potential human being.

The Standard Conservative Position

What I will call the standard conservative argument depends upon taking a hard line on the first of these two questions and finding it dispositive of the second. The standard conservative position is based on a philosophical premise that holds that the fetus should be protected as a person from the point of conception. This argument is sometimes made on theological grounds, on the assumption that conception is when ensoulment occurs.[10] On these grounds, many evangelicals and Christian fundamentalists, in particular, have adopted the view that abortion should be prohibited from conception on, barring endangerment of the life of the mother. Pat Robertson, for example, analogizes abortion at any time to murder: "We hold these truths to be self-evident that God has endowed us all with life, liberty and the pursuit of happiness, that we have life, the right to life. Life has become more and more cheap in the society we live in. But God says you shall not murder. In my opinion, abortion is murder. Once you begin to understand that the taking of an innocent life is murder, then that raises the bar from a 'constitutional right' to something that needs to be stopped."[11]

A second and more recent position holds that conception is morally significant because it is the point when a potential person with a unique and complete genetic identity is created. This latter, more sophisticated approach—which avoids metaphysical questions about the nature of the soul—has been the preferred argument of conservatives in recent years. John T. Noonan has argued, for example, that even if one does not accept the idea of ensoulment, the "positive argument for conception as the decisive moment of humanization is that, at conception, the fetus has received the complete genetic code. It is this genetic information which determines his characteristics, which is the biological carrier of the possibility for human wisdom, which makes him a self-evolving being."[12] Similarly, Sir William Liley, who developed the ultrasound technique, puts it this way: "From the moment a baby is conceived, it bears the indelible stamp of a separate distinct personality, an individual different from all other individuals."[13] Francis J. Beckwith has recently defended a slightly different version of this idea, arguing on philosophical grounds for a "substance" view of the person. The human organism, he maintains, is ontologically prior to its various properties and capacities—for example, its capacity for rationality or sentience or physical independence—which develop, change, and decay over time. "A human being is intrinsically valuable because of the sort of thing it is and the human being remains that sort of thing as long as it exists," Beckwith argues.[14]

It is understandable that anyone who believes that the soul enters the embryo at conception might adopt the standard conservative position in principle. Yet it is difficult to imagine even the staunchest advocates of embryonic rights accepting all the logical implications of their view of the embryo: If an embryo at two weeks' gestation is legally and morally equivalent to a person, then should abortion be prosecuted as first-degree murder? The logic of the standard conservative position suggests that it should. What about the use of spare embryos? Spare embryos generated for reproductive purposes could not be created at all unless we observed a strict requirement that these be rescued by gestating and bringing each one to term as a live human being. Moreover, not only could we not use these spare embryos for research purposes, as opponents of embryonic research would have it, but their destruction in the course of research would, again, be tantamount to murder. For the same reasons, the negligent but otherwise legal acts of women which result in miscarriage would have to be subject to the laws that protect living human beings from the negligent acts of third parties. A woman who causes her own miscarriage by drug or alcohol use, or for that matter by excessive exercise, would have to be subject to prosecution for manslaughter or negligent homicide. A third party who negligently causes the loss of the fetus in an automobile accident, for example, would also be prosecuted under a principle that treated the fetus as a person from conception on. Most defenders of the extreme conservative position balk at these implications, and for good reason. They intuitively understand that, as precious as an embryo is in its potentiality, it is not only physically and psychologically but also morally distinct from a living human being.

The argument from potentiality has other well-known difficulties as well. Why, for example, does the potentiality argument not prohibit contraception, which would prevent potential beings from being conceived? Indeed, what distinguishes this position on contraception, which orthodox Roman Catholics accept, from the still more extreme position that we all have a procreative duty to bring as many potential lives into existence as possible? The argument from potentiality has dizzying implications when taken to its logical extreme. Yet even if we grant Judge Noonan's claim that conception is the relevant point for thinking about potentiality, since it is only then that we find a particular individual being with an intact and complete genetic code, there is good reason for holding that potentiality is not enough to qualify an embryo as a person, morally and legally.[15]

An eight- or sixteen-cell blastocyst may be a complete genetic package, but it bears none of the physiological or psychological characteristics of a living person. Because the requisite neural-physiological system is not yet in place, zygotes and early embryos certainly do not have the subjective capacity to experience self-consciousness, or even the degree of sentience necessary to experience rudimentary pain sensations. It is precisely the capacity to be able to experience subjective conscious states that strikes many as the dispositive criterion for what it means to be worthy of at least a certain degree of moral regard and legal protection.

Perhaps these remarks will win over few on the pro-life side, particularly if they believe that the human soul enters the zygote at conception. For the rest of us, however, potentiality is a value, but it is not an absolute value. If it were, then we would have to take seriously the claims of all those potential people who are never born but who would be if we enjoined contraception. For the rest of us, human life is precious, but it becomes precious by *developing* into what is recognizably a human being. Before this point—and to some extent, even after this point (as even most conservatives will agree in contemplating abortion when the mother's life is endangered)—potentiality is something to be weighed against other competing interests.

The Standard Liberal Position

At the other liberal extreme, Michael Tooley has argued that to be recognized as a person a being must possess such characteristics as self-consciousness, along with "the capacity to envisage a future for itself" and the capacity to "have a concept of a continuing subject of experiences and other mental states." In sum, one must be (or have been) self-conscious and rational, with a high degree of conceptual capacity.[16] To be human, Tooley insists, is to be capable of rational self-consciousness. This has the unsettling if obvious implication that even the newborn baby—and perhaps a child one or two years old—does not have a moral claim to protection. Peter Singer has made similar suggestions, arguing that the unborn and, for that matter, the seriously mentally handicapped are not capable of experiencing forms of reflective consciousness similar to those of adults or even of animals. Thus, Singer argues that animals are more deserving of protection than are the unborn.[17] If Tooley's and Singer's views follow from the extreme liberal position, then that position will find few supporters beyond the lunatic fringe today.

Of course, most liberals today do not take such views. Rather, they adopt a pragmatic modus vivendi of their own. They will assert that, whatever one may think of the morality of abortion, every woman has a right to an abortion throughout pregnancy and up to the moment of delivery. The right may be predicated on the more general right of bodily integrity, analogous to her right to be free from any physical invasion. Or it may be conceived in moral rather than physical terms, as a right to live autonomously, to be able to make essential decisions about one's life. Before birth, the fetus is still part of the mother, the argument runs, and she may decide how to proceed. Only when the fetus is born does it acquire a right to life. Thus, the point at which the fetus should be legally protected and morally regarded is not conception, quickening, or viability, but birth. I will call this the standard liberal position on abortion.

The standard liberal defense of an unfettered right to an abortion gives a kind of absolute preference to the woman's right to decide over the fetus's right to life. It does so even though, in other contexts, we do not recognize an unlimited right of bodily integrity. The standard liberal position gives little or no weight to the potentiality of the fetus or to fetal sentience. It valorizes the claims of women as an oppressed minority while ruling out of court the possibility that the fetus represents the archetypal example of the "discrete and insular minority" that, in virtue of its physical differences from the rest of us, has no say in the political process. In fact, a small number of pro-life feminists have criticized the position taken by most feminists on the abortion issue. As Mary Meehan wrote in *The Progressive* twenty-five years ago:

> If much of the leadership of the pro-life movement is right-wing, that is due to the default of the Left. We . . . who marched against the War and now march against abortion would like to see leaders of the Left speaking out on behalf of the unborn. . . . We are dismayed by their inconsistency and we are not impressed by arguments that we should work and vote for them because they are good on such issues as food stamps and medical care. . . . The traditional mark of the Left has been its protection of the underdog, the weak and the poor; . . . abortion is a civil rights issue.[18]

Most who define themselves as liberals today do not accept Meehan's view. They may concede that the fetus has some value, and they may even suggest that they are troubled by the prevalence of abortion. But they will insist that the right to an abortion must remain inviolate as long as the fetus is physically within the body of the mother. But why are liberals and feminists afraid to concede anything to the interests of the developing fetus? One reason that suggests itself is that they are afraid of the *political* consequences of making this concession. Once one concedes that the fetus has an interest in being born or that the state has an interest in protecting potential life, the fear seems to be, there will be no logical stopping point. We will be on a slippery slope back to the days before *Roe*, when abortion was illegal everywhere.

This is the most understandable reason for refusing to make the concession, but it is, I believe, misplaced today. It is misplaced because a large majority of the U.S. public want to see abortion available either generally or under some circumstances. The U.S. public does not support the earlier restrictive approach to abortion. There is plenty of room at the political center for a sound and principled compromise.

Some on the left, of course, are not interested in compromise. Abortion has been so politicized that they either cannot conceive that the democratic process will faithfully track mainstream sentiments or they do not care—they want to see their position protected even if a majority cannot go the whole way with the standard liberal view. It is here that rhetoric sometimes fills the gap between logic and aspiration. Some of the claims of those favoring an unlimited right to choose rely upon strained analogies and questionable assumptions. One tack taken by some feminists is to justify an absolute right to abortion as a form of self-defense. Ellen Willis has argued, for example:

> Most people would agree . . . that killing in defense of one's life or safety is not murder. And most would accept a concept of self-defense that includes a right to fight a defensive war or revolution in behalf of one's independence or freedom from oppression. . . . The point is that . . . it makes no sense to discuss whether abortion is murder without considering why women have abortions. . . . Under these conditions [of social inequality] . . . the unwillingly pregnant woman faces a terrifying loss of control over her fate. . . . However gratifying pregnancy may be to a woman who desires it, for the unwilling it is literally an invasion. . . . Clearly, abortion is by normal standards, an act of self-defense.[19]

The metaphor of self-defense is seriously strained, however. It is strained not only because the woman has usually had a willing role in the sexual activity that has resulted in pregnancy (distinguishing her from the unwitting victim of an attack) but also, more importantly, because the fetus is not her assailant. The fetus's intentions are not wrongful nor does pregnancy normally threaten the life of the mother. When it does, even most conservatives agree that abortion should be available.

Lawrence Tribe and Andrew Koppelman have drawn a different analogy—one that compares laws prohibiting abortion to slavery. Tribe writes:

> A woman forced by law to submit to the anxiety of carrying, delivering and nurturing a child she does not wish to have is entitled to believe that more than a play on words links her forced labor to involuntary servitude. To give society—especially a male dominated society—the power to sentence women to childbearing against their will is to delegate to some a sweeping and un-accountable authority over the lives of others. . . . Even a woman who is not pregnant is inevitably affected by her knowledge of the power relationships thereby created.[20]

Tribe and Koppelman each suggest that we consider deploying the Thirteenth Amendment, passed in 1865 at the end of the Civil War to prohibit involuntary servitude in the United States, to constitutionalize the right to abortion.[21] Like the allusion to self-defense, the analogy to slavery may have rhetorical appeal for those who already accept Tribe's position, but to the rest of us it is simply a badly strained analogy. No one has "given society a right to sentence women to childbearing." No one can require a woman to become pregnant, and no one can require a woman to raise the child she bears. It is one thing to want to protect women's reproductive autonomy, as liberals do. It is quite another to suggest that anyone who takes a position that falls short of endorsing an unlimited right to an abortion at any time, and for any reason, up until the point of birth is a proponent of reproductive slavery. Analogizing pregnancy to slavery simply serves to inflate the rhetoric surrounding abortion, even as it seriously minimizes the plight of those who actually endured slavery.

We could multiply these examples but the point here will be clear: the winner-take-all effect of constitutionalizing abortion motivates each side to adopt extreme and unnuanced positions, and to bolster them with extremist rhetoric, false analogies, and, all too sadly, violence or the threat of violence.

The Constitutionalization
of the Standard Liberal Position

Roe v. Wade essentially constitutionalized the standard liberal position on abortion in a number of ways. The Court in *Roe* held, first, that a fetus is not a person within the meaning of any constitutional provision until it has been born.[22] Thus, birth represents the line between not having and having *constitutional* protection. This does not mean that states may not extend some protection to the fetus pursuant to their general police power, however; just as states can protect animals from cruelty, though they are not legally recognized as persons, the Court in *Roe* recognized the state's interest in protecting potential human life. Yet the state can pursue this interest only as long as this does not conflict with the mother's constitutional right to privacy. It is here that the Court got into the problem of balancing the interests of the state in protecting the unborn against the right of a woman to have an abortion. The balance the Court struck in *Roe* made viability the crucial line. The state's interest in protecting the fetus before viability is not sufficiently "compelling" to outweigh the woman's right of privacy. After viability, the balance shifts and the interests of the state in protecting the fetus become compelling. Theoretically, then, *Roe* seemed to say that the state may generally prohibit abortion after viability.

If the Court had stopped here, the ruling in *Roe* would have fallen short of the standard liberal position to the extent it permitted states to prohibit abortion during the last trimester of pregnancy, the period between viability and birth. Yet the Court did not stop here. It institutionalized the standard liberal position in a second and even more significant way. In *Roe* and a companion case, the Court held that even after viability, states may not proscribe abortion when a mother's "life or health" is in danger.[23] This life or health exception to the postviability rule, however, turns out to be the exception that swallows the rule.

Doe v. Bolton, a companion case decided with *Roe*, considered the meaning of the life or health exception. The more broadly we define "health," in particular, the less latitude there is for the state to protect the fetus even after viability. Could a woman obtain a postviability abortion because her *mental* health was in jeopardy— if, for example, she claimed that she would become depressed if she went through with the pregnancy? *Doe v. Bolton* answered yes.[24] In *Doe*, the Court ruled that it was interpreting the health exception in a broad way, to include not only physical but also "emotional, psychological and familial" factors. The plaintiff in *Doe*, for example, had argued that it would be "physically and emotionally damaging" for her "to bring the child into her poor, fatherless family."[25] Of course, if this is enough to satisfy the health exception, then virtually any claim is. *Doe* effectively extended the right to an abortion after viability to any single woman who could make the claim that her status as an unmarried woman makes her psychologically vulnerable. Moreover, since it is left to the doctor and patient to decide whether other conditions ought to fall within the exception, it is hard to imagine any condition or claim that could not be covered by the health exception.

The state's power to regulate abortion postviability thus proved to be a paper tiger. Any woman who, late in pregnancy, can find a doctor to confirm her claim that carrying the fetus to term will cause her any degree of emotional distress or that it will be damaging to her health in a familial way, whatever this might mean, has an absolute constitutional right to abortion up to the point of birth. Even Judith Jarvis Thomson, who wrote what is still today regarded as the definitive article defending a woman's right to an abortion, would not go this far:

> There may well be cases where carrying the child to term involves only Minimally Decent Samaritanism of the mother, and this is a standard we must not fall below. . . . [This] supports our sense that in other cases resort to abortion is even positively indecent. It would be indecent in a woman to request an abortion, and indecent in a doctor to perform it, if she is in her seventh month, and wants the abortion just to avoid the nuisance of postponing a trip abroad.[26]

While there is obviously a difference between desiring to take a vacation and claiming that one will be harmed in some emotional or familial way, how difficult is it for anyone with the former motive to claim the latter? While no one wants to second-guess the motives of a woman who is seeking a late-term abortion, the effect of the Court's reasoning leaves us only the choice between doing exactly this or admitting that there is no practical limit to the right to have an abortion up until the time of delivery.[27]

The constitutionalization of the standard liberal view was apparently solidified, at least in the short term, in 2000 with the Supreme Court's decision in *Stenberg v. Carhart*.[28] The Court in *Stenberg* decided that a state law that prohibited late-term abortions—what opponents of abortion call "partial-birth abortion"[29]—was unconstitutional because it did not include an exception for the health of the mother.

The decision also made clear that the woman and her doctor alone decide whether her condition qualifies under the health exception. This meant that states could place no pragmatic limit on the life or health exception, so abortion was protected as a constitutional right all the way up to birth. Yet in 2003, Congress responded to *Stenberg* by passing the Partial Birth Abortion Act, which makes it a crime to perform a late-term abortion using a proscribed form of the procedure unless a woman's life is in jeopardy.[30] Congress made factual findings that a "moral, medical and ethical consensus exists that the practice of performing a partial-birth abortion . . . is a gruesome and inhumane procedure that is never medically necessary and should be prohibited." It further determined that there was substantial medical disagreement about whether the procedure was ever necessary to preserve the health of the woman (since other abortion procedures are available).

The federal act was, in turn, challenged and in 2007 the Supreme Court narrowly upheld it (in a 5–4 decision) in *Gonzales v. Carhart*.[31] Despite the outcry by liberal critics of the decision, *Gonzales* only marginally cuts back on the constitutionalization of the standard liberal position. For one thing, the fetus remains a nonperson, constitutionally, until it is born. Further, even with respect to the limited number of late-term intact D&E abortions in which a mother's life is not endangered—the small class of cases reached by the Partial Birth Abortion Act—other procedures remain available to women seeking abortion at this late date. Justice Ginsburg admitted as much in dissent, observing that the act is unlikely to save even one life. Finally, while the Supreme Court upheld the Partial Birth Abortion Act "on its face," meaning that the act was not unconstitutional across the board, it left open challenges on a case-by-case basis where a woman could show that her health (but not her life) was seriously endangered by having to resort to another late-term procedure.

In sum, both liberals and conservatives have overestimated the significance of the decision. *Gonzales v. Carhart* is at best only a limited and symbolic victory for conservatives, and one that leaves intact the constitutionalization of the standard liberal position.

What's Wrong with the Standard Liberal Position?

The standard liberal position enshrined in *Roe* gives no weight to three considerations that many, including the large majority of Americans who believe that *Roe* goes too far, find significant. It ignores, first, the interests of society in protecting potential life. In particular, the standard liberal position pays only lip service to the interests of the fetus as a developing being who, particularly in the latter phases of pregnancy, is in no important way physically distinguishable from a live baby. Second, the standard liberal position pays little heed to the possibility that, at a certain point in pregnancy, the fetus develops the capacity for sentience or consciousness. It gives no weight to the possibility that the fetus feels pain and experiences the process of abortion in the latter phases of pregnancy for what it is: an excruciating way to die. Third, the standard liberal position does not take seriously enough society's collective interest in ensuring, in a moral and symbolic way, the value of life and a cultural ethos of caring and compassion that ought to be extended to the fetus as a developing human being.

In sum, the standard liberal position assigns an absolute value to the interests of privacy and reproductive autonomy—interests which, to be sure, are themselves worthy of protection—in a way that trumps every potential countervailing interest. People may reasonably disagree about how much weight these respective interests may be given. We may also draw different conclusions about the nature of fetal existence and at what point the fetus is capable of subjective experience (though a consensus is developing on this). But by relying on the idea of reproductive autonomy as a right that deserves absolute protection and by categorically denying that the fetus has any similar right, the standard liberal position refuses to give these other interests any weight. Yet it does so at a time when liberals themselves frequently question the notion of a right as a kind of absolute trump on all other countervailing interests, as with the modern liberal attack on absolute property and economic rights.

Most nonlibertarian liberals concede that individuals do not have an *absolute* right to do anything they wish with their own bodies. They agree that we don't have a right to shoot heroin or to contract away our sexual services or to sell a kidney to the highest bidder. Not only are these activities not protected by a right to privacy, but also they are illegal in most places.

No court has successfully elaborated a principle that can explain why abortion is absolutely protected as part of a right of bodily autonomy while prostitution is not, or why drugs prescribed for contraceptive purposes are protected while drugs prescribed for recreational purposes are not, or why normal sex is protected while consensual incest is not. And no court ever will find a principle—because the logic of self-ownership that underlies the right to privacy should reach all these activities even as the political consequences of taking these positions rules them out. This is why the Supreme Court has never come close to extending constitutional protection to prostitution or drug use or many other self-regarding activities—even when it cloaks its more nuanced privacy decisions in the gauzy garb of quasi-Millian rhetoric.

There is an additional irony in the modern rhetoric of privacy. Abortion is, in one very important way, arguably less private than many of these other activities not protected by the privacy right. Privacy extends to all activities that don't harm a third party. Consensual acts of prostitution or private drug use in the home arguably do not directly harm anyone else, but abortion does directly harm the fetus. The fetus may qualify only as a potential person or a potential third party, but abortion obviously affects its interests, whatever its status, in the most dramatic way imaginable—by ending its life. How ironic that the claims of privacy should be unequivocally accepted by so many in the abortion context but rejected in the context of prostitution, private soft drug use, or other arguably self-regarding activities where the interests of a third party are even less clearly affected!

Treating privacy as an absolute value when applied to abortion goes too far. Instead, women's legitimate interests in bodily autonomy during pregnancy should be balanced more sensibly against the three interests just mentioned the interest in protecting potential life, the interest in preventing fetal suffering, and the interest in preserving a social ethos of compassion and respect for life. Of the three interests, the second is the most important. The fetus's capacity for sentience—its ability to feel pain or, more generally, to experience rudimentary consciousness—is the single most plausible point to use in marking the point at which the fetus's life should be protected. To kill a conscious or sentient fetus is to kill a human being. Somewhere in the middle of the second trimester, perhaps around the twentieth week of pregnancy, society's interest in protecting the sentient fetus converges with its interests in protecting potential life and fostering an ethic of respect for life. It is at this point when the state's interest in prohibiting abortion becomes compelling.

Why is sentience or the capacity for consciousness morally important? First, each of the other four major criteria that one or another group has applied to draw the bright line designating moral and legal protection—conception, quickening, viability, and birth—are arbitrary. Each represents a *physical* event in pregnancy reflecting, respectively, the creation of the embryo, the point when the mother first feels movement, the point when the fetus can survive independently of the mother (with medical help), and the point of actual physical separation from the mother. But none of these lines tells us anything about the subjective experience of the fetus. Yet, isn't it our subjective capacity to be, as one moral philosopher has put it, "the subject of a life" that makes us worthy of moral and legal protection?[32] Shouldn't the capacity of the fetus to feel pain and to experience other conscious states warrant that it receive the protection that all other persons receive?

Interestingly, the common law rule, which drew the line at quickening, at least attempted to make the line depend upon an apparent morally relevant point in pregnancy. Quickening was thought relevant because common law lawyers, following medieval theologians, mistakenly believed that the fetus first moved at quickening, indicating that this was the point of ensoulment. Even the Roman Catholic Church followed the quickening rule until the nineteenth century, when medical science demonstrated that fetal movement occurs very early in pregnancy and that quickening is simply the point when the mother is first able to detect it. Thus, quickening turns out to be as arbitrary a point as the others. Unlike conception, quickening, viability, and birth, the development of the subjective capacity of the fetus to have conscious experiences is what strikes many moral philosophers (and many of the rest of us) as what should create the morally and legally protectable interest in one's own life.

What is our best understanding about when this occurs? As might be expected, conservatives and liberals have strained to push the point back or forward, depending upon their positions. Conservative judge John Noonan has argued plausibly that we should give the unborn at least the level of protection that we believe animals deserve. He goes on to suggest that this is quite early in pregnancy: "We may conclude that as soon as a pain mechanism is present in the fetus—as early as day 56—the [abortion] methods used will cause pain. The pain is more substantial and lasts longer the later the abortion is. It is most severe and lasts the longest when the method is saline poisoning."[33]

Recent evidence indicates, however, that the capacity of the fetus to experience pain begins much later. It is true that the fetus responds to external stimuli in what appears to be a stimulus-response manner as early as the seventh or eighth week of gestation.[34] Yet medical researchers have concluded that the mechanism responsible for stimulus-response reaction is neurologically distinct from the mechanism necessary to feel pain. For example, if one sticks one's hand in a pot of hot water, the stimulus-response mechanism causes one to react instantly and to withdraw the hand from the water; the subjective feeling of pain follows a half-second later. Thus, the pain does not cause our reaction but only accompanies it. One need not feel pain to have the stimulus-response mechanism intact. Researchers now believe that connections between the thalamus and the neocortex necessary for the fetus to experience pain develop from roughly twenty to twenty-four weeks of gestation, essentially a point in pregnancy just before viability.[35] This is the point when, according to the best research now available, the fetus is capable of experiencing pain and, perhaps more generally, of being "the subject of a life."

Not all agree, however. For example, there is still some debate concerning what the development of the thalamus-cortex connection means about the mental life of the fetus. Some have claimed that a level of conscious discrimination the fetus may not yet be capable of is necessary to register the experience as painful.[36] This conclusion is undercut by other experimental data that demonstrate that the fetus can "respond to sound from 20 weeks and discriminate between different tones from 28 weeks, among other things."[37] While the fetus is not capable of conceptual or rational ability, and will not be for several years after birth, it may still be capable of subjectively experiencing pain. While some will persist in claiming that the fetus cannot feel any pain, one is reminded of similar claims made by eighteenth-century vivisectionists who routinely dissected dogs and cats without anesthetic, maintaining that their violent reactions to the procedure were nothing but reflexes.

Perhaps the best indication that the fetus feels pain at this point is that it seems to react exactly as we do when we are threatened or in pain. Anecdotal experience of doctors and nurses who have participated in late-term abortions bears out the likelihood that the fetus is reacting not simply in a stimulus-response manner, but as the subject of experience. Because the late-term abortion is performed by partially removing the fetus from the body of the mother before killing it—thus the term "partial-birth" abortion—the effects on the fetus or baby are directly observable. As a nurse who testified before Congress described one such procedure:

> The baby's little fingers were clasping and unclasping, and his little feet were kicking. Then the doctor stuck the scissors in the back of his head, and the baby's arms jerked out, like a startle reaction, like a flinch, like a baby does when he thinks he is going to fall. The doctor opened up the scissors, stuck a high-powered suction tube into the opening, and sucked the baby's brains out. Now the baby went completely limp.[38]

While debate may continue about the nature of the fetus's experience, the state should be able to give the benefit of the doubt to the fetus in at least this case, to protect it from the very significant likelihood that it experiences such late-term abortion subjectively as a painful death, particularly since the state can do so without seriously burdening the woman's right to be free of the pregnancy.

It is also at this point that the other two interests become more significant. As I argued earlier, the first interest in protecting the potential life of the fetus develops as the fetus develops. This is why I rejected the conservative argument that gives this interest absolute priority from the time of conception. By the twentieth week, however, the fetus develops the capacity to feel pain, giving the potentiality claim more than symbolic significance. Similarly, the third interest concerns our desire to avoid the desensitization that seems to epitomize the type of abortion procedure usually performed at this time—the dilation and evacuation (D&E) or the dilation and extraction (D&X) or late-term procedure popularly known as "partial-birth abortion." This procedure, which may be performed beginning in the middle of the second trimester (around fifteen weeks), requires that the fetus be partially extracted from the woman's body before being killed. I will resist the temptation to characterize this procedure in any further detail, but it is fair to describe it, as Justice Scalia did in *Stenberg*, as "so horrible that the most clinical description of it evokes a shudder of revulsion."[39]

The Centrist's Approach

A fully defensible centrist position would recognize the right of a woman to have an abortion up until the twentieth week of gestation. We pick this point, halfway through pregnancy, because it a point that gives some breathing room to our interest in protecting the fetus. It ensures that the fetus will not suffer the excruciating agony of the later-term abortion while happily leaving women faced with the decision about whether to have a child ample time to make this decision. Since roughly 95 percent of all abortions occur by this time, it substantially protects the liberty interests of women. The proposal avoids the more barbaric and reprehensible consequences of late-term abortions, particularly the so-called partial-birth abortion. Given that this proposal reaches only a fraction of the total number of abortions performed each year in the United States, but reaches exactly those instances where the fetus deserves full moral and legal protection, it is difficult to understand how anyone can conclude that this would represent an undue burden on a woman's right to an abortion.

After the twentieth week, abortion should be permitted only when a woman's life or serious physical health is in danger. Even here, however, if it is possible to deliver the fetus after viability without jeopardizing the woman's life or physical health, this should be done. Since the fetus can live independently of the mother at the point of viability, postviability abortions vindicate the interests of a woman without entailing killing the fetus. The physical and autonomy interests of the woman can be completely vindicated by removing the fetus from her body, but her right to an abortion should guarantee no more than this. Specifically, it does not and should not be interpreted to include the right to end the life of the fetus. Even Thomson recognized this in her classic defense of abortion when she wrote that "while I am arguing for the permissibility of abortion in some cases, I am not arguing for the right to secure the death of the unborn child." Elaborating on her example in which an innocent woman is connected, without her consent, to a world-famous violinist for nine months, Thomson's analogy to pregnancy, she goes on: "I have argued that you are not morally required to spend nine months in bed [to sustain the life of the fetus]; but to say this is by no means to say that if, when you unplug yourself, there is a miracle and [the fetus] survives, you then have a right to turn around and slit his throat. You may detach yourself even if this costs him his life; you have no right to be guaranteed his death."[40] It is ironic that the logic of the standard liberal argument will not make even this very limited concession to the value of fetal life.

The conclusion I have drawn here will be unacceptable to some on the left. Feminists have occasionally argued that the right to an abortion must be understood to include a more general right *not to be a parent*, even in the biological sense. They contend that women who have postviability abortions will experience a range of psychological harms—the harm of having to decide whether to raise the child or give it up for adoption, and the psychological consequences in the event she does relinquish the child for adoption, knowing that she has a child somewhere out in the world. These psychological consequences militate in favor of giving a woman the right to decide to end the life of the fetus, the argument runs.[41]

Yet this position gives greater weight to these psychological harms, which may not even have any great significance for many women, than it does to the substantially more weighty interest of the fetus in being permitted to live. If the psychological interest of the woman consists in not being burdened with the fear that her child, now living out there in the world with its adoptive family, may be abused or otherwise not living well, how can it be better to extinguish the life of the fetus altogether? Whatever effect this apprehension may have on the mental state of the relinquishing mother, if it has much effect at all for some women, a weighing of the equities here clearly points in the direction of preserving the life of the postviable fetus even at the risk of this psychological effect on the mother. This conclusion is only buttressed by the fact that women will remain free to obtain an abortion before viability at any time without this risk.

Only in a world where one's position on abortion is made to bear the weight of much more general issues concerning the war between the sexes should our choices be limited to the standard, and equally extreme, liberal and conservative positions. It is time to reason our way to a more thoughtful, moderate conclusion.

Chapter 10
Race, Gender, and Reasonable Equality of Opportunity

EARLY IN MY TEACHING career at a law school in Chicago, as South Africa's regime of apartheid was in its death throes, the faculty had invited a white South African candidate to interview for a tenure-track faculty position teaching international law. BALSA, the school's black law student association, requested a hearing before the full faculty to oppose the hiring of this candidate. They opposed his hiring because they thought it somehow signaled our acceptance of the South African regime itself—that is, to hire a white South African was to endorse the policies of apartheid. Of course, the faculty wanted to do no such thing. We were uniformly opposed to racial apartheid. More importantly, our candidate was on the record as having fiercely opposed apartheid in various publications. Several of us pointed this out to the delegation from BALSA, yet these students remained undeterred in their opposition to him. Even if this particular white candidate was opposed to apartheid, they insisted, hiring him could bring some marginal symbolic or economic benefits to the regime. In any event, these students maintained, they would take this candidate's hiring as an offense, an indication of racial insensitivity on the part of the law school faculty.

By coincidence, however, the hiring committee had also extended an interview to a second South African—in this case a black candidate. The black candidate was interviewing for a different position and was in no way in competition with the white candidate. By the logic of the students' argument, one would expect them to equally oppose hiring the black candidate, since this would arguably have the same endorsement and economic effects as hiring the white candidate. Yet when presented with the case of the black candidate, the students retired en masse momentarily from the meeting to ponder the dilemma. When they returned, they announced that they were not opposed to the hiring of the black candidate, that this would, indeed, represent a blow struck in the name of social justice at the regime of apartheid. But what about the benefits to the regime? Why would it benefit the regime to hire a white who opposed apartheid, but not a black who had taken no position at all? No one could explain the apparent inconsistency, yet the faculty acceded to both demands, hiring the black candidate and rejecting the white.

A few years later, I witnessed an even more bizarre incident during a faculty meeting at another law school. The meeting had been called to consider the tenure and promotion of a female faculty member, but there were problems. On her resume, the candidate had failed to attribute to her husband coauthorship of several articles that she had written with him. The articles appeared on her resume as if she were the sole author, when in fact they were written jointly, and in an area in which he was a noted expert. Several faculty members considered this a clear instance of resume fraud. When asked about the discrepancy informally, our candidate at first said that she had written the articles herself, but that, upon completion, she had placed her husband's name on them in anticipation that this would bring offers from more prestigious journals, who would be familiar with her husband's work. Apparently realizing that this itself amounted to fraud, she later changed her story to say that the articles had indeed been coauthored with her husband, and that she had simply forgotten to attribute coauthorship on her resume.

A contentious debate followed—among the female faculty. No male faculty member spoke up either to defend or to indict this candidate. Among the female faculty who did have something to say, no one could explain or justify the candidate's initial omission or the change of story that followed. When the female faculty member who had initially discovered the discrepancy raised strong concerns about the veracity, not to mention the productivity, of the candidate, another female faculty member came to the candidate's defense. This second woman, a self-described feminist and progressive, could defend the candidate only in the following terms: Yes, it was hard to understand how the candidate could have accidentally omitted her husband's name from her resume on so many articles in which he had a role. And, yes, the change of story was very "troubling." Nevertheless, "in the end, I'm going to give her the benefit of the doubt—because she is a woman." She continued that if the candidate were a black male, she would give him the same moral benefit of the doubt as well. She then added, gratuitously, that she "would not give the benefit of the doubt to a white male."[1]

Anyone who has spent any time on an academic faculty in the United States in the past twenty-five years is familiar with this phenomenon. Hiring and tenure decisions have become explicitly race and gender conscious in most U.S. universities and law schools. I have been a member of five faculties in different parts of the country, and it has been true of each of them. Each year as the fall semester opens and the faculty contemplates its curricular needs, it is not uncommon to hear comments such as, "We have to identify a female business person," or "Let's find an African American who does patent law." And law school faculties, of all departments, frequently make decisions that are blatantly illegal. Recently my faculty considered two equally qualified tax candidates, one female and one male. Various faculty members openly and explicitly expressed preferences for the female candidate solely because of her gender. (This is illegal under Title VII of the Civil Rights Act.) We have even gone so far as to open and close faculty positions on the basis of race. In one case we opened two positions, made offers to two black candidates, and then closed down the second position, with a white next in line, when one of the two black candidates took another offer elsewhere. This, too, is illegal and, for a state school, probably a violation of the Constitution as well.

I include these vignettes to signal the momentous change in the way many think about equality today. If equality once meant that like cases be treated alike, many today, especially liberals, hold exactly the obverse view: they want the differently situated treated differently to achieve what liberals refer to as "substantive equality." This is where the Center cleaves from the Left on questions of equality. We are opposed to racism and to sexism and to heterosexism, and we further believe that it is acceptable for an admissions director or a hiring director to make individualized assessments of the kinds of obstacles particular individuals have overcome in their lives, since these tend to say something powerful about the character of the individual. But we are opposed to applying different standards in a nonindividualized way—by using quotas or other forms of preferential treatment—based on race, ethnicity, or gender among individuals competing for a job or a seat in a university. And we are certainly opposed to the more arbitrary ways described here by which one group receives the benefit of the doubt in matters that go to questions of character, reliability, or truthfulness.

I want to begin by comparing two distinct conceptions of equality—the conservative's "formal equality" and the liberal's "substantive equality"—each of which is flawed in important ways. Between these two ideas lies the centrist's conception of a reasonable equality of opportunity, which we will discuss at the end of this chapter.

The Conservative Ideal: Formal Equality

"All men have equal rights," wrote the father of modern conservatism, Edmund Burke, "but not to equal things."[2] With this, Burke expressed the formal conception of equality, the idea that equality requires that every individual be treated equally in the eyes of the law, but little else. Formal equality requires simply that neutral rules apply equally to all, regardless of circumstance. It prohibits punishing the wealthy or privileged less severely than the poor for a particular crime but, for this same reason, objects to giving the poor or disadvantaged a break by treating different cases differently. Strict adherence to formal equality would prohibit the progressive income tax, which taxes the wealthy at a higher rate than the middle class, and it forecloses affirmative action and other kinds of programs that apply different standards to those from different racial or ethnic groups. Formal equality also arguably has implications in specific areas of law. For example, formal egalitarians are more likely to find hate-speech bans unconstitutional on the theory that they discriminate against particular viewpoints, whereas substantive egalitarians argue that differential treatment for racially abusive speech is justified in light of the history of discrimination in the United States.[3]

The biggest problem with formal equality is not primarily the idea that rules should apply neutrally across the board, but rather its conception of the role of government in promoting equality. Formal egalitarians believe that the state should never intervene in the economic or social sphere to promote greater social or economic equality than that which would occur under conditions of the free market. They are opposed, for example, to antidiscrimination laws that require business owners to do business with people of all races and ethnic groups. Many formal egalitarians also opposed laws like the Americans with Disabilities Act, which requires private business owners to spend a portion of their own resources to make their businesses accessible to the handicapped. In a still larger sense, formal egalitarians believe that government should not engage in economic redistribution of any kind.

Why do conservatives take this hands-off approach to inequality, leaving each individual or group to fend for itself? Part of the answer is that formal egalitarians insist that any form of redistribution requires the government to depart from what should be its role as a neutral arbiter among different interests. In other words, formal egalitarians believe not only that the government should apply rules neutrally but also that it should not take sides between the rich and the poor, redistributing wealth from one group to another. Government must be completely neutral between competing interests. When government plays Robin Hood and takes from the rich to give to the poor, or when it requires white business owners to do business with minorities when they would prefer not to, or when it requires the (presumably well-off) business owner to construct wheelchair-accessible facilities to provide for the disabled individual, it is no longer acting neutrally. It is taking the side of one set of interests (often that of the poorer or more disadvantaged but more numerous) at the expense of another. As F. A. Hayek wrote: "equality before the law which freedom requires leads to material inequality"; thus, "the desire of making people more alike in their condition cannot be accepted in a free society as a justification for further and discriminatory coercion."[4] Of course, the consistent formal egalitarian is also opposed to corporate welfare, government tax breaks, and other incentives for the wealthy.

The formal egalitarians' insistence on government neutrality dovetails with their skepticism of concentrated government power and their tilt toward a free-market approach to economics. Neutrality requires that we let the free market run its natural course, that we let interest groups compete on their own terms with one another, and that we permit the chips to fall where they may so that government acts only to ensure that no one has broken the rules (by violating another's rights or by monopolizing a market). Formal egalitarians insist that government intervention to redistribute what liberals may regard as the windfall gains of inherited talents and wealth violates the property rights of others. Free-market economists Milton and Rose Friedman argue that the "society that puts . . . equality of outcome ahead of freedom will end up with neither equality nor freedom."[5] They also contend that intervention is usually wasteful, at least in a purely economic sense (e.g., if it were profitable to put in wheelchair-accessible ramps, businesses would have done it already).

But perhaps under all these utilitarian concerns lies a deeper cosmic objection. Some conservatives suggest that inequality is fundamentally ineradicable. It is part of the human condition. To the extent that government tries to equalize access to social goods and services, it operates on the material plane but leaves other (immaterial) inequalities untouched. As free-market economist Thomas Sowell puts it in *The Quest for Cosmic Justice*:

> Far from society being divided into those with a more or less standard package of benefits and others lacking those benefits, each individual may have windfall advantages and windfall disadvantages, and the particular combination of windfall

gains and losses varies enormously from individual to individual. Some are blessed with beauty but lacking in brains, some are wealthy but from an emotionally impoverished family, some have athletic prowess but little ability to get along with other human beings . . . and so on and so on. Add to this the changing circumstances of each individual over a lifetime—with relative advantages and disadvantages changing with the passing years—and the difficulties of merely determining the net advantages increase exponentially.[6]

Where the progressive government requires the materially wealthier person to subsidize the poorer, the poorer person may come from a more supportive family or be healthier or more physically attractive. It is unfair, the conservative seems to be saying, to shift the economic balance and leave the other inequalities untouched.

There may sometimes be something to this point: any attempt to achieve a condition of social equality will always leave untouched other kinds of inequality. But what Sowell and other conservatives ignore is that conditions like poverty and physical disability are usually correlated with many other negative conditions that *reinforce one another*: poverty is correlated with poor health, depression, a shorter lifespan. The disabled may find it difficult to earn a living, thereby reinforcing their isolation and social ostracism.[7] Just as one form of advantage—intelligence, good looks, wealth—can attract other resources (as when the attractive marry well, or the intelligent earn money which helps to keep them healthy), the opposite is also true: there is frequently a multiplier effect when it comes to being socially or physically disadvantaged.

Everyone's package of advantages and disadvantages, then, does not work out in some generalized egalitarian way. Centrists believe that a wealthy and compassionate society such as our own has an obligation to offset the maldistribution of social and personal disadvantages, though in a way most consistent with what we might call "individualism," in the best sense of the word. We believe that government should meet the individual halfway, helping to structure social conditions and to open up opportunities in ways that provide individuals a fair opportunity to achieve their personal best. We believe this is better for the individual and ultimately better for society, since a society benefits when its members' productive capacities are most fully actualized. For this reason, centrists believe that something more than formal equality is necessary.

The Liberal Ideal: Substantive Equality

Where formal egalitarians believe that like cases should be treated alike, substantive egalitarians believe that equality often requires that we treat the differently situated differently to achieve greater equality of outcome. "The law, in its majestic equality," Anatole France famously declared in criticizing the idea of formal equality, "forbids the rich as well as the poor to sleep under the bridges, beg in the streets and to steal bread." Holding everyone to the same standards ignores the fact that it is easier for some to meet them.

The liberal idea of substantive equality is not exactly total equality of condition, as is sometimes charged. Rather, moving toward substantive equality means trying to make things as fair as possible. Minimally, this means that government should intervene to offset some of the grosser forms of prejudice and discrimination, prohibiting racial discrimination, for example. It frequently also means that liberals take an aggressive stand in treating the disadvantaged in a preferential way by neutralizing as many unearned personal and social conditions that either disable or unfairly limit the individual, or that represent such windfall benefits as intelligence, being born into a wealthy family, or belonging to an ethnic or racial group with social advantages. For this reason, liberals favor more aggressive inheritance taxes and more progressive economic redistribution. At the further extremes, the more progressive thinkers may sanction inappropriate intervention into the private sphere of the family, for example, proposing that children be required to spend time in different geographical settings and economic circumstances to equalize their experiences.[8] And as I argued in Chapter 3, how far left a thinker or theory falls on the political spectrum has a great deal to do with how much equality one seeks, and how much government intervention one is willing to allow to achieve this.

One of the most regrettable casualties of substantive equality, however, is its tendency to foment corrosive cynicism concerning our ideas of merit and personal responsibility. Progressives frequently hold almost visceral contempt for the idea of merit, in part because they don't believe success is necessarily correlated with merit and in part because they are apprehensive about the social consequences of accepting the correlation between merit and success. In the nineteenth century, the anarchist Mikhail Bakunin derided the "aristocracy of the intellect" as the "last refuge of the spirit of domination."[9] In our own time, the linguist turned dissident Noam Chomsky writes that success in this society is a product less of intelligence than of "avarice, selfishness, lack of concern for others, aggressiveness," and so on, and that in a more decent society "the attributes that now lead to success would be recognized as pathological."[10]

Certainly success in any society is sometimes won by climbing over the backs of the more ethical or less aggressive, but to suggest that the genius of a cancer researcher, the brilliance of a great writer, or the intelligence and savvy of a Bill Gates is pathological is abundantly unfair. As much as liberals may wish to deny it, and as old-fashioned as it may sound, many who rise to positions of leadership do so because they are more intelligent, more motivated, more hard-working, or some combination of these. Of course, merit and success are far from perfectly correlated in our society, or in any society. Lack of intelligence is no bar to success in TV, film, or music. A smaller number of the intellectually limited may climb the corporate heights largely on the basis of connections or sheer aggressiveness. And occasionally one of these may even be elected president. But often when this happens (at least outside show business), it is not because we are too meritocratic, but because we sometimes aren't meritocratic enough.

Some progressives have suggested that neutral standards are inherently culturally subjective or insidiously biased for one or another reason. Critical race scholar

Richard Delgado concludes that "merit is what the victors impose" and "merit is comparable to etiquette," in that our standards are always revisable.[11] Alex Johnson, another critical race scholar, insists more pointedly that standards of merit are "a gate built by a white male hegemony that requires a password in the white man's voice for passage."[12] Manning Marable suggests in a similar way that the appeal to merit is a cynical ploy: "White conservatives were able to define 'merit' in a manner that would reinforce white male privilege, but in an inverted language that would make the real victims of discrimination appear to be the racists." This, Marable insists, was "a brilliant political maneuver."[13]

The cynics have a right to complain when objective criteria of merit are not applied equally and fairly—when a less qualified white person is given a position over a more qualified minority candidate. But the radical critique badly misses the mark when it attacks the idea of merit itself. There is nothing brilliant or cynical about using criteria long understood to qualify a person for a particular job or a seat at an institution of higher learning. If the qualifications are fair—if they adequately reflect what is required of a particular position or of a successful graduate school candidate, for example—and if they are applied neutrally, then this is all that we should have to appeal to in making these kinds of decisions.[14] Advocates of minority interests should insist upon a fair application of meritocratic standards rather than trash the idea of merit as inherently incoherent or racist.

If the critics just quoted share the view that success in our society has little to do with merit, others worry about the opposite, that our society may become too meritocratic—that an excessive focus on merit runs the risk of turning us into a hypercompetitive society. Feminist law professor Robin West argues that the "meritocratic imperative to maximize productivity, competency and performance" will lead to a "hyper-meritocracy" in which the "personal connecting virtues" of compassion, loyalty, and care will be lost.[15] Others worry that a true meritocracy may make inequality even more difficult to bear for the losers since they will not be able to shift the responsibility to the effects of nonmeritocratic factors. In his thoughtful book *The End of Equality*, Mickey Kaus writes that the goal of social egalitarians was "to eliminate gross environmental differences through civil rights laws, education and training." Yet, perhaps ironically, "the more we minimize gross environmental differences and eliminate class biases, the less success and failure will be influenced by environment and class, and the more they will be influenced by heredity." This leads to what Kaus calls "the Loser problem." Those "on the bottom, the losers, will feel somehow that they deserve to be on the bottom."[16] Having eliminated many of the last vestiges of the old class system in favor of a system of jobs open to talents, some liberals now believe that meritocratic equality has its own downside.

In many ways our economic trends bear out the rise of the new meritocracy. A recent study finds that only thirty-seven of *Forbes*'s richest four hundred in 2004 had inherited their fortunes, down from almost two hundred in the mid-1980s.[17] Another study a decade ago found that four-fifths of U.S. millionaires earned their fortunes in their lifetimes.[18] With the world having grown more competitive and meritocratic, some liberals now find themselves offering the kind of cautionary advice once confined to conservatives. As Herman Lubbe, a conservative sociologist pointed out a quarter century ago, the egalitarian society "is now by necessity an achievement society. . . . One will no longer be able to ascribe one's falling behind to social causes. Instead, one will have to ascribe it to what once would have been unself-consciously called 'stupidity.' "[19] Or as libertarian F. A. Hayek put it, strangely presaging the communitarian Kaus: "A society in which it was presumed that a high income was proof of merit, and a low income of the lack of it . . . would probably be much more unbearable to the unsuccessful ones than one in which it was frankly recognized that there was no necessary connection between merit and success."[20]

The lesson in all this is that for two hundred years progressives have fought to eliminate the unfair consequences of classism, racism, sexism, and discrimination against those who are disabled or otherwise different to create a society that was fairly and genuinely meritocratic. Now that we have begun to approach this kind of society, many liberals increasingly are having second thoughts.

Substantive equality is still occasionally defended on the older grounds—as a way of remedying the residual racism and sexism in our society to help achieve a more meritocratic society. Yet increasingly today it serves as a hedge against the consequences of meritocracy. By moving in the direction of an equality of results, as with the idea that every law school class, every medical school, every division within the workforce should be diverse racially and across genders, liberals hope to curb the effects of meritocracy. Certainly this is the understanding most liberals have of diversity as used in recent affirmative action policies. Diversity is a concept deployed today not to guarantee that the best get the position, but to ensure that every group is more or less equally represented in the workforce or student body.

Civil Rights, Yes; Affirmative Action, No

By "affirmative action" I mean any practice or program that gives preferential treatment to candidates on the basis of race or gender simply because they belong to a traditionally disadvantaged group. While affirmative action programs have been adopted both by public agencies and by private actors (corporations, nongovernmental organizations, etc.), and while they typically involve hiring, educational placement, or government contracts, here I primarily discuss affirmative action in admissions decisions in public universities. Centrists obviously support outreach and other similar programs intended to inform minorities about the availability of positions, to invite applications from minority candidates, and to otherwise assist qualified applicants in finding suitable positions. Since these programs do not in themselves entail that minority candidates will receive preferential treatment, they do not violate the centrist's commitment to equality.

Given that we centrists favor civil rights laws, why stop short of affirmative action? Indeed, is there a significant difference between supporting the civil rights laws and affirmative action? Cornel West associates the line we draw here with a neoconservative position and (rightly) observes that a commitment to merit lies behind our position. "By affirming the principle of equality of opportunity but trashing any mechanism that claimed to go beyond merit, neoconservatives drove a wedge between civil rights and affirmative action."[21] As West's suggestion makes clear, defending affirmative action often means attacking traditional notions of merit, since, by definition, "affirmative action" is the reliance on race or gender to give a position to a candidate who is arguably less qualified, according to traditional criteria, than a nonminority candidate. Ethicist James Sterba has also argued that those who endorse the civil rights laws "cannot consistently avoid endorsing" affirmative action, since affirmative action may be the only way to combat covert discrimination.[22] Yet centrists are concerned that the costs of fighting racism in this manner are too high and that affirmative action does more to exacerbate both the social and the racial divides today than it does to mend them.

Proponents of affirmative action usually offer one of two justifications for supporting preferential treatment for minorities. The first holds that affirmative action is required as a form of social compensation for previous discrimination or, more globally, to remedy the effects of educational and environmental deficits associated with being a minority in the United States. The second rationale, which has arguably become the dominant justification in recent years, is that affirmative action assures diversity within the classroom or the faculty.[23] Where the social compensation rationale is a form of corrective justice that seeks to give back to minorities what the legacy of racism and segregation has taken from them, the diversity idea is more pragmatic and utilitarian in character. Diversity is supposed to achieve several social benefits (to minorities and nonminorities alike) without regard to compensatory justifications.

Critical race scholars sometimes argue that the compensation idea is more radical than the diversity idea and seem to like to defend it, in part, for this reason alone. Charles R. Lawrence III, a law professor at Georgetown, argues that the diversity justification for affirmative action is "conservative" because it reinforces "elitist" conditions by integrating minorities into the existing social structure. Lawrence tells us that the Left should instead adopt a "radical vision of affirmative action, a vision which adopts the victim perspective and creatively shapes remedies that directly address remaining conditions of inequality."[24] He argues that a compensatory justification goes further than diversity in creating conditions of genuine equality. Manning Marable also insists that "affirmative action can and should be criticized from the Left, not because it was too liberal in its pursuit and implementation of measures to achieve equality, but because it was too conservative. It sought to increase representative numbers of minorities and women within the existing structure and arrangements of power, rather than challenging or redefining the institutions of authority and privilege."[25]

These arguments may simply be strategically radical in that they attempt to normalize the more conventional defenses of affirmative action by taking a more extreme approach to the issue. It is not at all clear, for example, why integrating minorities into "existing social structures" is "elitist," as Lawrence has it. If a fully integrated medical or legal profession remains elitist in some sense, then the problem is obviously no longer a problem of race. Similarly, Marable has something much more radical in mind than racial equality when he suggests that the Left ought to be "challenging or redefining the institutions of authority and privilege." For those who want to abolish these traditional standards entirely, what will take their place? Presumably a system that ensures racial proportionality in every professional and educational setting. But this is exactly what diversity advocates want. The central problem with the compensation rationale is that it either clamors for a trashing of all traditional standards of merit or collapses back into a demand for racial proportionality—in other words, diversity.

Using affirmative action to compensate victims of past discrimination raises some vexing questions. For starters, who should be compensated, and for what? Blacks? Hispanics? Any member of a "historically disadvantaged group," whatever this might mean? If affirmative action is limited to blacks, does it include new arrivals from Africa or the Caribbean, or is it limited to the descendants of African slaves? If compensation includes newer arrivals or nonblack minorities, then obviously we are not compensating because of the legacy of slavery alone. In this case, which conditions are eligible for compensation? Is it enough that a group has been badly treated by other groups at one point or another in the past? If so, wouldn't this require the inclusion of many other groups—Irish, Italians, Jews, and Chinese, among others? Would these different groups receive different levels of treatment, perhaps on a graded scale, depending on the seriousness of past discrimination? Or, if we limit compensation to those who have been the victims of de jure discrimination by the state, then who would we include? Would Hispanics and Asians have a claim since they have been victims of discrimination in the past and were even targeted by antimiscegenation statutes until the 1960s? And if we are compensating for the continuing effects of racism—for example, for the residual effects of segregation in inner-city schools—would white students who attend these schools have a right to compensation? Finally, to the extent that compensation is predicated on the idea that we want to make whole those who have been harmed by some combination of past or present social or political condition, would claimants have to prove that their present position is proximately traceable to these previous conditions (whatever we decide these should be)? For example, would the children of wealthy black parents have a right to compensation when it appears that their forebears have overcome the social and economic disadvantages of the past? And, for all those entitled to compensation, how far into the future would these claims remain viable?

These questions just begin to scratch the surface. Little wonder that the diversity idea has become increasingly popular, for it seeks outright racial proportionality in the classroom or the workforce without regard to issues of social compensation. And the diversity rationale, it turns out, is hardly a conservative idea, since diversity does not mean intellectual or religious or cultural diversity. It does not mean a diversity of viewpoints, for if it did, why not guarantee educational slots to anarchists and fascists, to members of the Black Panthers and the KKK? Nor does diversity imply a process of natural adjustment among a plurality of groups whose interests overlap and sometimes collide. No, diversity is engineered racial and gender proportionality and nothing else. In perfectly circular fashion, the word "diversity" is today used as a *justification* for racial proportionality in schools and other settings, when this racial proportionality is all that diversity *means* in the first place.

As Carl Cohen has written, "The only 'diversity' that is said to justify preference is racial diversity, and the standard by which it is decided whether diversity goals are adequately achieved is the *match* of the proportion of certain minorities entering college . . . to the proportion of those minorities in the population at large."[26]

Consider the *Grutter* and *Gratz* cases, the two most recent Supreme Court cases to address affirmative action.[27] In the *Grutter* case, the University of Michigan Law School claimed that it had used race as a "plus" factor in admissions decisions, meaning that race was used as one among other considerations in making admissions decisions. Yet the disparity between admissions standards for white and black applicants was striking. For students with GPAs between 3.25 and 3.49, and LSAT scores between 156 and 158 (placing these students somewhere roughly between the sixtieth and seventieth percentile of test takers), only one of fifty-one whites was admitted while ten of ten black applicants were admitted. The plaintiff, Barbara Grutter, was a returning student who ran a home health care business. Grutter's scores were truly exceptional. She had an undergraduate GPA of 3.8 and scored 161 on the LSAT, which placed her near the ninetieth percentile of test takers. Yet she was wait-listed and finally rejected by the law school.

The law school claimed that creating a "diverse" student body justified the disparities. The school's authorities denied that it was seeking to achieve racial proportionality among racial and ethnic groups, yet the school's director of admissions admitted that he would daily check the acceptance rates of minority groups and send out admissions letters accordingly. As a result, the correlation between the percentage of applications from each of the three minority groups (blacks, Hispanics, and Native Americans) virtually matched the percentage of acceptances for each group over the course of several years. Thus, in order to achieve proportionality, if 10 percent of the applicant pool was black, 10 percent of those admitted were black, notwithstanding the differences in grades and test scores among various groups. While administrators claimed that they sought to attain a "critical mass" of members of each group in order to enhance classroom diversity, it is difficult to see how admitting 13 to 19 Native Americans in a class of 350 can constitute a critical mass, as Justice Rehnquist pointed out.

In *Gratz*, the undergraduate department went even further, giving an applicant an automatic 20 points on a 150-point system simply for being a member of a minority. Yet 20 points was usually enough to guarantee the difference between automatic rejection and acceptance. Typically, a score of 75 meant a candidate's rejection, while a score of 100 usually was enough for admission. Thus, a white student with a score of 75 would be rejected, while a black student with the same grades and life experience would receive a 95, virtually guaranteeing admission. The Supreme Court ultimately upheld the use of race as a "plus" factor in the law school program but held unconstitutional the automatic point system used by the undergraduate school. Ironically, however, permitting the more intangible and indeterminate use of race may provide a cover for more overt attempts to engineer racial proportionality in the university system.

Defenders of affirmative action cite three kinds of social benefits fostered by commitment to diversity. They contend, first, that it is good for the learning environment in the classroom and, more generally, opens up lines of understanding between the races. Second, diversity is a gateway to positions of leadership for minorities. Guaranteeing larger numbers of minorities the opportunity to attend university, law school, or medical school ensures that more minorities will ultimately assume leadership positions in society. This, in turn, provides minority role models for the next generation of aspiring doctors, lawyers, and leaders. Third, diversity is supposed to promote greater minority access to basic legal and medical services as minorities return to serve and enrich their communities after graduation.

Of these three, only the second justification has any real merit. There is little evidence that adjusting upward the number of minorities (say from five to ten in a class of fifty) in a class in organic chemistry or civil procedure or even, for that matter, U.S. history will have any appreciable impact on the learning environment. How could it? How does tinkering with the racial mix of a class improve any student's understanding of class material—particularly in subject areas that have nothing to do with race? As for the claim that minorities who receive their degree will return to serve their communities, this usually does not happen.[28] In my own field, black law students who have performed well in school can write their own ticket, and most choose to do what nonminorities choose to do when they have the opportunity—they accept the big law firm job with the money and the benefits that go with it. Who can blame them? With student loan debt now frequently approaching six figures, this may be the only decision that makes sense for many.

So what is our justification for proceeding along race-conscious lines, and what are the costs of doing so? The individuals most likely to benefit from affirmative action in the educational context are the same individuals least likely to have been affected by overt discrimination or by the indirect, institutional effects of racism—women and middle- and upper-class blacks.[29] It is often the middle- and upper-middle-class student—the student who would have been admitted to the University of Illinois Law School on the merits—who is admitted to the University of Michigan instead as a result of the school's affirmative action program. From the applicant's side, being able to count oneself a minority is so advantageous in some contexts that the Plessys of yesteryear (Plessy claimed to be seven-eighths white) today insist upon being counted as black.[30] Indeed, rather than hoping to avoid being identified as a minority, minority applicants to universities and graduate schools today typically (and understandably) advertise their status precisely because they know that it means that they will be able to take advantage of the race preferences offered by the university.

Add to this the well-documented cases of abuse of the process, where individuals have misrepresented or exaggerated their status as a minority (e.g., the upper-middle-class white who claims to be Hispanic because one grandparent came from Spain). From the university's side, the designation of one group as an underrepresented minority is often an overtly political consideration. In *Grutter*, the effort to racially gerrymander the entering law school class reached comic proportions during a faculty debate at Michigan. When one faculty member wondered aloud whether Cubans should be considered Hispanic, another voiced the opinion that they should not be—because most Cubans are Republicans.[31]

Underlying all these objections, however, is the sense that engineering different standards for different races is profoundly wrong—that it violates the principle that government should do its best to prohibit discrimination, but should not get into the business of socially engineering racial and ethnic proportionality so that all professions mirror the racial constitution of society. Indeed, entertaining claims for racial and gender proportionality has produced a genuinely volatile and increasingly polarized social atmosphere in which minorities who make it legitimately, without the bump, are tainted as affirmative action babies, while nonminorities are increasingly suspicious that they have been victimized. And underneath this is the sense that we are no longer one society but instead a racialized and genderized version of Hobbes's "war of each against all."

This cannot be what equality means.

Reasonable Equality of Opportunity

The centrist's conception of a reasonable equality of opportunity charts a middle course between the conservative's formal equality and the liberal's substantive equality. Centrists recognize that some inequalities arise from externally imposed conditions—race, gender, the family and social condition into which someone is born, disabilities, and so on—which are in no way the product of the individual's own choices and which, in many cases, are irrelevant to one's true potential. Other inequalities arise from differences of "capacity, disposition and virtue"—differences that are substantially within the control of the person. Assuring each individual a reasonable equality of opportunity means that we make collective efforts, as much as is socially and politically practicable, to eliminate limitations imposed by the first, but not the second, source of inequalities.

This means that we centrists find ourselves in agreement with liberals at two points. We concur that affirmative government intervention is sometimes necessary to promote equality, as with antidiscrimination laws. And we agree that equality *sometimes* requires treating the differently situated differently. For example, we intuitively understand that legal penalties must be applied proportionately to a person's wealth in order for them to deter crime. A fine of twenty-five dollars for someone who has double-parked may be enough to deter a person of moderate means but may have no effect on the fabulously wealthy. Similarly, the progressive income tax is based on the idea that the rich can afford to pay a higher rate of taxation because there is a much larger margin between what they earn and what they need to survive than exists for the less wealthy. In some cases, equality may require eliminating basic hurdles that burden some, but not others, in the exercise of our basic rights. With this in mind, forty years ago the Supreme Court ruled that it was unconstitutional to charge voters a poll tax since this would skew the democratic process by discouraging poorer citizens from voting.[32]

We are in agreement with most conservatives, however, in opposing all quotas, all schemes intended to engineer racial proportionality and any procedures for decision making that automatically use differential standards for individuals in different groups or that give an automatic Michigan-style "bump" to members of one group rather than another. We are most strongly opposed to these measures when our own government, rather than a private corporation, engages in these practices. A reasonable equality of opportunity requires that all individuals be treated in the same way—equally—in making these decisions. In situations where individuals must compete for scarce occupational or educational opportunities, the competing qualifications and overall potential of competing candidates should be the touchstone for hiring and placement decisions. Does this mean that administrators cannot consider a person's having overcome the disadvantages of racial discrimination or an impoverished inner-city environment in making placement or hiring decisions? Absolutely not. What it means is that race should not be used as an automatic proxy. The disadvantages a person has overcome, whether in virtue of race, gender, disability, or economic background, may be powerfully relevant in telling us something about that person's potential in overcoming other problems relevant to the position for which they are chosen. But the "bump" for falling into a particular group should not be automatic and race should be no more deserving of any additional consideration than other types of limiting factors, including poverty and disability.

Particularly in educational settings, gauging a person's potential for success requires that we look beyond the objective criteria—tests and grades—and weigh the intangible factors that reflect the kinds of personal and social obstacles an individual has overcome. Overcoming an impoverished background, whether in white Appalachia or the black inner city, is relevant to gauging the applicant's grit and ability to overcome social and economic obstacles. Overcoming the effects of stigmatization says something about the character of the individual, a consideration that applies equally to the disabled student and the minority candidate. Candidates' backgrounds and what they have overcome often tell us something about their character, steadfastness and persistence, and the depth of their desire to succeed in various roles and pursuits.

A reasonable equality of opportunity requires that all positions be open to talent, regardless of race, gender, religion, ethnicity, or other background conditions. It is not necessarily offended when there are unintended disparities between groups. For example, women should not be foreclosed from physically demanding jobs such as police and firefighter positions, but the criteria for hiring must address what it takes to do the job competently. Height, weight, and strength requirements may result in more men being hired than women, since a higher proportion of men meet the minimum criteria. These qualifications should not be set artificially high so as to prevent otherwise qualified women from applying, but neither should they be relaxed to take in women who would not previously have qualified. (Of course, since there are different positions in the police or fire department, each with distinct qualifications, women who might not qualify for one position will be able to qualify for others.) In sum, a reasonable equality of opportunity requires that fair, uniform standards be set and that they be applied evenly to all across the board with a due recognition of a diversity of functions so that those foreclosed by physical or other limitations from one job have an opportunity to compete for other positions.

In contexts in which the focus shifts from a candidate's potential to the candidate's ability to perform, these background factors matter less, if at all. In deciding who should get the position as center on a professional basketball team, or neurosurgeon, or airline pilot, what we want is the ability to perform now. This highlights why race-conscious efforts in some areas strike many as so unseemly. For example, in 1994 the Detroit Symphony Orchestra abandoned its long-established practice of having those who audition play behind a screen so that they can be heard but not seen. The orchestra decided to remove the screen in order to increase the number of minority musicians accepted.[33] The orchestra's decision appears to be a frank concession that minorities weren't measuring up musically against the nonminorities they were competing against.

In the end, centrists disagree with proponents of affirmative action for the same reason that we object to racial profiling. Affirmative action benefits minorities while racial profiling disadvantages them, of course, but both operate on the same principle: both activities treat race as a proxy for other qualities. Affirmative action treats race as a proxy for having been socially disadvantaged, while profiling treats race as a proxy for having a greater propensity to commit crime. In both cases, there is some truth to the empirical generalization—blacks are more likely to commit crime than whites, and they are also more likely to have been socially disadvantaged. But if it violates our principle of equality to single out a particular individual who happens to be black as a means of crime prevention then it is equally wrong to do it in order to confer a benefit. The liberal is as wrong to support affirmative action while opposing racial profiling as the conservative is wrong to support profiling while opposing affirmative action.[34]

A commitment to a reasonable equality of opportunity means taking into consideration a whole host of factors—social class, economic background, disabilities, other personal hardships—among others. To the extent that individuals from minority groups have faced and overcome these factors, they ought to be considered on an individualized basis in educational and professional settings. And they ought to be taken into consideration not because we are compensating the person as victim, but because we recognize that the strength of character shown in overcoming these difficulties provides the most powerful evidence of their ability to succeed in the future.

Chapter 11
Crime and Punishment

A FEW YEARS AGO a joke floated around the Internet that captured in a visceral way the distinction between the liberal and conservative approaches to the problem of crime. It posited a liberal and a conservative, each confronted with the following scenario: A middle-aged family man is walking with his wife and children down a city street in a vaguely threatening urban setting. As dusk begins to fall, from out of the blue and around a darkened corner comes an apparently deranged maniac screaming shrilly and wielding a large knife. He sets his eyes upon the family and makes a line directly for them. The family man has just seconds to act, and he is given a loaded gun. Confronted with this menace the liberal, gun within his reach, ponders the reasons for the man's condition. Perhaps the knife isn't real. And even if it is, what has brought this poor soul to such a depraved moment? What awful set of events has set him on this path? Is he insane? Homeless? Or possibly a victim of some traumatic childhood experience? Am I justified in preferring my own life over his? the liberal wonders. Should I try to reason with him, or can I quickly maneuver my family out of the way? And so, on and on, the liberal continues to ponder the predicament as the madman strikes. In the same scenario, the response by the conservative is as unceremonious as it is immediate: Boom! While the joke was undoubtedly written by a conservative for conservatives, it captures something of the self-understanding of many liberals and conservatives.

The prevention and punishment of crime is for conservatives at the heart of the raison d'être of the state. If we had to boil down to one grand distinction liberals' and conservatives' contrasting understandings of the purpose of government, it would be that modern liberals believe that the state exists to protect the individual from society (from economic inequality, poverty, exploitation, ignorance, racism, sexism, and the like), whereas conservatives believe the reverse, that it is government's job to protect society from the individual (to preserve the social order from the predictable excesses and transgression of individuals). The essence of conservative political thought is that the state exists primarily to restrain and educate the individual. Failing these ends, the state must make good on its word and punish the criminal offender. In any of the various species of modern conservative thought, human nature is frail, fallen, or calculatingly self-interested. Authority and social constraint are indispensable to civilization. "Men are so constructed," wrote James Fitzjames Stephen, Mill's greatest nineteenth-century conservative critic, that "there are and always will be in the world an enormous mass of bad and indifferent people—people who do all sorts of things which they ought not to do, and leave undone all sorts of things which they ought to do."[1]

When these transgressions rise to the level where their consequences threaten the social order, society must be prepared to respond. The executioner "is the terror and the bond of human association," declared Joseph de Maistre. "Remove this mysterious agent from the world," he solemnly predicted, "and in an instant order yields to chaos, thrones fall, society disappears."[2] This may seem like conservatism at its most extreme, but it is not. Conservatives return to these themes routinely. Crime exists, they insist, because we permit it, because we fail to guard the social order and even our individual well-being against the predations of criminal offenders. Several years ago in *The Public Interest*, Jeffrey Snyder offered a startling explanation for the extent of crime in our society in "A Nation of Cowards":

> Crime is rampant in our society because the law-abiding, each of us, condone it, excuse it, permit it, submit to it. We permit it and encourage it because we do not fight back, immediately, then and there when it happens. Crime is not rampant because we do not have enough prisons, because judges and prosecutors are too soft, because police are hamstrung with absurd technicalities. The defect is there, in our character. We are a nation of cowards and shirkers.[3]

Snyder argued that the ordinary citizen should be armed, locked, and loaded, fully prepared to enforce the explicit terms of the social contract on an individual basis. Noting that 90 percent of all violent crimes are committed by offenders not carrying handguns, Snyder argued along the lines of a recent bumper sticker: "A well-armed society is a polite one." People should be prepared to defend themselves from crime. Crime "is an act of enslavement," he wrote.[4] Former New York City police commissioner Raymond Kelly drew the same analogy between crime and political oppression:

> The fight against crime in America, like that against Soviet domination, is now essentially a fight for freedom. Fearing crime, of becoming one of its victims, is to lose a fair amount of freedom. . . . Society's increasing tolerance of crime and anti-social behavior in general is abetting our own enslavement. The erosion of freedom caused by crime is so pervasive that we are in danger of failing to notice it at all.[5]

Contrast the liberal view. In 1976 Judge David Bazelon, on the federal court of appeals sitting in the District of Columbia, authored "The Morality of the Criminal Law," a classic liberal indictment of the criminal justice system. Bazelon contrasted the conservative's "law as external constraint" model, which "demands that criminal law punish disorder and make the cost of violating the law so great that few will dare to do so," with his own view. The liberal conception of criminal justice holds that "the only true moral order" is "order based on the internalization of control, that is, on the members of society obeying the law because they personally believe that its commands are justified." Punishment should never be used "to achieve repressive order." A society may not sit in judgment of an offender unless "society's own conduct in relation to the actor entitles it to sit in condemnation of him with respect to the condemnable act."[6]

Of course, contra Bazelon, conservatives want citizens to internalize the moral order as well, perhaps even more than do liberals. But liberals are more likely to feel that the U.S. system of criminal justice is repressive. They believe this, in part, precisely because they believe that many who become offenders have been victimized, disenfranchised, or abandoned by society. As Dr. Karl Menninger, a psychiatrist and founder of the Menninger Institute, explained in his book *The Crime of Punishment*, it is the criminal justice system itself that causes most of our crime:

> And there is one crime we keep committing over and over. I accuse the reader of this—and myself, too—and all the nonreaders. We commit the crime of damning some of our fellow citizens with the label "criminal." And having done this, we force them through an experience that is both soul-searching and dehumanizing. In this way we exculpate ourselves from the guilt we feel and tell ourselves that we do it to "correct" the "criminal" and make ourselves all safer from crime. We commit this crime every day that we retain our present stupid, futile, abominable practices against detected offenders.[7]

Just as there is often callousness in the conservative's view, there is more than a trace of utopianism in the liberal's. Influenced as it has been by nineteenth-century romanticism and Western European socialism, progressive liberalism echoes in a number of clearly discernable ways the utopian's insistence that criminals are the victims and that society is ultimately responsible for their acts. More than a century ago, the Russian prince turned anarchist Peter Kropotkin indicted all advanced criminal justice systems on much the same terms as Bazelon and Menninger. Take the most depraved murderer—Charles Manson, Ted Bundy, or John Wayne Gacy or, in Kropotkin's own time, Jack the Ripper. However horrible their crimes, they pale in comparison with society's crimes against them:

> But when we recall all the infamies which brought him to this; when we think of the darkness in which he prowls, haunted by images drawn from indecent books or thoughts suggested by stupid books, our thought is divided. And if we hear some day that Jack is in the hands of some judge who has slain a far greater number of men, women and children than all the Jacks put together, if we see him in the hands of one of those deliberate maniacs, then all our hatred of Jack the Ripper will vanish. It will be transformed into hatred for a cowardly and hypocritical society and its recognized representatives. All the infamies of a Ripper disappear before the long series of infamies committed in the name of law. It is these we hate.[8]

Modern liberals have inherited from their utopian forebears the quasi-Newtonian view that all crime represents a kind of equal but opposite reaction of offenders against the society that has blinkered their options. Not much distinguishes Kropotkin's indictment of "hypocritical society" from Menninger's declaration: "I suspect that all the crimes committed by all the jailed criminals do not equal in total social damage the crimes committed against them."[9]

Crime, liberals insist, is a symptom of systemic social dysfunction, not of individual moral failure, let alone sin. Criminals are trying to communicate something; they are our miner's canary—their acts tell us that there is something deeply askew

not with them but with our social institutions. The acts of the repeat criminal offender, Menninger wrote, are "signals of distress, signals of failure, signals of crises
which society sees primarily in terms of its annoyance, its irritation, its injury."[10] To
punish criminals is thus to doubly victimize them—once by inflicting their social
condition on them and a second time by punishing them when they react to their
condition. "In my opinion," Bazelon intoned, "it is simply unjust to place people
in dehumanizing social conditions, to do nothing about those conditions and then
to command those who suffer—"Behave—or else!"[11]

What Causes Crime?

One of the hallmarks of modern conservatism is to reject socially systemic explanations of human behavior. "Crime is not caused by society," conservative columnist
George Will declared. "Culpability resides in guilty individuals, not flawed institutions."[12] Yet no social scientist today, liberal or conservative, denies that there are
clear *correlations* between crime and poverty, race, unemployment, and other social
conditions. What are we to make of these?

Liberals like Menninger and Bazelon who wrote about crime during the 1960s
and 1970s operated from two central assumptions—a rationalistic conception of
human behavior and a tendency to concretize society. Both assumptions owed a
great deal to the influence of a form of behaviorism then prevalent among intellectuals. Their version of behaviorism held, first, that human behavior is fully
explicable in terms of a set of causes and conditions that are largely or entirely
external to individuals and that precipitate their behavior. "Behavior, both orderly
and disorderly, can be studied and scientifically appraised," Menninger assured us.
"The disciplines of psychology, psychiatry, sociology, ethnology, genetics, anthro-
pology and ekistics can be and are constantly applied to the behavior of human
beings. There really is such a thing as behavioral science."[13] Second, they presumed
that all these external causes and conditions emanate from society, which liberals
sometimes represent as a more or less concrete entity responsible for the condition
of each of its members. Bazelon suggested that "if . . . society itself were responsible
for any depredation or degradation that the actor had suffered, society might not
be entitled to condemn that actor."[14] Together these two tenets imply that the individual is a "product" of society and that society can make the individual better if
only it is willing to devote the necessary resources to that end.

As a judge, Bazelon advocated a conception of human nature that owed a great
deal more to the deterministic ideas associated with behaviorism than to the traditional free choice and individual responsibility paradigm that underlies criminal
law. There is an insuperable philosophical gulf between a view that insists that we
make choices about how we behave and a cause-and-effect conception of behavior
that holds us responsible for none of our actions. Mentioning a case he had pre-
sided over years earlier, Bazelon questioned "whether a free choice to do wrong
can be found in the acts of a poverty-stricken and otherwise deprived black youth
from the central city who kills a marine who taunted him with a racial epithet."[15]

Rather than interpreting the act as an expression of rage and overreaction, a voluntary choice precipitated by a provocative act (which might warrant a reduction in the crime from first-degree murder to voluntary manslaughter), Bazelon wanted to shift the focus to the offender's "deprived" background.

These intellectual peregrinations led Bazelon to author one of the most notorious opinions on the insanity defense. In *Durham v. United States*, he developed what has become known as the "product test" for excusing the putatively mentally disturbed offender.[16] The test required acquittal by reason of insanity if the accused's "unlawful act was the product of mental disease or defect." The product test was an exception broad enough to drive a truck full of psychiatrists through the more general free choice and individual responsibility rule. It was offered as an alternative to the old M'Naughten test, which excused the individual only when he did not understand "the nature and quality of his act" or the "difference between right and wrong with respect to the act."[17] The M'Naughten test was a necessary humanitarian concession to the free will model of human behavior. It meant that those who committed criminal acts because of an insane delusion were not acting "knowingly" and, thus, not voluntarily. The hornbook example is the offender who believes he is Babe Ruth in the 1928 World Series as he clubs his victim to death. Those of us who take the free will and individual responsibility model seriously recognize why it is both pointless and inhumane to punish the truly delusional.

Yet Bazelon's product test went much further. Indeed, it potentially conflicts with the traditional model, opening the way to excuse offenders who understood perfectly well what they are doing. They would be excused just as long as they could claim that their act was the product of a "mental disease or defect." The product test might provide an excuse for the likes of a Charlie Manson or a Ted Bundy, who murdered in cold blood but who could point to a background of child abuse, which could in turn be linked by a sympathetic psychiatrist to later criminal behavior. As Bazelon forlornly noted more than twenty years after the decision, the *Durham* product test "did not succeed," and Bazelon joined the other judges in abandoning the decision in 1972, eighteen years after its adoption.[18] Though the product test was supposed to limit the role of psychiatrists, it had just the opposite effect, as experts for every defendant could trace from the offense back to some childhood trauma or condition of social deprivation.

The deepest problem with a purely scientific approach to criminal law is not that it is wrong but that it proves too much. If all human behavior is determined by external causes and conditions rather than by the choices humans make, then it really doesn't matter whether our actions are precipitated by a poor environment or by the best of social conditions. Every action is equally excusable. Clarence Darrow's infamous defense of Leopold and Loeb, two privileged adolescents in the 1930s who murdered a mentally handicapped boy just to see if they could get away with it, was reminiscent of this thinking. Darrow argued that the two were victims of their upper-class background, that a life of wealth and privilege had left them insensate to the condition of the less well off. Thankfully, the jury did not buy his argument.

Explaining Crime without Excusing It

Understandably, most liberals today do not argue that all behavior should be excused. But they do argue that most crime is precipitated by social and economic factors, particularly poverty, and frequently seem to draw the implication that, from a social perspective, most criminals should be viewed as victims or otherwise compensated for their condition. If poverty causes crime, as they insist, how can we hold the criminal fully responsible?

The problem with the "poverty causes crime" formula is not simply that a majority of those who are poor do not commit crimes or even that many who are relatively well off do commit crimes—both white-collar and violent crime. Poverty could still be one of several influences on the crime rate without being a necessary or sufficient condition for crime. The real problem is that even when we can link poverty and crime, the connections are considerably looser than some liberals appear to believe.

Even when there is a correlation between poverty and crime, there may not be a causal relationship. Of course economic and social factors influence our options; our circumstances structure and limit our alternatives, so that we must make our choices from among the options that are open to us. In some cases, these options may be so constrained that we should be excused for our acts or have our punishment mitigated. A modern-day Jean Valjean, a father who steals to feed a starving baby, is certainly the kind of case where even the sensitive conservative will say, "There but for the grace of God go I." But most crimes today are not of this character, much as liberals want us to believe they are. When someone holds up and murders a cab driver for a couple of hundred dollars to go on a drinking spree, or rapes and brutalizes an innocent child, the crime is not caused by poverty and should never be excused. The liberal approach to criminal justice falters precisely in failing to draw commonsense normative distinctions between true economic exigency and blatant excuse making.

There is an even deeper problem with the "poverty causes crime" hypothesis: it doesn't square with history. If the level of poverty actually caused crime, one would expect the crime rate to be lowest when a populace is experiencing the greatest prosperity and highest at times of economic recession or depression. Yet just the opposite is often true. Though the United States today is the wealthiest country in the history of the world, our crime rate is much higher than at virtually any other time and place in history. And it often gets worse as economic circumstances get better, as more thoughtful liberals have acknowledged. Paul Krugman argues in *The Conscience of a Liberal* that the 1950s and 1960s represented the period of greatest prosperity in the United States. The median income of the average worker was higher than it had ever been before or has been since, and even the poorest classes were doing better in material terms than at earlier points in history. Yet, as Krugman points out, "the crime rate more than tripled between 1957 and 1970," just when the liberal hypothesis would expect it to have plunged. Conversely, even as average incomes stalled and began to fall relative to the cost of living in the 1980s and 1990s, crime fell, rather than rose.[19]

Recognizing that prosperity frequently seems to generate crime rather than prevent it, sociologists have arrived at a more refined explanation for the relationship between poverty and crime. Poverty, they point out, is a relative concept. Poor people in the United States are considerably wealthier by any material standard than are poor people who live in poor societies. Indeed, in many ways, they are better off materially than even the middle class a century ago. Given these developments, some sociologists have concluded that crime correlates not with poverty but with inequality, not with deprivation but with relative deprivation. As John Lea and Jock Young, two sociologists who have studied the phenomenon, put it, relative deprivation occurs "where individuals or groups subjectively perceive themselves as unfairly disadvantaged over others perceived as having similar attributes and deserving similar rewards."[20] Most criminals in our society have cars and homes, TVs and electronic appliances, and enough to eat. They are frequently driven not by economic exigency but by anger, resentment, and frustration. They see around them, almost within reach, a world that could be described as opulent, from the vantage point of a century ago, and they suspect that the more the rich get ahead, the more they fall behind.[21]

Sociologist John E. Conklin has persuasively shown that this phenomenon (he calls it "progressive deprivation") is also the most satisfactory explanation for violent crimes in times of rising prosperity. Relative deprivation is experienced when "value expectations" (what one feels entitled to) outpace "value capabilities" (what one feels capable of achieving).[22] The response is frequently frustration and rage aimed at symbols of the system. We see evidence of this when we consider the statistics concerning crimes of violence, many of which do not have an economic incentive at all. The murder rate almost doubled during the 1960s, and the rate of rape more than doubled during the same period. Even today, relative deprivation explains why the crime rate is substantially higher for minorities. In *Two Nations*, Andrew Hacker's exploration of race in the United States, Hacker tells us that blacks represent about 13 percent of the U.S. population, yet are responsible for just over 50 percent of criminal deaths in instances where the assailant was known. They also represent 34 percent of arrests for rape and assault.[23]

Relative deprivation serves to *explain* the relationship between poverty and crime without saying that economic factors operate above the heads of criminals. Conditions of relative deprivation do not give criminal offenders an excuse, let alone a justification, for acting as they do. Feeling aggrieved does not mean that you are justified in feeling aggrieved, and even if we could say that someone actually was justifiably aggrieved (relative to some social baseline of entitlements), this would not excuse criminal acts, particularly violent crimes perpetrated on innocent victims. Since relative deprivation is fully consistent with the view that offenders are often motivated by spite, envy, frustration, the quest for status, or sheer excitement, it doesn't excuse offenders or suggest that they are not responsible for their acts. It shifts the debate between liberals and conservatives from one about whether criminals should be excused for their acts to one about whether some of the precipitating social causes for crime warrant mitigation in punishment.

The Deterrent Effect

Relative deprivation provides only part of the answer to questions about what causes crime in our society. It cannot explain, for example, why the crime rate fell again so dramatically in the 1980s and 1990s, when our economic conditions were not greatly changed from a decade or two earlier. Conservatives point out that what changed was our tolerance for crime. Only when authorities were willing to get tough, as they did in the 1970s and 1980s—enacting tougher sentencing laws, building more prisons, providing for more policemen—did the crime rate begin to fall. There is something to this thesis, though conservatives have drawn some inapposite lessons from the effects of deterrence.

The commonsense conclusion that we can deter many kinds of crime is overwhelmingly supported by the literature. Four decades of research by criminologists bears out the conclusion that the higher the likelihood of arrest and conviction and, to a lesser extent, the more severe the criminal penalty, the greater the deterrent effect (though there is some disagreement about how much crime can be deterred through effective measures).[24] Most lawbreakers engage in at least some loose form of cost-benefit analysis. This doesn't mean that criminal behavior is optimally rational; clearly it usually isn't. But except in the case of addicts and psychopaths, as conservative sociologist Edward Banfield has observed, "there is an element of calculation—indeed, a very considerable one—in practically all criminal behavior." Even when criminal behavior appears irrational, "an element of rationality is hardly ever absent." Banfield notes that crimes of passion are hardly ever committed in front of police officers, and that those who impulsively shoplift usually steal something they want.[25] So when crime pays because of relaxed law enforcement, fewer police on the street, and an overburdened prison system, we should expect crime to increase.

Conservatives are right to insist that crime is, to a large extent, a measure of our response to it. But they often draw the wrong conclusions from this. Many conservatives have blamed the increase in crime during the 1960s on the judicial system. The problem began, many argue, with the liberalization of criminal law brought on by the Warren Court. "Between 1960 and 1965, the Court heard 75 cases in which criminals claimed that 'We the People' violated their rights," argues conservative blogger D. J. Connolly. "It ruled in favor of the crooks 64 of those 75 times." Conservatives point to cases like *Mapp v. Ohio*, which requires that evidence obtained without a search warrant be excluded from trial, and *Miranda v. Arizona*, which threw out the uncoerced confession of a rapist because the police had interrogated him without telling him that he could have an attorney present. Connolly points out that the incidence of burglary went from 900,000 nationwide in 1960, just before the period of constitutional liberalization, to 2.2 million in 1970, to 3.8 million in 1980, more than quadrupling in the twenty-year period. Moreover, violent crimes—especially murder and rape, which are frequently not perpetrated for economic reasons—skyrocketed during this period.[26]

Whatever role deterrence and punishment have—and there is good reason to believe they have an important role—conservatives have overestimated the impact of procedural decisions such as *Mapp* and *Miranda* in the mind of the average would-be criminal. The evidence is fairly conclusive that the most important aspect of deterrence is offenders' perception of the *likelihood of getting caught*, not how the evidence against them will be used in the event they are caught. The best deterrent to crime is the heightened presence of law enforcement—officers on the beat, community policing, and other mechanisms that raise the visibility of the agents of social order in crime-prone environments. Potential offenders who stop to calculate the risks and benefits of committing a crime are not likely to be encouraged in their endeavor by knowing that they can have illegally seized evidence excluded from their trial in the event they are apprehended, or that they will be entitled to call an attorney. What they think about is how likely they are to be caught and convicted.

Nor is strong deterrence always necessary for a low crime rate. If crime rates were invariably linked to levels of deterrence, we should expect the most socially permissive countries of the world—places such as the Netherlands or Sweden—to have much higher crime rates than we do in the United States. But they don't. In fact, their crime rates are much lower than ours. This leads some liberals, again, to draw the counterintuitive conclusion that repressive order actually *increases* crime. But this can't be right either, since the credible threat of punishment consistently deters many would-be offenders. So why do people commit less crime in some societies than in others, notwithstanding lower levels of deterrence?

Here we come to the deeper theme of our discussion of the causes of crime. Thoughtful liberals and sensitive conservatives understand that, to some extent, the crime rate is always inversely related to the level of social cohesion in a community. The more that people feel that we are all in this together, the less some (though certainly not all) will be drawn to violate the rights of others, particularly in violent and gratuitous ways. This is why liberals are right to point out that relative equality of condition seems to reduce the crime rate, even as conservatives are right to observe that a constant emphasis on social inequality promotes unrest. Sadly, it seems that the increase in crime during the 1960s was the flip side of the same social developments that led to the noblest achievements of that decade—the civil rights movement and heightened concerns that minorities had been unjustly denied an equal stake in U.S. society up to that time. The same zeitgeist that gave rise to the greater sensitivity of nonminorities to the plight of minorities also fueled heightened resentment and frustration on the part of minorities when these expectations remained partially unfulfilled.

The more that the disadvantaged feel aggrieved and react against the system—the greater the felt inequality and sense of relative deprivation—the greater will be our need for deterrence and what liberals regard as repressive control. And this is exactly what has happened since the 1970s.

White-Collar Crime, Blue-Collar Crime, and Proportional Punishment

If the poor and the socially disadvantaged have any right to complain about the criminal justice system, it is not because the system holds them responsible for their acts, but because it does so disproportionately, and often fails to hold the well-to-do equally accountable for their acts.

Over the past twenty-five years, there has been an alarming increase in the number of prisons and prisoners in the United States.[27] Our total prison population has increased on average over 3 percent a year since 1995, up roughly 40 percent since the mid-1990s.[28] In 2008 there were roughly 2.2 million persons in prison or jail in the United States, about 1 of every 136 people.[29] We have by far the highest prison population rate in the world: roughly 740 of every 100,000 people in the United States are incarcerated.[30] One in every thirty-two adults in the United States is behind bars, on probation, or on parole.[31] Social conservatives see in these figures the unmistakable signs of full-scale social decline, where liberals believe we have simply become a much more repressive society. There is more than a measure of truth in each view.

To some extent, these figures reflect our response to the rise in violent crime that took place in the 1960s and 1970s, and they may also explain why the crime rate began to fall by the 1980s. Yet many who are now behind bars are nonviolent offenders sentenced to lengthy prison terms under our drug laws or because of "three strikes" laws. Consider these statistics: roughly 55 percent of the 160,000 federal prison population today is incarcerated for drug offenses.[32] Under current mandatory minimum sentencing laws, a first felony drug conviction earns the offender five years in prison, escalating to ten years and then to life imprisonment for the second and third convictions. There are notorious asymmetries in drug sentencing; for example, it takes the possession of one hundred times more powder cocaine than crack cocaine to trigger the same mandatory minimum sentence of five years, a penalty schedule referred to as the "100 to 1" ratio.[33] Of course, the great majority of crack users are black, a statistic which only reinforces the perception that punishment is administered asymmetrically according to income level and race.[34] The average length of prison time served by a federal drug offender in the United States today is about six years, four months; violent offenders serve on average only five years, three months. Those who engage in white-collar crime, by contrast, frequently spend less than two years in jail.[35]

Since 1993, twenty-six states and the federal government have passed "three strikes" laws, which require life imprisonment (generally ensuring that the offender will spend at least twenty-five years in prison) for a third felony conviction. These statutes were passed to address the problem of habitual offenders, and they serve an important purpose when the offender is thrice convicted of violent crimes. But some states (e.g., California) apply the law to any third felony conviction, as long as the first two were either violent or "serious." These include cases where offenders have gone to prison for life for such third offenses as stealing golf clubs, filching nine videotapes, and taking a piece of pepperoni pizza from some children.[36] Even petty instances of blue-collar fraud sometimes garner unbelievably harsh sentences.[37] Yet someone who defrauds the government of millions of dollars in Medicaid bills may go to jail for little more than a year or two. Martha Stewart spent only five months in jail upon being convicted of lying to federal investigators and obstructing justice after engaging in insider trading (with which she was not charged). And President George W. Bush notoriously commuted the sentence of Lewis "Scooter" Libby only hours after judges announced that Libby would have to serve a thirty-month sentence for perjury and obstruction of justice pending appeal. In the past, commutations have almost universally taken place *after* a defendant has served some time in prison.

The reality is that even nonviolent blue-collar crime is frequently punished with longer sentences, which explains in part the increase in our total prison population. Yet in terms of the effects on social order, white-collar crime—embezzlement, bribery, fraud, insider trading, and other regulatory offenses—exacts a huge toll on us economically, and in more intangible ways. According to FBI figures, white-collar crime costs us $300 billion dollars annually—far more in economic terms than all street crime combined. Yet because the harms are nonviolent and diffused throughout society, and because corporations cannot go to jail, these crimes go underdeterred and (when uncovered) underpunished. When the Halliburton Company grossly overcharged the government for supplies it provided to our forces in Iraq, the crime took a toll on the economy and on our trust in the integrity of our government. When the officers of the Enron Corporation fraudulently pumped up the value of their stock, hid corporate liabilities in dummy corporations, and sold their private shares before the stock went into freefall, the consequences were painfully direct for the millions who held stock in the company and for the many employees who lost their retirement savings. When Arthur Andersen, Price Waterhouse, or other major accounting firms assist in manipulating the value of stock, there is an insidious but diffuse impact on the trust every investor ought to have in the market. But such crimes doesn't seem as real to judges, legislators, and the public as do more localized acts of viciousness and violence.

Conservatives in particular have a problem with these disparities. They applaud themselves for being tough on crime, but they frequently want to overlook the kinds of criminal activity committed by the powerful—activity that takes a higher toll in economic terms, and on our sense of social trust. While violent crimes have the most dramatic, felt human impact on particular individuals, white-collar crimes are in some ways even more corrosive of social order. When people in positions of trust and authority, officers of corporations or high-ranking government officials, embezzle, commit fraud, perjure themselves, or obstruct justice, their acts strike at the heart of what binds our society together—our faith and trust in the institutions of government and the economy. After President Bush commuted Lewis Libby's thirty-month sentence—a sentence the president thought was "excessive"—while leaving the door open for a full pardon in the future, the special prosecutor in the case, Patrick Fitzgerald, had this to say: "In this case an experienced federal judge considered extensive argument from the parties and then imposed a sentence consistent with the applicable laws. It is fundamental to the rule of law that all citizens stand before the bar of justice as equals."[38]

Liberals were absolutely right to criticize Bush's commutation of Libby's sentence as corrupt and hypocritical. Two weeks earlier the Bush administration's Justice Department had persuaded a court to uphold a sentence of eighty-eight months for perjury and obstruction of justice in a case that strikingly parallels the Libby case. If conservatives take seriously the idea that the criminal justice system exists to preserve the social fabric, they must be willing to deploy their law-and-order attitudes to the crimes committed by the wealthy and powerful in our society, not simply by the poor and disadvantaged.

The Death Penalty: Some Background

The most emotionally polarizing criminal justice issue today is capital punishment. The American Civil Liberties Union (ACLU) estimates that there have been roughly 14,000 legal executions in the history of the United States, and that about 3,350 people today are on death row.[39] About seven in ten Americans now support the death penalty.[40] Yet the death penalty is imposed rarely today, even in the narrowly defined set of cases for which it is available. When it is imposed, the average length of time between conviction and execution is now around twelve years. What the President's Commission on Law Enforcement and Administration of Justice said in 1967 is even more true today: the "most salient characteristic of capital punishment is that it is infrequently applied."[41]

Therein lies the dilemma. The more frequently the death penalty is imposed, the more the opponents of capital punishment insist that the practice should be curbed or eliminated. Yet the less frequently it is imposed, the more its opponents have been able to argue, with some plausibility, that the sheer infrequency of its imposition undercuts its deterrent value and makes imposing it on those who actually are sentenced to death all the more unfair.

Our current dilemma is a result of the history of capital punishment in the United States. After the American Revolution, all American states followed the English common law tradition that made the death penalty automatic in cases of murder, subject only to executive commutation on grounds of mercy. The jury had no discretion in deciding whether a death sentence should be imposed in a particular case: all convicted murderers were executed. By the mid-nineteenth century, however, most states changed the rule to leave the decision to impose death to the discretion of juries, an expression of our greater commitment to citizen self-government. Most states gradually circumscribed the class of cases for which capital punishment was available, and by the 1960s, most states permitted capital sentences only in cases of first-degree (premeditated) murder. Even among this smaller class of cases, the death penalty was seldom imposed and even less frequently carried out. By the mid to late 1960s, support for capital punishment plummeted, even as the crime rate skyrocketed. In 1966, there was only one execution in the entire United States, and in 1967 a Gallup poll put public support for capital punishment at around 40 percent. A few states abolished the death penalty during this period and, in various ways, the Supreme Court began to further circumscribe its use.

In 1972, the Supreme Court appeared to declare the death penalty unconstitutional. In *Furman v. Georgia*, two justices, Brennan and Marshall, argued that capital punishment always constitutes cruel and unusual punishment in violation of the Eighth Amendment; three others—Douglass, Stewart, and White—were more troubled by what seemed to them the arbitrariness with which the death penalty was imposed. As Justice Stewart summed it up: "These death sentences are cruel and unusual in the same way that being struck by lightning is cruel and unusual."[42] Paradoxically, juries' sparing use of the death penalty became the predicate for attacking it.

In 1976, in *Gregg v. Georgia*, the Supreme Court reversed itself, upholding a death penalty statute which carefully tailored death penalty decisions to first-degree murders that involve any of several aggravating circumstances—e.g., murder by an offender who has a previous capital conviction, murder involving torture, murder involving depravity of mind or aggravated battery, murder of a judge or police officer, or murder upon escape from lawful confinement, among others.[43] That the Court's purpose was more about narrowing the scope of the crimes for which the death penalty could be imposed than about juries' discretion was made clear in two cases decided the same day as *Gregg*. In these cases, the Court struck down statutes that required the death penalty in every case of first-degree murder.[44] The upshot of these decisions was that states could neither take away juries' discretion in cases of first-degree murder—an automatic rule was not acceptable—nor leave juries' discretion intact. The Court was saying that some discretion was required, but in a narrower subset of first-degree murders—those involving murder with aggravated circumstances. In subsequent cases, the Court further narrowed the scope of crimes for which the death penalty can be given. A year after *Gregg* it made clear that capital punishment was not available for crimes less serious than murder—in this case it spared an escaped convict who kidnapped, beat, raped, and robbed a woman at knifepoint.[45]

Today thirty-eight states and the federal government retain the death penalty, yet it is seldom carried out. Since the Supreme Court reinstated capital punishment in 1976, there have been, according to one death penalty expert, roughly 500,000 murders eligible for the death penalty in the United States. About 7,000 of these have resulted in a capital sentence. Of these 7,000 death sentences handed down, only about 950 had been carried out as of 2005.[46] This means that nationally, a murderer has perhaps a 1-in-500 chance of being executed for the crime. Even in the thirty-eight states that retain capital punishment, only about 1 percent of murderers are sentenced to death, and many of these death sentences are never carried out. Add to this the fact that the average waiting time between conviction and execution is now close to twelve years and one can understand why the death penalty might not pack a great deterrent wallop.

A few years ago author and lawyer Scott Turow, whom Illinois governor George Ryan appointed to a commission to study the death penalty, studied some 270 capital appeals in Illinois. Turow observed that he "was struck again and again by the wide variation in the seriousness of the crimes. There were some monstrous offenses, but also some garden-variety murders. The feeling that the system is an unguided ship is only heightened when one examines the first-degree homicides that have resulted in sentences other than death."[47] Conservative supporters of capital punishment respond that this variation indicates, if anything, that the death penalty should be more routinely and consistently imposed, not less frequently. No murder is a "garden-variety" murder, particularly since the death penalty can be imposed today only for willful, premeditated first-degree murders with aggravating circumstances. Rather than concluding that many who ought to receive the death penalty escape it, whether through the mercy of the jury or for other reasons, opponents of capital punishment pretend to insist that everyone in certain circumstances should receive it or that no one at all should. Conservatives plausibly suggest an alternative understanding: if you murder someone, you should expect the worst. Chances are, you will still escape the death penalty, but do not complain when you draw the joker.

The Arguments: A Brief Look

Conservatives and other supporters of the death penalty raise two arguments in support of their position. The first, based on retributive principles, holds that the death penalty is warranted on purely moral grounds as an expression of the community's instinctive revulsion to especially heinous murders. The second and more utilitarian argument holds that the death penalty deters murders and thus saves innocent lives. Each of these arguments stands on its own, though supporters of capital punishment frequently employ both. Opponents of capital punishment, on the other hand, deny that it deters serious crime and make at least four other arguments. They argue that the death penalty is administered in a racially biased way, that it is painful and barbaric and constitutes cruel and unusual punishment, that innocent people have sometimes been executed, and, finally, that it is always wrong to take a human life when not acting in self-defense. I hope to show that the prima facie case for the death penalty is much stronger than opponents believe, though I will propose an alternative to capital punishment at the end of the chapter.

(1) *The deterrence argument.* Supporters of deterrence claim that the death penalty deters murders and does so significantly better than life imprisonment. If this is true, then a failure to impose the death sentence is tantamount to contributing, by our omission, to the deaths of all those victims whose murders could have been deterred if capital punishment were available. This is a particularly difficult argument for death penalty opponents to respond to, at least if the death penalty does deter, since it means that they must accept as a cost of sparing the lives of convicted murderers the deaths of innocent victims whose murders could have been deterred.

So does the death penalty deter? The ACLU's website on the death penalty claims that "there is no credible evidence that the death penalty deters" and that "claims that each execution deters a certain number of murders have been thoroughly discredited by social science research." Each of these statements is patently false. The truth is that studies on deterrence have gone both ways.[48] Within the past few years, however, there have been a number of comprehensive studies that strongly indicate that capital punishment does have a dramatic deterrent effect. A 2004 study conducted by Joanna Shepherd concludes that each execution deters on average three murders and that capital punishment deters crimes thought to be undeterable—in particular, heat of passion murders and murders between intimates. She also found that longer wait times between conviction and execution decrease the deterrent effect of capital punishment—not a surprising conclusion since research has consistently shown that deterrence depends upon the likelihood and the swiftness of punishment.[49]

Other recent studies corroborate Shepherd's findings. A Texas study from 2001 found a sharp increase in the homicide rate when a moratorium was placed on the death penalty.[50] A 2003 study found an even more powerful rate of deterrence—as much as eighteen murders deterred for every execution.[51] A twenty-year nationwide study published in 2003 examined the 6,143 death sentences handed down between 1977 and 1997 and concluded not only that five murders were deterred for every death sentence imposed, but also that there was an increase of five murders for every commutation.[52]

Of course, for capital punishment to deter, it must be imposed consistently and swiftly enough to constitute a credible threat. But the death penalty today does not constitute a credible threat precisely because it is not used with any degree of consistency, frequency, or speed. Ironically, the deterrence value of capital punishment is undercut by opponents' efforts to reduce the frequency of executions and to increase the average waiting time between sentencing and execution. Given this reality, the question to ask now is not, Does the death penalty deter? but, Can we achieve more deterrence with other measures such as guaranteed life imprisonment for all capital offenses than we can with the system as it currently exists?

(2) *The argument regarding race and capital punishment.* One of the most powerful arguments against capital punishment is that blacks who commit death-eligible crimes are more likely than whites who commit these same crimes to receive the death penalty. While this may well have been true in the past, just the opposite is true today. Death penalty opponents frequently point to evidence such as that produced by David Baldus, whose findings of racial disparities in capital sentencing became the subject of a Supreme Court case challenging the death penalty in 1987.[53] The Baldus study examined death penalty sentencing in Georgia in the 1970s. It showed that the death penalty, there and then, was assessed 22 percent of the time in black-on-white murders, 8 percent in white-on-white murders, 1 percent in black-on-black murders, and 3 percent in white-on-black murders. While more than 90 percent of all murderers, black and white, escaped the death sentence, the disparity Baldus discovered is significant enough to be troubling. Yet recent nationwide figures drawn from the Department of Justice's Bureau of Justice Statistics by the researchers in what has become known as the "Cornell study" show that Baldus's findings do not now (if they ever did) reflect the national reality. African Americans, who represent about 14 percent of the U.S. population, committed about 51.5 percent of all murders in the United States during the period studied, yet make up only 41.3 percent of the death row population.[54] The study found that nationally a white person who commits a capital offense is twice as likely to receive

the death penalty as a black person who commits a capital offense, and that the proportion of black death row inmates relative to their share of homicides is lowest "where the conventional wisdom would least expect it—in the South." In twenty-eight states, including Georgia, South Carolina, and Tennessee, blacks are underrepresented on death row. Speaking of the so-called southern death belt, where juries are supposed to be more lenient to whites than to blacks, the researchers in the Cornell study—who were clearly surprised by their own findings—concluded that "the conventional wisdom about the death penalty is incorrect in some respects and misleading in others."[55]

What accounts for the bias against whites in death penalty sentencing? There are three possible explanations. One is that crimes committed by whites are, on average, even more savage than crimes committed by blacks. Infamous white killers Charlie Manson, Ted Bundy, John Wayne Gacy, Jeffrey Dahmer, Timothy McVeigh, and Dennis Rader, better known as the "BTK killer," certainly fit the mold. As Joshua Marquis, an expert on the death penalty, put it, "It may be shockingly politically incorrect to say, but the fact is that the most horrific murders—serial killings, torture murders and sex crimes against children—tend to be committed more frequently by white murderers than blacks."[56]

Another possibility, often cited by opponents of the death penalty, is that these figures reflect indirect racism against blacks. Since about 90 percent of all murders involve assailants and victims of the same race, opponents have suggested that these figures are a proxy for juries' attitudes toward the victim, rather than toward the offender.[57] As Scott Turow put it in discussing Illinois's experience, where whites who commit capital offenses are two-and-a-half times as likely as blacks to receive the death penalty, "In a racially divided society whites tend to associate with, and thus to murder, other whites. And choosing a white victim makes a murderer three and a half times as likely to be punished by a death sentence as if he'd killed someone who is black."[58] In other words, juries value black victims less than they value white victims.

Perhaps this explanation holds a kind of paradoxical appeal for those determined to find the signs of racism even in the face of evidence to the contrary. Apparently, death penalty opponents believe that capital punishment is administered in a way that tilts toward whites whether it is blacks who are disproportionately executed or whites who are disproportionately executed. Only by overlooking the greater leniency shown to blacks in capital sentencing can one reach this conclusion, however. More to the point, those who hold this view would not be mollified by increasing the number of black offenders who are given the death penalty for their crimes against black victims.

The third possibility is that juries have become so sensitized to racial issues that they sometimes overcompensate by sparing a greater number of blacks than whites. This is certainly at least as plausible an explanation as the second. At any rate, whatever the combination of reasons for the disparity, we should keep in mind that, in absolute terms, the number of murderers sentenced to death is marginal. In eight states that provide racial data, of 39,356 black murderers, 517 were sentenced to death (1.3 percent), as were 575 of the 20,650 white murderers (about 2.8 percent). Obviously, about 98 percent of black and white murderers were spared the death penalty.[59] At any rate, to the very marginal extent that race is an issue relevant to capital sentencing today, it is an issue for whites, not blacks.

(3) *The cruel and unusual punishment argument.* The focus has shifted more recently to an attack on the methods of execution. In the United States today, there are five legal methods of execution—hanging, firing squad, the electric chair, the gas chamber, and lethal injection—but lethal injection has become the most frequently used procedure. The Supreme Court recently upheld the constitutionality of lethal injection against an Eighth Amendment cruel and unusual punishment claim. The process, which requires three chemicals—an anesthetic that causes unconsciousness, a muscle relaxant that stops breathing, and the lethal ingredient, potassium chloride, that causes cardiac arrest—was challenged by death penalty opponents who claimed that if the first drug is administered in insufficient doses, the condemned will be conscious but paralyzed as they suffocate and suffer from the initial effects of the potassium chloride.[60]

Of course, other methods of execution present problems of their own. Hanging fractures the spine, paralyzes the diaphragm, and suffocates the prisoner, a process that can take several minutes and occasionally has had to be repeated. Electrocution, in use since New York introduced it as an alternative to hanging in 1890, causes deep burns and severe bleeding. Death by lethal gas is little better. The 1992 execution of Donald Harding, a convicted murderer in California, took eleven minutes and was so horrific that reporters who had witnessed it were reported to have been rendered "walking vegetables" for days afterward, the attorney general vomited, and the warden threatened to resign before he would conduct another similar execution.[61] Strangely, perhaps, the firing squad may be the fastest and least painful form of execution.

Whatever the form of execution, we must acknowledge that it is usually painful to die—occasionally as painful for murderers as for their victims. The more we have attempted to make executions humanitarian, the more we have medicalized death penalty procedures.

And the more we have medicalized these procedures, the more we are confronted with the *human* process of dying. We are forced, in other words, to confront the grim reality that dying is not pleasant, and that there may be insuperable limits to our efforts to make it less painful. Of course, in the end, opponents would regard the death penalty as cruel and unusual punishment even if we found a way for convicted murderers to die painlessly. It is not primarily the method of execution that motivates death penalty opponents but the fact that we are, after all, ending a person's life.

(4) *The argument from innocence.* How many innocent people have been wrongfully sentenced to death, and how many of these have been executed? There are, of course, disagreements here as well, but I will use the statistics cited by death penalty opponents even if their figures tend to overstate the problem. According to the ACLU, "since 1973 123 people in 25 states have been released from death row because they were not guilty." An additional "seven people have been executed even though they were probably innocent."[62] U.S. District Court judge Jed Rakoff, an

opponent of the death penalty who declared it unconstitutional in 2001, stated at a recent Federal Bar Council conference that his research puts the figure of innocents sentenced to death at about thirty, though it is not clear how many of these were executed.[63] Assuming the accuracy of these statistics, we can draw the following picture of the likelihood of an innocent person being executed: of the roughly 500,000 murders committed in the United States since Gregg, between 1 and 2 percent—about 7,000—have resulted in a recommendation that the death penalty be imposed. Of these 7,000, seven who were "probably innocent" were executed. So, if the ACLU is correct, one innocent person may be executed for almost every 100,000 death-eligible offenses. Additionally, precautions against sentencing the innocent—and the guilty—to death continue to grow. Several states have created a capital litigation bar that requires lawyers representing those facing the death penalty to be experienced in death penalty litigation. The increased use of DNA tests since the 1990s also serves to decrease the conviction of the innocent. Finally, the appeal process, which frequently lasts more than a decade, ensures that every capital case is scrutinized by judges at several levels. If being sentenced to death is like being struck by lightning, as Justice Stewart suggested thirty-five years ago, then being innocent and sentenced to death is like being struck by lightning two different times while standing in the same place.

Still, it happens. While capital punishment supporters are correct to insist that it happens very infrequently, they must be willing to accept that nothing in the system absolutely prevents innocents from being executed.

Supporters may be willing to weigh these innocent deaths, in utilitarian fashion, against the lives of innocent people whose murders were deterred by capital punishment. But if we can achieve greater deterrence today with mandatory life sentences than with the death penalty, which is administered in only 1 or 2 percent of capital crimes, then supporters have to give up this argument. Thus, a mandatory life sentence proposal has the advantage not only of saving the life of the occasional innocent person who is sentenced to death, but also of preserving the possibility that they may one day prove their innocence.

(5) *The argument from the immorality of capital punishment.* The deepest objection of all to capital punishment—one with which every sensitive proponent of capital punishment must come to terms—is this: if it is fundamentally wrong to take a human life for any reason, then it is wrong irrespective of the social, procedural, and empirical considerations that may surround the debate over capital punishment. All human life is precious. Death penalty opponents see a powerful paradox in the position that we take life in order to vindicate the value of human life. This is ultimately the reason underlying the Roman Catholic Church's opposition to the death penalty, as it is the position of many liberals and a few conservatives today. There is an undeniable moral appeal to the argument from the inviolability of human life. Yet there is a countervailing argument here—the retributive argument, which holds that we are permitted, or even morally required, to pay a murderer in kind for the crime committed.

Many of us are instinctive retributivists. The retributive idea is expressed, in its less refined version, in the biblical notion of an eye for an eye. Philosophers, most notably Immanuel Kant, have offered rationalized versions of the argument, favoring the death penalty on grounds that the principles of justice require executing those who intentionally kill others. While opponents may find it anachronistic, I believe that many Americans would find a pristine simplicity in Kant's sentiment that "he [who] has committed murder . . . must die." Kant wrote that "there is no parallel between death and even the most miserable life, so that there is no equality of crime and retribution unless the perpetrator is judicially put to death (at all events without any maltreatment)."[64]

Kant went so far as to argue that, even if a society were about to disband, "the last murderer in prison would first have to be executed," which was Kant's way of saying that the death penalty has a moral significance that transcends its social utility.[65] Others have argued in similar terms that the sheer malignity of murder, especially of brutal murders involving torture, sexual abuse, or multiple killings, requires an appropriately severe societal response. James Fitzjames Stephen declared that "it is morally right to hate criminals"; more recently, philosopher Jeffrie Murphy has argued persuasively that resentment is a healthy emotion, that it "is an emotional defense of attacks on self-esteem" which society should uphold, rather than discourage.[66]

In the end, of course, the retributive intuition is not provable—any more than the opposite view that capital punishment is inherently wrong is provable. I don't know whether Kant or Sister Helen Prejean, the author of *Dead Man Walking*, has the better argument, and I certainly don't wish to suggest that the two arguments offset one another. Yet this may be exactly the kind of situation where we can afford to relinquish philosophical purity in favor of a sound, pragmatic compromise that protects society, vindicates the interests of victims and their families, and yet preserves the moral concerns connected with the taking of innocent life.

A Centrist Approach to Capital Punishment

Neither liberals nor conservatives can be satisfied with the situation as it now stands, yet recent constitutional developments foreclose the possibility of reinstating the death penalty on a widespread basis even as public opinion opposes abolishing it. Our second-best alternative is not to muddle on in the present manner, applying the death penalty in a costly and piecemeal fashion, but to require that those convicted of crimes for which the death penalty is eligible go to prison for life without possibility of parole. Better to have 100 percent of all dangerous criminals serving life terms—and these must truly be life terms—than to have 1 or 2 percent executed and the rest subject to the scattershot vagaries of the criminal justice system, which now eventually frees a large percentage of these same convicted murderers. This solution will better satisfy conservatives' demand for deterrence than does the status quo, even as it satisfies liberals' concerns about the consistency and morality of capital punishment.

Call our proposal the civil death penalty. Offenders convicted of a violent murder forfeit their *civil* life, though not their physical existence. They would go to prison for life without any possibility of parole. This approach goes a considerable distance toward satisfying conservatives' two concerns: we can deter more crimes by sending 100 percent of those convicted of such crimes to prison for life than we can by sending 1 or 2 percent to death (and eventually releasing many of the remaining 98 percent). As for the retributive concern that these crimes merit serious punishment, what might be lost in terms of the gravity of the punishment (in accepting life imprisonment rather than death) would be more than offset by its consistent use. While strict retributivists who believe that justice requires the life of the murderer in exchange for the life taken may not be fully satisfied, some of the other benefits associated with the retributivist's outlook can be better realized. Punishment has an expressive function that requires broad social consensus that certain forms of punishment are morally justified in particular cases. Won't we send a stronger social message when a large segment of society agrees that heinous crimes warrant life imprisonment than we do now, when the controversy over the moral legitimacy of the death penalty overshadows the crimes themselves? Of course, opponents' major concerns (that the death penalty is cruel and unusual, that innocents are occasionally executed, and that it is always wrong to take human life) are satisfied as well.

Perhaps conservative supporters of the death penalty will object that they are giving more than they are getting—that death penalty opponents are giving nothing at all under this proposal—yet they would be mistaken. Liberals would have to give up any argument that a once-dangerous criminal is now rehabilitated, and certainly some liberals will find this unattractive. Conservatives would also be assured that dangerous offenders from among the 98 percent not sentenced to death under our current system will not be released to commit similar crimes in the future. This would also permit us to forgo the long, drawn-out, and immensely expensive death penalty appeal process (to the extent that more due process is accorded to these appeals than others). Yet it would also preserve the life of the occasional innocent person who is wrongly convicted and sentenced to death, permitting that person to seek exoneration in the event that new evidence turns up establishing his or her innocence.

The civil death penalty would permit us to do a much better job than we are now doing of getting tough on crime, even as it would enable us to give the highest form of respect to the value and the dignity of human life.

Chapter 12
The Debate over Illegal Immigration

IN THE PAST FEW years, Americans have witnessed a resurgence of often vitriolic debate on immigration policy, particularly concerning the problem of illegal immigration. We are profoundly ambivalent about immigration policy. On one hand, we are proud of our national heritage as a refuge from oppression and as the land of opportunity; on the other, we are understandably concerned about the rising tide of illegal immigration over the past ten to fifteen years. Reflecting this ambivalence, a recent poll indicates that 91 percent of those surveyed felt that illegal immigration was a "very serious" or "somewhat serious" problem. While 43 percent wanted to eliminate all forms of public benefits to those here illegally, including public education, medical services, and driver's license privileges, 60 percent favored granting undocumented aliens temporary worker status but rejected "amnesty" for those here illegally.[1] Ultimately, most U.S. citizens seem to believe that we have to secure our borders and stem the tide of illegal immigrants but also find humane and pragmatic ways of addressing the condition of those already here.

Perhaps more than with any other issue, the immigration debate has made for strange political bedfellows. Our national ambivalence concerning immigration is reflected in the way the debate unites those from otherwise clashing perspectives while dividing others who are normally political allies. On the liberal side, the debate unites libertarians and liberal U.S. bishops of the Catholic Church, probusiness interests, and pro-Hispanic groups. On the conservative side are arrayed traditional populists with environmentalists concerned about overpopulation, liberals worried about the economic effects of immigration on the American workforce, and nativist and xenophobic elements in U.S. society. In sum, the debate divides libertarians from traditional conservatives on the right, and liberal humanitarians concerned about the plight of those in the Third World from other liberal humanitarians concerned about the effects of immigration on the U.S. working class on the left. It is little wonder that these kaleidoscopic overlaps and divergences lead some to argue that the real divide in the immigration debate is between educated elites and defenders of the U.S. poor and working class. Historian Victor Davis Hanson writes that the debate cannot be framed in classic Left versus Right terms. Rather, "on one side are the elite print media, the courts and a few politicians fronting for employer and ethnic interests; on the other are the far more numerous, and rancorous, talk-radio listeners, bloggers and cable news watchers, the ballot propositions, and populist state legislators who better reflect the angry pulse of the country."[2] A 2007 Senate bill supported by President Bush, John McCain, and Ted Kennedy was a similar example of the strange-bedfellow phenomenon. The bill would have tightened border controls but given a "path to citizenship" or amnesty to immigrants here illegally upon payment of a $5,000 fine and back taxes. Bush and McCain took an extraordinary amount of heat from the conservative base, even as liberals criticized Kennedy and other liberal supporters for the hefty fine.[3]

Self-interest obviously plays a part in these political alignments, but it would be a mistake to dismiss the deeper philosophical convergences that bring libertarians and liberal Catholics together on this issue, and that divide them from other conservatives and other liberals. Through much of this book, I have linked the political positions on the ground of left liberals, libertarians, centrists, and various species of conservative to the deeper ideas that motivate those who hold these positions. The immigration debate affords a final opportunity to understand not just what distinguishes Left and Right, but to see how porous the modern Left-Right distinction itself is in some respects.

Philosophically, what divides liberals from conservatives in the immigration debate is their contrasting attitudes concerning two issues—how to manage social change, on one hand, and the tension between individualism and nationalism, on the other. Since the Enlightenment, the Left has usually championed a more relaxed and liberal attitude toward social change, while the Right has insisted on the need to slow the arc of history and to conserve culture. On the second front, the Left has routinely defended individualism and universal cosmopolitanism in the name of human rights, while the Right has remained rooted in the values of cultural particularism, nationalism, and the importance of the local. This is why conservatives stress the preservation of national borders and the stewardship of contemporary U.S. cultural values, and why liberals are less concerned about cultural change than they are about our humanitarian obligations to those of the Third World. Of course, these commitments are far from fixed on the Left-Right spectrum. Anarchists have taken a leading role in fighting globalism, while the Right is divided between libertarian modernists like F. A. Hayek who are prepared to let history run its course and conservatives like William F. Buckley who want to "stand athwart history, yelling Stop!"

We centrists, for our part, believe that these polar extremes—preservation versus change and universalism versus nationalism—present false dichotomies. It is futile to try to stop history, and we are too optimistic about our prospects for the future to want to do so in any event. We embrace the future, but it will be a future that we have shaped consciously. As for our humanitarian obligations to those of the Third World, we embrace these as well, but we do so with an understanding that our resources are not unlimited, and that our ability to remain a nation of refuge and hope depends crucially on our willingness to steward our resources and to provide for the descendants of those who are already here. For this reason, we reject both the utopian liberal call to throw open our borders and the pessimistic isolationism of conservatives.

Immigration in U.S. History: The Swinging Pendulum

Immigration policy in U.S. history is, as immigration law scholar Kevin Johnson puts it, "famous for its cyclical, turbulent and ambivalent nature."[4] Naturally enough, immigration policy was not a national priority at a point when much of the United States remained underpopulated. For the first century of our national existence, there were no substantial federal limitations on immigration, though some states imposed restrictions on criminals, vagrants, foreigners, and other "undesirables."[5] A combination of social and economic pressures, nativism, and xenophobia has intermittently played a powerful role in the passage of restrictive immigration laws from the point at which federal lawmakers began to address immigration. Congress passed the first series of major immigration laws, now colloquially known as the "Chinese exclusion acts," in the 1880s.[6] By the 1920s Congress had begun to experiment with immigration quotas. These culminated with the Immigration Act of 1924, which closed off immigration in a sweeping way for decades afterward. Aimed at potential immigrants from Asia and the poorer countries of southern and eastern Europe, the 1924 act limited annual immigration from any country to 2 percent of those from that country living in the United States as of 1890—a severe cap on all but those from Western Europe. The 1950s saw another wave of restrictions. In 1952 passports were for the first time legally required to enter the United States, and in 1954 President Eisenhower's Operation Wetback resulted in the expulsion of over a million Mexicans from the United States, some of them legal residents.

Yet by the 1960s the mood of the nation began to change. In 1965 Congress abolished the strict quotas on national origin in place since the 1924 act and relaxed the limits on immigration from poorer countries. The level of foreign-born in the United States, both legal and illegal, remained at historic lows until around 1970, when immigration began to rise.[7] In 1986, Congress passed the Immigration Reform and Control Act (IRCA). The IRCA originated as a restrictionist measure to cap immigration, yet by the time it was passed the law gave amnesty to close to three million illegal aliens then living in the United States. Four years later Congress passed the Immigration Act of 1990, which granted stays of deportation to family members of those who had been granted amnesty under the 1986 act. The 1990s saw several more circumscribed bills passed, including a 1994 act granting "temporary rolling amnesty" for close to 600,000 undocumented aliens; the 1997 Nicaraguan Adjustment and Central American Relief Act, which granted residence to about one million people from Central America; the Haitian Refugee Immigration Fairness Act of 1998, granting residence to about 125,000 from Haiti; and a 2000 act that extended amnesty to 400,000 claiming retroactive coverage under the 1986 act. This fifteen-year period during the Reagan, Bush, and Clinton administrations represents the recent high-water mark of liberal immigration policy.

Beginning in the mid-1990s, however, the pendulum began to swing back in a more conservative direction in some ways. In 1996 Congress passed legislation which expanded the grounds for barring entry of prospective immigrants into the United States and made deportation easier. In 2005 it passed the REAL ID Act, which imposed more stringent federal standards for issuing state driver's licenses. Still, these were moderate efforts in comparison with the various amnesties and similar measures granted during this period. Nor have the courts been immune from the effects of the pendulum of public sentiment concerning immigration. In

1982, the Supreme Court held unconstitutional a Texas law that barred children of undocumented aliens from public schools, the first case to give heightened constitutional protection to those in the United States illegally.[8] Yet in 2002, perhaps reflecting the changing mood of the country, the Court decided that undocumented aliens had no protection under federal labor law and could not recover back pay after an employer's clear violation of federal law.[9]

Under the amnesties given in the 1980s and 1990s, most of those here illegally were granted legal residency, and many have become U.S. citizens. But, of course, this did not end the tide of illegal immigration; if anything, it encouraged many more immigrants, in the hope that they, too, would be grandfathered in as legal residents. As Kevin Johnson, an unabashed advocate of open borders admits, "every effort to regularize the immigration status of undocumented immigrants through amnesty programs has been accompanied by the subsequent growth of a new undocumented immigrant population."[10] Today, some two decades after the IRCA was passed, there are at least twelve million people living illegally within U.S. borders—about 4 percent of the total U.S. population and perhaps three or four times the number of those here illegally in the 1980s.[11] About 56 percent of these have arrived from Mexico, with another 22 percent from the rest of Latin America.[12] Most are unskilled laborers; close to 75 percent lack a high school diploma.[13] The Department of Homeland Security estimates that 4.2 million, or over a third of those here illegally, have arrived since 2000, and that about two-thirds have entered since 1995.[14] According to the Center for Immigration Studies, there is a net increase of 1.25 million immigrants each year; about a third of these, or 450,000, are undocumented aliens who arrive here illegally.[15]

What most concerns many who study immigration trends is the rate of escalation of illegal immigration since about the mid-1990s. At current rates, the flow of undocumented aliens alone will add about 13 million to the U.S. population by 2030, and about 40 million by 2060.[16] It is important to remember that these figures reflect only *illegal* immigration and that the United States opens its doors to roughly twice this number, or about 800,000 legal immigrants, annually. In some states today, undocumented aliens make up a substantial proportion of the population; at least 8 percent of California's total population is here illegally, and 7 percent in Texas and Arizona.[17] These figures do not include the U.S.-born children of undocumented aliens who are entitled to automatic U.S. citizenship under the Fourteenth Amendment, conservatively estimated to be about 300,000 annually.[18]

To put things in perspective, the Center for Immigration Studies projects that at this rate, in a little more than fifty years, by 2060, the U.S. population will increase by 167 million people over our current 300 million. This projected increase represents more people than the entire U.S. population in 1950. Of these, 105 million will be due to legal and illegal immigration—more than the total population growth (through birth and immigration) during the first 130 years of our history.[19]

These figures are staggering and, if the trends continue, can only have a dramatic effect on U.S. society over the long haul. In response, conservatives want to close down the border with Mexico and deny those here illegally all public benefits and privileges, while libertarians and some liberals, motivated by humanitarian concerns, strongly advocate opening our borders. Each represents an unrealistic response to illegal immigration.

The Argument for Open Borders

"A border is an imaginary line between two nations separating the imaginary rights of one from the imaginary rights of the other." So quipped Ambrose Bierce in *The Devil's Dictionary*.

More recently, immigration analyst Richard Thompson Ford put it this way: "Borders are not inherently significant; they are significant because we attach meaning to them. We can change the significance of borders without changing their location by changing what they signify—what comes along with them."[20] There is a vast literature today in sympathy with these sentiments, which defends the right of free movement and attempts to make the case for open borders.[21] When made in philosophical terms, one strand of the argument originates in libertarian principles, the other in the Kantian liberal tradition. Other, more pragmatic approaches appeal to liberal and humanitarian grounds. Libertarians emphasize the right to travel as an inalienable freedom, while Kantian and humanitarian liberals frequently emphasize the moral arbitrariness of national borders and the hardships they impose on those left on the other side. The official website of the Libertarian National Committee quotes no less an authority than Thomas Jefferson, who maintained that there is a "natural right which all men have of relinquishing the country of which birth or other accident may have thrown them, and seeking subsistence and happiness wherever they may be able and hope to find them."[22] For the libertarian, there is no *collective* right to exclude; only individuals have rights to exclude someone from the property they own. Hillel Steiner thus concludes that "national borders possess no less—and no more—moral significance than the boundaries between my neighbor's land and mine." No "collectivity . . . can claim a non-contractual power to prevent [anyone] from allowing, or compel [them] to allow, another person onto her or his property."[23]

According to libertarians, government has no legitimate power to deny entry to individuals who are not violating others' rights to life, liberty, or property. This is another example of the radical methodological individualism of the libertarian discussed in Chapter 4. Libertarians assume that the protection of collective interests must be reducible to the protection of the property rights of particular individuals. Of course, libertarians also insist that open borders, like open markets, not only are a basic right, but also will work to the collective good in utilitarian terms in the long run. Immigrants will come only as long as there are jobs for them, libertarians argue, and there will be jobs for them only if there are others on this side of the border who benefit by giving them jobs. As Kevin Johnson puts it, in "an open borders regime, the immigration laws would more closely approximate market demand for immigration, with limited negative externalities and wasteful costs."[24] Or as Peter

Laufer, an advocate of opening the United States to Mexicans, writes: "As long as those agriculture, construction, restaurant and other positions are vacant, workers will come north. But that's good. We need the help. Our economy depends on its Mexican workforce. Economically driven immigration is self-regulating. When and if migrants fill the jobs U.S. citizens refuse to take, there will be little motivation for Mexicans to leave home."[25]

Centrists, however, do not find much merit in the argument that immigration will be naturally self-regulating. Indeed, it's a bit perplexing to see some nonlibertarian liberals embrace invisible hand assumptions in the immigration area when they are normally skeptical of these kinds of arguments in other economic contexts. Even assuming that potential immigrants in the Third World get the signal to stop coming when the economy is perfectly saturated with workers, at what point will this be? And at what cost to the economy? From the *ex ante* position of an impoverished laborer in the Third World, even a wage of one or two dollars an hour might be a sufficient inducement to travel north, yet there can be little doubt that at some point the effects of immigration may make it very hard on unskilled and low-wage U.S. workers—even if we're not quite there yet. So centrists are as skeptical of free-market arguments for open borders as we are in other economic matters.

Kantian and humanitarian appeals raise a deeper challenge to closed borders. Echoing Jefferson, Immanuel Kant wrote that "birth is no deed of him that is born" and talked of "the right all men have of demanding of others to be admitted into their society; a right founded upon the common possession of the surface of the earth."[26] In this Kantian vein, R. George Wright has argued that we have not "come to grips with the apparent moral arbitrariness of allowing many persons to undeservedly suffer absolute or relative poverty, rather than merely permit them to enter the United States, . . . where others with the equally undeserved good fortune to have been born in the United States resist" the entry of the less fortunate.[27] These arguments have a deep appeal because we all understand, as Kant and Jefferson did before us, that the place of one's birth is an accident from a cosmic point of view. What gives one group of people who, by sheer contingency of birth, happen to be born in a particular locale the right to exclude another group from a certain geographical area of the earth? As Yale law professor Bruce Ackerman insists: "Westerners are not entitled to deny this entry right simply because they have been born on the right side of the boundary line."[28] Open borders, Wright sums up, replace "the arbitrary contingencies of geographical natality" with "the unconditional dignity of each person."[29]

There is something undeniably attractive in this vision. Everyone understands the appeal of the United States, particularly to the poor of the Third World, and most of us intuitively feel that you can't blame people for trying to change their lives for the better. Laufer quotes an immigration judge who admitted: "You know, if I were in the same situation as most of these people, I'd come, too. . . . People don't voluntarily leave their surroundings unless there is a push factor."[30] In fact, whatever conservatives might say in vilifying undocumented aliens, I think many others will agree that there is something admirable and quintessentially "American" in the determination of any person willing to risk life and limb to come to a place which, at least initially, offers little more than an opportunity to eke out subsistence wages doing backbreaking work. Most undocumented workers come to the United States to work—and they work hard for wages that are considerably less than what most Americans will take. To the extent that the American spirit is supposed to embody the virtues of determination, hard work, and persistence through adversity, if anyone deserves the label "American," the great majority of these people do. Therein lies the heart of the appeal in the argument for open borders.

But alas, there is something of the smell of the lamp to calls to completely open our borders. No country in the world today has open borders, and for good reason. (At best some, like the European Union, have regional immigration agreements among fairly socially and economically homogenous nations.) What one commentator said twenty-five years ago seems even more evident today: "It is clear that advocacy of unlimited immigration into the United States cannot be taken seriously in a world in which three billion people are very poor and their numbers increasing rapidly."[31] In fact, many of the defenders of open borders hedge their arguments in various ways. Laufer wants to open the border to Mexicans but would restrict entry to those from Central and South America.[32] Wright concedes that "realistically," the only option to a more restrictive immigration policy would be "open entry with a minimally reduced benefits package." He adds that it may be "practically necessary or morally desirable to take the further first step of decoupling open entry even from voting rights for future first-generation immigrants."[33] And some libertarians concede that it is utopian to believe that we can workably combine an open border policy with a social service system that provides certain entitlements to all new arrivals. As Milton Friedman put it, "It's just obvious that you can't have free immigration and a welfare state."[34]

What each of these defenders of open borders seems implicitly to recognize is that, to the extent we open our borders, we will have to close our wallets. Worse still, open borders may lead to new forms of social balkanization and (as Wright suggests) to political stratification as the community tries to find new ways to shepherd its limited resources and to continue to give significance to the idea of citizenship. There is simply no way around the crucial central truth: in a finite world, opening one door usually means closing another. "To tear down the walls of the State is not . . . to create a world without walls," as communitarian Michael Walzer put it, "but rather to create a thousand petty fortresses."[35]

Johnson's call for open borders is one of the most recent, well-thought-out, and impassioned open border proposals. Yet his proposal self-consciously underscores the level of economic displacement and national self-sacrifice that an open border policy will require. He calls for the "de-regulation of immigration law" and advocates eliminating all numerical limits on entry, including current nation-by-nation caps on immigration, employment preferences, diversity visa rules, and priority for those who already have a family member in the United States. Instead, the borders would be open to all comers subject only to limited visa screening for criminal backgrounds and health risks. Once a visa is granted, new arrivals would have the same rights and privileges as lawful permanent residents and be eligible for similar public benefits, including public assistance. He defends extending due process protection under the Constitution to those who are denied admission to the United States, so that the government would bear the same burden of justifying exclusion as it now does in cases denying certain public benefits to U.S. citizens. He even goes so far as to suggest that we might extend the right to vote to noncitizen residents of the United States.[36]

Unlike various other advocates of open borders, Johnson does not balk at some of the likely consequences of open immigration. He recognizes the probable need for transfer payments or other forms of public assistance to poor and unskilled U.S. workers who would "lose ground" as a result of immigration. He foresees the need for increased federal assistance to states with large immigrant populations to help defray the costs of public education, medical services, and other benefits. He also argues that open borders will put an end to the unregulated market in immigrant labor.[37] Immigrants would presumably be protected by minimum wage and other labor laws, just as lawful residents are. Of course, this would obviously undercut their attraction as a source of cheap labor. With more people competing for the same number of jobs at the same wage, the unemployment rate of U.S. workers can be expected only to increase, perhaps dramatically, depending upon the number of new arrivals. And with greater unemployment among citizens and immigrants alike, both of which would be eligible for public benefits under Johnson's proposal, the drain on public resources could be overwhelming. There is simply no reason why the United States should run headlong to such a radical extreme rather than, for example, experimenting with a guest worker program or with higher lawful immigration quotas aimed at Mexico and Central America.

We live in a very different world than that of Jefferson, Kant, and other eighteenth-century forebears of the modern liberal tradition. They lived at a time when nine-tenths of the North American continent was uninhabited, and when even Europe was vastly underpopulated. They wrote when individualism was an economic reality rather than a shibboleth, when immigrants had to make it on their own without benefit of an extensive social service network. Open border conditions did not pose the threat of destabilizing social change or swamping the lifeboat as they threaten to do in the not-too-distant future. Similarly, the greater differential in wealth between the United States and the Third World today relative to two centuries ago makes it likely that more will come, including some who live relatively comfortable lives in their home countries. Even with the reality of dangerous border crossings, modern transportation makes movement to and from the border considerably easier than it ever was.[38] The point is that the realities and dynamics of immigration are very different today than in Jefferson's day. And even Kant in his munificent cosmopolitanism insisted that immigration cannot interfere with the rights of those already present.[39]

To sum up, centrists reject the libertarian's radical individualism and the liberal's argument for unlimited immigration for basically the same reason that we reject Mill's harm principle. What the harm principle says about the internal policy of the state, the argument for open borders says about the state's external policy. Both are based on a highly individualistic understanding of social harm. Both claim (or imply) that society has no right of self-regulation beyond the prevention of direct, material harm to individuals. Both the harm principle and the open border argument assume that society or the state lacks a *collective* right of self-preservation—that is, a right that transcends the right of society to protect particular individuals. Yet just as society may legitimately act to prevent certain kinds of internal collective harms that occur without harm to specific individuals, as with the Nirvana drug example earlier in the book, it can act to preserve the general tenor and character of our national community from external threats. To put it slightly differently, communities have no more an obligation than individuals do to sacrifice themselves to rescue others. It may be morally good and right for a community to decide to open its borders to those who need it, or need it most, but there is no general moral obligation for a community to open its borders to all. As Michael Walzer put it twenty-five years ago: "No one on the outside has a right to be on the inside." The right of every national community to choose whom to admit is the most essential mark of political sovereignty—arguably more essential than even the right to enter into international alliances or to choose one's trading partners. What is at stake is nothing less than the shape of the community. "Admission and exclusion," Walzer declared, "suggest the deepest meaning of self-determination."[40]

Nothing I have said implies that we should not have a generous immigration policy. It is simply to say that we have done all that we *should* when we have done all that we reasonably *can*. We as a polity have the right to decide on what terms, and how many, newcomers may arrive. Since all who come should have a right to work toward full citizenship—and to the extent that defenders of open borders recognize that citizenship rights might have to be limited, the case for open borders is hardly as inclusive as we might hope—the nation must have the right of self-regulation. If immigration is the road to citizenship, as it should be, and if citizenship continues to mean something more than residency, as it must, then open borders cannot be the answer.

The Conservative Counterattack:
The Arguments against Illegal Immigration

Conservative consternation over illegal immigration stems from three principal concerns—one cultural, one economic, and one legal or philosophical. Paleoconservatives, traditionalists, and communitarians are concerned, first, with the cultural and political consequences of immigration, particularly the way in which immigration threatens to alter what they see as the unique cultural identity of the United States. Second, conservatives (and some liberals) are troubled by the economic toll of illegal immigration. They fear that competition from undocumented workers drives down the wages of less skilled U.S. workers, contributes to unemployment, and more generally burdens the service sectors as untaxed illegal aliens use medical and educational services for which they don't pay. Along these lines are also concerns about overpopulation, crime, and the increased burden placed on the environment by an expanding population. Finally, conservatives usually attach great significance to the moral values associated with fidelity to law and preserving the integrity of the legal system. They fear that granting benefits to those here il-legally sends a signal for more to cross the border in violation of the law and, more symbolically, they believe that policies which support those who are here illegally undermine the rule of law. For these reasons, they are considerably less likely than are most liberals to accept humanitarian justifications for helping undocumented aliens.

As I mentioned at the outset of the chapter, most conservatives have historically been inclined to cherish the values of cultural particularism over humanitarian universalism, of localism over globalism. Why did Edmund Burke prefer the "little platoons" to the larger apparatus of the state? Why did Alexander Hamilton insist that all men naturally favor their families over their communities, their communi-ties over their nation, and their nation over other nations? Some cast these senti-ments in the form of a quest for community, as modern communitarians would have it, but others seem to find in the ties of blood, language, and culture an authenticity that can never be synthesized in a polyglot society. Consider the re-marks of Johann Gottfried Herder, the eighteenth-century defender of the German cultural *volkgeist* in reaction to the universalism of other Enlightenment thinkers: "The savage who loves himself, his wife and his child . . . and works for the good of his tribe as for his own . . . is in my view more genuine than that human ghost, the . . . citizen of the world who, burning with love for all his fellow ghosts, loves a chimera. The savage in his hut has room for any stranger. . . . The saturated heart of the idle cosmopolitan is a home for no one."[41]

Where for Herder and latter-day communitarians, local attachments are based on communal ties, paleoconservatives go much further, essentializing national identity. "During my life, I've seen Frenchmen, Italians, Russians, and so on," de-clared Joseph de Maistre, "but I must say, as for man, I have never come across him anywhere; if he exists, he is completely unknown to me."[42] In his book *State of Emergency*, firebrand conservative Pat Buchanan virtually echoes Maistre's sentiments:

> Language, faith, culture and history—and, yes, birth, blood and soil—produce a people. . . . After the ideologies and creeds that seized Germany, Italy and Russia by the throat in the twentieth century . . . Germans remained German, Italians remained Italian and Russians remained Russian. After three decades of Maoist madness the Chinese remain Chinese. Had America succumbed to dictatorship in the Cold War, we would still be Americans, recognizable by far more than the political beliefs we profess.[43]

For paleocons today, to say that one is an American, or that someone else is not, is to say something more than to indicate whether they have been born or natural-ized in the United States. Beneath even the commitment to a shared philosophy grounded in the American way of life lies something deeper still—deeper and po-tentially more ominous. It is a pungent tribalism that is frequently infused with nationalism, xenophobia, and racism. Praising the efforts of Californians who voted in favor of Proposition 187, which sought to withdraw all public benefits, including public school education, from undocumented aliens and their children,

Buchanan mordantly declared that these people "were not part of our nation, they did not belong here, they were not entitled to the benefits of U.S. citizens, and they ought to go back where they came from." And this was among the more moderate of his sentiments. The book plays on some of the most hyperbolic fears (e.g., "How many American women must be assaulted, how many children molested, how many citizens must die . . . before our government does its duty?"); jingoism ("Chicano chauvinists and Mexican agents have made clear their intent to take back through demography and culture what their ancestors lost through war"); and outright racism ("When it comes to the ability to assimilate into a nation like the United States, all nationalities, creeds and cultures are not equal").[44] It is in this essentialized, almost spiritualized, conception of ethnicity, I believe, that the much overused comparison between paleoconservatism and fascism finds its greatest force.[45]

In some of the less virulent strains, race and ethnicity are linked to culture, and it is this more acceptable target—the cultural effects of immigration—which is attacked. In *Who Are We? The Challenge to America's National Identity*, Harvard political scientist Samuel Huntington draws an analogy from our situation to population shifts in the fourth century that he believes may have contributed to the fall of Rome. More generally, he is concerned about the fragmentation of U.S. culture brought about by immigration and warns that we could become a "culturally bifurcated Anglo-Hispanic society with two national languages."[46] Victor Davis Hanson worries more pointedly that illegal immigration from Mexico serves to import Mexico's endemic forms of cultural and social dysfunction. He argues that "half of all children born to Hispanic parents in America were illegitimate" and that "illegitimacy is far more common in Mexico than it is in the United States. Likewise, fewer students per capita graduate from high school in Mexico than they do here."[47] Other conservatives have written extensively on the problems of culture and assimilation posed by increased immigration.[48]

Centrists tend to view these same concerns in a broader historical perspective. On one hand, it is true that illegal immigration over the last two decades is at a historic high. For this reason, we advocate getting the border under control to stem the tide of illegal immigration. On the other hand, we recognize that these kinds of nativist concerns have a cyclical nature. Each wave of new arrivals historically— Irish, Germans, Chinese, Italians, eastern Europeans, and now, Hispanics—has been met with similar pronouncements by those voicing nativist, xenophobic, and frequently apocalyptic fears. We are not in the least troubled by the influence of Hispanization on our general culture. Quite to the contrary, we find in Mexican and South American culture richness and vitality that have served only to enliven U.S. culture generally. What troubles us is not where immigrants come from, or whether they are brown rather than white, but that they come illegally, with costs that will have to be borne by the rest of us, and in numbers that may make assimilation difficult. We want to see new arrivals become U.S. citizens. We want to see them embrace U.S. ideals, learn English, and become good citizens even as they maintain their native culture—just as every previous wave of immigrants has done. Immigration, in sum, should lead to assimilation and citizenship; it should be more than a bridge to second-class status with a marginally better economic situation than one had in one's homeland.

What about the economic costs of illegal immigration? Reviewing liberal and conservative assessments of the effects of undocumented aliens on the economy is a bit like looking into two mirror universes simultaneously. Liberals claim that undocumented workers take only jobs that no U.S. citizen will do, while conservatives respond that they take jobs that citizens won't do *at the same wages*. Conservatives claim that illegal workers don't pay taxes but use public services (they send their children to public schools, use emergency medical services, and frequently receive food assistance and Medicaid dollars), while liberals point out that many undocumented workers pay taxes, including Social Security taxes that they will never benefit from, and receive less than half the assistance from federal programs that citizens do. Conservatives are apprehensive of the effects of growing numbers of low-skilled workers in an increasingly complex technology- and information-based economy, and worry that they will form a permanent underclass of alienated and disenfranchised persons who will create the kinds of social and cultural problems reminiscent of disenfranchised Muslims in Germany and France today. Liberals respond that it is precisely the complementarity of necessary low-skilled workers to an increasingly high-skilled workforce that will make our economy more efficient. Liberals point to the positive effects of undocumented workers in lowering prices on agricultural and other goods, generating GDP and sales taxes, consuming U.S. goods and services, and helping prevent U.S. companies from leaving for cheaper labor markets. Conservatives respond that these considerations ignore the way illegal immigrants displace U.S. workers, drive up unemployment rates, and drive down wages for unskilled and semi-skilled U.S. workers.[49]

Where does the truth lie? According to a report by the Center for Immigration Studies, in 2002 undocumented aliens cost the federal government about $10 billion. They paid roughly $16 billion in taxes ($7 billion of which went to Social Security), but they consumed about $26 billion in federal services.[50] Costs at the state and local level vary widely depending on location. A study by the Federation for American Immigration Reform (FAIR) found that in California illegal immigration costs the state $10 billion dollars and the average household about $1,200 a year. This includes almost $8 billion to school the children of undocumented aliens, who now make up 15 percent of California's public school population, with the rest divided between health care and incarceration.[51] A much cited but now dated 1998 report by the National Academy of Sciences estimated that the costs of illegal immigration to the average household in the United States were around $200 a year. We should expect these costs to have risen, perhaps dramatically, with the absolute numbers of immigrants here illegally over the course of the past several years.

What about the effects on employment and prices? In certain low-skill industries, particularly in border states, the effects have been significant. As radio talk-show host Terry Anderson put it in describing the effects in Los Angeles, "In the '70s, the auto-body repair business in South Central was pretty much occupied by blacks. Those jobs are gone now. They're all held by Hispanics and all of them are illegals. And those $25 jobs that blacks used to hold in the '70s now pay $8 to $10."[52] Kenyon College economists found that the influx of roughly thirty-five thousand mostly Vietnamese women into the nail salon business in California from the late 1980s, a number that equaled the total number of jobs in the industry until then, drove out ten thousand native-born workers.[53] In many industries—restaurants, construction, gardening, and roofing—the influx of new workers creates a labor surplus that drives down wages and drives up unemployment. One estimate is that close to two million unskilled U.S. workers are displaced from their jobs every year at a cost of about $15 billion in public assistance to these workers.[54] For those who remain, particularly in unskilled occupations, the effects on wages are fairly substantial. In a study of the effects of legal and illegal immigration, economist George Borjas estimates that by 2000, competition from illegal immigrants had undercut wages for U.S. citizens who had not completed high school by about 8 percent, or $1,800 annually.[55]

It also forces some U.S. citizens to stay competitive by cutting costs and receiving pay under the table, which siphons off tax dollars.[56] While the downward pressure on wages does have a positive effect on U.S. income, it is not as significant as some have suggested. A University of Iowa study has shown that undocumented labor cuts agricultural prices only by 2 or 3 percent. The National Academy of Sciences study from a decade ago concluded that undocumented aliens boost U.S. spending power by an average of $120 per household annually.[57]

What can we conclude about the economic costs of illegal immigration? First, they are borne most heavily by those living in border states and by unskilled U.S. workers, where the effects are substantial. For the rest of us, the costs are modest—but will only increase with the influx of growing numbers of poorly educated immigrants. The 1998 National Academy of Sciences study found that the average immigrant without a high school education creates a lifetime net fiscal burden of about $89,000, while an immigrant with a high school degree will impose a net $31,000 burden.[58] Given that two-thirds to three-fourths of illegal immigrants do not have a high school degree, the costs to the average U.S. citizen will be perhaps $3,000 over the course of a lifetime at the current number of twelve million illegal immigrants. These are costs—and they are not insignificant—that will be borne by all citizens. To the extent the trends continue, the costs will mount.

Conservatives' third concern is both more symbolic and more practical. Many U.S. citizens are incensed at what they take to be the flagrant violation of national sovereignty and U.S. law by those who enter the country illegally. They oppose lax enforcement of immigration laws as well as internal policies that implicitly reward those who are here illegally, including making driver's licenses available to undocumented workers or providing them with in-state tuition or other public benefits. They are concerned because they believe these undermine the legal system generally and because nonenforcement sends a signal that encourages many others to cross the border illegally. *National Review* writer John O'Sullivan calls this the "broken windows problem of law enforcement writ large."[59] As a statement by the American Conservative Union Foundation put it, "Conservative values require that the rule of law be adhered to or there will be anarchy. For immigration, therefore, there must be some penalty for those who do not obey the law and enter illegally."[60] Even some liberals oppose amnesty for this reason. As one writer to the *New York Times* put it, "This is one liberal who believes that amnesty (or whatever euphemism you prefer) in addition to fostering a diminution of respect for the law, will serve as a signal to millions of others that if they can get here, they are home free."[61]

Proponents of a liberalized immigration policy argue either that humanitarian concerns should trump rule-of-law arguments or, more paradoxically, that giving amnesty to those here illegally is "the only way to restore the integrity of the immigration code."[62] But this is more than a little like saying that we can reduce the crime rate by taking criminal offenses off the books. Others seem not to want to acknowledge that the violation of law warrants any consideration in the immigration calculus. At a panel on immigration at the annual Association of American Law Schools conference in January 2008, three speakers addressed recent local and state laws that target employers, landlords, or others who provide jobs and resources to undocumented aliens. All three were opposed to these laws—two seemed ideologically committed to open borders, and a third questioned the efficacy of these laws. But no one on the panel or from among the audience of law professors even raised what ought to be the most obvious question for lawyers: in discussing immigration policy, should we give *no weight* to the fact that undocumented aliens are, after all, here illegally?

The Centrist Approach: Five Proposals

A strong but humanitarian immigration policy places many liberals and centrists in a catch-22. Most will agree that unrestricted immigration cannot be sustained and seem to agree that we have a corresponding need to limit immigration. For this reason, conservatives want to take a hard line on domestic policies by denying to undocumented aliens any public privilege or benefit that might encourage more illegal immigration or signal a weakness of will to get tough on immigration. Yet few conservatives want to go the full way—rounding up and deporting those who are here and closing down businesses that employ undocumented aliens. This confronts each of us who believes in limiting illegal immigration while rejecting scorched earth policies aimed at driving out undocumented aliens with the same obvious tension. Rather than embracing a foolish consistency in immigration policy, we should acknowledge that hard lines have to be drawn.

Yet in some ways the tension presents us with an opportunity. As even most advocates of open borders admit, there will always be a trade-off between the liberality of our immigration policies and the level of generosity with which we are able to respond to those who are already here illegally. The more seriously we take our commitments to enforcing the border, the more we will be able (and inclined) to do for those who are already here. The less seriously we take the border, the less we will be able to do—for immigrants and for U.S. citizens. The following five proposals spell out a sound, centrist approach to illegal immigration.

(1) *Get serious about border enforcement.* In a Pew Center study, 46 percent of Mexicans said they would like to live in the United States and 20 percent admitted that U.S. laws prohibiting entry would not deter them.[63] Each year around half a million Mexicans—roughly fifteen thousand a day—come illegally, though

at least as many are apprehended trying to enter the United States. Congress has appropriated money to build a border fence but to date, for reasons that remain unclear, there has been little progress on it. The total cost of building the fence, $8 billion, is less than the annual cost of illegal immigration to taxpayers at the federal level alone. Advocates of open borders insist that a fence will not dissuade those desperate enough to want to come. Yet when a fourteen-mile fence was constructed across the San Diego–Tijuana border in 1994, the number of those caught trying to cross fell by 98 percent. The proposed fence would consist of two fifteen-foot fences separated by a stretch of highway patrolled by border control agents. Motion sensors would notify agents of an attempted crossing and permit a quick response. Beyond these fences there would be another eight-foot fence of coiled wire and beyond that fence would lie ditches to stop trucks that might crash the fence. There is no doubt that the fence would dramatically reduce border breaches. The only question is whether we have the will to erect it.

Some inside and outside the United States denounce the idea. Open borders advocate Kevin Johnson writes that "the floodgates concern betrays an attitude of U.S. superiority and the assumption that, if the opportunity existed, people the world over could not resist coming to the best of all nations."[64] But, of course, plenty do want to come and continue to make the crossing. Mexico's former president Vicente Fox called the idea "shameful" and other Mexican politicians lambasted the fence as "stupid" and "under-handed." The irony, however, is that Mexico defends its own southern border with Guatemala by using the military and by incarcerating illegal aliens as felons.[65]

No doubt some recoil from the idea of the fence because, at a symbolic level, it runs counter to America's vaunted self-image as a haven for the huddled masses. But there are only three options on the table for us, ultimately: we either continue to accept the flow of illegal aliens; we get tough internally by deporting those who are here illegally, targeting businesses that employ them, landlords that rent to them, and so on; or we stop illegal immigration at the border. The advantage of the third approach is that it does the least to upset the status quo while vindicating rule-of-law concerns. Those who are here already can be treated with humanity, and those who have yet to cross will not be able to rely on the claims of settled expectations—that they have lived here for years, that they have a place in the community, et cetera.

The fence is not a symbolically attractive option, but it has become a necessity. It is the second worst of all alternatives—while everything else ever proposed is among the worst.

(2) *Do not grant amnesty to those here illegally.* Proponents of liberal immigration policy insist that it would be draconian of us to refuse amnesty to those already here. As Tamar Jacoby, a proponent of free-market immigration policies puts it, refusing to grant amnesty to those already here

> would create a permanent caste of second-class workers, people trusted to cook Americans' food and tend their children but not to call themselves Americans or participate in politics. They would live in permanent limbo, at risk of deportation if they lost their jobs, afraid of bargaining with employers, and unlikely to take the

all-important emotional leap that is essential for assimilation. Surely this is not the answer for a proud democracy such as the United States.[66]

Yet four reasons militate strongly against giving amnesty to the twelve million people who are now here illegally. It is, first of all, not fair to those who have waited in line to come here legally to give priority to those who have come illegally. Amnesty clearly rewards those who have broken the law and penalizes those who have obeyed it. Second, the best way to vindicate the value of fidelity to law and the significance of national sovereignty is to withhold from those who have broken the law the greatest plum of all, U.S. citizenship. Third, the costs of amnesty would increase the tax burden, as those receiving amnesty would then be eligible for a wider panoply of public benefits. A Center for Immigration Studies report indicates that it costs the federal government alone $2,700 per year per undocumented household—the difference between the costs of public services used and the taxes paid by undocumented workers. With amnesty, the deficit would rise to about $7,000 per household annually. While these now legalized workers would be paying somewhat more in taxes, the tax increases would be more than offset by their access to the full range of public services and transfer payments eligible to legal residents.[67]

Finally, nothing sends a stronger signal for more illegal immigrants to come than the hope that the next wave, too, will be covered under some future amnesty. While Jacoby refers to amnesty as a "one-time transitional measure," in fact it would be the fourth or fifth such measure in the last twenty years—and certainly not the last. While the hope of economic gain may motivate many to come, it is the longer-term hope of citizenship that motivates most to stay. Take this possibility off the table and we substantially undercut the primary pull factor that brings many here. Of course, there is no reason to oppose any plan that permits those here to return to their country and wait in line with others to become citizens. But most centrists will oppose giving adults who have come here illegally spots at the front of the line.

I would make one exception to the "no amnesty" rule. Those who can prove that they were brought here as children by their parents should have the opportunity to become citizens. We could attach special conditions to this, including the condition that these children complete their high school education or a skills-training program—a condition which would ensure that these children have the opportunity to assimilate fully, culturally and economically. Some of the reasons that militate against amnesty for adults—that they should not be rewarded and that fidelity to law requires precluding a path to citizenship—simply don't apply for those who are brought here as children. Moreover, the costs of amnesty for those who are uneducated can be mitigated by conditioning the children's path to citizenship on their obtaining a marketable skill. This seems to strike the best balance between our humanitarian obligations and the necessity to deter further illegal immigration.

(3) *Liberalize our immigration quotas and our refugee policies in particular.* Currently, roughly 800,000 persons immigrate legally to the United States each year. We could raise this number and increase the number of low-skilled workers now permitted here legally, directing our efforts at Mexico and Central America and

combining this with a path to citizenship for those who remain employed and learn English. Not only would this help to infuse the labor force particularly in low-skill but necessary occupations, but it would provide a positive incentive for others to take the legal rather than the illegal path to entry. Faced with the choice between immigrating legally, with all the benefits of legal residency and an open route to citizenship, and arriving illegally, many will see the benefit in taking the legal route.

We should also immediately expand our commitment to admitting bona fide refugees and asylum seekers—those fleeing oppressive political conditions in other countries around the world. Currently, only a limited number of people win asylum or refugee status each year in a process that is severely stacked against the asylum seeker.[68] Indeed, conservative judge Richard Posner, who has recently and repeatedly criticized immigration judges for their incivility and incompetence, overturned an asylum denial because of its "factual errors, bootless speculation and errors of logic" and the general "weirdness" of the judge's findings.[69] If our moral commitment to remaining a refuge for the politically oppressed means anything, here is one area where liberals and conservatives should be able to agree that we can do much more.

(4) *Once the border is secured, grant driver's licenses to those here.* Opponents of liberalized immigration policies contend that giving driver's licenses to undocumented aliens subverts federal immigration policy and encourages others to come. In fact, most U.S. citizens—77 percent according to one recent poll—oppose granting undocumented aliens driver's licenses.[70] This is sound policy now. Granting licenses to those here illegally will certainly only encourage more to come and will further undermine integrity-of-law concerns. But once we have secured the borders, these concerns are significantly less pressing. Moreover, it is in our national self-interest to license undocumented aliens who drive. Denying those here licenses prevents them from obtaining automobile insurance, since a license is usually required for insurance. When undocumented aliens who are poor and uninsured are injured, the costs are now borne by hospitals and the public at large, rather than by insurance companies.

A driver's license is also the best way to identify and locate those here illegally. As Maria Pabon Lopez puts it, permitting undocumented aliens to remain unlicensed does "not further post-9/11 safety concerns, since the undocumented drivers will remain unidentifiable by law enforcement."[71] Driving privileges should be linked to employment, to the payment of taxes, and to registering with a national database. To obtain a driver's license, the undocumented alien will have to find an employer who registers him or her with the national database. Once registered, the worker will have taxes deducted from his or her paychecks and can be issued a driver's permit. The permit should be renewed on an annual basis with a fee charged to cover administrative costs. Providing driver's permits linked to workers' employment status means insuring them and providing at least minimal insurance coverage to third parties injured in accidents involving undocumented aliens. It also permits these workers to drive legally, open a bank account, or cash a check and reduces their exposure to fraud and to theft of undeposited money. Even a minimal humanitarian obligation requires that we permit the undocumented to protect themselves in this essential way. Those who drive without the permit should be subject to deportation, one way to effect border enforcement internally.

(5) *Register undocumented workers and tax their employers.* Several states and localities have passed laws which penalize businesses for employing undocumented workers. Arizona's recent law, for example, fines employers for a first offense and withdraws their license to do business for the second—the business equivalent of the death penalty. Some localities that initially took a hard line on employing illegal aliens have abandoned such policies upon discovering how costly they are. Rather than penalizing employers, however, we should simply tax them for the costs their employees impose on the infrastructure—in terms of emergency hospital services and public schools. Employers should be required to register undocumented employees, at which point the worker will be issued the necessary documents to obtain a driver's license. Employers should then pay an annual tax on hours worked by illegal workers, which will help defray the costs imposed on U.S. taxpayers. Of course, these requirements will drive employers' costs up to some extent and may incidentally limit the employment of undocumented workers. But that's fine. They will serve to narrow the advantages of hiring illegal workers over U.S. citizens and, to that extent, shift employment back to U.S. citizens. Employers who violate the policy should be subject to paying back taxes and serious fines.

Once the tax burden is shifted to those who benefit most from illegal immigration, and with the escalating influx of illegal immigrants under control, the U.S. public will feel less under siege. Under these circumstances, there is every reason to believe that the cyclical nature of immigration policy will permit U.S. citizens again to embrace more generous policies for illegal immigrants who are here, particularly their educational and health needs. For example, while the children of illegal immigrants have a constitutional right to attend K-12 public education, state legislatures should be more willing to permit in-state college tuition breaks similar to those proposed in various DREAM acts for those who can show that they were brought here by their parents at a young age. As recent legislative activity shows, it is the states that are most under stress from illegal immigration—California, Arizona, and Texas—that have frequently embraced the most severe and often counterproductive restrictions in these areas. In Arizona, for example, voters passed Proposition 300, a ballot initiative that requires proof of U.S. citizenship to get in-state tuition or financial aid. The initiative does not prevent undocumented students from attending classes, but they are required to pay out-of-state tuition, which some have linked to a sharp decline in enrollment. One consequence of the law was to force several thousand students to drop out of college.[72] The effect is most apparent in ESL (English as a second language) courses, which are obviously essential to promoting cultural and linguistic assimilation. Since the children of undocumented aliens would be eligible for citizenship, we should want to do everything we possibly can to promote their cultural and economic assimilation.

Before we can contemplate extending social benefits to those here illegally and to their children, however, we must have the big picture under control. This means closing off the border and taking amnesty off the table for those who have violated U.S. immigration policy.

Notes

Introduction

1. The Left-Right political spectrum is usually represented in something like the following way:

   Anarchism ⟷ Socialism ⟷ Liberalism ⟷ Conservatism ⟷ Authoritarianism ⟷ Fascism

   Of course, each genre of political thought can be broken down further. Liberalism is usually divided between left-wing (or progressive) liberalism and right-wing (or classical) liberalism. Conservatism is similarly broken down among the neoconservatives, traditionalists, and paleocons, among others. I examine these distinctions in some detail in Part I.

2. The two most famous of these accounts are Hannah Arendt, *The Origins of Totalitarianism* (1948) (showing the parallels between totalitarianism on the Left and Right), and F. A. Hayek, *The Road to Serfdom* (1944) (pointing out the similarities between Nazism and Stalinism). Hayek later argued that political orientation is best represented by a triangle, with socialism, conservatism, and his own libertarian liberalism at the corners. All other theories, he argued, fall between these—for example, modern liberalism is intermediate between socialism and libertarianism. Hayek, "Why I'm Not a Conservative," in *The Constitution of Liberty* (1960), 398.

3. Paul Waldman, "The Liberal Moderates," *American Prospect* (October 18, 2005), *www. prospect.org/cs/articles?articleld=10438*, citing data showing that 21 percent of voters in 2004 called themselves liberal and 34 percent self-defined as conservative. A 2006 Gallup poll found that 24 percent of Americans defined themselves as liberals while 27 percent self-defined as conservative. David Boaz, "The Libertarian Option," *Wall Street Journal* (January 31, 2006).

4. Russell Kirk, *Prospects for Conservatives* (1989), 33.

5. Hayek, *The Constitution of Liberty*, 399.

6. Noam Chomsky, "Equality," *The Chomsky Reader*, ed. James Peck (1987), 190.

7. John Zerzan, *Running on Emptiness: The Pathology of Civilization* (2002), 142.

8. For a cogent modern application of this older, truer conservative tradition, see George F. Will, *Statecraft as Soulcraft* (1993).

9. Maurice Duverger, *Political Parties: Their Organization and Activity in the Modern State* (1954).

Chapter 1

1. F. A. Hayek concluded that Smith first used the word to refer to "the liberal system of free exportation and importation" and the exhortation to permit "every man to pursue his own interest his own way, upon the liberal plan of equality, liberty and justice." Hayek, *The Constitution of Liberty*, 530, note 13.

2. Boaz, *The Libertarian Reader* (1997), xiii.

3. See, for example, Randy E. Barnett, "The Moral Foundations of Modern Libertarianism," in *The Varieties of Conservatism in America*, ed. Peter Berkowitz (2004).

4. Fox News Online, December 5, 2006.

5. For recent conservative criticism of the cross-influences of left liberalism and right-wing totalitarian movements, see Jonah Goldberg, *Liberal Fascism: The Secret History of the American Left from Mussolini to the Politics of Meaning* (2007).

6. In the most famous case from that era, *Lochner v. New York*, 198 U.S. 45 (1905), the Court struck down a New York law that limited a baker's hours to sixty per week.

7. *West Coast Hotel Co. v. Parrish*, 300 U.S. 379 (1937).

8. John Locke, *Second Treatise of Government*, ed. C. B. Macpherson (1980), chap. 2, para. 6 (emphasis in original).

9. Murray N. Rothbard, "What Is Libertarianism?" *Modern Age* (Winter 1980), reprinted in *Conservatism in America since 1930*, ed. Gregory L. Schneider (2003), 266.

10. This is the point of MacIntyre's critique of liberal conceptions of rationality. Alasdair C. MacIntyre, *Whose Justice? Which Rationality?* (1989).

11. I am deliberately avoiding a deeper issue that troubles philosophers: whether any form of moral realism requires belief in God. Moral realism is the idea that moral propositions like "Murder is wrong" or "Rights should not be violated" can be true or false in the way that facts are. Some philosophers believe that they have provided secular versions of moral realism, but many others (theists and agnostics alike) have their doubts.

12. Locke, *Second Treatise*, chap. 9, para. 124 (emphasis in original). And by "property" he meant all that we own in a physical and in a moral sense—not simply our physical possessions, but our rights to life, liberty, and estates. Where today we speak of "a right to property," Locke would have reversed this, insisting that we have "property in our rights."

13. Ibid., paras. 36–40.

14. Ludwig von Mises, *Socialism* (1922); F. A. Hayek, *The Road to Serfdom* (1944).

15. Jeremy Bentham, "Anarchical Fallacies," *Works of Jeremy Bentham*, vol. 2, ed. John Bowring (1843), art. 2, pp. 503, 501.

16. Ibid. Political conservatives like David Hume in the eighteenth century and James Fitzjames Stephen in the nineteenth always insisted that government was formed by force, and that the individual had no right to foment rebellion. See Chapter 2.

17. Ronald Dworkin, *Taking Rights Seriously* (1977).

18. Bentham, "Anarchical Fallacies," art. 2, p. 501.

19. Ibid., 503.

20. Robert L. Hale, "Coercion and Distribution in a Supposedly Non-Coercive State," in *American Legal Realism*, ed. William W. Fisher, Morton J. Horwitz, and Thomas A. Reed (1993).

21. John Stuart Mill, *Autobiography*, ed. John Robson (1990), 80.

22. John Stuart Mill, *Autobiography*, ed. Jack Stillinger (1969), 81.

23. *On Liberty* opens with Mill's acknowledgment of Harriet's contribution to the work. Harriet had died a year before *On Liberty* was published. See Jo Ellen Jacobs, *The Voice of Harriet Taylor Mill* (2002), 195–254, examining this debate and defending Harriet's contributions to Mill's work.

24. John Stuart Mill, *On Liberty* (1985), 69–70.

25. Ibid., 68–69.

26. Mill himself made clear that "harm" was an ambiguous concept. It included acts that violate the rights of others. (There is a circularity here that has not escaped the notice of critics.) See Steven Smith, "Is the Harm Principle Illiberal?" *American Journal of Jurisprudence* 51 (2006).

27. Mill, *On Liberty*, chap. 5.

28. *Zablocki v. Redhail*, 434 U.S. 374 (1978).

29. Thomas Hobbes, *Leviathan* (1968), 189.

30. Mill, *On Liberty*, 128, 123. "Self-individuation" is the term I use to characterize the modern conception of freedom shared by many progressives. See J. L. Hill, "The Five Faces of Freedom in American Political and Constitutional Thought," *Boston College Law Review* 45 (2004): 499, 561–79.

31. Mill, *On Liberty*, 123.

32. Thomas Paine, *Common Sense* (1995), at 1.

33. Mill, *On Liberty*, 68.

34. *Planned Parenthood of Southeastern Pennsylvania v. Casey*, 505 U.S. 833, 851 (1992).

35. See, e.g., T. H. Green, "Liberal Legislation and Freedom of Contract," in *Liberty*, ed. David Miller (1991), 21, 22, 23.

36. L. T. Hobhouse, *Liberalism* (1911), 73.

37. John Dewey, *Liberty and Social Action* (1935), 48 (emphasis in original).

38. Carl Becker, *New Liberties for Old* (1941), 112.

39. *The Public Papers and Addresses of Franklin D. Roosevelt*, ed. Samuel Rosenman (1950), 13:40–42.

40. John Rawls, *A Theory of Justice* (1971), 75.

41. Ibid., 179 (my emphasis).

42. Ronald Dworkin, "Liberalism," *A Matter of Principle* (1985), 195; see also Dworkin, "Why Liberals Should Care about Equality," ibid., 205–20.

43. Letter from Thomas Jefferson to P. S. DuPont de Nemours, April 24, 1806, cited in David N. Mayer, *The Constitutional*

Thought of Thomas Jefferson (1992), 77. See ibid., 76–85, for a discussion of Jefferson's conception of political rights.

44. Isaiah Berlin, "Two Concepts of Liberty," *Four Essays on Liberty* (1969), 125.

45. Alexis de Tocqueville, *Democracy in America*, trans. George Lawrence (1969), 692.

Chapter 2

1. Robert Blake, *The Conservative Party: Peel to Majors* (1998), 6.

2. This is the central point of Louis Hartz's great book *The Liberal Tradition in America* (1955). Hartz argued that liberalism and conservatism in the United States are two strains of the broader liberal tradition, the first more Jeffersonian and democratic, the second traceable from the Federalists to the Whigs to modern Republicans.

3. See Herbert Storing, *What the Anti-Federalists Were For* (1983).

4. In *The Conservative Mind*, 7th rev. ed. (1985), 8–9, Russell Kirk concluded that conservatism consists of six elements: "belief that a divine intent rules society," preference for the "proliferating variety" of cultural forms over uniformity and egalitarianism, the view that "society requires orders and classes," the conviction that property and freedom are "inseparably connected," faith in tradition, and, finally, distrust of change and recognition that "change and reform are not identical." Anthony Quinton, in contrast, argues that conservatism does not depend upon particular theological or institutional commitments but consists of three principles: belief in the continuity of social and political institutions, skepticism about the possibility of rational political knowledge, and the view that "human beings in society are organically or internally related" (i.e., conservatism is essentially an anti-individualistic doctrine). Anthony Quinton, "Conservatism," in *A Companion to Contemporary Political Philosophy*, ed. Robert C. Goodin and Philip Petit (1997), 244–46. Quinton's more academic and general definition of conservatism abstracts enough from contemporary culture to avoid the difficulties presented by the mixture of influences on contemporary conservative thought. Yet for this very reason it may not capture the quality of U.S. or British conservatism today. A more culturally specific definition of contemporary conservatism in the United States is provided by John Micklethwait and Adrian Wooldridge, the authors of a recent study of the attitudes of U.S. conservatives. The authors argue that conservatism consists of six basic principles, including suspicion of the power of the state, preference for liberty over equality, patriotism, belief in "established traditions and hierarchies," skepticism regarding progress, and, finally, an element of elitism. Micklethwait and Wooldridge, *The Right Nation* (2004), 13.

5. Jerry Z. Muller distinguishes "orthodoxy" from "conservatism," arguing that orthodox thinkers believe in some religious or transcendental conception of reality and morality with which political institutions must conform, whereas the conservative is a metaphysical skeptic. Muller, ed., *Conservatism: An Anthology of Social and Political Thought from David Hume to the Present* (1997), 4–9; see also Peter Berger and Richard J. Newhouse, *Movement and Revolution* (1970), 21, which contrasts "conservatives by faith" with "conservatives by lack of faith." Other conservatives insist that a belief in a transcendent order is essential to being a conservative. Russell Kirk argued, in fact, that belief in God was the first and most essential element of any theory worthy of the label "conservative." Kirk, *Conservative Mind*, 8. Many skeptical conservatives will admit, nevertheless, that shared religious belief has great social utility (Muller, *Conservatism*, 13), even where they may remain doubtful of the truth lying behind religious commitment.

6. While classical liberal versions of modern conservatism represent a limited-state philosophy, most other conservatives have traditionally believed that the state needed to be strong and at least expansive enough to be able to shape the character of its citizens. For two recent examples of the conservatism of the strong state, see Roger Scruton, *The Meaning of Conservatism* (1980), 38–63, for a neo-Hegelian conservatism; and George F. Will, *Statecraft as Soulcraft* (1993), 22, which finds conservative values "threatened less by big government than by an abdication of government." Compare these with Robert Nisbet, *Conservatism: Dream and Reality* (1986), 34–41, which advocates a "bounden state" that leaves the traditions of civil society alone.

7. Edmund Burke, *Reflections on the Revolution*

in France, vol. 2, *Select Works of Edmund Burke,* (1999), 193.

8. Pocock quoted in Muller, *Conservatism,* 22–23. Liberalism and socialism embody some of these same contradictions—e.g., socialism has both anarchistic and totalitarian versions. But there is at least a core set of values that seems to animate liberals or socialists, in contradistinction to conservatism.

9. Samuel Huntington, "Conservatism as an Ideology," *American Political Science Review* 51 (1957): 454.

10. "For the conservative, the desirability of specific institutions is dependent upon time and place" so that "conservatism tends to be procedural and methodological, rather than substantive." Muller, *Conservatism,* 12. I discuss the skeptical conservative tradition at the end of this chapter.

11. This seems to be the heart of F. A. Hayek's "decisive objection" to conservatism—that conservatism offers only resistance to change without proposing any substantive direction of its own. Hayek, "Why I'm Not a Conservative," *The Constitution of Liberty* (1960), 398.

12. Plato, *The Republic,* bk. 8.

13. Ibid., lines 562–63; cf. Niccolò Machiavelli, *The Discourses,* bk. 3, chap. 29; Vilfredo Pareto, *The Rise and Fall of Elites* (2006).

14. Polybius, "The Roman Constitution," bk. 4, in *The Portable Greek Historians,* ed. M. I. Finley (1959), 474, 476.

15. Cicero, *Republic,* bk. 5, paras. 1–2.

16. See Plato, *Phaedo,* 82 A, B; *Phaedrus,* 270.

17. George Will concludes that Aristotle "is the first consciously conservative philosopher" because he was a realist whose politics nevertheless "take[s] its bearings from what ought to be." Will, *Statecraft as Soulcraft,* 24.

18. Aristotle, *Politics,* bk. 1, chap. 2, 1253a, 19–20.

19. Ibid., bk. 7, chap. 2.

20. As Hannah Arendt pointed out, the Greeks had no word for the "social" as distinguished from the "political." The Romans first drew this distinction. Hannah Arendt, *The Human Condition* (1958), 24. For the Greeks, including Aristotle, "the state" included the socializing institutions of the community, everything outside the private sphere of the household.

21. Aristotle, *Politics,* bk. 1, chap. 2, 253a, 31–33.

22. Jean-Jacques Rousseau, *The Social Contract,* in *The Social Contract and the Discourses,* ed. G. D. H. Cole (1973), 116.

23. Ibid., 84; Aristotle, *Politics,* bk. 1, chap. 2, 253a, 30.

24. Aristotle used the term "eudaimonia" to refer to the state of satisfaction attained by the person who lives in accordance with our given purpose in the world. While eudaimonia is sometimes mistakenly translated as "happiness," it is probably better understood as a natural contentment or fulfillment that arises from living according to nature's purpose for us. Aristotle, *Nicomachean Ethics,* bk. 1, chaps. 8–9.

25. Ibid., bk. 2, chap. 1.

26. Cicero, *Republic,* bk. 3, para. 33.

27. John Phillip Reid, *The Concept of Liberty in the Age of the American Revolution* (1988).

28. Isaiah Berlin, "Joseph de Maistre and the Origins of Fascism," in *The Crooked Timber of Humanity,* ed. Henry Hardy (1990). Berlin bases this characterization of Maistre on, among other things, a number of rather striking passages in which Maistre paints a brutal picture of human bloodlust throughout history. In one such passage, Maistre praises the executioner as "the terror and the bond of human association . . . [without which] thrones fall, societies disappear" (117). Yet even Mussolini saw that fascism "has not taken de Maistre as its prophet." Benito Mussolini, *Doctrine of Fascism* (1935), 36.

29. Joseph de Maistre, *On God and Society: Essay on the Generative Principle of Political Constitutions and Other Human Constitutions,* ed. Elisha Greifer (1967), 83, 40.

30. Numerous writers have drawn the distinction between the reactionary right and the radical right. Paul Gottfried, *The Conservative Movement,* rev. ed. (1993), 143–66; Roger Eatwell and Noel O'Sullivan, *The Nature of the Right* (1989), 63–70, 79–98, 124–45; Muller, *Conservatism,* 27–30. The radical right, represented by fascism, is anything but conservative. Like the radical left, its goal is to remake society, though on very different lines than what the Left would prefer to see.

31. Maistre, *On God and Society,* 63, 15, 18, 42. Succeeding cites of this work appear in the text.

32. Ibid., 4, 6.

33. Ibid., 59, 55, 54, 57.

34. Ibid., 55, 60–61, 40, 33, 9.

35. Ibid., 85, 52, 90.

36. Hayek, *The Constitution of Liberty,* 407.

37. Blake, *The Conservative Party*, 7.
38. Hartz, *The Liberal Tradition in America*, chaps. 3, 7.
39. Burke, *Reflections*, 193, 122.
40. Ibid., 122.
41. Edmund Burke, "An Appeal from the New to the Old Whigs," in Daniel Richie, *Edmund Burke: Further Reflections on the Revolution in France* (1992), 163; Edmund Burke, "Tracts Relating to the Popery Laws" (1765), in R. B. McDowell, ed., *The Writings and Speeches of Edmund Burke*, vol. 9 (1991), 456; Burke, *Reflections*, 151.
42. Burke, *Reflections*, 193.
43. The conservative ambivalence toward economic and materialist values is the subject of Irving Kristol, *Two Cheers for Capitalism* (1978).
44. Burke, *Reflections*, 193, 194–95.
45. Quoted in Nisbet, *Conservatism*, 36–37.
46. Quoted in Kirk, *Conservative Mind*, 26.
47. Burke, *Reflections*, 154.
48. Ibid., 239.
49. Ibid., 152.
50. Ibid., 121.
51. Kirk, *Conservative Mind*, 7.
52. Maistre, *On God and Society*, 85.
53. Stephen Holmes, *The Anatomy of Anti-Liberalism* (1993), 14 (discussing Maistre's attitude toward Hume).
54. Leslie Stephen quoted in Donald W. Livingston, *Hume's Philosophy of Common Life* (1984), 306.
55. David Hume, *An Enquiry Concerning the Principles of Morals* (1751), sec. 3, part 1; ibid., sec. 3, part 11.
56. Ibid., Appendix 3.
57. David Hume, *The History of England* (1954), 6:346, quoted in Livingston, *Hume's Philosophy of Common Life*, 321. Livingston calls this "Hume's law."
58. David Hume, "Of Passive Obedience," *Essays Moral, Political and Literary*, ed. Eugene F. Miller (1985), 489. Adopting the epigraph of Locke's *Second Treatise of Government*, Hume declares: "*Salus populi suprema Lex*" (the safety of the people is the supreme law). Ibid.
59. Hume, *Enquiry*, sec. 3, part 2.
60. Ibid. (emphasis in original).
61. Ibid.
62. Hume, "Of the Origin of Government," *Essays Moral, Political and Literary*, ed. Eugene F. Miller (1985), 38–39.
63. Hume, "Of the Original Contract," *Essays Moral, Political and Literary*, ed. Eugene F. Miller (1985), 471.
64. Ibid., 472.
65. James Fitzjames Stephen, *Liberty, Equality, Fraternity*, ed. Stuart D. Warner (1993), 70.
66. Andrew Sullivan, *The Conservative Soul* (2006), 173, 233.
67. Ibid., 180.
68. Sullivan, *Conservative Soul*, 254.
69. Michael Oakeshott, "On Being Conservative," *Rationalism in Politics and Other Essays* (1991), 408–9.
70. Oakeshott quoted in Sullivan, *Conservative Soul*, 217.

Chapter 3

1. Douglas Murray, *Neoconservatism: Why We Need It* (2006), 34.
2. Irving Kristol, "A Conservative Welfare State," in *The Neocon Reader*, ed. Irwin Stelzer (2004), 143–48; Daniel Bell, *The Cultural Contradictions of Capitalism* (1996), xii–xiii.
3. H. W. Brands, *The Strange Death of American Liberalism* (2001), viii.
4. Richard Rorty, "Trotsky and Wild Orchids," *Philosophy and Social Hope* (1999), 17 (my emphasis).
5. Paul Krugman, *The Conscience of a Liberal* (2007), 11.
6. I discuss these issues in Chapter 8.
7. Edmund Burke, *Reflections on the Revolution in France*, vol. 2, *Select Works of Edmund Burke* (1999), 189, 142.
8. Robert P. George, "Religious Values and Politics," *The Clash of Orthodoxies* (2001), 231.
9. *Lawrence v. Texas*, 539 U.S. 558 (2003).
10. Recent political thinkers have used the term "paleoconservative" in two distinct ways that reflect the uncertain boundaries between conservatism and more authoritarian and fascist thought. Paul Gottfried, a self-described paleoconservative, insists that paleocons are opposed to what they regard as the "anti-humanist" elements in modern democracy: they loathe equality and democracy and are "far more Nietzschean than neo-Thomistic." Paul Gottfried, *The Conservative Movement* (1993), 155. The problem with this view is that it mistakes a form of postmodern authoritarianism for true conservatism. The true conservative is profoundly dubious of political revolutions and downright despises social revolutionary movements (including right-wing movements) because these rend the fabric

of social traditions and practices prized by conservatives. True paleoconservatives also believe that there is a natural moral order in the world, manifest by God's will or a natural law. It is difficult to see how a conservative could ever be a Nietzschean. Closer to the target, Adam Wolfson writes that the paleoconservative is "not so much a conservative as a reactionary" who "despises much of American life." Adam Wolfson, "Conservatives and Neoconservatives," in *The Neocon Reader*, ed. Irwin Stelzer (2004), 219. Yet even Wolfson underemphasizes the paleocon's neo-Thomism. See Stephen Tonsor, "Why I Am Not a Neoconservative," in *Conservatism in America since 1930*, ed. Gregory L. Schneider (2003), for an example of a fundamentalist paleoconservative attack on newer forms of conservatism.

11. Similarly, political commentator and erstwhile Republican presidential candidate Pat Buchanan may be counted among modern paleoconservatives. Pat Buchanan, *Where the Right Went Wrong* (2004).

12. Leonard Read and other limited-state liberals began calling themselves "libertarian" in the 1950s. David Boaz, *The Libertarian Reader* (1997), xiii. The neo- and paleo- prefixes to conservatism also emerged around this time, when, according to one source, Michael Harrington began using the term "neoconservative" to describe apostate liberals such as Irving Kristol. E. J. Dionne, *Why Americans Hate Politics* (1991).

13. Tonsor, "Not a Neoconservative," 378.

14. Leo Strauss, the intellectual progenitor of neoconservatism, who was famously concerned about the disintegrating effects of moral relativism, argued that political order depends upon maintaining some noble myths, among them a shared religious belief that binds the political order. Leo Strauss, *The City and Man* (1964). See Shadia B. Drury, *Leo Strauss and the American Right* (1999), for a critique of Strauss's philosophy.

15. Tonsor, "Not a Neoconservative," 376, 375.

16. Russell Kirk has argued that neoconservatives have been disproportionately Jewish liberals who broke with the liberal establishment on the question of Israel. John B. Judis, "The Conservative Wars," *New Republic* (August 11 and 18, 1986): 16. Stephen Tonsor claimed that true conservatism is "culturally unthinkable" within a secularized Jewish intellectual milieu. He argued that true (paleo)conservatism is "Roman or Anglo-

Catholic in its political philosophy." Tonsor, "Not a Neoconservative," 378.

17. Jeffrey Hart describes this in his remembrance of William F. Buckley. Jeffrey Hart, "Right at the End," *American Conservative* (March 24, 2008): 19.

18. Robert Nisbet's *Twilight of Authority* (1975) provides a classic example of the conservative's indictment of modern society in this respect. The antiauthoritarianism of libertarians, for their part, is evident in their permissive attitudes toward pornography, homosexuality, and drug legalization, and the opposition of many to the death penalty and to criminal sanctions generally.

19. Murray N. Rothbard, "What Is Libertarianism?" *Modern Age* (Winter 1980), reprinted in *Conservatism in America since 1930*, ed. Gregory L. Schneider (2003), 264.

20. Frank S. Meyer, *In Defense of Freedom and Related Essays* (1996), 127.

21. See Ernest van den Haag, "Libertarians and Conservatives," *National Review* (June 8, 1979): 725–39 (for a conservative attack on libertarianism.)

22. F. A. Hayek recognized this fifty years ago when he pointed out that "the fate of conservatism is to be dragged along a path not of its own choosing" and that "the tug of war between progressives and conservatives can only affect the speed, not the direction, of contemporary developments." Hayek, *The Constitution of Liberty* (1960), 398.

23. Both Rousseau and Hobbes began from the individualistic premise only to reach very illiberal conclusions. Rousseau anticipated the modern radical left, Hobbes, modern utilitarian liberalism. Rousseau thought that a genuine commitment to freedom meant that citizens could place no constitutional limits on the state, while Hobbes concluded that the Leviathan was necessary to guarantee individual security. See Isaiah Berlin, *Freedom and Its Betrayal: Six Enemies of Human Liberty* (2002), examining the ways in which Rousseau's thought and others begin from a commitment to freedom and lead to the opposite.

24. L. T. Hobhouse, *Liberalism* (1911), 66.

25. John Stuart Mill, *On Liberty* (1985), 56.

26. Stephen quoted in Jerry Z. Muller, ed., *Conservatism: An Anthology of Social and Political Thought from David Hume to the Present* (1997), 188.

27. James Fitzjames Stephen, *Liberty, Equality, Fraternity* (1874), at 10, 14.

28. *Planned Parenthood v. Casey*, 505 U.S. 833, 851 (1992).

29. Kirk, *The Conservative Mind*, 7th rev. ed. (2001), 8.

30. Ralph Waldo Emerson, "Self-Reliance," *Selected Lectures, Essays and Poems*, ed. Robert D. Richardson Jr. (1990), 159.

31. Karl Marx, "For a Ruthless Criticism of Everything Existing," *Marx-Engels Reader*, ed. Robert C. Tucker (1978), 13 (emphasis in original).

32. Hayek, *The Constitution of Liberty*, 400. These comments appear tellingly in a postscript entitled, "Why I Am Not a Conservative."

33. Letter to Samuel Kercheval, July 12, 1816, in *The Portable Thomas Jefferson*, ed. M. Peterson (1975), 558–59.

34. See, e.g., Michael Oakeshott, "Rationalism in Politics," *Rationalism in Politics and Other Essays* (1991); Anthony Quinton, *The Politics of Imperfection* (1978).

35. Thomas Sowell, *A Conflict of Visions: Ideological Origins of Political Struggles* (2007).

36. John Kekes, *A Case for Conservatism* (2001), 41.

37. Richard Weaver, *Ideas Have Consequences* (1948), 10.

38. Russell Kirk, *Prospects for Conservatives* (1989), 31, 38.

39. This is the essence of the epistemological side of the classical liberal's attack on collectivism. See Ludwig von Mises, *Socialism* (1922) (predicting socialism's failure for this reason); F. A. Hayek, *The Road to Serfdom* (1944).

40. Tonsor, "Not a Neoconservative," 378.

41. T. S. Eliot, Choruses from *The Rock*, 6, quoted in Douglas Murray, *Neoconservatism: Why We Need It* (2006), xxi.

42. See Chapter 11, looking at the asymmetries of the criminal justice system.

43. Irving Kristol, "The Spiritual Roots of Capitalism and Socialism," in *Capitalism and Socialism: A Theological Inquiry*, ed. Michael Novak (1991), at 14.

44. Robert Nisbet, *Conservatism: Dream and Reality* (1986), 47.

45. Kirk, *Conservative Mind*, 8–9; John Micklethwait and Adrian Wooldridge, *The Right Nation* (2004), 13.

46. Democraticus, "Loose Thoughts on Government," *American Archives*, 4th series, ed. Peter Force, 6:730 (cited in Gordon S. Wood, *The Creation of the American Republic, 1776–87* [1969], 71).

47. William A. Galston, "The Legal and Political Implications of Moral Pluralism," *Maryland Law Review* 236 (1998): 57.

48. In *Roberts v. United States Jaycees*, 468 U.S. 609 (1984), the Jaycees, a historically male-only organization, voted to admit female members but reserved full membership status, including the privilege of voting on the Jaycees' policies, to men between the ages of eighteen and thirty-five. Older men and all women were eligible only for secondary, nonvoting membership status. Minnesota's Human Rights Act forbade discrimination on the basis of gender. The Supreme Court sided with the women members, upholding the law and deciding that the state's purpose of achieving equality trumped the members' right of association. In *Boy Scouts of America v. Dale*, 530 U.S. 640 (2000), the Supreme Court held that the Boy Scouts had the right to exclude Dale, an adult scoutmaster who was openly homosexual and a gay activist. The Court tried to reconcile this ruling with the Jaycees case by suggesting that the Scouts have a long-standing policy holding that homosexuality is "not morally straight," whereas the Jaycees' central message would not be diluted by the inclusion of women voting members.

Chapter 4

1. Murray N. Rothbard, *For a New Liberty* (2006), 49. He wrote that "libertarians regard the State as the supreme, the eternal, the best organized aggressor, against the persons and property of the mass of the public. All states everywhere, whether democratic, dictatorial, monarchical, whether red, white, blue or brown." Ibid., 48.

2. *Journal of Political Economy* (December 1938): 869, quoted in F. A. Hayek, *The Road to Serfdom* (1944), 152.

3. See, e.g., Milton Friedman, *Capitalism and Freedom* (1982), for the definitive libertarian defense of an unregulated economy in these areas.

4. These are spelled out in chap. 5, "Applications," of *On Liberty*.

5. Murray N. Rothbard, "What Is Libertarianism?" *Modern Age* (Winter 1980), reprinted in *Conservatism in America since 1930*, ed. Gregory L. Schneider (2003), 265.

6. See Thomas A. Spragens Jr. "The Limits of Libertarianism," in *The Essential*

Communitarian Reader, ed. Amitai Etzioni (1998), for a critique of the libertarian conception of freedom.

7. See Alan Wertheimer, *Coercion* (1990), for a defense of a moralized conception of freedom and coercion.

8. Richard Cornuelle, "The Power and the Poverty of Libertarian Thought," in *The Libertarian Reader*, ed. David Boaz (1997), 364.

9. There are several excellent recent anthologies and compilations of different genres of conservative thought: Russell Kirk, ed., *The Portable Conservative Reader* (1982) (mainly a traditionalist focus); Irving Kristol, *Neo-Conservatism: The Autobiography of an Idea* (1995) (neoconservatism); Gregory L. Schneider, ed., *Conservatism in America since 1930* (2003) (eclectic collection of all forms of conservatism); Jerry Z. Muller, ed., *Conservatism: An Anthology of Social and Political Thought from David Hume to the Present* (1997) (neo- and skeptical conservative focus).

10. After denying the reality of global warming for years, President Bush eventually stated that he had come to believe that it is indeed a reality. Even a conservative magazine acknowledged in 2008 that most conservatives are still in denial. Rammesh Ponnuru, "Senator Empirical," *National Review* (May 18, 2008): 17.

11. Norman Podhoretz, "The Case for Bombing Iran," *Commentary* (June 2007); see also "The Case for Bombing Iran: Norman Podhoretz and Critics," *Commentary* (October 2007): 8.

12. Patrick Buchanan, *A Republic, Not an Empire: Reclaiming America's Destiny* (1999); Robert Nisbet, *The Present Age* (1986), especially chap. 1.

13. Joshua Muravchik, "The Past, Present, and Future of Neoconservatism," *Commentary* (October 2007), argues that neoconservatism is motivated by four commitments—moralism that inclines adherents toward interventionism, internationalism, belief in the efficacy of military power, and belief in the virtue of democracy. All but the third of these are closely linked to a hard Wilsonian liberalism. Paleocons and more traditional conservatives are skeptical of the first three commitments and lukewarm on the fourth. Neocons view their Middle East policy as an extension of the Cold War fight against Communism to the extent that both are motivated by a moral commitment to

fighting tyranny and aiding democracy. See Douglas Murray, *Neoconservatism: Why We Need It* (2006), chap. 2.

14. Peggy Noonan, "You'd Cry Too, If It Happened to You," in *Backward and Upward: The New Conservative Writing*, ed. David Brooks (1995), 150–51.

15. The Supreme Court upheld this law by a 6 to 3 vote in April 2008. *Crawford v. Marion County Election Board*, 128 S.Ct. 1610 (2008).

16. Catharine A. MacKinnon, *Only Words* (1993), 3.

17. Martha A. Field, *Surrogate Motherhood* (1990). Andrea Dworkin, *Intercourse* (1998). We look at some of the arguments regarding abortion in Chapter 9.

18. Richard Delgado, *The Rodrigo Chronicles* (1995), 11–13.

19. Martha Albertson Fineman, "Cracking the Foundational Myth: Independence, Autonomy, and Self-Sufficiency," *Journal of Gender, Social Policy and the Law* 13, 28 (2000): 8.

20. Hillary Rodham Clinton, "Children under the Law," *Harvard Educational Review* 43, 4 (1973): 487, 492, 503, 509–10.

21. Quoted in Janah Goldberg, "A Half Century's Slander," *National Review* (January 28, 2008): 38.

22. John Patrick Diggins has argued that U.S. politics have been influenced by three waves of political leftism—the "lyrical left" of the utopians in the early twentieth century, the Communist movement in the 1920s and 1930s, and the New Left of the 1960s and 1970s. John Patrick Diggins, *The Rise and Fall of the American Left* (1992).

23. Rawls, *A Theory of Justice*, 179 (my emphasis).

24. Ronald Dworkin, "Liberalism," *A Matter of Principle* (1985), 195.

25. James Madison, "Federalist 10," *The Federalist Papers*, ed. Clint Rossiter (2003), 130 (my emphasis).

26. Richard Rorty, "Trotsky and Wild Orchids," *Philosophy and Social Hope* (1999), 17.

Chapter 5

1. Walter Lippmann, *Public Opinion* (1965), 80.

2. I take up this aspect of the contrast between liberals and conservatives in Chapter 11.

3. Christopher Hitchens, *God Is Not Great: How Religion Poisons Everything* (2007).

4. Iris Murdoch, "Existentialists and Mystics," *Existentialists and Mystics: Writings on Philosophy and Literature*, ed. Peter Conradi (1997), 226.

5. Richard Dawkins, *The God Delusion* (2006), 14.

6. Letter to Harold Laski, January 11, 1929, excerpted in *The Essential Holmes*, ed. Richard A. Posner (1992), 107–8.

7. See Raymond Martin and John Barresi, *The Rise and Fall of Soul and Self: An Intellectual History of Personal Identity* (2006).

8. Michael Oakeshott, "Rationalism in Politics," *Rationalism in Politics and Other Essays* (1991), 9.

9. The term "fundamentalism" came into use in the early twentieth century after two devout oil magnates, Milton and Lyman Stewart, funded a series of widely distributed religious tracts, entitled "The Fundamentals: A Testimony of Truth," from their base in California. Malise Ruthven, *Fundamentalism* (2004), 10–11. The term later came to be applied to any literalist religious system, Christian or otherwise. Some today maintain a distinction between evangelicals and fundamentalists. Both are supposed to be rigorous religious literalists, but evangelicals are supposed to be more engaged in bringing religious values to the political sphere. John W. Dean, *Conservatives without Conscience* (2007), 94–95.

10. The Coalition on Revival, "Manifesto for the Christian Church," *www .americanfundamentalists.com/cast/manifesto .pdf*.

11. Bob Altmeyer, *The Authoritarian Specter* (1996); John C. Green, *The Christian Right in American Politics: Marching to the Millennium* (2003); Ruthven, *Fundamentalism*.

12. Both Weber and Emile Durkheim linked secularization and modernization, as have such recent sociologists as Peter Berger. Ruthven, *Fundamentalism*, 194.

13. See the Pew Research Center polls on religion in America, *people-press.org/reports/ display.php3?PageID=386*.

14. See the website for the National Association for Evangelicals, *www.nae.net*.

15. Pew Research Center for People and the Press, "Bush's Gains Broad-Based: Religion and the Presidential Vote" (December 6, 2004). Polls and other data are quoted in Dean, *Conservatives without Conscience*, 96.

16. Cathy Young, "Jerry Falwell's Paradoxical Legacy," *Reason* 39, 4 (August–September 2007): 19.

17. C. S. Lewis, "Meditation on the Third Commandment," *God in the Dock*, ed. Walter Hooper (1970), 198 (my emphasis).

18. On the crèche and law school Christmas tree, see John C. Gibson, *The War on Christmas* (2006).

19. John Rawls, *Political Liberalism* (1993), 217.

20. Most scholars read Rawls to require that laws and other political decisions comport substantively with shared public reason—that laws cannot be passed for reasons that fall outside the range of reasons that we can all agree upon. A few scholars read him more narrowly to require only that political outcomes comport with *procedures* we can all agree about. Even these scholars, however, admit that Rawls can be read the other way. See, e.g., Fabienne Peter, "Rawls' Idea of Public Reason and Democratic Legitimacy," *Journal of International Political Theory*, 3 (April 2007): 129–43.

21. Rawls, *Political Liberalism*, 58, 61, 63.

22. Rawls cites three criteria for a worldview to count as a "comprehensive doctrine," his term for an overarching religious or philosophical belief system that cannot be defended in purely positivistic terms. First, it is an "exercise of theoretical reason" that provides a comprehensive worldview. Second, it organizes and prioritizes values into an "intelligible view of the world." Finally, "it normally draws upon a tradition of thought and doctrine" which evolves slowly. Ibid., 59. It is not at all clear why this couldn't be a description of the secular paradigm itself.

23. See *Planned Parenthood of Southeastern Pennsylvania v. Casey*, 505 U.S. 833 (1992).

24. In the strict philosophical sense, determinism is the view that everything that happens in the world has been precipitated by a set of conditions and causes that bring about the event. In other words, determinism implies that nothing could ever happen except what does happen; there is no contingency in the world. What appears to be contingency is simply a product of our lack of understanding. See Ted Honderich, *Consequences of Determinism: A Theory of Determinism*, vol. 1 (1990).

25. B. F. Skinner, *About Behaviorism* (1974), 54 (my emphases).

26. Ibid., 208.

27. Some have argued on utilitarian grounds that the threat of punishment, not the

old-fashioned function of punishing the blameworthy, should serve preventative and deterrent functions. Richard B. Brandt, "The Utilitarian Theory of Punishment," *Ethical Theory* (1959), reprinted in *Readings in the Philosophy of Law*, ed. John Arthur (2006), at 246.

28. Letter to Harold Laski, December 17, 1925, in Posner, *The Essential Holmes*, 216.

29. Robert A. Dahl, *Democracy and Its Critics* (1989), 100.

30. Cass R. Sunstein, "Legal Interference with Private Preferences," *University of Chicago Law Review* 53 (1986): 1129.

31. Ibid., 1133, note 16; 1170.

32. Charles Fried, *Modern Liberty and the Limits of Government* (2006), 100.

33. This was central to the economic liberalism of John Rawls and Ronald Dworkin, as we saw in Chapters 1 and 3.

34. Skinner, *About Behaviorism*, 218; B. F. Skinner, *Beyond Freedom and Dignity* (1971), 39.

35. I take up these questions in different ways in Chapter 10, where I address racial and gender equality, and in Chapter 11, where I examine liberals' and conservatives' explanations for the causes of crime.

Chapter 6

1. The conclusions I draw in this chapter, written before the economic meltdown of 2008 and 2009 and the subsequent efforts to spend our way back to economic health, have taken on an even greater urgency in the wake of these events. Many of the figures I cite here concerning federal spending and deficits now significantly understate the problem.

2. Frederic Bastiat, "The State," *Selected Essays in Political Economy*, trans. Seymour Cain (1968), para. 5.20.

3. Curtis S. Dubay and Scott A. Hodge, "Tax Foundation Special Report: America Celebrates Tax Freedom Day" (April 2007), table 1, *www.taxfoundation.org*.

4. With the recent Bush tax cuts and the effects of the alternative minimum tax, taxpayers who earn between $100,000 and $200,000 annually now pay the highest overall percentage of their incomes in federal taxes relative to any other class, including those who make more than $10 million a year. Correspondents of the *New York Times, Class Matters* (2005), table, 190–91.

5. Dubay and Hodge, "Tax Foundation Special Report," table 2.

6. Brandon R. Julio, "Tax Foundation Special Report: The Growth of Government Spending in the Twentieth Century" (March 2000), 93:7; table 5, 93:11.

7. Just one example: we spent $50 million to construct an indoor rainforest in Coralville, Iowa. Brian M. Riedl, "How to Get Federal Spending under Control," Heritage Foundation, Backgrounder #1733 (March 10, 2004), *www.heritage.org*.

8. Michael Hampton, "Why You're Always Broke: 40 Percent of Your Money Goes to Taxes" (October 11, 2005), *www.homelandstupidity.us*; Brian M. Riedl, "A Victory over Wasteful Spending? Hardly," Heritage Foundation, Web Memo #839 (September 14, 2005), 1, *www.heritage.org*.

9. These and related figures are cited in Andrew Sullivan, *The Conservative Soul* (2006), 144–47; they are borne out by Riedl's study. See Riedl, "A Victory over Wasteful Spending?"

10. Riedl, "A Victory over Wasteful Spending?" 2.

11. Riedl, "Get Federal Spending under Control," 11–12.

12. Ronald D. Utt, "The Bridge to Nowhere: A National Embarrassment," Heritage Foundation, Web Memo #889 (October 20, 2005), *www.heritage.org*.

13. Congressional Budget Office, "A 125-Year Picture of the Federal Government's Share of the Economy, 1950–2075," revised July 3, 2002.

14. Russell Roberts, "If You're Paying, I'll Have Top Sirloin," in *The Libertarian Reader*, ed. David Boaz (1997), 312–14.

15. *DeShaney v. Winnebago County Dept. of Social Services*, 489 U.S. 189 (1989).

16. The dissent was written by Justice Brennan and was joined by Justices Thurgood Marshall and Harry Blackmun. Ibid., 203–12.

17. Mary Otto, "For Want of a Dentist," *Washington Post* (February 28, 2007).

18. Sullivan, *The Conservative Soul*, 119.

19. Liam Murphy and Thomas Nagel, *The Myth of Ownership* (2006), 8, 9.

20. Robert Hale, "Coercion and Distribution in a Supposedly Non-Coercive State," reprinted in *American Legal Realism*, ed. William W. Fisher III, Morton J. Horwitz, and Thomas A. Reed (1993), 102–3.

21. Richard A. Posner, *Overcoming Law* (1995), 281.

22. Robert William Fogel, *The Escape from Hunger and Premature Death, 1700–2100* (2004), xv.

23. Ibid., 67.

24. Libertarian David Boaz, for example, argues that property rights are protected as an extension of the principle of self-ownership. David Boaz, *Libertarianism: A Primer* (1997), 65. But some forms of property are more closely connected to the persona than others.

25. Benjamin Barber, for example, argues in favor of a more egalitarian, participatory, and communitarian conception of politics that, he believes, would transform "private into public, dependency into interdependency, conflict into cooperation, license into self-legislation, need into love, and bondage into citizenship." Benjamin Barber, *Strong Democracy* (1984), at 119–20. This vision asks too much of politics.

26. Billionaire Warren Buffett recently observed that he pays a lower effective income tax rate than a secretary of his who earns $30,000 annually.

27. *U.S. Term Limits v. Thornton*, 514 U.S. 779 (1995) (Kennedy, J., concurring).

28. Cass Sunstein writes, for example, that "the original constitutional structure of dual sovereignty was a large mistake, allied with anachronistic goals of limited government." Cass R. Sunstein, "Beyond the Republican Revival," *Yale Law Journal* 97 (1989): 1578.

29. One way to put this is that centrists would adapt the principle of "subsidiarity" to our political institutions. Communitarians and Catholic social theorists use this term to refer to the principle that "no social task should be assigned to an institution that is larger than necessary to do the job. . . . What can be done at the local level should not be passed on to the state or federal level." "The Responsive Communitarian Platform: Rights and Responsibilities," in *The Essential Communitarian Reader*, ed. Amitai Etzioni (1998), xxx.

Chapter 7

1. *Gonzales v. Carhart*, 550 U.S. 124 (2007).

2. *Stenberg v. Carhart*, 530 U.S. 914 (2000).

3. Linda Greenhouse, "In Steps Big and Small, Supreme Court Moved Right," *New York Times* (July 1, 2007).

4. Richard John Neuhaus, "The Supreme Court and Reasonable Hope," *First Things* (April 20, 2007), *www.firstthings.com/onthesquare/?p=709*.

5. Dewy Kidd, "Will Recycled Senate Impeach Bad Federal Judges?" *worldnetdaily.com* (November 12, 2004).

6. Joanna Grossman, "The Consequences of *Lawrence v. Texas*," *findlaw.com* (July 8, 2003).

7. Greenhouse, "In Steps Big and Small."

8. *Lochner v. New York*, 198 U.S. 45 (1905), struck down a New York law which limited to six ten-hour days the maximum number of hours a baker could work. The Court decided that this violated the freedom of contract of bakers and their employers to contract to work longer hours.

9. The term "realist" is confusing here, since it implies that realists believe that the body of rules that make up the law is "real," when they believe just the opposite. It is as if someone asked, "Does the law exist as a set of objective rules and standards that are binding on judges?" and the realist responds (perhaps in the voice of the proverbial Valley Girl), "Get real!"

10. Jerome Frank, *Law and the Modern Mind*, 6th ed. (1963), 259–69, discussing the need to rid ourselves of the rigid need for "father-authority" in our conception of law.

11. *San Antonio Independent School District v. Rodriguez*, 411 U.S. 1 (1973).

12. Learned Hand, *The Bill of Rights* (1958), 73.

13. Robert H. Bork, *The Tempting of America: The Political Seduction of the Law* (1990), 298.

14. Alexander M. Bickel, *The Least Dangerous Branch: The Supreme Court at the Bar of Politics* (1962), 16.

15. See, e.g., *Swann v. Charlotte-Mecklenburg Board of Education*, 402 U.S. 1 (1971), endorsing busing to desegregate schools; *Shapiro v. Thompson*, 394 U.S. 618 (1969), holding that states cannot impose a one-year waiting period before a newcomer to a state can receive welfare benefits. The Court's ruling made it impossible for states with more generous welfare policies to protect against a sudden influx of those drawn to the state by higher welfare payments.

16. *Goodridge v. Dept. of Public Health*, 798 N.E.2d 941 (Mass. 2003). California's supreme court reached a similar conclusion, mandating a constitutional right to gay

marriage under the California constitution, in May 2008.

17. *Baker v. Carr*, 369 U.S. 186 (1962); *Reynolds v. Sims*, 377 U.S. 533 (1964).

18. *Bush v. Gore*, 531 U.S. 98 (2000).

19. See Jeffrey Toobin, *The Nine* (2007), 141–44.

20. Jeffrey Rosen, *The Most Democratic Branch* (2006), xiv.

21. Antonin Scalia, *A Matter of Interpretation: Federal Courts and the Law* (1997), 23.

22. Robert H. Bork, *The Tempting of America: The Political Seduction of the Law* (1990), 144.

23. Scalia, *A Matter of Interpretation*, 38.

24. Bork, *The Tempting of America*, 143.

25. Scalia, *A Matter of Interpretation*, 37–38.

26. *Reed v. Reed*, 404 U.S. 71 (1971).

27. Robert Bork, for example, does intellectual backflips to try to show that the result in *Brown v. Board of Education* is consistent with his philosophy after all, even as he concedes that the ratifiers of the Fourteenth Amendment "probably assumed that segregation was consistent with equality." Bork, *The Tempting of America*, 82.

28. John Hart Ely, *Democracy and Distrust* (1981).

29. Ronald Dworkin, *Taking Rights Seriously* (1977) and *Law's Empire* (1988).

30. Ronald Dworkin, *A Matter of Principle* (1983).

31. Stephen Breyer, *Active Liberty* (2005), 8.

32. Ibid., 18.

33. Ibid., 82–83.

34. *Griswold v. Connecticut*, 381 U.S. 479 (1965).

35. *Eisenstadt v. Baird*, 405 U.S. 438 (1972).

36. *Roe v. Wade*, 410 U.S. 113 (1973).

37. Compare *Cruzan v. Director, Dept. of Public Health*, 497 U.S. 261 (1990), which recognizes a limited right to refuse medical treatment, with *Washington v. Glucksburg*, 521 U.S. 707 (1997), which holds no right to "assisted suicide."

38. Speech by William J. Brennan Jr. at the "Text and Teaching Symposium," Georgetown University Law Center (October 12, 1985), reprinted in Federalist Society, *The Great Debate: Interpreting Our Written Constitution* (1986), 23.

39. This was the very measured centrist approach of Justice Stewart in *Reynolds v. Sims*, where the Court formally embarked on administering the "one person, one vote"

rule. *Reynolds v. Sims*, 377 U.S. 533 (1964; Stewart, J., dissenting).

Chapter 8

1. Jeremy Bentham, *The Principles of Morals and Legislation* (1988), 171–72. Bentham called this "cases in which punishment is groundless."

2. Wilhelm von Humboldt, *On the Limits of State Action* (1791).

3. John Stuart Mill, *On Liberty* (1985), 68–69.

4. For example, Mill argued that prostitutes could not advertise their services and that pimping could be regulated or prohibited. Mill, *On Liberty*, chap. 5.

5. Mill thought that individuals could react to offensive but nonharmful conduct by those who are conceited or boorish or of "low manners" by avoiding them or even warning others away from them. But this, he thought, should be the extent of their punishment, aside from the natural punishment that follows as a consequence of their behavior. Ibid., chap. 4.

6. James Fitzjames Stephen, *Liberty, Equality, Fraternity* (1874), 23, 10.

7. Ibid., 14, 21.

8. The best and most recent attempt to defend an updated version of the harm principle which recognizes the need for significant amendments and qualifications is Joel Feinberg's *The Moral Limits of the Criminal Law*, 4 vols. (1984–1988). See especially volume 1, *Harm to Others*.

9. Mill has a nuanced response to this. At one point he agrees that whenever "there is a definite damage, or definite risk of damage, either to an individual or to the public, the case is taken out of the province of liberty and placed in that of morality or law." Mill, *On Liberty*, 149. But he seems to have in mind such things as the power to regulate the sale of poisons or other dangerous articles. A page earlier, he writes that a man may never be punished for drunkenness or intemperance, but only for the public consequences of these conditions. Ibid., 148. And at other points he indicates a preference for the more individualistic approach of severely punishing the person who repeatedly commits crimes while under the influence of a drug to the more collectivistic approach of making the drug off limits to everyone on

grounds that it leads to crime in a certain percentage of cases. Ibid., 167.

10. See Feinberg's "ride on the bus" for a harrowing and escalating list of potentially offensive activities in *Moral Limits of the Criminal Law*, vol. 2, *Offense to Others* (1986). Even Mill thought prevention of offense was acceptable. These "offenses against decency," he wrote, "may rightly be prohibited." Mill, *On Liberty*, 168.

11. Patrick Devlin, *The Enforcement of Morals* (1965), 10, 9, 11, 13–14, 15, 94.

12. Hart distanced himself from Mill's harm principle: "I myself think there may be grounds justifying the legal coercion of the individual other than the prevention of harm to others." H. L. A. Hart, *Law, Liberty and Morality* (1963), 5. His book attacks morals legislation but, like many other contemporary liberals, Hart accepted the need for paternalism.

13. Ibid., 50–52.

14. Ibid., 81.

15. Mill concluded that laws may not be used to prevent bad examples or the spread of injurious dispositions. Society is "armed with the powers of education," "the authority of a received opinion," and "the natural penalties" that fall upon those whose activities represent a social harm. This should be enough. Mill, *On Liberty*, 150.

16. William Blackstone, *Blackstone's Commentaries* (2006), 4:215. These sentiments, as we have seen, are quoted in Justice Burger's concurring opinion in *Bowers v. Hardwick*, 478 U.S. 186, 197 (1986).

17. *Lawrence v. Texas*, 539 U.S. 558 (2003). Interestingly, however, the Court did not find a constitutional right to consensual acts between gays; rather, it overturned the sodomy law on the more limited ground that it did not meet the "rational relation test," the lowest or least exacting form of judicial scrutiny. Thus *Lawrence* has an ambiguous legacy: in favor of gays it says that "this law is not even defensible on the most minimal grounds required for a law to be upheld," yet it does not actually protect these consensual acts as a right.

18. Jonathan Rauch, *Gay Marriage: Why It's Good for Gays, Good for Straights, and Good for America* (2005), 7, 20, 22. The book review quoted is Christopher Caldwell, "Vows," *New York Times Book Review* (April 11, 2004).

19. Quoted in ibid., 4–5.

20. Ibid., 89.

21. Richard A. Posner, *Sex and Reason* (1993), 132.

22. Robert M. Hardaway, *No Price Too High: Victimless Crimes and the Ninth Amendment* (2003), 24. While Hardaway's studies date from the 1980s, it is unlikely that these numbers have gone down.

23. Researchers have found that married customers seek "kinky" sex, or sex with a different partner, while unattached customers may simply be shy or unable to form a relationship with a partner. Marilyn C. Moses, "Understanding and Applying Research on Prostitution," *National Institute of Justice Journal*, no. 255 (November 2006).

24. Priscilla Alexander, "Prostitution: A Difficult Issue for Feminists," in *Sex Work*, ed. Priscilla Alexander and Frederique Delacoste (1987), 209.

25. I have reached exactly the opposite conclusion Mill reached on some of these issues. He argued that customers may have liberty interests in purchasing certain kinds of goods and services, while the sellers do not. Ultimately, however, he concluded that the buyer's interest should be enough to protect prostitution from state interference, though the state could prevent its public nuisance aspects. Mill, *On Liberty*, chap. 5.

26. The next most serious crime was that of a store owner knowingly placing large eggs in a container marked "extra large." Hardaway, *No Price Too High*, 24.

27. Evelina Giobbe, "Confronting the Liberal Lies about Prostitution," in *The Sexual Liberals and the Attack on Feminism*, ed. Dorchen Liedholdt and Janice Raymond (1990), 72.

28. Margaret Jane Radin, *Contested Commodities* (1996), 133.

29. George Gilder, *Men and Marriage* (1986), 47, 45.

30. Linda R. Hirshman and Jane E. Larson, *Hard Bargains: The Politics of Sex* (1998), 287.

31. Even when Congress passed the Mann Act, commonly referred to as the "white slave act," in 1910, the Bureau of Investigations (the forerunner to the FBI) interviewed 1,106 prostitutes as a prelude to its passage. Only six reported that they were prostitutes involuntarily. Hardaway, *No Price Too High*, 154.

32. Alexander, "Prostitution," 209.

33. Hardaway, *No Price Too High*, 156–57. Some countries, including Sweden, have

recently tightened their laws to prevent international trafficking in sex slavery.

34. "Off with Their Heads: Thoughts from the Drug Czar," *Washington Post* (June 20, 1989).

35. See Gary S. Becker, Kevin M. Murphy, and Michael Grossman, "The Market for Illegal Goods: The Case of Drugs," *Journal of Political Economy* 38 (2006): 114.

36. One example of this hybrid approach is the adoption in many states of drug courts, tribunals designed to deal with drug offenders by monitoring their behavior.

37. Boaz, *Libertarianism*, 238, 79.

38. David A. J. Richards, *Sex, Drugs, Death, and the Law* (1982), 172, 176–77.

39. Ibid., 177. Kant's central contribution to the moral psychology of modern liberalism is the tenet that some choices are more rational than others—that acts motivated by addictions, strong desires, irrational impulses, etc., are not fully "free." In fact, Richards's ultralibertarian view of human personality, which seems to hold that just about any choice is autonomous, is diametrically opposed to the view of progressives such as Cass Sunstein, who seem to doubt that we ever act autonomously. See Chapter 5. (This ambivalence regarding the concept of human freedom is one of the deeper paradoxes of modern liberalism.)

40. National Highway Traffic Safety Administration, U.S. Department of Transportation, "Traffic Safety Facts 2000: Alcohol" (2000).

41. James A. Inciardi, "The Case against Legalization," in *The Drug Legalization Debate*, ed. Inciardi (1991), 57, 56.

42. Smoking one marijuana cigarette is equivalent to smoking four tobacco cigarettes in terms of the harm done to the lungs. Ibid., 50 (citing studies).

Chapter 9

1. The poll, conducted in April 2006, can be found at *www.gallup.com/poll/22222/ Religion-Politics-Inform-Americans-Views-Abortion.aspx*. This is broadly consistent with the results of a CBS News Poll taken a few years earlier, which found that 25 percent opposed abortion under all circumstances, 37 percent thought that it should be available but with stricter limits

than those imposed in *Roe v. Wade*, and 36 percent favored the general availability of abortion. CBS News Poll (May 20–23, 2003).

2. The intermediate group is likely to include people with broadly diverging opinions, including those who might wish to see abortion permitted up to a point late in pregnancy as well as those who may only permit exceptions in order to save the life of the mother or in cases of rape.

3. U.S. Department of the Census, *Statistical Abstract of the United States*, "Vital Statistics" (2007), chap. 2, table 96.

4. In 2003, about 61 percent of abortions occurred before the ninth week, another 18 percent between the ninth and eleventh weeks, with another 10 percent between the eleventh and thirteenth weeks. "Abortion Surveillance—United States, 2003," *www.cdc.gov/mmwr/preview/mmwrhtml/ss5511a1.htm*.

5. Belinda Bennett, ed., *Abortion* (2004), 313–42; Linda R Hirshman and Jane E. Larson, *Hard Bargains: The Politics of Sex* (1999).

6. Rachel Benson Gold, "Lessons from before *Roe*: Will Past Be Prologue?" *The Guttmacher Report on Public Policy* 6, 1 (March 2003).

7. The Planned Parenthood organization estimated that, in the 1960s, before abortion was legalized, as many as 17 percent of all deaths related to pregnancy and childbirth were the result of abortions.

8. Steven D. Levitt and Stephen J. Dubner, *Freakanomics: A Rogue Economist Explores the Hidden Side of Everything* (2006).

9. Judith Jarvis Thomson, "A Defense of Abortion," reprinted in Joel Feinberg, *The Problem of Abortion* (1973). Thomson analogizes pregnancy to the problem of rescue. She imagines one has awakened to find that one has been connected to a famous violinist, who will die unless permitted to remain connected for nine months. Though it would be morally generous to remain connected to the violinist (or the fetus) for nine months in order to save a life, one (or the pregnant woman) has no affirmative duty to save the violinist (the fetus). The article also responds to a number of possible objections.

10. Until the mid-nineteenth century, the Catholic Church held that ensoulment did not take place until quickening, the point at roughly twelve to sixteen weeks in pregnancy when the mother is first able

to sense the movement of the fetus. When medical developments demonstrated that movement takes place much earlier but is not sensible to the mother, a Church council determined that ensoulment must take place at conception.

11. Pat Robertson, *www.patrobertson.com/teaching/shallnotmurder.asp.*

12. John T. Noonan, "An Almost Absolute Value in History," in *The Problem of Abortion*, ed. Joel Feinberg (1973), 15.

13. John T. Noonan, *The Morality of Abortion: Legal and Historical Perspectives* (1970), 58.

14. Francis J. Beckwith, *Defending Life: A Moral and Legal Case against Abortion Choice* (2007), 132. Beckwith's view depends on accepting the controversial Aristotelian assumption that things in the world (including human beings) consist of a substance which is prior to and independent of the properties of this substance.

15. Arguments against the potentiality principle were advanced by Michael Tooley in "A Defense of Abortion and Infanticide," in *The Problem of Abortion*, ed. Joel Feinberg (1973), 86–87.

16. Ibid., 89.

17. Peter Singer, *Practical Ethics* (1993), 135–74.

18. Mary Meehan, "Abortion: The Left Has Betrayed the Sanctity of Life," *The Progressive* (September 1980), *groups.csail.mit.edu/mac/users/rauch/nvp/consistent/meehan_progressive.html*. Also see Rosemary Bottcher, "Pro-Abortionists Poison Feminism," in *Pro-Life Feminism: Different Voices*, ed. Gail Grenier Sweet (1985).

19. Ellen Willis, "Abortion: Is a Woman a Person?" in *Powers of Desire*, ed. Ann Snitow, Christine Stansell, and Sharon Thompson (1983), 473, excerpted in Mary Becker, Cynthia Grant Bownan, and Morrison Torrey, *Feminist Jurisprudence* (1994), 402–3.

20. Lawrence H. Tribe, *American Constitutional Law*, 2nd ed. (1988), 1354.

21. Tribe argues that the "thirteenth amendment's relevance is underscored by the historical parallel between the subjugation of women and the institution of slavery." Ibid., 1354, note 113. Andrew Koppelman, "Forced Labor: A Thirteenth Amendment Defense of Abortion," *Northwestern University Law Review* 480 (1990): 84.

22. *Roe*, 410 U.S. 153, 158.

23. Ibid., 164–65.

24. *Doe v. Bolton*, 410 U.S. 179 (1973).

25. Ibid., 192, 190.

26. Thomson, "A Defense of Abortion," 138.

27. States may regulate abortion in less restrictive ways but they may not prohibit it. For example, in *Planned Parenthood of Southeastern Pennsylvania v. Casey*, 505 U.S. 833 (1992), the Court upheld the state's power to insist that a woman be provided with information about abortion and adoption to permit her to make an informed choice about whether to proceed with abortion. The law also requires a twenty-four-hour waiting period between receiving this information and obtaining an abortion. Pro-choice advocates had argued against upholding the law, claiming that it unduly burdened women's decisions concerning abortion.

28. *Stenberg v. Carhart*, 530 U.S. 914 (2000).

29. The procedure, known as the "intact D&E," or dilation and evacuation, is described at greater length later.

30. The act reaches only those late-term abortions in which the fetus's head is entirely outside the body of the mother or, in the case of a breach presentation, when the fetus must be extracted to the point where its navel is outside the body of the mother. If the abortion can be performed without this degree of extraction, even it if means pulling apart the body of the fetus, the law does not reach it.

31. *Gonzales v. Carhart*, 550 U.S. 124 (2007).

32. Tom Regan, *All That Dwell Therein: Animal Rights and Environmental Ethics* (1982).

33. Noonan is quoted in Jeff Hensley, *The Zero People* (1983), 152.

34. Andre Hellegers states that, by the eighth week, "if we tickle the baby's nose, he will flex his head backwards away from the stimulus." Andre Hellegers, "Fetal Development," *Theological Studies* 3, 7 (1970): 26.

35. Stuart W. G. Derbyshire, "Can Fetuses Feel Pain?" *British Medical Journal* 909 (April 15, 2006): 15; David J. Mellor, Tamara J. Diesch, Alistair J. Gunn, and Laura Bennet, "The Importance of 'Awareness' for Understanding Fetal Pain," *Brain Research Reviews* 455 (November 2005): 49.

36. Derbyshire, for example, argues that "pain must consist of such experienced concepts as the location, feel and cognition associated with the pain." Derbyshire, "Can Fetuses Feel Pain?" 911.

37. See a discussion of the mental capacities of the late-term fetus in "The Science, Law, and Politics of Fetal Pain Legislation," Note,

Harvard Law Review 115 (2002): 2010, 2013–15.

38. This testimony is quoted in Justice Thomas's dissenting opinion in *Stenberg v. Carhart*, 530 U.S. 914, 1007.

39. *Stenberg v. Carhart*, 530 U.S. 914, 952. A description of the procedure appears in this opinion, 958–60.

40. Thomson, "In Defense of Abortion," 139.

41. Mothers who relinquish children for adoption have reported feelings of guilt, remorse, and depression. See Arthur D. Sorosky, Annette Baran, and Reuben Pannor, *The Adoption Triangle* (1978), chaps. 4, 13; Rochelle Friedman and Bonnie Gradstein, *Surviving Pregnancy Loss* (1982), 3–25.

Chapter 10

1. The faculty ultimately voted 31 to 2, with one abstention, to grant tenure. The candidate is no longer a member of the faculty.

2. Edmund Burke, *Reflections on the Revolution in France*, vol. 2, *Select Works of Edmund Burke* (1999), 56.

3. See Cass R. Sunstein, *Democracy and the Problem of Free Speech* (1995), for an in-depth review of the debate and a defense of the substantive egalitarian's approach.

4. F. A. Hayek, *The Constitution of Liberty* (1960), 87; see also F. A. Hayek, *The Road to Serfdom* (1994), 87: "Formal equality before the law is in conflict, and in fact incompatible with any activity of the government aiming at material or substantive equality of different people."

5. Milton Friedman and Rose Friedman, *Free to Choose* (1980), 148.

6. Thomas Sowell, *The Quest for Cosmic Justice* (1999), 13–14.

7. See Janny Scott, "Life at the Top Isn't Just Better, It's Longer," in Correspondents of the *New York Times*, *Class Matters* (2005), for an extended discussion of the social and emotional advantages of wealth.

8. See Martha Albertson Fineman, "Cracking the Foundational Myth: Independence, Autonomy, and Self-Sufficiency," *Journal of Gender, Social Policy, and the Law* 13, 28 (2000): 8.

9. *The Basic Bakunin: Writings, 1869–1871*, ed. Robert Cutler (1992), 79.

10. Noam Chomsky, "Equality," *The Chomsky Reader*, ed. James Peck (1987), 190.

11. Richard Delgado, "Rodrigo's Tenth Chronicle: Merit and Affirmative Action," *Georgetown Law Journal* 83 (1995): 1711, 1721.

12. Alex M. Johnson Jr., "The New Voice of Color," *Yale Law Journal* 100 (1991): 2007, 2052.

13. Manning Marable, "Staying on the Path to Racial Equality," in *The Affirmative Action Debate*, ed. George E. Curry (1997), 7–8.

14. Of course, people can to some extent disagree about what the qualifications of a good lawyer or a good doctor or a good student are—e.g., how compassionate or public spirited or intellectually curious should they be? But such discussions usually involve disagreements about the relative value of different virtues—for example, IQ versus "social intelligence," compassion versus assertiveness, the importance of life experience—that all agree are (to one degree or another) important. See John Lawrence Hill, "A Theory of Merit," *Georgetown Journal of Law and Public Policy* 1, 1 (2002): 15, where I develop an idea of merit that looks beyond the "objective" indicia of personal qualifications to underlying indicia of personal potential.

15. Robin West, "Constitutional Fictions and Meritocratic Success Stories," *Washington and Lee Law Review* 53 (1996): 995, 1018–19.

16. Mickey Kaus, *The End of Equality* (1992), 46–47.

17. Janny Scott and David Leonhardt, "Shadowy Lines That Still Divide," in Correspondents, *Class Matters*, 4.

18. Thomas J. Stanley and William J. Danko, *The Millionaire Next Door* (1996), 16.

19. Hermann Lubbe, "The Social Consequences of Attempts to Create Equality," in *Conservatism: An Anthology of Social and Political Thought from David Hume to the Present*, ed. Jerry Z. Muller (1997), 394.

20. Hayek, *The Constitution of Liberty*, 98.

21. Cornel West, "Affirmative Action in Context," in Curry, *The Affirmative Action Debate*, 32–33.

22. Carl Cohen and James P. Sterba, *Affirmative Action and Racial Preference: A Debate* (2003), 253–54.

23. See, e.g., Charles R. Lawrence, "Two Views of the River: A Critique of the Liberal Defense of Affirmative Action," *Columbia Law Review* 101 (2001): 928, which complains that the now-dominant diversity

24. Ibid., 940, 969.

25. Marable, "Staying on the Path," 11–12.

26. Cohen and Sterba, *Affirmative Action and Racial Preference*, 38.

27. *Grutter v. Bollinger*, 539 U.S. 306 (2003), upholding the University of Michigan Law School's use of race; *Gratz v. Bollinger*, 539 U.S. 244 (2003), striking down the University of Michigan's College of Literature, Science, and the Arts undergraduate affirmative action program.

28. Robert L. Woodson Sr., "Personal Responsibility," in Curry, *The Affirmative Action Debate*, 113, argues that affirmative action has redistributed minorities from small and medium-sized to large firms.

29. Ibid., 112; Woodson argues that the prime beneficiaries of affirmative action have been middle- and upper-class blacks; Heidi Hartmann, "Who Has Benefitted from Affirmative Action?" in Curry, *The Affirmative Action Debate*, 77, argues that white women are the real beneficiaries of affirmative action policies; Glenn C. Loury, "Performing without a Net," in Curry, *The Affirmative Action Debate*, 53, argues that "economic disparities among blacks are actually greater than those among Americans as a whole," so that "the principal beneficiaries of affirmative action are relatively well-off blacks."

30. See *Plessy v. Ferguson*, 163 U.S. 537 (1896), in which the Court upheld "separate-but-equal" policies.

31. Reported in Justice Kennedy's concurring opinion in the *Grutter* case.

32. *Harper v. Virginia State Board of Elections*, 383 U.S. 663 (1966).

33. *New York Times* (November 29, 1994), cited in Cohen and Sterba, *Affirmative Action and Racial Preference*, 179, note 250.

34. Michael Brus, "Proxy War: Liberals Denounce Racial Profiling, Conservatives Denounce Affirmative Action: What's the Difference?" *Slate.com* (July 9, 1999), reprinted in *Justice: A Reader*, ed. Michael J. Sandel (2007), 261.

Chapter 11

1. James Fitzjames Stephen, *Liberty, Equality, Fraternity* (1874), 23. Richard Posner called Stephen "the first neoconservative." Richard Posner, "The First Neoconservative," *Overcoming Law*, 259–70.

2. See Isaiah Berlin, "Joseph de Maistre and the Origins of Fascism," in *The Crooked Timber of Humanity*, ed. Henry Hardy (1990), 117.

3. Jeffrey R. Snyder, "A Nation of Cowards," *Public Interest* (Fall 1993).

4. Snyder cites statistics that in 98 percent of cases where a potential victim brandishes a gun, this is all that is required to deter an attack. Only in 2 percent of cases did the would-be victim shoot his assailant. Ibid.

5. Kelly is quoted in George Will, "Darnell Gets a Gun," *The Leveling Wind* (1994), 89.

6. David L. Bazelon, "The Morality of the Criminal Law," *Southern California Law Review* 49 (1976): 385, 386, 388.

7. Karl Menninger, *The Crime of Punishment* (1966), 9.

8. Peter Kropotkin, *Anarchism: A Collection of Revolutionary Writings*, ed. Roger N. Baldwin (2002), 102, 104.

9. Menninger, *The Crime of Punishment*, 28.

10. Ibid., 29.

11. Bazelon, "Morality of the Criminal Law," 401–2.

12. George Will, "The Journey Up from Guilt," *The Leveling Wind* (1994), 145.

13. Menninger, *The Crime of Punishment*, 17.

14. Bazelon, "Morality of the Criminal Law," 388, note 4.

15. Ibid., 389, referring to *United States v. Alexander*, 471 F.2d 923 (D.C. Cir. 1972).

16. *Durham v. United States*, 214 F.2d 862 (D.C. Cir. 1954).

17. M'Naughten's Case, 8 Engl. Rep. 718 (1843).

18. Bazelon, "Morality of the Criminal Law," 395; *United States v. Brawner*, 471 F.2d 969 (1972) (Bazelon, C.J., concurring in part and dissenting in part).

19. Paul Krugman, *The Conscience of a Liberal* (2007), 87. Krugman attributes the 1960s boom in crime to a post–baby boom "multiplier effect" caused by high concentrations of "crime-prone young males" in the inner city who adopted "new, dangerous norms for behavior." Joblessness and racism contributed to a wave of frustration and rage that generated the pernicious and self-destructive social conditions that developed in inner cities at the time. Ibid., 88–89.

20. John P. Lea and Jock Young, *What Is to Be Done about Law and Order?: Crisis in*

the Nineties (1993). The locus classicus of the idea is W. G. Runciman, *Relative Deprivation and Social Justice* (1966).

21. I say it is not true that they have been left behind economically, because, as economists such as Robert William Fogel have shown, it is precisely the lower classes that have gained the most in the last century relative to the rest of society. We all are doing much better, but the lot of the poorest has improved the most. Robert William Fogel, *The Escape from Hunger and Premature Death, 1700–2100* (2004), especially chap. 2. This may say nothing more than that the condition of the poor was once abominable and today is considerably less so.

22. John E. Conklin, *Robbery and the Criminal Justice System* (1972), 30; Isaac Ehrlich, "The Deterrent Effect of Criminal Law Enforcement," *Journal of Legal Studies* 1 (1972): 276.

23. Andrew Hacker, *Two Nations* (2003), 211, 213.

24. Christopher Cornwell and William N. Trumball, "Estimating the Economic Model of Crime with Panel Data," *Review of Economics and Statistics* 76, 2 (May 1994): 360; John B. Taylor, "Econometric Models of Criminal Behavior," in *Economic Models of Criminal Behavior*, ed. John M. Heineke (1978).

25. Edward C. Banfield, *The Unheavenly City Revisited* (1990), 181.

26. D. J. Connolly, "Judicial Activism Causes Crime," *ttokarnak.home.att.net/Crime.html*.

27. There were fewer than 600 state prison facilities in the early 1980s. Today there are more than 1,000, an increase of about 70 percent over this period. Sarah Lawrence and Jeremy Travis, *The New Landscape of Imprisonment: Mapping America's Prison Expansion* (2004), 2. In Texas alone, an average of 5.7 new prisons were built each year between 1979 and 2000. During this same twenty-one-year period, the total number of prisons in ten states, including Texas, Florida, and California, went from 195 to 604 facilities. This far outpaced the population growth of these states. Ibid.

28. Paige M. Harrison and Allen J. Beck, Bureau of Justice Statistics, U.S. Department of Justice, "Prisoners in 2005" (2006), 2.

29. Ibid., 1. "U.S. Prison Population Sets Record," *Washington Post* (December 1,

2006). This is close to one in every one hundred adults.

30. Roy Walmsley, "World Prison Population List," International Center for Prison Studies, 7th ed. (2007), 1. Russia was the next highest, with 611 per 100,000. But the great majority of countries have prison rate populations well below 150 per 100,000. Ibid. These figures are projected to increase another 200,000 in the next five years. Steven Ohlemacher, "Study: Prison Population on the Rise," Associated Press (February 14, 2007).

31. "U.S. Prison Population Sets Record."

32. Harrison and Beck, "Prisoners in 2005," 10, table 14.

33. U.S. Sentencing Commission, "Report to Congress: Cocaine and Federal Sentencing Policy" (May 2007), 3–4.

34. In 2006, about 82 percent of crack users were black; only about 9 percent were white. Ibid., 19.

35. Those convicted of fraud received 22.5 months on average, while white-collar offenders of regulatory laws spend 28 months in prison on average. Bureau of Justice Statistics, U.S. Department of Justice, "Federal Criminal Case Processing: 2000" (November 2001), 12, table 6.

36. Linda Greenhouse, "Justices Uphold Long Sentences in Repeat Cases," *New York Times* (March 6, 2003).

37. In *Rummell v. Estelle*, 445 U.S. 263 (1980), the Supreme Court held that a life sentence after being convicted, successively, of fraudulent use of a credit card to obtain $80 worth of goods, passing a forged check in the amount of $28.36, and obtaining $120 by false pretenses did not violate the Eighth Amendment's "cruel and unusual punishment" clause.

38. Scott Shane and Neil A. Lewis, "Bush Commutes Libby Sentence, Saying '30 Months Is Excessive,'" *New York Times* (July 3, 2007).

39. American Civil Liberties Union [ACLU], "The Death Penalty: Questions and Answers" (March 2007).

40. An October 2007 Gallup Poll places U.S. support for the death penalty at 69 percent, up a few points from a few years earlier. Support for the death penalty has waxed and waned over the years. Previous polls shown in this survey indicate that support for capital punishment hit an all-time low

of 40 percent in 1967 (just as the national crime rate had exploded) and a recent high of about 80 percent in the mid-1990s. *www.gallup.com/poll/101863/Sixtynine-Percent-Americans-Support-Death-Penalty.aspx.*

41. President's Commission on Law Enforcement and Administration of Justice, *The Challenge of Crime in a Free Society* (1967), 143, cited in *Furman v. Georgia*, 408 U.S. 238 (1972), 436, note 18 (Blackmun, H., dissenting).

42. *Furman v. Georgia*, 408 U.S. 238, 309.

43. *Gregg v. Georgia*, 428 U.S. 153 (1976).

44. *Woodson v. North Carolina*, 428 U.S. 280 (1976); *Roberts v. Louisiana*, 428 U.S. 325 (1976).

45. *Coker v. Georgia*, 433 U.S. 584 (1977).

46. Joshua Marquis, "The Myth of Innocence," *Journal of Criminal Law and Criminology* 95 (2005): 501, 518.

47. Scott Turow, "To Kill or Not to Kill," *New Yorker* (January 6, 2003): 44.

48. These studies are collected in Hugo Adam Bedau and Paul G. Cassell, *Debating the Death Penalty* (2005).

49. Joanna M. Shepherd, "Murders of Passion, Execution Delays, and the Deterrence of Capital Punishment," *Journal of Legal Studies* 33 (June 2004): 283.

50. Dale O. Cloninger and Roberto Marchesini, "Execution and Deterrence: A Quasi-Controlled Group Experiment," *Applied Economics* 33 (2001): 569.

51. Hashem Dezbhaksh, Paul H. Rubin, and Joanna M. Shepherd, "Does Capital Punishment Have a Deterrent Effect?" *American Law and Economics Review* 5 (2003): 344.

52. H. Noci Mocam and R. Kaj Gittings, "Getting off Death Row," *Journal of Law and Economics* 46 (2003): 453. The authors of this study make it clear that they still oppose the death penalty because of misgivings about the disparate impact of capital punishment on whites and blacks.

53. *McClesky v. Kemp*, 481 U.S. 279 (1987). For an updated version of Baldus's findings: David C. Baldus, George Woodworth, David Zuckerman, Neil A. Weiner, and Barbara Broffitt, "Racial Discrimination and the Death Penalty in the Post-Furman Era: An Empirical and Legal Overview with Recent Findings from Philadelphia," *Cornell Law Review* 83 (1998): 1638.

54. John Blume, Theodore Eisenberg, and Martin Wells, "Explaining Death Row's Population and Racial Composition," *Journal of Empirical Legal Studies* 1, 1 (2004): 165, 189–90.

55. Ibid., 166.

56. Marquis, "Myth of Innocence," 507.

57. Of white victims, 86 percent are murdered by whites, while 94 percent of black victims are murdered by blacks. Blume et al., "Explaining Death Row's Population," 192.

58. Turow, "To Kill or Not to Kill." 44.

59. Marquis, "Myth of Innocence," 507, note 39, citing Blume, "Explaining Death Row's Population," 197, table 8.

60. See *Morales v. Tilton*, 465 F.2d 972 (N.D. Cal. 2006), where a court found the chemical regimen posed exactly this risk. Deborah W. Denno, "The Lethal Injection Quandary: How Medicine Has Dismantled the Death Penalty," *Fordham Law Review* 76, 49 (2007), 55–56.

61. Denno, "The Lethal Injection Quandary," 63.

62. ACLU, "Death Penalty," 3. This report mentions a study that concluded that 350 innocent people have been sentenced to death over the course of the twentieth century, 25 of whom were executed. Most of these occurred during the first third of the century, before the addition of a court-mandated defense counsel and the panoply of constitutional protections erected since the 1960s. In the period since the reinstatement of capital punishment in 1976, the figure is much smaller.

63. Marquis, "Myth of Innocence," 520.

64. Immanuel Kant, "The Theory of Right, Part II," in *Kant: Political Writings* (1995), 156.

65. Ibid.

66. Jeffrie G. Murphy and Jean Hampton, *Forgiveness and Mercy* (1988), 91, citing Stephen, *Liberty, Equality, Fraternity.*

Chapter 12

1. Fox News/Opinion Dynamics Poll (May 3, 2003), *www.foxnews.com/projects/pdf/050305_poll.pdf*, cited in Kevin Johnson, *Opening the Floodgates* (2007), 4.

2. Victor Davis Hanson, "Mi Casa Es Su Casa: America's Porous Border Enables Mexico's Misrule," *Wall Street Journal* (January 1, 2006).

3. "Bush Takes on Conservatives over Immigration," *New York Times* (May 30, 2007).

4. Johnson, *Opening the Floodgates*, 45.

5. See Gerald L. Neuman, "The Lost Century of American Immigration Law (1776–1875)," *Columbia Law Review* 93 (1993): 1833, detailing state immigration restrictions in the nineteenth century.

6. The Chinese exclusion law was challenged and upheld in *Chae Chan Ping v. United States*, 530 U.S. 581 (1889). In fact, this case developed the "plenary power" doctrine, which held that Congress's power to regulate immigration is unreviewable by the courts. Thus, Congress can establish immigration quotas on nationality that would otherwise violate equal protection and other constitutional principles.

7. By 1970, according to one estimate, less than 5 percent of adults in the United States were foreign born. Krugman, *The Conscience of a Liberal*, 133.

8. *Plyler v. Doe*, 457 U.S. 202 (1982).

9. *Hoffman Plastic Compounds, Inc. v. N.L.R.B.*, 535 U.S. 137 (2002). Where *Plyler* was decided on constitutional grounds, *Hoffman Plastics* was decided on statutory grounds.

10. Johnson, *Opening the Floodgates*, 73.

11. The best estimates are consistent on this figure. The Office of Immigration Statistics places the figure at 11.6 million undocumented aliens as of 2007. Michael Hoefer, Nancy Rytina, and Bryan C. Baker, "Estimates of the Unauthorized Immigrant Population Residing in the United States," Office of Immigration Statistics, Department of Homeland Security (August 2007). The Pew Hispanic Center also places the 2007 number at between 11.5 and 12 million, *pewhispanic.org/files/reports/61.pdf*. Roughly 450,000 undocumented aliens arrive annually; the number has probably passed 12 million at this printing. The Center for Immigration Studies estimated 35 million foreign-born living in the United States as of March 2005. Steven A. Camarota, "Immigrants at Mid-Decade: A Snapshot of America's Foreign Born Population at 2005," *www.cis.org/articles/2005/back1405.pdf*.

12. Hoefer et al., "Estimates of Unauthorized Immigrant Population," 1.

13. "Prospects for America's Workers: Immigration's Impact," Hearing before the Subcommittee on Immigration, Border Security and Claims, 108th Congress (2003).

14. Hoefer et al., "Estimates of the Unauthorized Immigrant Population," 2, table 1.

15. Center for Immigration Studies, Backgrounder, "100 Million More: Projecting the Impact of Immigration on the U.S. Populations, 2007 to 2060," 6. The Center found that annually 1.6 million immigrate to the United States and another 350,000 leave, for a net increase of 1.25 million persons each year. One-third of these are illegal immigrants. Ibid., 1.

16. Ibid., 6.

17. These are figures from 2000. Office of Policy and Planning, U.S. Immigration and Naturalization Service, "Estimates of the Unauthorized Immigrant Population Residing in the United States, 1990–2000" (2003), 8.

18. This figure is based on the crude birth rate (33 births in 1,000) multiplied by the total population of twelve million. Colorado Alliance for Immigration Reform, "Economic Costs of Legal and Illegal Immigration," *www.cairco.org/econ/econ.html*, 3.

19. Center for Immigration Studies, "100 Million More," 2.

20. Richard Thompson Ford, "Beyond Borders: A Partial Response to Richard Bradfault," *Stanford Law Review* 48 (1996): 1173, 1194.

21. Some representative examples include Johnson, *Opening the Floodgates*; R. George Wright, "Federal Immigration Law and the Case for Open Entry," *Loyola Los Angeles Law Review* 27 (1994): 1265; Joseph H. Carens, "Aliens and Citizens: The Case for Open Borders," *Review of Politics* 49 (1987): 251; and see the essays in Brian Barry and Robert E. Goodin, eds., *Free Movement* (1992); and in Mark Gibney, ed., *Open Borders? Closed Societies? The Ethical and Political Issues* (1988).

22. Interestingly, as a young man Jefferson had written against open immigration. In his 1782 "Notes on Virginia," he worried about the effects of immigrants on U.S. democracy. "In proportion to their numbers, they will share with us in the legislation. They will infuse into it their spirit, warp and bias its direction, and render it a heterogeneous, incoherent and distracted mass." As in other areas, however, Jefferson's republicanism gave way to a more libertarian philosophy as he grew older.

23. Hillel Steiner, "Libertarianism and the Transnational Migration of People," in Barry and Goodin, *Free Movement*, 93–94.

24. Johnson, *Opening the Floodgates*, 41.
25. Peter Laufer, *Wetback Nation: The Case for Opening the Mexican-American Border* (2004), xvi.
26. Wright, "The Case for Open Entry," 1294–95, quoting Immanuel Kant, *Perpetual Peace*, ed. Nicholas Murray Butler (1939), 24.
27. Wright, "The Case for Open Entry," 1294.
28. Bruce A. Ackerman, *Social Justice in the Liberal State* (1980), 95.
29. Wright, "The Case for Open Entry," 1295.
30. Laufer, *Wetback Nation*, 34.
31. Michael S. Teitelbaum, "Right versus Right: Immigration and Refugee Policy in the United States," *Foreign Affairs* 59, 21 (1980): 55.
32. Laufer, *Wetback Nation*, xviii, 244.
33. Wright, "The Case for Open Entry," 1287, 1288
34. Peter Brimelow, "Milton Friedman at 85," *Forbes* (December 27, 1997), 52.
35. Michael Walzer, *Spheres of Justice* (1983), 39.
36. Johnson, *Opening the Floodgates*, 37–43.
37. Ibid., 42–43.
38. This is not to gainsay the danger of crossing the desert from Mexico to the United States today, but see Laufer, *Wetback Nation*, 6–7, recounting the story of Juana Maria, an undocumented Mexican woman who flew from El Paso to Dallas, and Dallas to California, en route to being reunited with her husband.
39. Kant qualified his stand for open borders by insisting that immigration is permissible only so long as "the private ownership of the land of the natives is not diminished." Immanuel Kant, *The Metaphysical Elements of Justice*, ed. John Ladd (1965), section 50. In a society in which wealth has shifted from real property to other forms of wealth, Kant's qualification would seem to apply to significant effects on taxes and other social resources.
40. Walzer, *Spheres of Justice*, 41, 62.
41. Johann Gottfried Herder, *Idea for the Philosophy of a History of Mankind*, 3:5, quoted in John Dunn, *Western Political Theory in the Face of the Future* (1979), 79.
42. Joseph de Maistre, *Considerations on France* (1994), 53.
43. Patrick J. Buchanan, *State of Emergency* (2006), 162–63.
44. Ibid., 12, 146.
45. Buchanan quotes with approval the French historian Ernest Renan, who wrote that "a nation is a living soul, a spiritual principle." The common possession of a rich heritage and common interests are the "soul" of a nation. Ibid., 140.
46. Samuel P. Huntington, *Who Are We? The Challenge to America's National Identity* (2004), 211.
47. Victor Davis Hanson, "Rethinking Illegal Immigration," *Tribune Media Services* (November 13, 2006).
48. In addition to Buchanan's and Huntington's works, see Peter Brimelow, *Alien Nation: Common Sense about America's Immigration Disaster* (1995); Victor Davis Hanson, *Mexifornia: A State of Reckoning* (2003); *National Review* Reports on Immigration and Assimilation, *The Melting Pot Boils Over* (2006).
49. Compare Tamar Jacoby, "Immigration Nation," *Foreign Affairs* (November–December 2006), for the liberal view, with Steven Malanga, "How Unskilled Immigrants Hurt Our Economy," *City Journal* (Summer 2006).
50. Center for Immigration Studies, "The Costs of Illegal Immigration," *www.cis.org/articles/2004/fiscalrelease.html*, 1–2.
51. Robert Longley, "Illegal Immigration Costs California over Ten Billion Annually," About.com (December 2004), *usgovinfo.about.com/od/immigration naturalization/a/caillegals.htm*.
52. Fred Dickey, "Undermining American Workers: Record Numbers of Illegal Immigrants Are Pulling Wages Down for the Poor and Pushing Taxes Higher," *Los Angeles Times* (July 20, 2003).
53. Malanga, "How Unskilled Immigrants Hurt," 4.
54. Colorado Alliance for Immigration Reform, "Economic Costs," 2.
55. George J. Borjas, "Increasing the Supply of Labor through Immigration," Center for Immigration Studies report (May 2004), 6–7.
56. A U.S. painting contractor was willing to cut his price 20 percent if payment was made under the table, according to Dickey, "Undermining American Workers."
57. Malanga, "How Unskilled Immigrants Hurt," 5.
58. Colorado Alliance for Immigration Reform, "Economic Costs," 2.
59. John O'Sullivan, "Tearing Up the Country," in *National Review* Reports, *The Melting Pot Boils Over*, 53.
60. American Conservative Union Foundation,

"A Conservative Immigration Policy?" *acuf .org/issuesissue3/040108news.asp*, 1.

61. Carl Menoff, "The Power of Immigration to Divide," letter to the editor, *New York Times* (January 4, 2008).

62. Tamar Jocoby, "Immigration Nation," *Foreign Affairs* (November–December 2006), 61.

63. Roberto Suro, "Attitudes toward Immigrants and Immigration Policy: Surveys among Latinos in the U.S. and Mexico," Pew Hispanic Center Report (August 16, 2005).

64. Johnson, *Opening the Floodgates*, 26.

65. Buchanan, *State of Emergency*, 256.

66. Jacoby, "Immigration Nation," 64.

67. Center for Immigration Studies, "The Costs of Illegal Immigration," 1.

68. In 2006, about 67,000 persons won asylum or refugee status. Kelly Jefferys, "Refugees and Asylees: 2006," Annual Flow Report (May 2007). See Linda Kelly-Hill, "Holding the Due Process Line for Asylum," *Hofstra Law Review* 36, 85 (2007).

69. See, e.g., *Pramatarov v. Gonzales*, 454 F.3d 764 (7th Cir., 2006).

70. William Gheen, "It's Illegal Immigration, Stupid: Why McCain and Hillary Will Never Be President" (November 20, 2007), *www .theconservativevoice.com/article/29359.html*.

71. Maria Pabon Lopez, "More Than a License to Drive: State Restrictions on the Use of Driver's Licenses by Non-Citizens," *Southern Illinois University Law Review* 29, 91 (2004): 108.

72. Anne Ryman, "3,850 College Students Denied In-State Tuition, *Arizona Republic* (January 9, 2008).

Index